"A fascinating, readable, and ~~well-researched book about a movement that has~~ done most to shape an influe~~ntial segment of evangelical Christianity and~~ the role of Christianity in Am~~erican higher education.~~"

George Marsden, author of *The Outrageous Idea of Christian Scholarship*

"*To Think Christianly* is a pioneering work of scholarship which sheds light on a movement richly deserving of historical attention. Over the past few years Charles Cotherman has interviewed many people who have been part of Christian communities of study, and in doing so he has refreshed our memories and offered the clear-eyed view of a knowledgeable observer who cares. As the director of a Christian study center for more than twenty-five years as well as a regular visiting professor and former board member at Regent College, I'm grateful that what has been, largely, a scattered oral history now is written in this thoughtful and respectful book. It will guide all of us who hope to invite people to 'think Christianly.'"

Susan S. Phillips, sociologist and professor of Christian spirituality, executive director of New College Berkeley, an affiliate of the Graduate Theological Union

"Richly informative and superbly written, Cotherman's study fills in a huge gap in understanding evangelicals. But it also raises a titanic question, What is the state of evangelical thinking, and its influence on churches across the country, as evangelicals confront the far deeper challenges of the present moment?"

Os Guinness, author of *Last Call for Liberty*

"Charles E. Cotherman has written a fascinating history of a type of Christian higher education that has been growing in importance: Christian study centers, often adjacent to secular campuses. The first such work, *To Think Christianly*, contextualizes the movement and in so doing provides wisdom for its future development. This history is sympathetic but not hagiographic; Cotherman points out both strengths and weaknesses. He is also particularly attentive to how these centers have facilitated women's theological training. I commend the book to all those interested in the development of Christian higher education."

Andrea L. Turpin, author of *A New Moral Vision: Gender, Religion, and the Changing Purposes of American Higher Education, 1837–1917*

"Charles Cotherman chronicles the history of one of the most important elements of the Christian project in America today, and he does it well. The Christian study center movement is so extensive and variegated, it would be impossible to give exhaustive voice to every contributor to its success, but Cotherman has marshaled his material well and given us an accurate, fulsome, and well-written account that is both credible and accessible. Extremely well-researched but easily read, I cannot imagine a better recounting of this fascinating story of God's kingdom work in higher education today."

Andrew H. Trotter Jr., executive director of the Consortium of Christian Study Centers

"Cotherman not only shares the rich history of the Christian study center movement, but he also gives us hope for the future spiritual and intellectual engagement among evangelicals at the university. This is a must-read primer for those wanting to learn about study centers and the holistic flourishing of Christians on college campuses."

Tom Lin, president and CEO of InterVarsity Christian Fellowship/USA

"As a Christian study center director serving a large public research institution, I am grateful for this exceptional book that provides rich historical context for the changing contours of faith, vocation, and learning within secular higher education. Those of us in the study center movement seek influence through thoughtful intellectual engagement, deep relational connection, and hospitable service. This faithful and consistent presence does not always garner front-page headlines, but it does change the lives of faculty, staff, and students, and even the academy itself. Dr. Cotherman's book tells the story of how this holistic approach has evolved over the past fifty years, and why it offers so much promise for the future."

John R. Terrill, executive director of Upper House and the Stephen & Laurel Brown Foundation, serving the University of Wisconsin-Madison

"This important new book tells the story of a cultural force that observers of American evangelicalism have generally underestimated: the Christian study center movement. Beginning with the 1950s, Cotherman painstakingly traces the intellectual networks, alliances, and struggles among evangelical thought leaders, evangelists, and professors who have been eager to rethink conservative Christian engagement with the life of the mind. He adds complexity and richness to our understanding of Christian intellectual life in modern America."

Molly Worthen, associate professor of history at the University of North Carolina at Chapel Hill, author of *Apostles of Reason: The Crisis of Authority in American Evangelicalism*

"Deep research and interviews with many key individuals make this book a stimulating history of efforts to overcome evangelical anti-intellectualism. Cotherman presents the work of Francis (and Edith) Schaeffer at L'Abri in Switzerland, and then of James (and Rita) Houston at Regent College in Vancouver as the sparks stimulating broader, deeper, and wider Christian cultural engagement—culminating now in the Consortium of Christian Study Centers and other important initiatives. Good reasons abound to be pessimistic about the future of Christian intellectual life. This well-written and compelling book, by contrast, is a sign of hope."

Mark A. Noll, author of *Jesus Christ and the Life of the Mind*

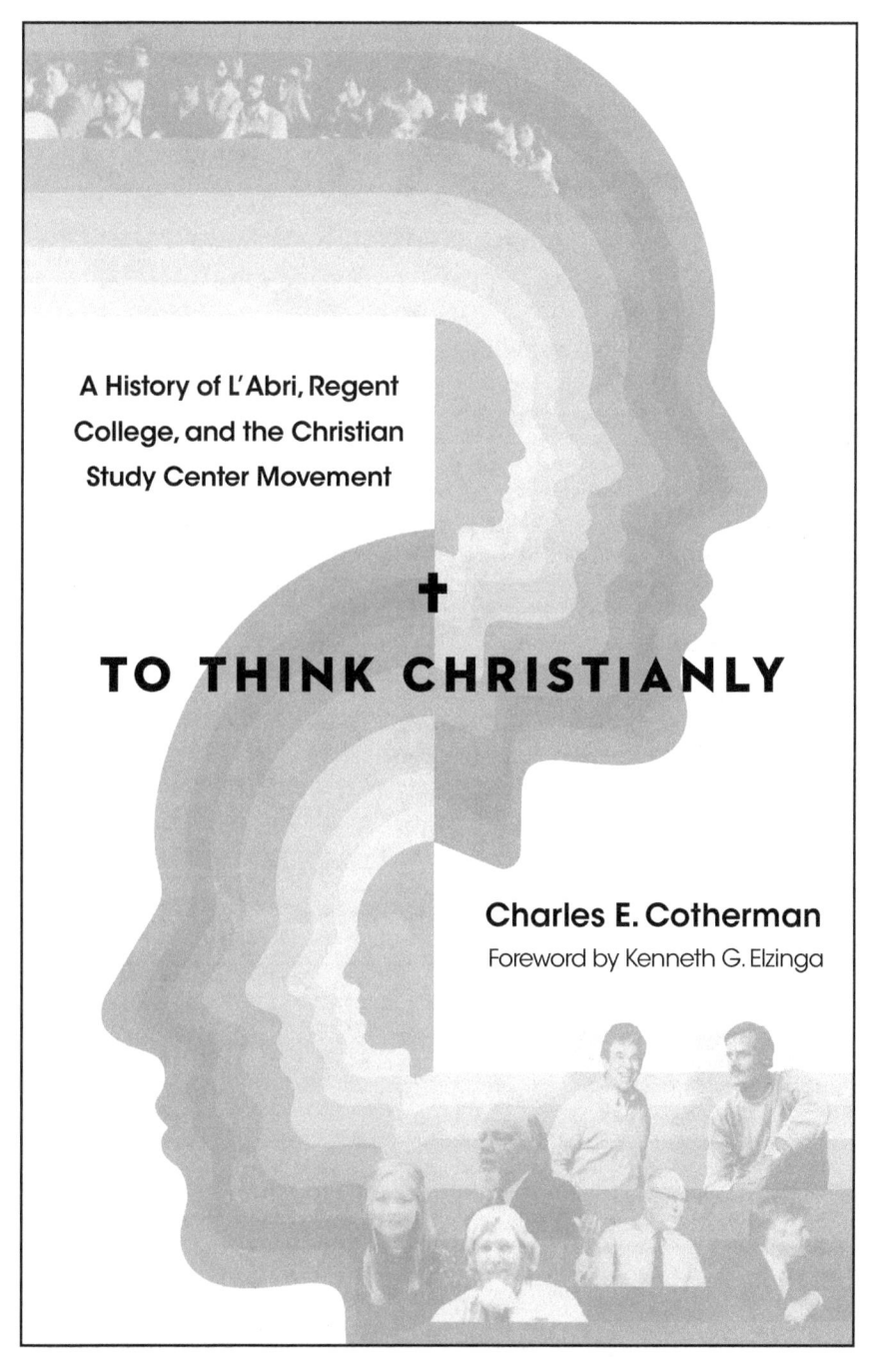

A History of L'Abri, Regent
College, and the Christian
Study Center Movement

TO THINK CHRISTIANLY

Charles E. Cotherman

Foreword by Kenneth G. Elzinga

ivp
Academic

An imprint of InterVarsity Press
Downers Grove, Illinois

InterVarsity Press
P.O. Box 1400, Downers Grove, IL 60515-1426
ivpress.com
email@ivpress.com

©2020 by Charles E. Cotherman

All rights reserved. No part of this book may be reproduced in any form without written permission from InterVarsity Press.

InterVarsity Press® is the book-publishing division of InterVarsity Christian Fellowship/USA®, a movement of students and faculty active on campus at hundreds of universities, colleges, and schools of nursing in the United States of America, and a member movement of the International Fellowship of Evangelical Students. For information about local and regional activities, visit intervarsity.org.

All Scripture quotations, unless otherwise indicated, are taken from The Holy Bible, New International Version®, NIV®. Copyright © 1973, 1978, 1984, 2011 by Biblica, Inc.™ Used by permission of Zondervan. All rights reserved worldwide. www.zondervan.com. The "NIV" and "New International Version" are trademarks registered in the United States Patent and Trademark Office by Biblica, Inc.™

Cover design and image composite: David Fassett
Interior design: Jeanna Wiggins
Images: old textured paper: © Katsumi Murouchi / Moment Collection / Getty Images
    old textured paper: © R. Tsubin / Moment Collection / Getty Images
    abstract watercolor: © marthadavies / E+ / Getty Images

ISBN 978-1-5140-0428-9 (paperback)
ISBN 978-0-8308-5282-6 (hardcover)
ISBN 978-0-8308- 3924-7 (digital)

Printed in the United States of America ∞

InterVarsity Press is committed to ecological stewardship and to the conservation of natural resources in all our operations. This book was printed using sustainably sourced paper.

Library of Congress Cataloging-in-Publication Data

Names: Cotherman, Charles E., 1983- author.
Title: To think Christianly: a history of L'Abri, Regent College, and the
    Christian study center movement/ Charles E. Cotherman.
Description: Downers Grove, IL: InterVarsity Press, [2020] | Includes
bibliographical references.
Identifiers: LCCN 2019059217 (print) | LCCN 2019059218 (ebook) | ISBN
    9780830852826 (hardcover) | ISBN 9780830839247 (ebook)
Subjects: LCSH: Christian study centers—History | Christian study
    centers—United States—History. | L'Abri (Organization) | Regent
    College. | Church work with students—United States. |
Evangelicalism—United States—History—21st century.
Classification: LCC BV4487.S78 C68 2020 (print) | LCC BV4487.S78 (ebook)
    | DDC 267/.13—dc23
LC record available at https://lccn.loc.gov/2019059217
LC ebook record available at https://lccn.loc.gov/2019059218

| P | 23 | 22 | 21 | 20 | 19 | 18 | 17 | 16 | 15 | 14 | 13 | 12 | 11 | 10 | 9 | 8 | 7 | 6 | 5 | 4 | 3 | 2 | 1 |
| Y | 40 | 39 | 38 | 37 | 36 | 35 | 34 | 33 | 32 | 31 | 30 | 29 | 28 | 27 | 26 | 25 | 24 | 23 | 22 | 21 |

FOR SCOTT W. SUNQUIST AND

MATTHEW S. HEDSTROM,

guides who opened doors

to the past and future

CONTENTS

Foreword by Kenneth G. Elzinga	ix
Acknowledgments	xiii
List of Abbreviations	xvii
Introduction	1

PART 1: INNOVATION

1 L'Abri	13
2 Regent College	48

PART 2: REPLICATION

3 The C. S. Lewis Institute	91
4 The Ligonier Valley Study Center	120
5 New College Berkeley	152
6 The Center for Christian Study	189

PART 3: MULTIPLICATION

7 The Consortium of Christian Study Centers	221
Conclusion	255
Bibliography	271
Archives List	292
Interview List	293
Figure Credits	294
Index	295

FOREWORD

Kenneth G. Elzinga

TO THINK CHRISTIANLY is a book of intellectual history that also is a pleasure to read—no easy task for an author. Charles Cotherman shows how the confluence of Francis Schaeffer at L'Abri and James Houston at Regent College helped initiate and shape the study center movement in the United States. While not a manual on how to start a study center, the book advocates the value of study centers as places where individuals—often college students—are encouraged to use their minds to know God and to understand contemporary culture.

For those who want to learn about study centers, this book is a great place to start. For those involved with study centers, this book is a carefully researched and engagingly written account of how it all began. A thesis of the book is that L'Abri and Regent College were at the taproot of the study center movement. Schaeffer and Houston take center stage, but Cotherman includes many others who played important supporting roles.

Cotherman frequently mentions the Center for Christian Study at the University of Virginia as one of the first study centers to be (unlike L'Abri) physically adjacent to a university and (unlike Regent) not administratively connected to a university. Full disclosure—I was involved in the start of this center. I have observed several ways in which it has enriched the DNA of the University of Virginia and the surrounding community. Let me comment on this.

First, the Center for Christian Study is a *center*. This means there is a place, a geographical footprint. In addition, I have often heard the UVA study center described as a "safe place." It is safe not just in the sense of physical safety but also in the sense of being a safe place where one can bring disagreements and doubts.

When a man named Nathanael first heard about Jesus, he scornfully asked, "Can anything good come out of Nazareth?" (Jn 1:46 NRSV). Colleges and universities today are full of people like Nathanael. Can anything good come out of Christianity? A study center is a place to ask that question. When a man named Thomas heard of Jesus' resurrection from the dead, he had doubts whether this were true. Study centers should be safe places for the scornful Nathanaels and the doubting Thomases.

The Christian faith makes much of the words *following* and *sending*. When Jesus began his public ministry, he went up to strangers—Matthew, James, John, Peter, and Andrew—who were busily engaged in their lives, and said, "Follow me." And they did. At one point in his public ministry Jesus said, "Whoever wants to be my disciple must deny themselves and take up their cross daily *and follow me*" (Lk 9:23, emphasis added). Fast-forward two thousand years, and people are still following Jesus.

Jesus also used the word *send*. In one of the most remarkable statements Jesus ever made, he said, "Peace be with you! As the Father has sent me, I am *sending* you" (Jn 20:21, emphasis added). In what many Christians now call the Great Commission, Jesus sends his followers out into the world with these instructions: "Therefore go and make disciples of all nations" (Mt 28:19).

Study centers, such as the one at the University of Virginia, meet at the confluence of following and sending. This interplay represents what study centers should be about. They should produce *followers* of Jesus and also should *send* followers of Jesus out into the world.

As biblical literacy dwindles and as the institutional church becomes less commonly a place where people go to be catechized and learn about Christianity, study centers become even more important. Indeed, in a post-Christian era, study centers can be places where students who know nothing about the story of Jesus hear the good news, perhaps for the first time, and are invited to become followers of Jesus. Then study centers can be places that embrace Jesus' words, "As the Father has sent me, I am sending you."

To be sent is different from wandering or taking a stroll. To be sent means there is a mission, a reason, a purpose, an objective to accomplish. How should this influence the way study centers think about sending in their engagement with students?

The place to start is helping students understand the difference between being sent and choosing a career. Christian study centers, not university career centers, are places where followers of Jesus can learn to understand that they are sent out to be the aroma of Christ in the world. Indeed, study centers are uniquely positioned to help college students understand that being sent is different from a career. John Ortberg said that a calling is "something I do *for* God," while a career "threatens to *become* my god."[1]

One of the most remarkable contributions of the Reformation was to recapture the idea that ordinary people, living ordinary lives, doing ordinary work, also are those to whom the word *send* applies. In line with this, for most students engaged with a study center, being sent will not mean to the foreign mission field; it will not mean seminary; it will not mean going on staff with a parachurch organization. It will mean taking a job with General Mills or Deloitte, with Wells Fargo or Pfizer, with the Metropolitan Museum of Art or Black & Decker.

Preparing to send is a special role a study center can play at a college or university. It prepares followers of Jesus to be sent to all the corners of the earth, to full-time ministry and to the marketplace, knowing that in both instances they are being sent on mission.

Another metaphor I hear describing the Center for Christian Study at the University of Virginia is that of a hub. The center is a physical hub where other Christian ministries are welcome to meet with students for conversation and coffee, for prayer and Bible study. Often UVA students will say, "I'll meet you at the Stud." The center also serves as a source of synergy with other Christian ministries. It does not compete with them but rather complements them. Some parachurch ministries that do not have a physical space have used office space at the center.

One more word that should describe the DNA of Christian study centers is *irenic*. Indeed, a theme of Cotherman's book is that study centers are to be marked by relational warmth and hospitality as well as making followers of Jesus and sending them on mission. Part of the genius of Schaeffer and Houston and their spouses was developing a physical place where mind and heart came together.

Dozens of Christian study centers—often adjacent to universities—now dot the continent. This book is the first to tell us how and why.

---

[1] John Ortberg, *If You Want to Walk on Water, You've Got to Get Out of the Boat* (Grand Rapids: Zondervan, 2001), 71.

ACKNOWLEDGMENTS

THE HISTORY THAT FOLLOWS centers on open doors and the power of relationships. As such, it is fitting that the six-year journey of discovering and then telling this history has been defined by the same things—open doors (both symbolic and literal) and a network of relationships.

Among the most significant doors to this history are those who lived it and who have taken time to share their stories with me through email, coffee conversations, and formal oral-history interviews. A full list of interviewees can be found in the back matter, but it is perhaps worth calling special attention to Walter and Virginia Hearn, Daryl Richman, and R. C. Sproul, who have each passed away since our conversation. It was an honor to be able to hear and record their stories. This book also benefited greatly from the foresight and generosity of individuals such as Edith Black and James Houston, who had the wisdom to commit a lifetime of letters and personal material to carefully curated archives and then had the good faith to allow a young scholar freedom to use them. In this same vein, I want to acknowledge the immense help I received in navigating these treasures of history from archivists such as Cindy Aalders (Regent College), Thomas Brewer (Ligonier Ministries), David Stiver (Graduate Theological Seminary), and Bill Youngmark (Southeastern Baptist Theological Seminary), who proved exceedingly capable guides to well-organized and valuable collections. Bill Wilder and the Center for Christian Study staff supported my work over the course of these many years by an ongoing willingness to answer questions and grant open access to the study center's archives. In addition to formal archival collections, this book was supplemented in significant ways by Carl Armerding, Jane Spencer Bopp, David Gill, Dale Myers, Beat Steiner, and Drew Trotter, who each provided helpful resources from personal collections.

Because many of these study centers have never been treated at length in a published work, the photographs included in this book record an important, sometimes never-before-seen historical record that moves through this volume as a kind of history within a history. For their help in the procurement of photos I am especially indebted to Cindy Aalders, Elisa Bricker, Brittany Fan, Rachel Gaffin, David Gill, Sammy Godo, Jim and Lorain Hiskey, Sylvester Jacobs, Karl Johnson, Per-Ole Lind, Kenneth McAllister, Linda Mercadante, Polly Schatz, Stephen Sparks, and John Terrill.

Research and writing are not just mental labor but fully embodied pursuits. The hospitality of Carl and Betsy Armerding, Paul and Jane Bopp, Brian and Lydia Dant, James Houston, Steve and Susan Phillips, Michael and Amy Raburn, Richard and Portia Schneider, and Drew Trotter was a blessing and a joy to me at points throughout this journey. By opening the door to shared meals and guest bedrooms, they not only helped bring this project to fruition but lived out hospitality like that traced in these pages. My body and mind were also sustained through the early stages of this project by the Jefferson Scholars Foundation, whose generosity, hospitality, and commitment to fostering scholarly community made the work of compiling this book not merely possible but extremely enjoyable.

I am also deeply thankful to the individuals who chose to invest in me in the formative stages of this journey. Jon Boyd and the folks at IVP Academic have demonstrated a constant balance of professional aptitude and personal warmth. Heather Warren and Matthew Hedstrom extended a welcome to a program and a field, and Grace Hale and Charles Marsh were extremely helpful conversation partners as this project took shape. Throughout my time at the University of Virginia Matt's shepherding was invaluable for helping me bring the scope of this narrative into focus.

That I am a historian at all is attributable to my teacher and friend Scott Sunquist. I could not have asked for a better guide to pursuing a holistic balance of scholarship, faith, and life.

I am also deeply grateful for the friendship and encouragement of Garrett and Autumn Heath, Josiah Micklos, Chris Starcher, Matt Ace, Joe Carrico, Tom Carothers, Dylan Ziegler, Luke Braughler, Richard and Portia Schneider, Ben and Jess Lewis, Paul and Jane Bopp, Rick Osberg, Mike Nilon, Michael Houle, Josue and Shannon Barrios, Jason Hansford, Joel Seymour, and Rita Joyce, who were always supportive of my academic endeavors and who were often willing to read more of my writing than the basic duties of friendship demanded. Our Willoughby community group was a constant source of encouragement through the early stages of this process and our Oil City Vineyard family through the latter. As a scholar I have also been sustained by friendships cultivated through involvement in the Society of Vineyard Scholars. I am especially indebted to Caleb Maskell, who has been a friend, encourager, and an academic sounding board in the days when I had few others. This project began to come into clearer focus during a breakfast conversation we had at SVS in spring 2015.

Finally, it is hard fathom the myriad ways in which this book and my life in general hinge on the support and love of my family. From meals and childcare to words of encouragement, Jim and Jeanene Cotherman and Dale and Barb Myers have been tremendous allies in all of my endeavors. Andy and Jenna Cotherman, Todd and Emily Shumaker, and Josh and Alison Albright have similarly been regular sources of encouragement, joy, and support. I am also grateful to my three amazing children—Elliana, Anneliese, and Benton—for their love, prayers ("Help Daddy with his book"), and the perspective they bring to my life by reminding me on a daily basis that there are things more important than academic positions and books.

Above all, I am grateful for the love, wisdom, and companionship of Aimee Cotherman. For over ten years she has been a partner in all of life, from parenting and multistate moves, to graduate school and the ups and downs of church planting and ministry. There is no one else with whom I would rather walk through life's many doors.

Soli Deo Gloria

ABBREVIATIONS

CCSA	Center for Christian Study Archives, Center for Christian Study, Charlottesville, VA
CWLFC	Christian World Liberation Front Collection, Graduate Theological Union Library, Berkeley
FSC	Francis A. Schaeffer Collection, Southeastern Baptist Theological Seminary, Wake Forest, NC
JHF	James Houston Fonds, Regent College, Vancouver
KSGC	Keith Shepherd Grant Collection, Regent College, Vancouver
MCF	Michael G. Collison Fonds, Regent College, Vancouver
NCBA	New College Berkeley Archives, New College Berkeley, Berkeley

INTRODUCTION

WHAT DOES IT MEAN to think Christianly? For anyone familiar with the recent history of North American evangelicalism this question has an almost haunting quality. From Richard Hoftstadter's 1964 Pulitzer Prize–winning *Anti-intellectualism in American Life*, to Mark Noll's oft-cited 1994 cri de coeur *The Scandal of the Evangelical Mind*, to Molly Worthen's more recent *Apostles of Reason*, the connection between evangelically inclined Christianity and truncated thinking has functioned as an assumed, even unavoidable, feature of American evangelicalism at both a popular and academic level.[1] But does a movement defined historically by a reaction to modernism via commitments to the centrality of the cross, personal conversion, the authority of Scripture, and an abiding inclination toward activism have to surrender intellectual vitality—the ability to think not only well but "Christianly" about all of life—in the process?[2]

This book offers a glimpse into a small but significant network of individuals and Christian communities, or study centers, that have chosen to answer this question not with reasoned theological statements—though there have been a few who have taken up the task to set this out in writing—but with living

---

[1] Richard Hofstadter, *Anti-intellectualism in American Life* (New York: Vintage, 1966); Mark A. Noll, *The Scandal of the Evangelical Mind* (Grand Rapids: Eerdmans, 1994); Molly Worthen, *Apostles of Reason: The Crisis of Authority in American Evangelicalism* (New York: Oxford University Press, 2013). Other notable and pertinent critiques of Christian intellectual engagement in the late twentieth and early twenty-first century include Harry Blamires, *The Christian Mind* (Ann Arbor, MI: Servant Books, 1978); Charles Malik, *Of Two Minds* (Westchester, IL: Cornerstone Books, 1980); Os Guinness, *Fit Bodies, Fat Minds: Why Evangelicals Don't Think and What to Do About It* (Grand Rapids: Baker Books, 1994); J. P. Moreland, *Love Your God with All Your Mind: The Role of Reason in the Life of the Soul* (Colorado Springs: NavPress, 2012); Mark A. Noll, *Jesus Christ and the Life of the Mind* (Grand Rapids: Eerdmans, 2011); Todd C. Ream, Jerry Pattengale, and Christopher J. Devers, eds., *The State of the Evangelical Mind* (Downers Grove, IL: IVP Academic, 2018).

[2] For evangelicalism as a reaction to modernity, see Bruce Hindmarsh, *The Spirit of Early Evangelicalism: True Religion in a Modern World* (New York: Oxford University Press, 2018). When I use the word *evangelical* in this study I am referring to those who are shaped by the four emphases Bebbington identifies: crucicentrism, conversionism, biblicism, and activism. See David Bebbington, *Evangelicalism in Modern Britain: A History from the 1730s to the 1980s* (London: Routledge, 1993), 2-3.

and learning communities or study centers founded on the conviction that all of life (the life of the mind included) falls necessarily within the purview of Christian discipleship.[3] None of the individuals and communities treated in these pages achieved this integration of life, faith, and mind perfectly, but they all held up this type of holistic life-mind engagement as an ideal.

For a generation of evangelical baby boomers faced with unprecedented levels of educational and vocational opportunity alongside unavoidable social unrest, the ideal—even if never perfectly achieved—made a profound difference as they joined their peers in the nation's burgeoning universities.[4] As some of these individuals began to work out the implications of these ideals in their own lives and careers, they helped to spur a vocational revolution within American evangelicalism that resulted in numerous evangelicals moving into careers in academics, the arts, and business—fields that had seldom come within the evangelical horizon of possibility in such a powerful way.[5] In the process individuals such as Francis A. Schaeffer (1912–1984) and James M. Houston (b. 1922), along with communities they led—L'Abri (founded 1955) and Regent College (founded 1967), respectively—launched a Christian study center movement that eventually touched the lives of individuals at some of North America's most influential institutions with a version of evangelical Christianity that was as much at home in the pew as in the library, classroom, or art gallery.

---

[3]For such theological statements, see David W. Gill, *The Opening of the Christian Mind: Taking Every Thought Captive to Christ* (Downers Grove, IL: InterVarsity Press, 1989); David C. Mahan and C. Donald Smedley, "University Ministry and the Evangelical Mind," in Ream, Pattengale, and Devers, *State of the Evangelical Mind*, 59-99.

[4]Between 1960 and 1970 university enrollment in the United States grew 139 percent as the first of the baby boomers entered universities and the US government poured 2.9 percent of the gross national product into research and development. By 1970, 8.6 million students were attending college. See Robert Wuthnow, *The Restructuring of American Religion: Society and Faith Since World War II* (Princeton, NJ: Princeton University Press, 1988), 155. For the most part these students were white "children of plenty," the beneficiaries of postwar affluence; see Grace Elizabeth Hale, *A Nation of Outsiders: How the White Middle Class Fell in Love with Rebellion in Postwar America* (New York: Oxford University Press, 2011).

[5]Mark Thomas Edwards, *The Right of the Protestant Left: God's Totalitarianism* (New York: Palgrave Macmillan, 2012), 164. L'Abri's influence across the four key spheres of society (art/culture, politics, education, business) has been well documented by Michael Lindsay; see D. Michael Lindsay, "Evangelicals in the Power Elite: Elite Cohesion Advancing a Movement," *American Sociological Review* 73, no. 1 (February 2008): 60-82; Lindsay, *Faith in the Halls of Power: How Evangelicals Joined the American Elite* (Oxford: Oxford University Press, 2007).

God's Avant-Garde

The Christian study center movement did not emerge in a vacuum, nor were efforts such as Regent College or L'Abri the first efforts to cultivate Christian communities marked by faith, intellectual pursuit, and hospitality. In some sense Christianity had always held the seeds for expressions of this kind through monasticism's longstanding dedication to prayer and work (*ora et labora*) within the context of study and community.[6] Protestants, through their explicit rejection of monasticism, had less access to a legacy of praying and working communities, but even within Protestantism, there were always a few who picked up on reverberations of this long stream within the church by founding intentional communities (with varying levels of orthodoxy) and educational endeavors rooted in common prayers and shared life.[7] By the middle decades of the twentieth century, the example of dissenting German theologian Dietrich Bonhoeffer (1906–1945) and his underground seminary community, Finkenwalde, described in his book *Life Together*, had become an inspiration for many who sought to combine spirituality with theological learning and deep community.[8]

One of the most significant of these communities was the Christian Faith-and-Life Community at the University of Texas in Austin. Founded in 1952 by Presbyterian minister W. Jack Lewis as an effort to take part in the wider post–World War II lay renewal, the community soon became "a model for lay education and campus ministry known around the country and even the world" as a means for adapting Christianity to the demands of a modern age.[9] In 1965 theologian Harvey Cox described a church that was able to contextualize the good news of the gospel to the modern age as "God's *avant-garde*," and the Christian Faith-and-Life Community's work gave it a right to lay claim in practice to this title even prior to Cox's use of the term.[10] During the

---

[6]This combination was crystallized by St. Benedict and the monastic tradition he founded. See Timothy Fry, trans., *The Rule of Saint Benedict in English* (Collegeville, MN: Liturgical Press, 1982); Kenneth Scott Latourette, *A History of Christianity: Beginnings to 1500*, rev. ed. (Peabody, MA: Prince, 1953), 334-36.
[7]Catherine L. Albanese, *American Religions and Religion* (Boston: Wadsworth Cengage, 2007), 154-75.
[8]Charles Marsh, *Strange Glory: A Life of Dietrich Bonhoeffer* (New York: Vintage, 2014), 227-62; Dietrich Bonhoeffer, *Life Together* (New York: Harper & Row, 1954); Doug Rossinow, *The Politics of Authenticity: Liberalism, Christianity, and the New Left in America* (New York: Columbia University Press, 1998), 54.
[9]Rossinow, *Politics of Authenticity*, 56.
[10]Harvey Cox, *The Secular City* (New York: MacMillan, 1965), 108-29; Rossinow, *Politics of Authenticity*, 53-84.

community's first three years, programming at the study center primarily focused on biblical and theological studies, but this changed in 1954 as Lewis began to grow disenchanted with traditional Christian orthodoxy. The community's transformation continued the next year when Joseph Mathews, a onetime fundamentalist preacher who had gradually moved toward mainline Christianity, became the director of the Christian Faith-and-Life Community curriculum. Under Mathews, the community functioned for students as a "robust experiment in community intellectual living that was in such stark contrast to the comfortable campus life of the 1950s."[11]

As existentialist thought from Europe began to influence American campuses such as the University of Texas in Austin in the 1950s through literature and the Beat movement, the Christian Faith-and-Life Community functioned less as a center of spiritual formation and more as an incubator of intellectual inquiry free from college or parental constraints. As the next decade proved, the influence from one study center could be significant. Not only did clergy at schools such as Duke, Brown University, the University of Montana, and the University of Wisconsin model experiments similar to the Christian Faith-and-Life Community, but a number of leaders at the community also went on to exert national influence. Within the Christian Faith-and-Life Community students honed their intellects with a steady diet of existentialist and counterculture authors and primed themselves for action first in the civil rights movement and then in the emerging New Left, where the connections between the community and organizations such as Students for a Democratic Society (founded 1960) were undeniable. In 1961 future Students for a Democratic Society leaders and contributors to the influential 1969 Port Huron Statement Tom and Casey Hayden were married at the Christian Faith-and-Life Community, a place Tom Hayden later referred to as "*the* liberated spot on the silent campus."[12]

An understanding of the Christian Faith-and-Life Community—and the wider religious and cultural impulses that drove its formation, development, and eventual dissolution as students in the New Left eventually opted for more narrowly political organizations such as Students for a Democratic Society—provides a helpful launching point into a discussion of L'Abri and the evangelical study center movement the Swiss experiment helped to catalyze. On a

---

[11]Willie Morris in Rossinow, *Politics of Authenticity*, 54.
[12]Rossinow, *Politics of Authenticity*, 54.

personal level, Schaeffer's faith journey followed several of the same general contours as that of Lewis and Mathews at the Christian Faith-and-Life Community. Schaeffer began his ministry within fundamentalist Presbyterianism but shifted away from separatist fundamentalism when he encountered European theological and philosophical currents that fueled his own doubts and eventually a personal theological upheaval in the early 1950s. These experiences prompted Schaeffer, like Lewis and Mathews after him, to develop a ministry deeply committed to contextualizing the gospel to the needs of the day by creating a hospitable community dedicated to spiritual development and intellectual engagement with ideas such as existentialism and the nascent postmodernity that questioned the very idea of truth. In the process Schaeffer, like his contemporaries at the Christian Faith-and-Life Community, also embodied Cox's idea of God's avant-garde by contextualizing the gospel in a way that spoke to the needs of his time more compellingly than almost anything else within English-speaking evangelicalism.

Like Lewis, Schaeffer inspired a host of imitators across the United States and around the world. Yet for all their similarities, there was a crucial difference between the Christian Faith-and-Life Community and L'Abri and between their founders. Schaeffer differed from Lewis in that he came out of this season of exploration and doubt having shed fundamentalist separatism but not orthodox Christianity and a belief in absolute truth. This made all the difference for L'Abri and the network of individuals and study centers it inspired. At L'Abri, students imbibed plenty of Francis and Edith Schaeffer's eccentricities (a few students at L'Abri even took to wearing Swiss knickers like Schaeffer), but they also encountered the Schaeffers' deep conviction that there was truly a "God who is there" and who "is not silent."[13]

In addition to their status as *the* epitome of the evangelical's bohemian avant-garde during L'Abri's first decade and a half (1955–1970), the Schaeffers were able to exert lasting influence on a generation of evangelicals in part because their contextualization was not an end in itself but a door to a theologically robust worldview—a word Schaeffer popularized through his lifetime—rooted in the Reformed theological tradition. By placing distinct emphasis on the

---

[13]Schaeffer emphasizes these aspects of God repeatedly and used them in the titles of his early books. For imitators of Schaeffer's dress, see Linda Mercadante, *Bloomfield Avenue: A Jewish-Catholic Jersey Girl's Spiritual Journey* (Cambridge, MA: Cowley, 2006), 120.

sovereignty of God over all of creation, Reformed theology—most often associated with the work of sixteenth-century Reformer John Calvin—carried within itself seeds of cultural engagement that bore significant fruit within twentieth-century American evangelicalism. At L'Abri the Schaeffers helped students imagine what a gospel that touched and informed all of life looked like. Many of the young evangelicals who sat at Francis Schaeffer's feet during a discussion or who observed Edith Schaeffer cultivating beauty in the everyday left their experience inspired by the sheer breadth of worthwhile Christian endeavor. In case after case, L'Abri proved to be an open door to the immense possibilities available for meaningful Christian engagement. In this way, L'Abri functioned, like the Christian Faith-and-Life Community, as a launching pad where a generation learned to aspire to meaningful action. Unlike at the Christian Faith-and-Life Community, however, the action L'Abri inspired—at least in its first two decades of existence—managed to avoid being co-opted by politics.

As significant as L'Abri was for the formation of the intellectual, spiritual, and even relational aspirations of a generation, the Christian study center movement would look much different today if not for the influence of another learning community—Regent College. It was Regent College, led by Oxford-trained geographer and influential lay Christian James Houston and a group of well-connected Plymouth Brethren scholars and businessmen, that helped give academic heft to the fledgling study center movement and strengthened its emphasis on helping everyday lay Christians think Christianly about their vocations, whatever they might be. At the same time, the experiment in graduate lay theological education at Regent also set a new precedent for evangelical efforts to engage the secular university not as a foe to be conquered but as a meaningful—even necessary—academic and cultural partner. Whereas the Schaeffers' L'Abri was to a certain extent an insular, sheltered community (as even the name L'Abri, French for "shelter," could imply), Houston's unabashed esteem for the university and Christian academic pursuits became an exemplar to many at a time when more evangelicals than ever before were entering college. Furthermore, Houston's personal emphasis on theological education aimed at the laity combined with Regent's Plymouth Brethren heritage to open the door to theological education for many—including many women—who could not gain access to traditional seminary education or in other cases found seminary to be a poor fit. Because study centers did not, by and large, offer degrees leading to ordination, most of them, even those that did not affirm women's ordination, offered equal learning opportunities to both men and women at a time when many evangelical seminaries still did not.

By the early 1970s it was becoming clear that L'Abri and Regent College had become inspirations for a growing number of people who desired to found study centers of their own in places ranging from college towns such as Berkeley, California, and Charlottesville, Virginia, to global cities such as Washington, DC, and tucked-away hamlets such as Stahlstown, Pennsylvania. In each of these settings individuals who had come into contact with L'Abri, Regent College, or in many cases both, did their best to build on the legacy of these early study centers as hospitable places marked by spiritual and intellectual vibrancy. As this history will show, the reality seldom matched the ideal. Indeed, virtually every study center treated in these pages struggled with issues related to student recruitment or financial solvency at one point or another. There were also plenty of missteps and personality conflicts along the way. In some cases ambitions and promptings from publicists and consultants proved too powerful to resist, and study centers were transformed beyond recognition. In other cases, study centers held on to a founding vision almost to the brink of collapse before shifting their strategies to meet the changing demands of their context.

Amid these challenges and difficulties, the models that early study center leaders found in L'Abri and Regent College proved to have enduring value. As individuals such as Jim Hiskey, R. C. Sproul, David Gill, and Beat Steiner worked to adapt these models to their own contexts, they launched a loosely connected study center movement that eventually resulted in the development of a formal network of university-based Christian study centers called the Consortium of Christian Study Centers. Founded in 2008 by Andrew Trotter (longtime director of the Charlottesville-based Center for Christian Study) and a small team of other study center directors, the Consortium of Christian Study Centers has become the institutional umbrella for a renewed study center movement aimed at cultivating holistic flourishing and promoting the values of faithful "institutional presence" and "the life of the mind" on some of the nation's most prestigious academic institutions.[14]

---

[14]Mahan and Smedley, "University Ministry and the Evangelical Mind," 70-71. In 2011 these developments led Mark Noll to cite the existence of "self-standing study centers at Cornell, Illinois, Michigan, Michigan State, Minnesota, [and] Virginia" along with "the newly formed Consortium of

A Note on Definitions, Scope, and Sources

Before we dive into the history of how the ministry of an American couple in a Swiss chalet and a handful of Plymouth Brethren scholars in rented basement rooms in Vancouver launched a relational network and corresponding movement that is currently growing in numbers and influence, it will be helpful to offer a definition of a study center and then to define the scope and sources of this history.

What is a Christian study center? A Christian study center in its most basic form is a local Christian community dedicated to spiritual, intellectual, and relational flourishing via the cultivation of deep spirituality, intellectual and artistic engagement, and the cultivation of hospitable presence. To be a study center, each of these four elements—spiritual, intellectual, relational, and spatial—must be cultivated. Though one can grow intellectually and spiritually through online courses or individualized study, and though a ministry that devotes its energies to developing media for individualized, anonymous consumption may play a role in developing an individual's ability to think Christianly, such a ministry could not be called a study *center*. Place—and more specifically a place marked by relational warmth and hospitality—is essential.

In addition to a sense of place as defined by the built environment and welcoming ethos of a study center, the geographical location of a study center also exerts an important influence on the contours of each study center's ministry. Trotter has developed a helpful typology that accounts for these differences in the function and goals of four unique types of study centers: church-based study centers, city-based study centers, university-based study centers, and destination study centers. While examples of each of these different types of study centers appear in this history, the primary focus within this study is on the development of a university-based study center movement as represented by the Consortium of Christian Study Centers and its members. Not only are these study centers, by virtue of their proximity to academic institutions, representative of the most intellectually engaged study centers, but they also represent the growing edge of today's study center movement as it encounters

---

Christian Study Centers" as notable contributors to "the growing Christian presence at the nation's pluralistic universities"—a development that, Noll argued, should give evangelicals a reason "for thinking more optimistically about evangelical intellectual life." See Noll, *Jesus Christ and the Life of the Mind*, 156-57.

questions of religious liberty on campus and as it grows in terms of influence, representation, and financial resources.

A note on sources. The narratives that fill the following pages have been collected from a wide array of sources. Though it is easy to envy colleagues who write on individuals from the distant past who cannot be offended or offer critiques, during the course of this project it has been a privilege to enter into the history of these study centers through the stories of those who experienced them firsthand during their formative years. Oral-history interviews, personal letters, and more than one trip to personal collections in tucked-away corners, attics, or musty basements have added the joy of building relationships to the joy of intellectual discovery. This history is also richer thanks to those who experienced these communities and had the good sense to contribute the publications, letters, brochures, and so on to archives and the care of dedicated archivists. While this history benefited from the holdings of numerous archives, it is worth noting that this book is among the first to make extensive use of the recently cataloged James M. Houston Fonds at Regent College. This study is also the first to offer extended historical investigation of many of the study centers whose stories come up in this narrative.

The scope of this study. While the histories that follow trace the contours of some of the most influential study centers within North America and the rise of a university-focused study center movement more specifically, it is important to note from the start that this history does not claim to be exhaustive. There is plenty of room for further historical and quantitative work on the study center movement in its diverse forms. From the start, study centers were formed in church basements, homes, retreat centers, and virtually anywhere an enterprising and intellectually inclined individual could gather a small library of books and tapes and a few friends. Many of these study centers were short lived, but others had longer life spans, and some continue to function today. A simple internet search will demonstrate that there are many study center–like communities today that are dedicated to the training of lay Christians and in some cases clergy in the United States and around the globe. Perhaps the most notable North American study center to be left out of this study is the Institute for Christian Studies, which was founded in 1967 in Toronto by Dutch Calvinists. From the start the Institute for Christian Studies was a community defined by innovative methods, an ethnically Dutch culture, and a strict emphasis that its professors use the Reformational philosophy of Herman Dooyeweerd (1894–1977) as the foundation of all instruction—all of which led to misunderstandings and curtailed the institute's influence on the wider study center movement.[15] Thus while the Institute for Christian Studies proved an enduring institution and fruitful conversation partner for a subset of American evangelicals—especially scholars with ties to Calvin College and the Dutch Reformed community in Michigan—its influence on the Christian study center movement represented by the Consortium of Christian Study Centers is minimal in comparison to L'Abri and Regent College.

It is also worth noting that the following history makes no claims of delimiting all, or even the most important, currents in the development of a Christian or even more specifically evangelical mind. To claim to do so would not only be an act of hubris, but it would also be a venture whose scope would far exceed the parameters of a single book. Spurring Christians toward deep and sustained intellectual engagement is not the work of a day, nor is it the task of a single organization or movement. The story of the Christian study center movement is one small—but significant and often overlooked—means through which Christians have joined together to face the intellectual and spiritual demands of their times. In the process these communities have helped form an influential and growing network of individuals and institutions dedicated to living out a spiritually and intellectually engaged faith through a commitment to faithful presence and a desire to cultivate holistic flourishing on the campuses they call home. It is to their story that we now turn.

---

[15]For a monograph on the history of the Institute for Christian Studies, see Robert E. VanderVennen, *A University for the People: A History of the Institute for Christian Studies* (Sioux Center, IA: Dordt College Press, 2008). On the institute as an innovative and misunderstood venture, see VanderVennen, *University for the People*, 22-27.

PART 1
INNOVATION

1

L'ABRI

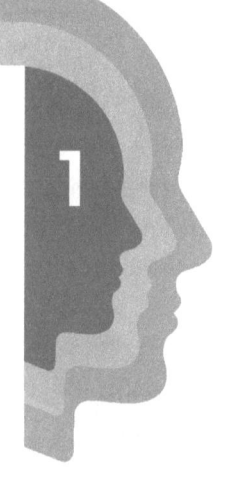

IN FEBRUARY 1970 Francis Schaeffer, an American pastor, missionary, bestselling evangelical author, and founder of the increasingly influential Christian community L'Abri in Huemoz, Switzerland, received a letter from a young American named David Gill. Gill, two years out of the University of California, Berkeley, was working as a high school history teacher in the San Francisco Bay Area. He was also an emerging leader in Berkeley's countercultural Christian World Liberation Front. In less than two years he would serve with Sharon Gallagher as the coeditor of the front's underground newspaper, *Right On!*, and help found a free university known as the Crucible. In his letter, Gill outlined how Schaeffer's 1968 book *The God Who Is There* had "revolutionized my testimony at UC Berkeley." Then he came to his main question: "Have you ever considered a sort of 'Farel House West' in Berkeley?" In Gill's opinion, Berkeley seemed just the place for a branch of L'Abri and its residential study center Farel House. "Berkeley," he enthused, "would be an ideal place to take over an old fraternity house and use it to confront modern men . . . with the person of the Lord Jesus Christ."[1]

Gill was not the only evangelical interested in re-creating Schaeffer's innovative learning community. Between winter 1970 and summer 1971 Schaeffer received similar letters from a number of individuals who went on to become leading players in the development of an evangelical study center movement in North America. In June 1970 Jim Hiskey, a former PGA golfer who in collaboration with the National Prayer Breakfast had started a L'Abri-style campus ministry at the University of Maryland, wrote to tell Schaeffer "how grateful

---

[1]David Gill to Francis A. Schaeffer, February 13, 1970, box 56, file 6, FSC.

we are for your ministry."[2] From the other side of the continent Jim Houston, founding principal of Vancouver's Regent College, a newly formed venture in lay theological education, wrote in August 1970 to ask Schaeffer whether he would speak at the next Regent summer school. "We really need you at this critical time," Houston noted. "The launching of any orbital mission requires tremendous thrust to begin with and we feel that you alone can provide some of this [thrust] by supporting us next summer."[3] During spring 1971, while Schaeffer was speaking at the first US L'Abri conference at Lookout Mountain, Tennessee, he met R. C. Sproul, a young Presbyterian minister from Cincinnati who had studied for a doctorate at the Free University in Amsterdam. Within a week Sproul wrote Schaeffer to follow up on a discussion the two had regarding Sproul's desire to start a L'Abri-type study center near Ligonier, Pennsylvania.[4] In September of the same year, Beat Steiner, a student leader in Action Ministries at the University of Virginia, struck up a correspondence with Schaeffer. Steiner hoped Schaeffer might agree to conduct a series of lectures the next spring at the University of Virginia.[5]

As the correspondence between Schaeffer and a veritable who's who of evangelicals in the early study center movement demonstrates, it is virtually impossible to talk about the emergence of a Christian study center movement in North America without referencing Francis and Edith Schaeffer's L'Abri Fellowship.[6] From its founding in 1955 L'Abri (French for "shelter") offered a generation of evangelicals the chance to discuss ideas and receive what the

---

[2]Jim Hiskey to Francis A. Schaeffer, June 25, 1970, box 56, file 12, FSC.
[3]James M. Houston to Francis A. Schaeffer, August 7, 1970, box 52, file 26, FSC.
[4]Sproul's first letter: R. C. Sproul to Francis A. Schaeffer, March 18, 1971, box 56, file 6, FSC. Sproul referred to Schaeffer as a mentor in 1979; see R. C. Sproul to Francis A. Schaeffer, June 21, 1979, box 56, file 6, FSC.
[5]Beat Steiner to Francis A. Schaeffer, July 27, 1971, private collection.
[6]Many biographical accounts of Schaeffer's life already exist. The most thoroughly researched is Barry Hankins, *Francis Schaeffer and the Shaping of Evangelical America* (Grand Rapids: Eerdmans, 2008). Two biographies written by individuals with close personal interactions with Schaeffer are Collin Duriez, *Francis Schaeffer: An Authentic Life* (Wheaton, IL: Crossway Books, 2008), and Louis Gifford Parkhurst, *Francis Schaeffer: The Man and His Message* (Wheaton, IL: Tyndale House, 1985). Several family members have also told Schaeffer's story. These include Edith Schaeffer, *The Tapestry: The Life and Times of Francis and Edith Schaeffer* (Waco, TX: Word Books, 1981), and Frank Schaeffer's memoirs: *Crazy for God: How I Grew Up as One of the Elect, Helped Found the Religious Right, and Lived to Take All (or Almost All) of It Back* (New York: Carroll & Graf, 2007) and *Sex, Mom, and God: How the Bible's Strange Take on Sex Led to Crazy Politics, and How I Learned to Love Women (and Jesus) Anyway* (Cambridge, MA: Da Capo, 2011).

Schaeffers described as "honest answers to honest questions."[7] Not a commune but certainly a spiritual and intellectual community, L'Abri gave the Schaeffers a place to hone their thinking and a platform from which to launch into a global ministry as writers and speakers, and eventually filmmakers and political activists.[8] Based out of their home, L'Abri was the canvas on which the Schaeffers' deep appreciation for beauty (from table settings to classic and modern art), their firm conviction that Christians need never fear pursuing the truth, and their embodiment of the Reformed idea that the lordship of Christ extends to all of life cast a vision for the flourishing life that inspired a generation of evangelicals to reconsider the spiritually, intellectually, and culturally stunted versions of Christianity many had encountered in their homes and churches. As hundreds and then thousands of American evangelicals read the Schaeffers' books, made the pilgrimage to L'Abri, and enjoyed food and conversation around the Schaeffers' table, many developed a taste for the intellectually and culturally engaged Christianity the Schaeffers espoused. For some this hunger led to advanced academic study. For others it led to engagement in spheres of society such as the arts, business, or formal ministry. For a few, however, L'Abri was more than a stopping place; it was a model to be replicated in the places they called home. It was the start of an evangelical Christian study center movement.

New Vistas: The Schaeffers' Break with Separatist Fundamentalism

In many ways the Schaeffers were unlikely candidates and an alpine village in Switzerland an unlikely place to launch a movement. Indeed, when the Schaeffers quietly started the ministry of L'Abri out of their home in June 1955 few outside their inner circle of prayer partners (or praying family, as Edith referred to them) even took note. By 1955 Francis Schaeffer seemed well past his most influential days. The onetime agnostic who had come to faith in high school and impressed his professors in college and seminary with his natural intellectual abilities and zeal had at one point been a rising star in the Bible Presbyterian Church (founded 1937), having served in increasingly influential

---

[7]Francis A. Schaeffer, *Two Contents, Two Realities*, in *Complete Works of Francis A. Schaeffer: A Christian Worldview*, vol. 3, *A Christian View of Spirituality* (Westchester IL: Crossway Books, 1982), 403-27.

[8]Longtime L'Abri worker and Schaeffer friend Jerram Barrs describes it as "a cross between an extended family and a study center." See Jerram Barrs, Francis A. Schaeffer: The Early Years (course, Covenant Theological Seminary, fall 1989), lecture 23.

pastorates beginning with tenures in Grove City and Chester, Pennsylvania, before eventually landing a post at the large Covenant Church in St. Louis. While there, his star continued to rise as he and Edith had demonstrated an impressive ability to develop and lead ministry to children, eventually founding Children for Christ as a separatist version of Child Evangelism Fellowship. These experiences led to a call by the Independent Board for Presbyterian Foreign Missions in 1948 to serve as missionaries to children and their families in postwar Europe. Francis seemed poised to become a national leader within fundamentalist circles in North America.

But Europe changed Schaeffer. Like American artists, writers, and jazz musicians who flocked to Paris decades earlier, Europe seemed to offer Schaeffer a freedom to develop his taste for art, philosophy, and even good conversations in a context that reverberated with the newest currents in thought while simultaneously distanced from the internecine struggles that dominated American fundamentalism.[9] As Schaeffer found a new voice and sensibility in Europe, he forfeited a portion of his standing within American fundamentalism. By 1955 Schaeffer found himself outside his previous denomination and increasingly marginalized by the Independent Board for Presbyterian Foreign Missions, which did not approve of his growing emphasis on evangelism through home-based hospitality and spiritual conversation. Both emphases had been shaped by the Schaeffers' longstanding practice of inviting people into the family's home for meals and conversation as well as his own spiritual crisis, which occurred in the winter and spring of 1951, when he had attempted to root out doubt by returning to his teenage agnosticism in order to rebuild his faith on a firmer foundation.[10]

In some ways it was Schaeffer's own struggle with doubt that made L'Abri possible by pushing the pastor-turned-missionary to consider ways to better reach his European neighbors with a message that emphasized an intellectually honest quest for truth and a deep spirituality built on genuine love for God and neighbor. While the combination of these traits was not common within American evangelicalism in the 1950s and early 1960s, there were evangelicals, such as Harold J. Ockenga (1905–1985) and Carl F. H. Henry (1913–2003), who were attempting to balance intellectual and spiritual vitality through endeavors such

---

[9]Jerrod Seigel, *Bohemian Paris: Culture, Politics, and the Boundaries of Bourgeois Life, 1830–1930* (New York: Viking, 1986), 367-68.
[10]Francis A. Schaeffer, "True Spirituality," in Schaeffer, *Christian View of Spirituality*, 195.

as Fuller Theological Seminary (founded 1947) and *Christianity Today* (founded 1956). Like many neo-evangelical efforts, which built on World War II sensibilities toward mobilization and large events, many of these ministries tried to carry out the formation of minds and hearts with large programs or crusades fueled by equally large ambitions and a handful of deep-pocketed donors.[11] The Schaeffers' approach was different. Rather than making evangelicalism bigger through sheer numbers and name recognition, the Schaeffers made evangelicalism different by combining and expanding neo-evangelical efforts to engage the intellect and culture with L'Abri's key innovation—their decision to base a robust and holistic appreciation for the intellect, culture, and Christian spirituality not within the context of a mass rally or accredited theological institution but in a community built around home-based hospitality and the rhythms of everyday life. Inadvertently harking back to the monastic model of prayer and work in the context of study and community, L'Abri was a working, living, studying, praying community before communal living became a countercultural standard.[12]

Before not only their evangelical peers but also most Americans, the Schaeffers seemed to intuit that a home-based ministry of hospitable presence was the vehicle through which they could carry the message of a God who was truly there to a world that had lost all sense of absolute truth and crossed what Schaeffer described as "the line of despair."[13] To a certain extent the Schaeffers' work at L'Abri was an extended and multifaceted effort to help a generation dealing with this loss of truth and the fallout of the postmodern shift, which deprivileged all universal truth claims (or metanarratives) in favor of a relativized understanding of reality in which individuals came to understand truth in terms of their personal experiences and the communities to which they belonged.

Building a Shelter

L'Abri was the Schaeffers' means of confronting this shift in truth and the accompanying fallout in individual lives. Francis first landed on the name L'Abri for

---

[11]For more on the influence of Ockenga and the neo-evangelical movement, see Garth Rosell, *The Surprising Work of God: Harold John Ockenga, Billy Graham, and the Rebirth of Evangelicalism* (Grand Rapids: Baker Academic, 2008); George M. Marsden, *Reforming Fundamentalism: Fuller Seminary and the New Evangelicalism* (Grand Rapids: Eerdmans, 1987); Owen Strachan, *Awakening the Evangelical Mind: An Intellectual History of the Neo-evangelical Movement* (Grand Rapids: Zondervan, 2015).
[12]Between 1965 and 1970 over two thousand communal groups were formed. Robert Houriet, *Getting Back Together* (New York: Coward, McCann & Geoghegen, 1971), xiii.
[13]Francis A. Schaeffer, *The God Who Is There* (Downers Grove, IL: InterVarsity Press, 1968), 14-16.

a new missionary outreach in fall 1954. The name symbolized his hope that their home could function as a spiritual shelter where individuals could come for help. Edith liked the idea and immediately spun into her characteristic action by beginning to compile a folio decorated with pine trees on a hillside and inscribed with the words "L'Abri . . . come for morning coffee, or afternoon tea, with your questions."[14]

Before L'Abri could move beyond the pages of Edith's sketchbook, however, there were practicalities to consider. First, the couple had to navigate a series of obstacles, the most notable of which were two letters they received on February 14, 1955. The first informed them that they were evicted from the canton of Valais due to their work as Protestant missionaries in a Catholic canton. The second letter took the eviction further by requiring that the Schaeffers leave Switzerland entirely. It seemed like the Schaeffers' dreams for L'Abri were coming to an end. Yet what seemed at first like an abrupt end to their European ministry actually marked an important beginning. While they were forced to leave the Catholic canton of Valais, the family was eventually permitted to remain in Switzerland provided that they find a house in the Protestant canton of Vaud by March 31, 1955. In the nick of time, they were able to make a down payment on a house, Chalet les Melezes, just outside the village of Huemoz in the Protestant canton of Vaud.[15] Situated at an altitude of over three thousand feet, the long balconies and many windows of the chalet provided panoramic views of the Rhone Valley and the famous Dents du Midi mountain range. In the years to come, account after account from those who visited L'Abri contained reference to the significance of the alpine beauty that surrounded the chalet.[16]

Convinced that God had provided them with favor to stay in Switzerland and a chalet that was ideally situated for the ministry of conversations and hospitality they felt drawn to, the Schaeffers severed their last official tie to American fundamentalism by resigning from the Independent Board for Presbyterian Foreign Missions on June 5, 1955.[17] By resigning from the board, the Schaeffers freed themselves from the organization's oversight and severed their lifeline of financial support at the same time. Drawing on the legacy of "faith"

---

[14]Edith Schaeffer, *Tapestry*, 404.
[15]Edith Schaeffer, *L'Abri* (Worthing, UK: Norfolk, 1969), 77-112.
[16]Os Guinness, interview with author, October 19, 2015, Mclean, VA.
[17]Duriez, *Francis Schaeffer*, 131-33.

Figure 1.1. The view looking out from a chalet at L'Abri.

missionaries before them such as George Mueller and Hudson Taylor, the family would now rely on God to provide not just "the people of God's choice" for their ministry but also the necessary funds to sustain their family and to feed and house the people God sent.[18] Because one of the primary guiding principles of L'Abri was that the ministry existed primarily to serve as a demonstration of God's existence in the world, the Schaeffers decided that they would never explicitly ask for funds or advertise their ministry in order to attract students.[19] They were putting themselves in God's hands and would wait for him to provide.

As far as the Schaeffers and the small community that assembled at Chalet les Melezes were concerned, God held up his end of the bargain. Though money was often tight, there seemed always to be just enough. For their part, the Schaeffers did all they could to help God in his task of provision by stretching

---

[18]Edith Schaeffer, *The Tapestry*, 394. See also Edith Schaeffer, *Dear Family: The L'Abri Family Letters, 1961-1986* (San Francisco: Harper & Row, 1989), 32, 85.

[19]In February 1956 Francis Schaeffer described the work of L'Abri by noting, "I do believe He is giving a demonstration here of His existence. I believe more and more that *this* is truly the central task of the Christian—to give the Lord the opportunity to exhibit his existence." See Francis Schaeffer, *The Letters of Francis Schaeffer: Spiritual Reality in the Personal Christian Life*, ed. Lane T. Dennis (Wheaton, IL: Crossway, 1986), 63-64, letter of February 8, 1956.

resources as far as possible. They used the phrase "active passivity" to describe the way in which through their work at L'Abri they sought to balance the tension between waiting on God to demonstrate his existence through miraculous provision while all the while doing their part to live with the utmost frugality.[20]

For those who stayed with the Schaeffers during the 1950s and 1960s, L'Abri's somewhat fragile financial status was obvious. Hurvey and Dorothy Woodson, the first L'Abri workers from outside the Schaeffer family, describe L'Abri in the 1950s as "very poor" and extremely cold in the winter. Hurvey, who was often in charge of regulating the house's temperature when Schaeffer was away, remembers being assigned to guard the stockpile of firewood so that visitors would not use too much. Edith would sometimes dig in the coals from the previous day's fire for bits that might still be useful. "It was really a very tight situation," Hurvey remembers. "We ate a lot of cornflakes, and we didn't have much."[21]

Within the L'Abri community individuals were classified as belonging to one of four or sometimes five categories based on the duration and purpose of their stay in Huemoz. Among the earliest distinctions made at L'Abri was the basic distinction between guests and workers. Guests were able to stay for a short time (usually no more than a week) at L'Abri for free. According to Edith, the absence of a guest fee played an important role in fostering the "'enlarged Family' feeling" at L'Abri. "No one who comes to L'Abri as a guest pays for board and room. It is not a 'conference,' it is a place where doors are open, as a private home would be, to those whom the Lord sends with special spiritual needs."[22] Unlike temporary guests, workers functioned as permanent staff and were paid minimally—usually around twenty-five to thirty-six dollars a month—based on personal need.[23] Beginning in 1960 with the development of L'Abri's Farel House—a part of L'Abri specifically devoted to study through private tutoring and listening to audio tapes—the Schaeffers also accepted "students." L'Abri students paid two dollars a day for meals and personalized instruction by Schaeffer or a L'Abri worker.[24] Students spent roughly four hours a day listening to Schaeffer's tapes. They then

---

[20]Duriez, *Francis Schaeffer*, 125.
[21]Duriez, *Francis Schaeffer*, 141-42.
[22]Edith Schaeffer, *Dear Family*, 22, letter of July 21, 1961.
[23]Guinness, interview. See also Hankins, *Francis Schaeffer and the Shaping of Evangelical America*, 58. For more on workers' pay, see Jerram Barrs, Francis Schaeffer, the Later Years (course, Covenant Theological Seminary, 1989), lecture 3, "Life at L'Abri."
[24]Originally Schaeffer himself oversaw the students' course of study. As student numbers grew, he gradually transferred this duty to a handful of L'Abri workers such as Os Guinness.

spent another four hours working in the L'Abri kitchens, gardens, woodworking shops, and so on. Students could stay for up to three months. Eventually, however, enough students and guests requested to stay longer that L'Abri established the position of helper. Students who became helpers at the end of their three-month stay could remain at L'Abri for an additional six months.[25] The real power brokers at L'Abri were L'Abri members. In order to become a member, one had to be elected to membership after serving at least three years as a worker.[26]

The Schaeffers never took out ads to find L'Abri guests, workers, or students. The draw of L'Abri, especially prior to the publication of Francis's first books,

---

[25] Frank Schaeffer, *Crazy for God*, 92.
[26] Frank Schaeffer, *Crazy for God*, 92; Hankins, *Francis Schaeffer*, 58.

Figure 1.2. L'Abri student Linda Mercadante works in a garden outside a L'Abri chalet. L'Abri students typically spent half the day listening to Schaeffer's recordings and half the day working on various community projects.

in 1968, was carried along relational networks through word of mouth and personal interactions with the Schaeffers and other L'Abri members and workers. Even before all the boxes were unpacked in Chalet les Melezes, the Schaeffers began to receive guests at their home. Word began to spread both at the University of Lausanne, where the Schaeffers' daughter Priscilla was studying, and in the United States, where the Schaeffers maintained connections with friends, family, and former congregants through Edith's regular letters to their "praying family." Within a few months of officially launching L'Abri, their home was seldom empty, especially on the weekend. By the time L'Abri marked its official one-year anniversary in July 1956, the number of visitors had increased to over 175 people from mid-June through July.[27]

Of the hundreds of guests who spent time at L'Abri during summer 1956, perhaps none was as influential as Dutch art historian Hans Rookmaaker. Ever since Schaeffer and Rookmaaker had met at the 1948 meeting of the fundamentalist International Council of Christian Churches in Amsterdam, the two enjoyed a close friendship based on their mutual passion for great art and Reformed theology.[28] On the basis of this friendship, the Rookmaakers and their three young children came to L'Abri in summer 1956 for an extended stay. During this time both Hans and Anky Rookmaaker were impressed by the Schaeffers' deep spirituality, especially their emphasis on prayer.[29] In the years to come the Rookmaakers' involvement in the ministry of L'Abri grew significantly. Eventually they became full L'Abri members, and in 1971 they launched Dutch L'Abri in the farming village of Eck en Wiel near Amsterdam.[30]

While there is some debate as to the degree to which Schaeffer and Rookmaaker's friendship was marked by intellectual reciprocity, there is little doubt that both men benefited greatly from each other.[31] Schaeffer helped the Dutch Rookmaaker tweak the English of his dissertation in order to make it acceptable

---

[27] Edith Schaeffer, *With Love, Edith: The L'Abri Family Letters* (San Francisco: Harper & Row, 1988), 362, letter of July 31, 1956.
[28] Laurel Gasque, *Art and the Christian Mind: The Life and Work of H. R. Rookmaaker* (Wheaton, IL: Crossway Books, 2005), 72-74. See also Linette Martin, *Hans Rookmaaker: A Biography* (Downers Grove, IL: InterVarsity Press, 1979).
[29] Duriez, *Francis Schaeffer*, 148-49.
[30] Gasque, *Art and the Christian Mind*, 98-99.
[31] For differing views on Rookmaaker's influence on Schaeffer, see Molly Worthen, *Apostles of Reason: The Crisis of Authority in American Evangelicalism* (New York: Oxford University Press, 2013), 211; Gasque, *Art and the Christian Mind*, 96, 102-3; William Edgar, *Schaeffer on the Christian Life: Countercultural Spirituality* (Wheaton, IL: Crossway, 2013), 51.

to his committee and provided a sounding board for Rookmaaker's thoughts. For his part, Rookmaaker stood behind Schaeffer as a kind of scholar-at-large for L'Abri. Indeed, he was one of the few academic voices Schaeffer permitted into his inner circle of advisers, a group primarily made up of family members and far younger acolytes. Convinced of the quality of Rookmaaker's thought, Schaeffer used L'Abri conferences and his frequent lectures to InterVarsity Christian Fellowship groups in England as platforms to introduce Rookmaaker and his work. Once given the stage, Rookmaaker's engaging style and deep knowledge were on full display. By 1970, when Rookmaaker published his crossover bestseller *Modern Art and the Death of a Culture*, his Schaeffer-aided transition from Dutch academic to public intellectual stardom was complete.[32] Until his early death, in 1977, Rookmaaker was one of the most sought-after lecturers on the interaction of art and modern culture within English-speaking evangelicalism on both sides of the Atlantic.

Before Schaeffer could play a role in introducing Rookmaaker in Britain, however, he needed to be introduced on English soil himself, something that did not happen in a meaningful way until he and Edith traveled to London in late May 1958. In typical L'Abri fashion, Schaeffer's introduction on the British scene came via a relationship he and Edith formed with a L'Abri guest who wanted to give some of her friends back home a chance to experience the challenging conversations she had enjoyed at Chalet les Melezes. The short trip paved the way for future trips, English L'Abri conferences, and eventually a separate English L'Abri branch, which benefited in its early years from the leadership of Swiss L'Abri–trained individuals such as Jerram and Vicki Barrs and Ranald and Susan (Schaeffer) Macaulay.

Open Doors: L'Abri and the Schaeffers' Rise to International Fame, 1960–1974

As significant as the 1950s were for the development of rhythms of life and deep relationships at L'Abri, it was during the 1960s that L'Abri began to gain wider exposure as an intellectual and countercultural Christian community. In 1960 a journalist whose daughter attended high school with one of the Schaeffers' daughters tipped off a friend at *Time* magazine about the Schaeffers' work. The

---

[32]Gasque, *Art and the Christian Mind*, 100-101, 181.

resulting article, titled "Mission to Intellectuals," in the January 11, 1960, issue of *Time*, introduced the Schaeffers' heretofore relatively unknown ministry to thousands of readers in the United States and around the world. By calling L'Abri "one of the most unusual missions in the Western world," the article presented Schaeffer as anything but a staid fundamentalist type. The article highlighted Schaeffer's passion to present "the Bible's historical truth in such a way that it is acceptable to today's intellectuals," along with his assessment that "Protestantism has become bourgeois."[33]

Recognition in *Time* helped raise L'Abri's profile, but it was not until 1965, when Francis and Edith traveled to Boston at the invitation of Harvard graduate student and Park Street Church collegiate pastor Harold O. J. Brown (1933–2007), that Francis Schaeffer began to reestablish himself and the ministry of L'Abri as an influence within American evangelicalism.[34] During the twelve-day trip Schaeffer lectured as often as three times a day to audiences numbering as many as four hundred students. Describing the trip in a family letter written just before she and Francis headed back to Europe, Edith enthused, "It is as if *suddenly* both in England and here doors have swung open in a new degree."[35]

Edith's instincts proved correct. Over the next two decades open doors defined the work of the L'Abri Fellowship like never before. As his February 1965 Boston trip showed, the first of these newly opened doors was increased opportunity for travel—especially travel to the United States. A few months later Schaeffer followed up his Boston lectures by presenting his views of contemporary society in even greater depth at Wheaton College, near Chicago, and at California's evangelical Westmont College. These trips were harbingers of things to come. In 1968 the Schaeffers were joined by their teenage son, Frank, and Os Guinness on a fourteen-city tour with stops at places such as Wheaton and Westmont while also including new destinations such as Michigan's Calvin College.[36] Later Schaeffer followed up these American trips by holding the first American L'Abri Conference at Covenant College in Lookout

---

[33]"Mission to Intellectuals," *Time*, January 11, 1960. For Edith Schaeffer's take, see Edith Schaeffer, *With Love, Edith*, 447, letter of February 12, 1960.
[34]Brown earned his PhD from Harvard in 1967. For more biographical information on Brown, see John D. Woodbridge, "Harold O. J. Brown," *First Things*, July 10, 2007, www.firstthings.com/web-exclusives/2007/07/harold-oj-brown.
[35]Edith Schaeffer, *Dear Family*, 88.
[36]Hankins, *Francis Schaeffer*, 77; Guinness, interview.

Mountain, Tennessee, in March 1971. From that point on, the door to the United States never remained closed for long.

Schaeffer's success on the American evangelical lecture circuit led to openings in the world of publishing. As early as 1965, demand for tapes and the 55,000-word, 130-page transcript of his lectures at Wheaton turned his mind toward publishing a book based on the "Speaking Historic Christianity into the Twentieth-Century World" lecture series that he had been developing and adapting for several years. In 1968 Schaeffer published a minimally edited version of his 1965 Wheaton lecture transcripts as *The God Who Is There*. The same year he also published *Escape from Reason*, based on reworked transcripts from lectures he delivered in the United Kingdom in 1966 and 1967. Both books were published in the United Kingdom by Hodder and Stoughton a few months before Inter-Varsity Press made them available for US markets. Schaeffer went on to publish twenty more books, twelve of which were published through InterVarsity Press.[37]

Schaeffer was not alone in his efforts to publish material related to the work of L'Abri. As early as 1963 Edith had decided to turn what she often described as "the story of L'Abri" into a book.[38] Published in 1969 by London's Norfolk Press, the book did much to highlight and better describe L'Abri as a multifaceted community in the wake of the substantial increase in publicity the ministry was receiving due to Francis's more theoretical publications. As Francis Schaeffer noted in the brief forward to *L'Abri*, Edith's book presented an important supplement to the image of L'Abri one might get from reading *The God Who Is There* or *Escape from Reason*. His books stemmed from L'Abri's emphasis on providing "an honest answer to honest questions." Edith's book, however, offered readers a glimpse into the ways "the Personal-Infinite God" demonstrated his reality at L'Abri. They were, to Francis Schaeffer's mind, "the two sides of a single coin."[39]

As the Schaeffer's sphere of influence expanded through speaking engagements and writing, so did the number of people who wanted to visit L'Abri. Edith noticed a shift as early as fall 1966: "L'Abri seems to be growing, with more people *coming* here all the time, and more calls coming for us to go to a scattered number of places to speak." As the ministry expanded, it seemed that "'private life' is

---

[37] Hankins, *Francis Schaeffer*, 161, 164-72, 79. Tyndale House, Fleming H. Revell, and Crossway also published Schaeffer's books.
[38] Edith Schaeffer, *Dear Family*, 55, letter of August 28, 1963.
[39] Francis Schaeffer, foreword to Edith Schaeffer, *L'Abri*.

fading out from any of our daily schedules."[40] The situation only became more frenzied in the next few years. October 1969—when Chalet les Melezes and L'Abri's multiple other chalets were still full after a busier-than-usual summer—signaled a new normal.[41] As Edith noted for readers of her October 1969 family letter, "We have all suddenly and with a great feeling of dismay, awakened to the fact that there is *not* going to be a difference between summer, autumn, winter, and spring as far as numbers of people coming to L'Abri."[42] The demand for time at L'Abri and interaction with Schaeffer only grew in the early 1970s as the Schaeffers continued to write and as ministries such as InterVarsity Christian Fellowship continued to make sure that a generation of college students had access to their books. Even when Edith tried to downplay the allure of L'Abri in early 1972, noting, "L'Abri is *not* a rosy glow of excitement and perfection, not even for one day," letters still poured in from individuals around the globe who wanted "to come to L'Abri, to sell homes, furniture, leave all, and 'join the community.'"[43]

Shifting Scenes: Film, Politics, and L'Abri, 1975-1984

As the Schaeffers underwent a transformation from a relatively unknown couple to some of the brightest stars within twentieth-century evangelicalism, life at L'Abri changed. Perhaps the most noticeable and significant change was the increasing absence of the Schaeffers from daily life at Chalet les Melezes. In the two decades since the founding of L'Abri, the Schaeffers had transitioned from a relatively unknown missionary couple to internationally known authors and evangelical celebrities. Along the way they encountered both the benefits and the costs of success. The sale of millions of books brought huge royalties, which, because the Schaeffers donated much of the profit from their publications to L'Abri, provided a significant boon to the ministry's financial stability throughout much of the 1970s.[44] Fame, however, also meant that personal space virtually disappeared. Though Edith had once described L'Abri as a type of extended

---

[40]Edith Schaeffer, *Dear Family*, 110.
[41]By 1969 Swiss L'Abri consisted of several chalets and a chapel building used for Sunday morning services and L'Abri's educational ministry, Farel House.
[42]Edith Schaeffer, *Dear Family*, 140, letter of October 13, 1969.
[43]Edith Schaeffer, *Dear Family*, 180, letter of March 4, 1972, emphasis original.
[44]On royalties, see Hankins, *Francis Schaeffer*, 57; Barrs, "Life at L'Abri." In 1991 James Davison Hunter reported that Francis Schaeffer had sold three million copies of his books in the United States alone; see James Davison Hunter, *Culture Wars: The Struggle to Define America* (New York: Basic Books, 1991), 244.

family, by January 1973 this was no longer the case. "At some time in the past years, the balance has changed, a line was crossed, and Melezes ceased really to be a shared home." Instead, "the hall became a kind of youth hostel or entrance to a pension in atmosphere at times. One could not walk through without being asked dozens of questions, or without having a picture snapped." In the face of such constant attention, the Schaeffers found that the small apartment they had been renting as a getaway and writing retreat was no longer sufficient. The Schaeffers purchased Chalet le Chardonnet, which was located about ten minutes up the mountain from Chalet les Melezes, and moved into their new home on January 26, 1973.[45] From that point on the Schaeffers primarily saw individual L'Abri students and guests at their new home by appointment.[46]

A new house was not the only thing that kept the Schaeffers away from Chalet les Melezes during these years. International celebrity meant a demand for international travel. Books demanded book tours. The Schaeffers spent much of fall 1972 on the road as Francis spoke to groups at Princeton University; Geneva College, in western Pennsylvania; the American L'Abri branch in Los Gatos, California; the University of Hawaii; and universities in multiple Japanese cities, Hong Kong, and India.[47] By 1973 a new home and a full travel itinerary meant that students who traveled to L'Abri to sit at Schaeffer's feet were now facing the prospect of learning not from Schaeffer himself but from one of his sons-in-law or a L'Abri worker.

By far the most significant change at L'Abri, however, came in 1975, when Francis Schaeffer followed Frank's lead and entered the world of film. Since at least 1974 Schaeffer had been working on a book about "the rise and decline of western thought and culture."[48] Originally the project, which eventually became Schaeffer's widely popular *How Should We Then Live?* book and film series, was conceived as only a more expansive print version of the declension narrative that Schaeffer had already charted in books such as *The God Who Is There* and *Escape from Reason*. Frank, however, had other ideas. He was convinced that his father needed to expand the reach of his ideas and that film was the best means to this end.[49] Working

---

[45]Edith Schaeffer, *Dear Family*, 201-2, letter of February 10, 1973.
[46]Edgar, *Schaeffer on the Christian Life*, 73.
[47]Edith Schaeffer, *Dear Family*, 203.
[48]Edith Schaeffer, *Dear Family*, 225, letter of November 26, 1974.
[49]As he admits, the suggestion also fit with his own ambition to direct and film movies; see Frank Schaeffer, *Crazy for God*, 258.

together with Gospel Films producer Bill Zeoli—the son of evangelist Anthony Zeoli, whom Schaeffer had met shortly after coming to Christ—Frank convinced his father to venture beyond the printed word.[50] That Zeoli was a convincing salesman, the son of a significant evangelist, believed in Frank's potential, and had access to the huge fortune of Amway cofounder Richard DeVos did not hurt.[51] As Frank later recalled, "Until Billy Zeoli showed up, Dad, with his preference for the small-is-beautiful hippie ethos . . . had avoided the temptation to capitalize on his growing fame." Comparing Schaeffer's allure for evangelicals to that of the era-appropriate allure of the Grateful Dead for Deadheads, Frank notes that Schaeffer felt his work would lose its meaning if he "sold out" when he was "on the cusp of going big-time" by taking "the last step" toward celebrity.[52]

But with the prodding of his son and Zeoli, Schaeffer took more than a step into filmmaking. With characteristic abandon, he and Edith threw themselves wholeheartedly into the production of a *How Should We Then Live?* documentary film. Francis and Edith hit the road for film shoots across Europe in August 1975, and the rigors of prepping for daily shoots took up nearly all of the Schaeffers' energy for much of the next year and a half.[53] After the filming was finally completed, the Schaeffers readied themselves for a fourteen-city North American film tour in which Schaeffer would host question-and-answer sessions after viewings of the film. The first of these showings took place before fifty-six hundred people in Oakland, California, on January 30, 1977—Schaeffer's sixty-fifth birthday.[54] From this point on, Schaeffer shifted his focus increasingly away from the one-on-one conversations and small group exchanges that had been the hallmark of L'Abri and instead focused on gathering large crowds for a handful of big events and on an interest in politics—especially the issue of abortion—which defined the remaining years of his life and dramatically shaped his legacy. L'Abri continued to welcome guests and students for decades to come, but something had shifted. L'Abri's golden age had passed.

---

[50]At the very least Edith saw it as significant that Zeoli was the son of Anthony Zeoli. See Edith Schaeffer, *Dear Family*, 235, letter of July 4, 1975; Edith Schaeffer, *Tapestry*, 55.
[51]Frank Schaeffer, *Crazy for God*, 256-69; Hankins, *Francis Schaeffer*, 161-65.
[52]Frank Schaeffer, *Crazy for God*, 257.
[53]For a thorough treatment of the rigor of these months spent filming, see Edith's account in *Tapestry*, 583-92.
[54]Edith Schaeffer, *Tapestry*, 592.

A Multifaceted Community and Its Legacy

What was it that made Francis and Edith Schaeffer and the L'Abri Fellowship so magnetic? And what did those who found their way to L'Abri during the ministry's most significant decade (1965–1975) find when they arrived at Chalet les Melezes? For many, what they encountered was not just one celebrity teacher or family but a multifaceted community where spirituality and the search for beauty and truth through art and intellectual engagement were set within a context of relationship and openhanded hospitality. As powerful as each of these dimensions of L'Abri was in its own right, taken together they endued L'Abri with a magnetism—especially during the late 1960s and early 1970s—that was second to none within evangelicalism. A visit to L'Abri became a kind of credential for a generation of evangelicals aspiring to make the trip. For the many who realized this dream, L'Abri frequently became the doorway to even greater hopes.

L'Abri as a Spiritual Community

While spirituality was not always the first thing writers and photographers noted when they visited the Schaeffers in Huemoz, L'Abri's most foundational identity was not its intellectualism or its engagement with art and culture. Rather, these traits were the natural outflow of L'Abri's primary identity as a spiritual community dedicated to prayer and the belief that the gospel affected every facet of one's life and vocation. These emphases were the natural result of Schaeffer's own experiences. Before he was frequenting museums, pontificating on Søren Kierkegaard, or functioning as an icon of countercultural evangelicalism, he was a pastor dedicated to aiding people in their journey toward "the God who is there." For Schaeffer, the truth of the gospel meant not only that God was Lord of *all* aspects of life but also that hell was real.[55] These spiritual realities drove the Schaeffers to risk the "costly" and "unantiseptic" hospitality that left their wedding presents broken and tattered and that led them to allow young people whom they suspected had venereal diseases to sleep between their sheets.[56]

---

[55] Francis A. Schaeffer, *The Church at the End of the Twentieth Century*, in *Complete Works of Francis A. Schaeffer: A Christian Worldview*, vol. 4, *A Christian View of the Church* (Westchester, IL: Crossway Books, 1982), 93.

[56] Reflection on the costliness of hospitality, Francis Schaeffer noted, "In about the first three years of L'Abri, almost all our wedding presents were wiped out. Our sheets were torn. Holes were burned in our rugs." See *Church at the End of the Twentieth Century*, 92–93.

The Schaeffers' faith undergirded it all. As longtime L'Abri worker Jerram Barrs later noted, "understanding spirituality" was "essential for understanding anything at all about the work of L'Abri."[57]

Understanding spirituality at L'Abri begins with understanding the centrality of prayer to the Schaeffers' work and the common life of those who stayed at L'Abri. In many ways L'Abri necessitated a life of prayer. "When we say we pray, looking directly to the Lord to supply funds and workers, we really mean it," Edith emphasized to the thirteen hundred members of the Schaeffers' praying family in 1959.[58] Prayer marked out L'Abri's days, weeks, and years and showed Schaeffer to be anything but a cool rationalist. Throughout the first two decades of L'Abri's existence (and much of its subsequent history), a day per week was set aside for staff prayer.[59] During these days the staff selected half-hour blocks of time for prayer in L'Abri's prayer room, where they interceded for L'Abri, the Schaeffers, the needs of L'Abri guests, and other pressing concerns.[60] Prayer was not reserved for the weekly day of prayer alone but extended into almost every part of L'Abri. Prayers took place as guests and workers kneeled around living room coffee tables, hiked, or sat around the Schaeffers' fireplace. At dinnertime prayers were often so long and detailed that kitchen workers sometimes worried that the soup would get cold. As William Edgar remembers, "I would have to get used to smelling the excellent savors of the great cooking at L'Abri while the praying person went from Genesis to Revelation, then the cosmos."[61] Each year L'Abri set aside at least one whole day for fasting and prayer, thereby freeing "all the Workers for prayer and quiet meditation without any of the usual work."[62] Few were more deeply affected by the Schaeffers' emphasis on prayer than Hans and Anky Rookmaaker. When the Rookmaakers traveled to L'Abri for three weeks in summer 1956, they found that "the Schaeffers prayed, prayed actually much more than the Dutch churches" and that their prayers were often answered.[63]

---

[57] Barrs, Francis Schaeffer, the Later Years.
[58] Edith Schaeffer, *With Love, Edith*, 442, letter of September 1, 1959.
[59] Wade Bradshaw, *By Demonstration, God: Fifty Years and a Week at L'Abri* (Carlisle, UK: Piquant Editions, 2005), 25.
[60] More descriptions of prayer at L'Abri appear in Barrs, Francis Schaeffer, the Later Years; Barrs, Francis A. Schaeffer: The Early Years; Edith Schaeffer, *L'Abri*; Edith Schaeffer, *With Love, Edith*; Edith Schaeffer, *Dear Family*; Edgar, *Schaeffer on the Christian Life*, 30.
[61] Edgar, *Schaeffer on the Christian Life*, 24.
[62] Edith Schaeffer, *Dear Family*, 48, letter of August 28, 1963.
[63] Duriez, *Francis Schaeffer*, 149.

Prayer also played a role in shaping hospitality at L'Abri. "The warm welcome was genuine," Edgar notes. "Indeed, it resulted from a prayer that was often said at L'Abri: 'Lord bring us the people of your choice.'" Edgar believes this prayer played a significant role in helping the Schaeffers and other workers at L'Abri treat "every guest . . . as if he or she was a special envoy" sent in God's providence.[64] Thus it was no surprise that Schaeffer and many L'Abri workers were known to spend large amounts of time in conversations, all the while acting as if the individual in front of them was the most important person on the planet. In some sense he or she was. In the eyes of the Schaeffers *this* person at *this* time was a specific answer to their prayers. As Dorothy Jamieson Woodson notes, "When Mr. Schaeffer would talk to you, there was nothing else in the world that was going on. He was totally focused on you."[65]

The Schaeffers' efforts to make L'Abri a countercultural community marked by prayer and vibrant spirituality often had lasting ramifications. There was a sense for many that God was truly present and actively involved in directing and sustaining life at L'Abri. For many the sense that a relational God answered prayer in tangible ways was extremely compelling. Together the deep spirituality and authentic community that many experienced at L'Abri made it relatively easy for individuals to commit themselves to the God whom the Schaeffers said made it all possible. Conversions and reconversions to Christianity abounded at L'Abri. Indeed, to at least one atheist-turned-Christian at L'Abri, "It seemed everyone was becoming a Christian."[66]

L'Abri as an Intellectual Community

While spirituality undergirded everything at L'Abri, it was not spirituality that most shaped L'Abri's reputation. Even though many left L'Abri with new or renewed faith and a deeper appreciation for prayer, it was L'Abri's intellectual appeal that received the widest acclaim and set the ministry apart in the minds of many. From at least the publication of the 1960 article in *Time*, which declared L'Abri to be a "mission to intellectuals," Schaeffer joined a small company of evangelically sanctioned intellectuals. Throughout the 1960s and much of the

---

[64]Edgar, *Schaeffer on the Christian Life*, 25.
[65]Duriez, *Francis Schaeffer*, 145.
[66]Linda Mercadante, who arrived at L'Abri as an atheist and left as a Christian, was one of those who converted. See Mercadante, *Bloomfield Avenue: A Jewish-Catholic Jersey Girl's Spiritual Journey* (Cambridge, MA: Cowley, 2006), 127.

1970s, L'Abri was among the leading destinations in the world for intellectually curious evangelicals who wanted to explore their questions, understand their culture, and embrace their intellectual curiosity within the framework of traditional Christian orthodoxy.

One of the most amazing things about this phenomenon was that Schaeffer never technically claimed to be, and in fact was not, a trained scholar. Though he did have a divinity degree from Faith Theological Seminary, his doctorates were honorary (Highland College, CA, 1954; Gordon College, MA, 1971), and his approach to scholarship sometimes seemed eccentric. To many who were close to him, it seemed Schaeffer got his information almost exclusively from decades of talking with European university students and his obsessive reading of magazines rather than monographs. According to longtime L'Abri worker Os Guinness, even though "Schaeffer was wrong on certain details and issues," he was "a brilliant thinker," who had "an extraordinary knack of connecting things no one had connected before." Yet during several years of living at L'Abri Guinness "never saw him open a single book except the Bible. Much of his reading came from magazines such as *Newsweek* and *The Listener*."[67] Schaeffer's reading preferences reflected his isolation from scholarly discourse. With the exception of his close friendship with Rookmaaker, Schaeffer functioned seemingly without much sustained interaction with the larger scholarly world.

By the early 1970s Schaeffer's apparent intellectual isolation was starting to be a cause for concern among some evangelical academics. For George Marsden, a budding evangelical scholar who was present for Schaeffer's 1968 visit to Calvin College and wrote positively of Schaeffer's ability to "make Christianity appear intellectually relevant to the contemporary era," Schaeffer's seeming disregard for the wider scholarly community was a surprising and then frustrating reality.[68] During a 1969 trip to L'Abri, Marsden managed to track down Schaeffer—whom, even then, Marsden remembers as being "very inaccessible"—and asked him about his intellectual influences. Schaeffer named Westminster Theological Seminary's Cornelius Van Til as a partial influence but claimed to have worked out most of his material on his own. Two years later Marsden and

---

[67] Guinness, interview. According to Barrs, Francis Schaeffer "did study a great deal" (Francis Schaeffer, the Later Years, lecture 4, question and answer session). Schaeffer "took advantage of every moment he had. He was an extraordinarily self-disciplined person" (Francis Schaeffer, the Later Years, lecture 5, "The Ministry the Lord Gave the Schaeffers").
[68] Hankins, *Francis Schaeffer*, 78.

Richard Mouw, another promising young scholar at Calvin College, approached Schaeffer about the possibility of taking a group of Calvin College students to L'Abri for January term. Schaeffer turned down their request. The students were welcome to come, Schaeffer informed them, but not Marsden or Mouw. Schaeffer, insistent on being the sole authority at L'Abri, told the two junior professors that their presence might foster confusion regarding leadership at L'Abri.[69]

By the early 1970s Marsden and Mouw were not the only evangelical scholars who were uneasy about the intellectual path Schaeffer was taking. As the decade wore on, James Houston also began to be concerned that Schaeffer's intellectual isolation (as well as his inability to recognize it) seemed to increase as his fame and authority grew. Houston had been writing to Schaeffer on a semiregular basis since August 1970. In early letters Houston extended multiple requests that Schaeffer speak at Regent's Summer School or annual convocation and compared notes with Schaeffer on topics such as biblical ecology and the place of the creative arts within North American evangelicalism.[70] Over the next few years, however, Houston became worried about Schaeffer and the intellectual isolation Houston believed marked not just Schaeffer but L'Abri as well. When Schaeffer finally agree to visit Regent College in May 1975, Houston had the chance to discuss his concerns with Schaeffer over breakfast.[71] To Houston, Schaeffer seemed unconvinced.

Shortly after their Vancouver exchange, Houston spelled out his fears to Schaeffer in a letter. Again Houston urged Schaeffer to expand his thinking by broadening the circle of his advisers: "Within the body of Christ we need each other and the way in which others can cross-fertilize, or indeed correct our own perspective, and certainly in this day of highly specialized skills to help each other in specialties that are not our own." Houston then raised his concern that L'Abri had become the wrong kind of shelter—a ghetto instead of a temporary resting place: "L'Abri has been your strength; please do not let it be a source of weakness because it became too much of a ghetto of thought. It is a shelter for those from outside but do not let it be a ghetto for the thought that comes from within."[72]

---

[69]George Marsden, email to author, August 11, 2015.
[70]James M. Houston to Francis A. Schaeffer, August 7, 1970, box 52, file 26, FSC.
[71]James M. Houston, interview with author, October 24, 2015, Vancouver.
[72]James M. Houston to Francis A. Schaeffer, May 1, 1975, box 52, file 26, FSC.

Schaeffer, by this time well into the production of his first film and riding a still-growing wave of celebrity, did not think Houston's assessment well founded. After noting that he did "appreciate" Houston's "concern," Schaeffer continued,

> I realize the danger but really Jim, I think that either you, or someone who is giving you this impression, have really missed the actual situation. I'm really anything but isolated. Endless theologians and other thinkers come here to talk with me and on top of that, in my time away lecturing, I have long conversation with almost the whole spectrum of theological and intellectual thought.... Of course, none of us can have too much inter-contact but I don't think the possible danger in my case is realized. For example, in my new book and film which I'm working on, we've had about ten competent researchers in every possible area not only check my work but make input into it.[73]

This time it was Schaeffer who failed to convince Houston. This exchange marked the last correspondence between the two men.

But the middle-aged Houston, with his PhD and long career as a geographer at Oxford, was not Schaeffer's typical student. Much more typical was Sharon Gallagher, an American evangelical who spent time at Swiss L'Abri in 1971 after her graduation from Westmont College. Gallagher originally met the Schaeffers and Guinness during their 1968 lectures at Westmont. For Gallagher, Schaeffer was a tour guide to artistic and intellectual realms the evangelical subculture she grew up in had little interest in or time for. Gallagher experienced L'Abri as a community that was profoundly "intellectually stimulating." For Gallagher, Schaeffer himself was a large part of L'Abri's allure. Gallagher remembers being "very impressed" by Schaeffer and found his "idea of integration of worldview" to be "very exciting."[74]

For thousands of young evangelicals such as Gallagher, it was precisely Schaeffer's ability to make the Reformed principle of the lordship of Christ in all spheres of society seem applicable for contemporary culture that made him so inspirational on an intellectual and cultural level. Inspired by an Abraham Kuyper–like emphasis on the importance of the gospel for all of life, Schaeffer never equivocated regarding the need for Christians to be involved in all aspects of society.[75] It was precisely his ability to convincingly teach and model the expansive

---

[73]Francis A. Schaeffer to James M. Houston, June 19, 1975, box 52, file 26, FSC.
[74]Sharon Gallagher, interview with author, December 3, 2015, Berkeley.
[75]See James D. Bratt, *Abraham Kuyper: Modern Calvinist, Christian Democrat* (Grand Rapids: Eerdmans, 2013), 195.

relevance of the gospel throughout the course of his ministry that exerted such a significant impact on those who encountered his books or stayed at L'Abri. Os Guinness provides insight into the way in which Schaeffer's influence worked:

> Francis, for me as for thousands of English and American young students who were Christians, was a door opener. It was not only okay but right and proper and responsible, as a Christian, to understand the whole of life—"All truth is God's truth," as the early Christians said. So whether it's art or philosophy or culture or the films of Ingmar Bergman or the music of John Cage, the whole of life is fair game to think about freely as a Christian.[76]

Thena Ayers, a Canadian Inter-Varsity leader who spent a year at L'Abri following her graduation from the University of British Columbia, describes her time with the Schaeffers as "a hugely integrative, productive time" for similar reasons: "Dr. Schaeffer was like a breath of fresh air for evangelicals because he was talking about literature, and film, and philosophy, and the whole world of ideas, and doing so with a confidence and a kind of godly authority." Ayers's experiences in Inter-Varsity during her student years had helped her cultivate the conviction that all truth was rooted in Christ, but it was Schaeffer's ministry that showed her what this concept actually looked like. "He took us into his thinking," Ayers remembers, as "he would embrace all of these fields and wrestle with it as a Christian, and think it through as a Christian." For Ayers, the entire experience was "totally rich" and "inordinately stimulating."[77]

Guinness and Ayers were not alone. For many others whose own stories read similarly in the larger contours if different in the exact details, time spent at L'Abri was often the foundation on which they then added further academic work and a lifetime of influence as standard-bearers for thoughtful evangelical engagement with culture and the life of the mind. In so doing L'Abri played a significant role in fueling an intellectual and vocational reorientation within American evangelicalism.

Schaeffer's influence was not limited to his ability to motivate the hundreds who flocked to L'Abri. As historians such as Michael Hamilton have noted, Schaeffer's books were also extremely influential in fanning the intellectual imagination of young evangelicals. From the late 1960s through much of the

---

[76] William C. Martin, *With God on Our Side: The Rise of the Religious Right in America* (New York: Broadway Books, 1996), 160.
[77] Thena Ayers, interview with author, October 26, 2015, Vancouver.

Figure 1.3. Students reading outside Chalet les Melezes circa 1975.

1980s, evangelical young people who showed intellectual promise were frequently given copies of books by two authors—C. S. Lewis and Francis Schaeffer. As "church youth leaders and campus ministers introduced their brighter students to Schaeffer's books," they ended up playing a part in "launching scores of evangelical scholars on their careers."[78] For Regent College professor Steven Garber, who first encountered Schaeffer's ideas as an "intellectually curious" twenty-year-old and recent University of California, Berkeley, dropout, it was an encounter with the work of Schaeffer and others from L'Abri in the early 1970s that first lit "a match . . . in my heart," which led to a stay at L'Abri the next year and continued to illuminate his life as a campus minister, vocational consultant, and college professor for decades to come.[79] Like Garber, many of those who experienced this multifaceted and integrative approach to theological education eventually went on to pass on these insights to a new generation

---

[78]Michael S. Hamilton, "The Dissatisfaction of Francis Schaeffer: Thirteen Years After His Death, Schaeffer's Vision and Frustrations Continue to Haunt Evangelicalism," *Christianity Today*, March 3, 1997, 28.

[79]Steven Garber, *The Fabric of Faithfulness: Weaving Together Belief and Behavior* (Downers Grove, IL: InterVarsity Press, 2007), 43. Garber went on to work with the C. S. Lewis Institute before founding the Washington Institute for Faith, Vocation & Culture. In 2018 he joined the faculty of Regent College.

through pastorates, college professorships, and involvement in study centers and other entrepreneurial and integrative communities.[80]

Right theology and an expansive vision were only part of Schaeffer's allure. Content mattered, but so did style and tone. For countercultural young people, it mattered that Schaeffer seemed more a "swashbuckling" rebel than a collected seminary professor who doled out knowledge in measured tones.[81] Schaeffer advanced classical Reformed convictions regarding the need for the integration of the gospel in all of life, but in his books, lectures, and conversations these concepts were charged with intense conviction, theatrical gusto, and an unflinching confidence in the truth of the Christian worldview. Unlike many evangelicals of his day, Schaeffer offered educationally inclined baby boomers reassurance that they could pursue intellectual inquiry without fear: "*The truth of Christianity is that it is true to what is there.* You can go to the end of the world and you never need be afraid, like the ancients, that you will fall off the end and the dragons will eat you up."[82]

For Schaeffer this meant that one could "carry out your intellectual discussion to the end of the discussion because Christianity is not only true to the dogmas, it is not only true to what God has said in the Bible, but it is also true to what is there."[83] For evangelicals raised on the stock questions and predictable answers of Sunday school curricula and flannelgraph boards, this sentiment was liberating. Suddenly the whole range of intellectual and vocational options—including, but not limited to, professional scholarship—were open for legitimate Christian endeavor. It is no wonder that later scholars used phrases such as "vocational revolution" to describe his influence.[84] Through his books and the example of L'Abri, Schaeffer invited a generation of evangelicals to engage their minds and the world with a scope as wide as creation and a confidence rooted in the trustworthiness of God.

---

[80]It is impossible to fully quantify Francis Schaeffer's influence in this regard. However, a partial list of those who went on to be influential in the Christian study center movement after being influenced by Schaeffer includes Steve Garber, Jim Hiskey, Andrew Trotter, David Turner, Beat Steiner, Sharon Gallagher, David W. Gill, and R. C. Sproul.

[81]David W. Gill, "A Marginal Life," David W. Gill, www.davidwgill.org/autobio/ (accessed October 5, 2016).

[82]Francis A. Schaeffer, *He Is There and He Is Not Silent* (Carol Stream, IL: Tyndale House, 1973), 17, emphasis original.

[83]Francis Schaeffer, *He Is There and He Is Not Silent*, 17. See also Francis A. Schaeffer, *A Christian View of the Bible as Truth* (Westchester, IL: Crossway Books, 1982), 376.

[84]Mark Thomas Edwards, *The Right of the Protestant Left: God's Totalitarianism* (New York: Palgrave Macmillan, 2012), 164.

L'Abri as a Hospitable Community

In the day-to-day it was the Schaeffers' emphasis on making L'Abri a hospitable space that made room for both the spiritual and intellectual development of those who stopped by. Again, this emphasis traced back to the Schaeffers' own priorities and experiences in ministry. Even before the founding of L'Abri or their move to Europe, the Schaeffers had an intuitive grasp on the importance of building relationships inside their home. The practice that began during Schaeffer's pastoral career and the development of Children for Christ continued during the Schaeffers' time in Europe and then expanded to an even greater extent with the founding of L'Abri and the decision to open their home to anyone whom God might bring. For those who came through the doors of Chalet les Melezes, the hospitality of the L'Abri staff was undeniable. "I had never experienced anything like it," Linda Mercadante noted when reflecting on the hospitality she encountered

Figure 1.4. Visitors to L'Abri often made memories and friendships that lasted a lifetime.

Figure 1.5. Francis and Edith Schaeffer on the way to the chapel in the mid-1970s. By this point the celebrity culture that had built up around the Schaeffers meant that they were frequently photographed as they went about the daily rhythms of life.

at L'Abri in 1973. Mercadante had shown up at the Schaeffers' door with almost no knowledge of Schaeffer, no winter coat, and little money after several harrowing experiences hitchhiking through Europe. Within her New Jersey, Jewish-Italian family hospitality was reserved for family members and seldom if ever extended to strangers. At L'Abri, however, Mercadante found that the Schaeffers and other L'Abri workers "were very self-consciously hospitable." The worker who opened the door took Mercadante in, spent time talking with her, and, upon learning that she had no coat, quickly pointed her in the direction of the L'Abri "grab bag," where guests and students could choose from an assortment of clothing items for free.[85]

In addition to housing, feeding, and even clothing those who came to their door, the Schaeffers' extended hospitality to a generation of seekers through subtle but important decisions about contextualization. By drawing on the methods of Christian missionaries such as Hudson Taylor (1832–1905) and Amy Carmichael (1857–1951), whom the Schaeffers especially esteemed, they contextualized the gospel to the cultural milieu without compromising the historic truth of the Christian message.[86] More than a mere missionary strategy, the decision to cultivate L'Abri as a place with room for culturally attuned variations in dress and hairstyle implicitly functioned as a method through which the Schaeffers extended hospitality to those who visited L'Abri. For individuals such as Christian rock star Larry Norman, who visited L'Abri on his honeymoon in late 1971, L'Abri—unlike much of the American evangelical subculture Norman had experienced—was a place where his long golden locks and his desire to create meaningful art were both welcomed.[87] By adapting their lives, schedules, and even appearance the Schaeffers signaled not only that L'Abri was in step with the times but also that it was a place open to individuals who might seem too eccentric for a traditional evangelical church.

More than any other individual at L'Abri, Schaeffer's unique ability to contextualize the Christian mission was something one could both hear and

---

[85] Mercadante, *Bloomfield Avenue*, 117.
[86] It is important to think of Francis Schaeffer within the context of the Christian missionary movement. For Edith's reflections on the influence of Hudson Taylor's China Inland Mission on her parents' mode of dress, see Edith Schaeffer, *The Hidden Art of Homemaking* (Wheaton, IL: Tyndale House, 1985), 189-90.
[87] Gregory Alan Thornbury, *Why Should the Devil Have All the Good Music? Larry Norman and the Perils of Christian Rock* (New York: Convergent, 2018), 111-12. Norman was so inspired by L'Abri that he even attempted to form a community for artists on the L'Abri model (p. 69).

see. He spoke the language of the Beats and the countercultural generation that followed them. He called the middle class "bourgeois" and "plastic," and he railed against the emptiness of a consumerist and individualistic middle class that valued "personal peace and affluence" above all else.[88] He often spoke convincingly on the writings of Camus and Sartre, the films of Fellini and Bergman, and the music of Bob Dylan, the Beatles, and Jefferson Airplane. Schaeffer also adopted the dress of those he was trying to reach. Well before most evangelical churches welcomed long-haired, shoeless hippies into their sanctuaries, Schaeffer himself "took to wearing beige Nehru jackets, odd linen shirts, and mountain climbing knickers" while wearing his hair long and growing a goatee.[89] For countercultural visitors to L'Abri, Schaeffer's physical appearance—and the similar appearance of many L'Abri guests and workers—was an extension of hospitality that signaled that L'Abri had room for them. Of course, these clothing choices didn't hurt L'Abri's cool factor. When folks such as budding feminist and future Pulitzer Prize–winning author Jane Smiley visited L'Abri, they found that "everyone—teachers, students, helpers—was good-looking and well dressed."[90]

Figure 1.6. Francis Schaeffer addresses a group near Santa Cruz, California, in fall 1971.

---

[88]Francis A. Schaeffer, "The New Super Spirituality," in Schaeffer, *Christian View of Spirituality*, 385.
[89]Frank Schaeffer, *Crazy for God*, 208. The exception was Sunday, when Schaeffer, unable to fully detach himself from his fundamentalist past, donned a black suit and tie; see Mercadante, *Bloomfield Avenue*, 120.
[90]Jane Smiley, "Frank Schaeffer Goes Crazy for God," *The Nation*, September 27, 2007, www.thenation.com/article/frank-schaeffer-goes-crazy-god/.

L'Abri as an Aspirational Community

Perhaps the most significant way in which Schaeffer and L'Abri shaped evangelicalism in its North American context was by modeling a cosmopolitan version of evangelicalism that proved immensely alluring. From the way they dressed and talked to the company they kept and how they kept it, Francis and Edith Schaeffer played a significant role in shaping the cultural, theological, vocational, and even social imagination of an entire generation of evangelical young people who were experiencing unprecedented levels of affluence and opportunity. L'Abri made all this possible. Through much of its first two decades of existence, L'Abri necessitated daily, sometimes hourly, interactions between the Schaeffers and their young admirers. Guests at L'Abri had front-row seats as the Schaeffers performed cosmopolitan evangelicalism before their eyes on a daily basis.

Interactions with the Schaeffers at L'Abri stoked guests' aspirations in a variety of ways. For some, such as Hans and Anky Rookmaaker, it was the Schaeffers' deep spirituality as expressed through prayer that cultivated aspirations of deepening their own faith and prayer life.[91] Similarly, the Schaeffers inspired many to cultivate their minds through study at L'Abri's Farel House, seminary, or a university. In the late 1960s and early 1970s there was a virtual pipeline from L'Abri to places such as Regent College, Westminster Theological Seminary, and Covenant Theological Seminary.[92] Furthermore, even though Schaeffer himself never formally studied for a doctorate, his ability to be conversant and surprisingly informed on a wide array of topics was a capacity that many of his students respected and sought to cultivate in their own lives. These aspirations led many leading evangelical thinkers and innovators, including Os Guinness, David Wells, and William Dyrness, among others, to enter PhD programs after spending time at L'Abri.

The Schaeffers' cultural sensibilities and artistic tastes also provided plenty of aspirational fodder for aesthetically deprived American evangelicals. While Schaeffer's appreciation for the music of Bach may have seemed perfectly normal to L'Abri guests such as William Edgar, who grew up in a wealthy cosmopolitan home before entering Harvard as a musicologist, for most of the Americans who streamed through Chalet les Melezes, Bach, Cézanne, and Rembrandt

---

[91]This is reflected in many letters held in the Francis A. Schaeffer Collection.
[92]Edith Schaeffer, L'Abri, 214.

were hardly familiar.[93] Because of this, perhaps no realm of Schaeffer's influence was more liberating and captivating for middlebrow evangelicals than his affinity for fine art. Nowhere was Schaeffer more at home, more of a tour guide, or less a prototypical American evangelical than when he was immersed in some form of artistic expression. As Mel White, a prominent evangelical ghostwriter who worked with Schaeffer on some of his later projects, notes, in the area of art as with much that Schaeffer discussed, "It wasn't what he said but what he was talking about that made the difference." Unlike virtually every other evangelical White knew, Schaeffer "was pointing at art, at music, at film, at theater, at government; he was talking about . . . all of these issues that had been on the off-list for evangelicals." At that time evangelicals largely avoided movies and high culture, but Schaeffer "was talking about the great films and the way they've changed our lives and was visiting museums." "Francis was opening the whole world to us," White recalls. "I think Francis was the first voice that said, 'Reclaim everything in God's creation: It's yours.'"[94]

Schaeffer's culturally attuned intervention could hardly have come at a better time for American evangelicals. By unlocking the gates to artistic realms outside what most evangelicals would have ever encountered unaided, Schaeffer stoked the imaginations and aspirations of a generation by teaching them how to appreciate fine art just as they found that their increased educational attainment and a shifting American culture offered them greater social mobility than ever before. For many, the lessons they learned at L'Abri held personal, social, and even professional benefits. Students at L'Abri stood to increase their ability to derive joy from art, but they also learned how to handle themselves in the world of fine art frequented by social elites.

As important as Francis himself was for the development of L'Abri, no one helped cultivate L'Abri as an aspirational and artistic *community* more than Edith. Indeed, for some who were close to L'Abri, Edith was "the secret of L'Abri."[95] Unlike Francis, who hailed from a working-class background, Edith grew up in a genteel, well-educated missionary family, where she developed an early love of art, stylish dress, and high culture that endured throughout her life. But

---

[93]Edgar, *Schaeffer on the Christian Life*, 24-25.
[94]Martin, *With God on Our Side*, 160.
[95]Os Guinness, "Fathers and Sons," *Books and Culture*, 2008, www.booksandculture.com/articles/2008/marapr/1.32.html. Edgar calls Edith "the 'hidden artist' who held L'Abri together" (Edgar, *Schaeffer on the Christian Life*, 62).

Edith's eye for art was not limited to the highbrow art that filled the world's top museums. Rather, her passion for art extended to everyday aesthetics.[96] She was a lifelong champion of all forms of human creativity, including "everyday" forms of art such as cooking and sewing, because she saw all art as stemming from the creativity of God. "We have been created in His image, so we can be, and are *made* to be, creative," Edith told her readers. This theological conviction undergirded her call for Christians to live "artistically, aesthetically, and creatively" in their daily lives by dressing more carefully, cultivating musical ability, or simply working to make their handwriting more visually appealing.[97] In her own way Edith was making her husband's argument—*all* of life, including seemingly mundane tasks, fell within the scope of God's concern.

L'Abri was the canvas where Edith's ideas came to life as she worked to make Chalet les Melezes an artistic masterpiece. From the designer fashions she wore and the classical music she and Francis relished to her zest to put fresh flowers on the table and offer meals that were attractive both to the palate and the eye, Edith modeled what she described as "hidden art" for a generation of young evangelicals.[98] Her entire life was a performance of aesthetics and class that few who stopped at L'Abri could miss. "At mealtimes every effort was made to provide a gracious setting that would facilitate intense but civilized conversation," Mercadante remembers. "Tables were beautifully laid with table clothes, fabric napkins, flowers, and even candles.... There was no grabbing food, boisterousness, or interrupting allowed. Instead, everyone sat up straight, stayed in their seats, and politely contributed to the conversation."[99] The photography of Sylvester Jacobs offers a visual demonstration of Edith's careful cultivation of class and beauty at L'Abri meals; carefully folded cloth napkins, flowers, and place settings laid out with elegant simplicity abound.[100] Through her cultivation of

---

[96] Frank Schaeffer, *Crazy for God*, 12-19. According to Frank Schaeffer, it was Edith who took Francis to an art museum for the first time (19).

[97] Edith Schaeffer, *Hidden Art of Homemaking*, 25, 32.

[98] She published her reflections on this theme in 1971. See Edith Schaeffer, *Hidden Art of Homemaking*. For more examples of Edith's concern for everyday beauty at L'Abri, see Edith Schaeffer, *L'Abri*; Edith Schaeffer, *With Love, Edith*; Edith Schaeffer, *Dear Family*; Hankins, *Francis Schaeffer and the Shaping of Evangelical America*, 68-69.

[99] Mercadante, *Bloomfield Avenue*, 118.

[100] Sylvester Jacobs, *Portrait of a Shelter* (Downers Grove, IL: InterVarsity Press, 1973), 60, 71-72, 78, 105. For more on Jacobs's experience as an African American at L'Abri, see Duriez, *Francis Schaeffer*, 165-66; Sylvester Jacobs and Linette Martin, *Born Black* (London: Hodder and Stoughton, 1977), 100-104.

a cultured, aesthetically conscious home, Edith's presence in Chalet les Melezes provided a fitting complement to Francis's wide-ranging lectures on art and his guided museum tours. Together Edith and Francis modeled the dignified, artistically aware cosmopolitanism that prepared young L'Abri guests to navigate the halls of power where more than a few of them would eventually find themselves.[101] For some detractors, L'Abri seemed little more than "a high-class cult"; for many evangelicals, however, it was the gateway to a new world.[102]

The significance of Edith's presence as an example of Christian womanhood was also a profoundly influential—and remarkably complex—part of life at L'Abri. While Edith assumed a traditional "helpmeet" role in many ways as she worked behind the scenes to enable Francis's ministry while hiding his short temper, she was no wallflower.[103] Fittingly described as "a force of nature," Edith wowed L'Abri visitors with more than her artistic sensibilities and culinary flair. The possessor of enduring physical beauty, natural confidence, and personal charm—all magnified by her herculean stamina and capacity for work—Edith Schaeffer was, as Guinness notes, "one of the most remarkable women of her generation."[104] Often staying up all night to write her family letter or finish one of her various other projects, Edith never showed signs of weariness or even took a nap.[105] Rather, she flaunted her stamina, frequently telling readers of her family letter how late she stayed up to write them.

Her work ethic was matched by her genuine love for people. Multiple guests at L'Abri remember Edith taking time to extend personal kindness through a sympathy letter written to a young woman she had never met or a picnic lunch made special for a newly engaged couple.[106] "I have never met such a great heart of love, and such indomitable faith, tireless prayer, boundless energy, passionate love for life and beauty, lavish hospitality, irrepressible laughter, and seemingly limitless time for people—all in a single person," Guinness later remarked.[107] A second mother to many, an inspiration to more, Edith Schaeffer was one of the most powerful, multitalented women within postwar American evangelicalism.

---

[101] D. Michael Lindsay, "Evangelicals in the Power Elite: Elite Cohesion Advancing a Movement," *American Sociological Review* 73, no. 1 (February 1, 2008): 60-82.
[102] Smiley, "Frank Schaeffer Goes Crazy for God."
[103] Frank Schaeffer, *Crazy for God*, 216.
[104] Guinness, "Fathers and Sons."
[105] Frank Schaeffer, *Crazy for God*, 112.
[106] Ayers, interview; Barrs, "Life at L'Abri."
[107] Guinness, "Fathers and Sons."

It was not only the power of the Schaeffers' personalities, however, that affected the aspirations of L'Abri guests. Those who visited L'Abri in the 1960s and 1970s found themselves thrust into a diverse web of relationships that included people whose fame, social standing, and educational and racial backgrounds would have likely precluded their interaction in other contexts.[108] In so doing L'Abri helped expand the aspirational imagination of its guests, especially those who came from backgrounds with fewer resources (be they cultural, social, educational, or economic), while simultaneously forming the relational network they needed to advance in domains ranging from education to politics, art, media, and business.[109] Demonstrating the burgeoning power of parachurch organizations to connect evangelical power brokers and build influential

Figure 1.7. Edith Schaeffer blended a rigorous work ethic with natural elegance as she cultivated an appreciation for community, prayer, and beauty at L'Abri.

interpersonal networks, L'Abri functioned as the unofficial hub of American evangelical influence throughout much of the 1970s.[110] Billy Graham, Jack Sparks, Bob Dylan, Larry Norman, Chuck Colson, and George H. W. Bush's mother, Dorothy Walker Bush, were some of the most famous evangelicals who came into L'Abri's orbit during these years, but there were many others, including graduates of Ivy League schools, sons and daughters of prominent American

---

[108] L'Abri welcomed guests from around the world, including many non-Western and non-European countries in Africa and Asia. African Americans such as photographer Sylvester Jacobs also found the Schaeffers' lack of racial prejudice refreshing. For Jacobs's reflections on L'Abri, see Jacobs and Martin, *Born Black*.

[109] Lindsay, "Evangelicals in the Power Elite," 71.

[110] The Schaeffers began transitioning their primary residence to Rochester, Minnesota, in 1978 and 1979, when Francis Schaeffer underwent several rounds of extensive treatment for lymphoma at the Mayo Clinic.

pastors, businessmen, and politicians, who also touched the lives of average evangelicals at L'Abri. Few other venues within American evangelicalism offered similar opportunities for friendship and networking among individuals from such a wide range of backgrounds.

L'Abri's identity as an evangelical melting pot where the mores of the more culturally astute classes were both taught and caught meant that the once-isolated retreat was perfectly poised to be a principal mediator of American evangelicals' growing social, intellectual, cultural, and political ambitions in the years to come. L'Abri became a credential, a passport into an unofficial but nevertheless important evangelical club. As onetime L'Abri guests, students, and workers fanned out across the globe, they often continued to cherish the relationships they made in Huemoz. These relational connections bore lasting fruit. As sociologist Michael Lindsay notes, the relational network that L'Abri forged still exerted significant influence within American life decades after Francis Schaeffer's death. Of the 360 elite informants Lindsay interviewed for his 2007 book *Faith in the Halls of Power*, "13 percent mentioned L'Abri, its founder Francis Schaeffer, or his writings as having a profound influence on their lives." Furthermore, the result of this L'Abri connection was significant. Lindsay found that "through L'Abri, a number of leaders from different sectors built inter-personal networks that have remained important to them throughout their lives. These connections helped informants get job interviews, meet future business partners, and develop supportive friendships as they moved to new cities."[111] Important for much more than the political legacy most studies of Schaeffer foreground, L'Abri—as a spiritual, intellectual, and aspirational community—served as glue that held many of the most influential voices of twentieth-century evangelicalism together.

A Final Aspiration: Re-creating L'Abri

For a few of those who read the Schaeffers' books or made their way to L'Abri during L'Abri's first two decades, however, the Schaeffers inspired aspirations of a different type. The allure and influence of L'Abri meant that many evangelicals

---

[111] Lindsay, "Evangelicals in the Power Elite," 70. For a more detailed study of the way in which American evangelicals gained power across several sectors of society between 1976 and 2006, see D. Michael Lindsay, *Faith in the Halls of Power: How Evangelicals Joined the American Elite* (Oxford: Oxford University Press, 2007).

in America and around the world wanted a chance to access L'Abri more regularly and expand its ministry beyond Huemoz, Milan, Amsterdam, California, and the United Kingdom. For these individuals, L'Abri inspired aspirations of launching similar experiments in spiritually deep and intellectually robust communities on university campuses, at retreat centers, and in cities across North America. By the late 1960s L'Abri was by far the most famous and ready-made model for evangelicals who aspired to take part in helping to bridge the deep-seated evangelical head-heart divide and rescue the evangelical mind from the shallow obsession with personal piety that defined much of the Jesus movement.

Schaeffer's Swiss retreat was not, however, the only innovative attempt to take thoughtful Christianity to North American evangelicals. Just as L'Abri reached what some consider its zenith in 1968, other significant and innovative educational communities were beginning to emerge. A few of these new ventures eventually vied with L'Abri for pride of place within intellectually engaged North American evangelicalism. One of the most influential of these communities was located not in Europe or the United States but in the Canadian city of Vancouver.

REGENT COLLEGE

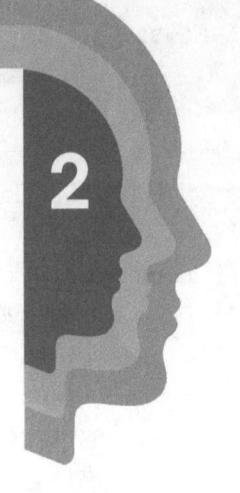

2

As the Schaeffers took their first steps back into the North American orbit in the mid-1960s and began directing their energy toward lecture tours and the publications that carried the influence of L'Abri around the world, a group of Plymouth Brethren leaders in Vancouver were beginning to lay the groundwork for a different kind of Christian learning community, one that would soon stand alongside L'Abri as the most significant catalysts for lay intellectual and theological engagement within North American evangelicalism. Unlike L'Abri, however, the goal of the Vancouver committee was not an informal series of Bible studies, lectures, and tape-listening sessions but a school capable of offering graduate-level theological education to the laity.[1]

Marshall Sheppard and the Founding of Regent College

The idea that eventually became Regent College captured the imagination of Marshall Sheppard in the early 1960s. Sheppard, a successful shoe merchant and Plymouth Brethren leader in the Vancouver area, represented both the financial stability and visionary impulse that had come to define Vancouver's large Brethren population. For years Sheppard had worked to mentor young Brethren

---

[1] Histories of Regent College include John G. Stackhouse, *Canadian Evangelicalism in the Twentieth Century: An Introduction to Its Character* (Toronto: University of Toronto Press, 1993), 154-64; and Robert K. Burkinshaw, *Pilgrims in Lotus Land: Conservative Protestantism in British Columbia, 1917–1981* (Montreal: McGill-Queen's University Press, 1995), 215-22. The most in-depth treatment of Regent's founding (circa 1961–1970) is Kenneth V. Botton, "Regent College: An Experiment in Theological Education" (PhD diss., Trinity Evangelical Divinity School, 2004), http://search.proquest.com/pqdtglobal/docview/305080117/abstract/FE2B427B616E4F05PQ/1. Regent's own publications and archival holdings contain numerous historical accounts. This chapter makes use of three archival collections housed at Regent College: the Michael G. Collison Fonds, the Keith Shepherd Grant Collection, and the James Houston Fonds.

leaders through personal concern and the publication of the Vancouver-based Brethren quarterly *Calling*, which he launched in 1958.[2] By 1963 Sheppard was discussing his idea of a Brethren graduate school with like-minded men from local Brethren assemblies and a few promising young Brethren leaders such as W. Ward Gasque (b. 1939) and Don Tinder (b. 1938).[3] Both were students at Fuller Theological Seminary, and both had their eye on doctoral work.[4]

From their first involvement Gasque and Tinder provided an important link between Sheppard's idea and younger Brethren and evangelical college students. In 1964 both Gasque and Tinder attended the InterVarsity missions conference at Urbana, where they talked to nearly one hundred Brethren college students and were encouraged by the level of interest these students showed in the proposed theological school.[5] After hearing Gasque and Tinder's report, Sheppard and a group of Brethren businessmen, most of whom belonged to the Granville Chapel Brethren assembly, officially formed a School of Theology Committee, chaired by Sheppard, in order to bring this vision to fruition.[6] Shortly thereafter he invited another young Brethren scholar, Carl E. Armerding (b. 1936), to join the project as well. Armerding, who was a member of one of North America's most influential Brethren families, was beginning a PhD in biblical studies at Brandeis at the time.[7]

Sheppard's ability to inspire was not limited to rising Brethren scholars. Sheppard cultivated a cohort of leaders for the project that included members of the Brethren community with extensive business and administrative acumen. Individuals such as Brian Sutherland, a former executive in the large mining firm Comico who had recently moved back to Vancouver from Montreal, and Ken Smith, whose successful real-estate business provided early and sustained financial backing for the project, brought significant administrative experience and economic support to Sheppard's project. With others such as Dick Richards

---

[2] Stackhouse, *Canadian Evangelicalism in the Twentieth Century*, 155.
[3] Botton, "Regent College," 128. See Susan S. Phillips and Soo-Inn Tan, *Serving God's Community: Studies in Honor of W. Ward Gasque* (Vancouver: Regent College Publishing, 2015), xx-xxi.
[4] Tinder eventually completed a PhD in church history with Sydney Ahlstrom at Yale, and Gasque completed a PhD in biblical studies under F. F. Bruce at the University of Manchester.
[5] Stackhouse, *Canadian Evangelicalism in the Twentieth Century*, 155; Carl Armerding, "Theological Education in the Brethren: 1934–1984," unpublished paper.
[6] Alister E. McGrath, *J. I. Packer: A Biography* (Grand Rapids: Baker Books, 1997), 224.
[7] Armerding's uncle, Hudson Taylor Armerding (1918–2009), was the president of Wheaton College from 1965 to 1982.

and John Cochrane rounding out the early planning committee and board, Sheppard's team represented an early and enduring source of stability.

Sheppard's desire to form a new Brethren school likely stemmed from both religious commitment and shifting social realities. While most Plymouth Brethren in North America were known for their hostility toward the academy, by the early 1960s many in Vancouver's Plymouth Brethren assemblies were aware that the academy could not be ignored. For the affluent, socially prominent Vancouver Brethren, these changes hit close to home: their children, like those of middle-class parents across North America, were going to college in ever-increasing numbers.[8] In fall 1965 John Cochrane, a young Vancouver businessman and friend of Sheppard, took to the pages of the *Calling* with an assessment of the changing cultural landscape. In response to cultural changes, he made a proposal that included the first public description of Sheppard's school.[9]

Titled "The Effect of Increased Education—And a Proposal!," Cochrane's article cut to the chase. Citing US statistics that projected the number of college students to nearly triple from 2.7 million in 1955 to 8.6 million in 1975, Cochrane predicted "the emergence of a more academic church congregation." Cochrane then made the implication of these trends explicit: "It seems likely that the new college generation will expect the twentieth-century church to meet certain standards. Our theology will have to be related to the world around us." Cochrane continued on with a statement especially pertinent for a sect historically opposed to professional clergy: "Preachers will have to possess qualifications sufficient to command the respect of their audiences." In light of these trends, Cochrane offered a proposal—a Brethren school, perhaps in Vancouver, that would help the heirs of John Nelson Darby (1800–1882), the nineteenth-century founder of dispensationalist theology and the Plymouth Brethren movement, adapt to the times without losing their souls. Cochrane proposed that the school be a

---

[8]To some degree this was because a majority of Vancouver's Brethren assemblies were "open," therefore largely eschewing the strict sectarianism and anti-intellectualism that marked the more exclusive assemblies in the sect. Berkinshaw notes that not only was Vancouver home to "one of the strongest concentrations of Open Brethren in North America, if not in the world," but many of these Brethren were individuals of "considerable means." See Burkinshaw, *Pilgrims in Lotus Land*, 216-19, 313n55. College enrollment in the United States more than doubled between 1950 and 1960, from 168,043 to 393,553. Between 1960 and 1970 enrollment increased fivefold, eventually coming in at about 2.1 million. These trends did not stop until the mid-1970s. See John R. Thelin, *A History of American Higher Education* (Baltimore: Johns Hopkins University Press, 2004), 326.
[9]Stackhouse, *Canadian Evangelicalism in the Twentieth Century*, 155.

graduate institution, located on the campus of the University of British Columbia (thus with access to the university's library), and open to "men and women" from all Christian traditions. As far as programming was concerned, Cochrane foresaw "a one-year course for the student who plans a business or professional career... and three-year course for those who believe the Lord may be leading them into full-time ministry at home or abroad." Cochrane compared the school favorably to Fuller Theological Seminary but was careful to make one distinction that reflected the ecclesiological views of his audience: the program would emphasize "the training of laymen rather than the development of professional clergy."[10] Cochrane closed the article by offering an address to which interested individuals could write to the Vancouver committee. For the first time Sheppard's idea was out to an international Brethren audience.[11]

James Houston and the Vancouver Committee

One of those who read Cochrane's article was James Mackintosh Houston, an Oxford University geographer who was also the son of Plymouth Brethren missionaries and a leader in British Open Brethren circles. Houston wasted little time drafting a reply.[12] Unbeknownst to the Vancouver group, he had been mulling over the idea of a similar center for lay theological study since at least the Cuban Missile Crisis of 1962.[13] For Houston, a changing world demanded that Christians fit their pedagogy to the times. By the time Houston read Cochrane's article in 1965, emerging problems in Vietnam and the beginnings of international student protest only increased his empathy for a generation of students growing up under the shadow of war and potential nuclear holocaust.[14]

---

[10] John Cochrane, "The Effect of Increased Education—And a Proposal!," *Calling* (Fall 1965): 9-11.
[11] Criticism of Cochrane's article soon appeared among Brethren leaders. See J. M. Davis, "Concerning the Proposal for a Post Graduate Study Center," *Letters of Interest* (October 1965): 14; Neil M. Fraser, "Regarding a Post-graduate Study Center," *Letters of Interest* (November 1965): 13.
[12] James M. Houston, "The Inside Story of Regent College," circa 1970, JHF.
[13] Houston had been a university lecturer in the School of Geography since 1947. In 1964 he became a fellow of Hertford College, Oxford. He became bursar (i.e., second in authority) of Hertford College in 1967. He kept this position until he resigned from Oxford University in 1970. No full biography of Houston has been published at this time. One of the best treatments of Houston's life can be found in Arthur Dicken Thomas's two-part article in *Crux*. See Arthur Dicken Thomas, "James M. Houston, Pioneering Spiritual Director to Evangelicals," *Crux* 29, no. 3 (September 1993): 2-10; Thomas, "James M. Houston, Pioneering Spiritual Director to Evangelicals," *Crux* 29, no. 4 (December 1993): 17-27.
[14] James M. Houston, interview with author, October 24, 2015, Vancouver. See also Botton, "Regent College," 126.

He was ready to try his hand at something new, something very much like the venture Cochrane suggested. But he was not completely convinced the timing was right. His Plymouth Brethren piety had conditioned him to wait on God's timing. Convinced that God would make it perfectly clear whether he should enter this venture, Houston decided to wait. He never sent the letter.[15]

He did not have to wait long. At the suggestion of young Plymouth Brethren scholar and planning committee member Ward Gasque and on the recommendation of renowned Brethren biblical scholar F. F. Bruce, the Vancouver committee wrote to Houston in November 1966 with the request that he consider serving as the yet-to-be-named graduate school's first principal.[16] Houston, already in North America where he was serving as a visiting professor in geography at the University of Texas, consented to visit the committee in January 1967.

Once in Vancouver, Houston outlined three elements essential to his vision for the proposed school. In Houston's opinion the college should be a graduate institution, on the campus of the University of British Columbia (and affiliated with the university), that could transcend denominational lines.[17] In virtually every point Houston's vision echoed Cochrane's 1965 article. The differences that did exist between the two proposals were largely differences of degree. While Cochrane had never used the word *affiliation*, he had assumed that the school would be on the University of British Columbia campus and gain access to the University of British Columbia library. Likewise, while Houston agreed with Cochrane's emphasis that the school needed to transcend denominational lines, he went beyond Cochrane by insisting that the school exist free from any explicit ties to the Plymouth Brethren.

Houston's visit convinced Sheppard and the Vancouver committee that they had found the right man for the job. A couple of months later Sheppard wrote Houston confirming the committee's decision: "We are sure you are the man

---

[15] Houston, "Inside Story of Regent College."

[16] The committee had originally asked F. F. Bruce to head the institution in August 1966, but Bruce was not willing to leave his position as the John Rylands Professor of Biblical Criticism and Exegesis at Manchester University; see Laurel Gasque and W. Ward Gasque, "Frederick Fyvie Bruce: An Appreciation," *Ashland Theological Journal* 23 (1991), http://biblicalstudies.org.uk/pdf/ashland_theological_journal/23-1_01.pdf. Houston did not know Bruce had been offered the job until years later: Houston, "Founding Days at Regent," JHF. For Ward Gasque's role in getting Houston to Regent, see Phillips and Tan, *Serving God's Community*, xxiv-xxv.

[17] The wording of these three points differs slightly depending on which account one reads. This is taken from the earliest firsthand accounts of Houston, "Inside Story of Regent College" (which does not mention affiliation). See also Stackhouse, *Canadian Evangelicalism in the Twentieth Century*, 157.

needed.... Every finger pointed in your direction." He went on, framing Houston's decision in heroic terms: "I think we all recognize it would be a difficult decision for you to leave secure, secular employment in your profession to head a school which is nothing at the moment but a dream. But were not all the great men of faith faced with similar decisions?" Houston initially hesitated, but after spending the summer in Vancouver, he agreed to serve as the school's first principal.[18] On April 4, 1968, the provincial government of British Columbia granted the newly christened Regent College a charter to grant theological degrees.[19] Regent's first summer school was scheduled for summer 1969. Houston was at the helm. Regent College was launched.

Making Regent College

A provincial charter and a founding principal with Oxford University connections gave the Vancouver venture hope for success but no certainty of it. Throughout the first years Houston was leading what in a candid moment he termed "a survival venture," dependent on contributions from board members such as Ken Smith and a seemingly endless round of marketing and traveling on the part of Houston and other faculty members to keep the school afloat.[20] From the time Houston accepted the position at Regent until he officially gave his notice of resignation to Oxford and moved with his wife, Rita, and their four children to Vancouver in 1970, Houston balanced his life as bursar of Hertford College, Oxford, with multiple trans-Atlantic trips and intracontinental trips across North America.[21] Throughout this time Houston found himself talking and writing about Regent College constantly. In speeches, sermons, and long personal letters he laid out his hopes for the college. In the process Houston offered his audiences models on which to compare Regent and a vision for what Regent could become.

---

[18]Marshall Sheppard to James M. Houston, March 31, 1967, box 1, folder 8, JHF; James M. Houston to Marshall Sheppard, April 26, 1967, box 1, folder 8, JHF.

[19]After having failed to find a good geographical, biblical, or Plymouth Brethren (e.g., Gasque's suggestion of "Chapman Hall") name, the committee settled on Regent—the name of fellow planner Ken Smith's real-estate company. See Houston, "Founding Days at Regent." For Gasque's suggestions see W. Ward Gasque to Brian P. Sutherland, April 24, 1967, box 1, folder 12, JHF.

[20]James M. Houston to Mr. and Mrs. Victor Adrian, November 24, 1970, box 2, folder 3, JHF. For board contributions, see James M. Houston to Marshall Sheppard, September 24, 1969, box 1, folder 8, JHF.

[21]Houston did not officially resign from Oxford until 1971. James M. Houston, email to author, March 29, 2016.

Ironically, nearly all of his models for the innovative new venture came from the Old World. One of the readiest models was Tyndale House, Cambridge. Founded in 1945 by the evangelically minded Tyndale Fellowship (founded 1938), by the late 1960s the residential study and research center was playing a significant role in Britain's postwar evangelical renaissance.[22] As Tyndale House developed, it was able to acquire a top-notch library for biblical research and thereby attract some of the brightest established and up-and-coming evangelical scholars in the world. Many important scholars with Regent connections, including J. I. Packer, F. F. Bruce, and William J. Martin, were involved in Tyndale Fellowship at some level.[23] With its residential, university-centered location and a quality library, Tyndale House provided the Tyndale Fellowship with a geographical base capable of scholarly synergy.

Houston liked much of what he saw at Tyndale House, especially its ability to bring together scholars, especially senior scholars, and thereby advance evangelical scholarship. He did, however, want to push Regent in a broader direction beyond Tyndale House's specific focus on biblical studies and theology. Houston laid out his dream for Regent College in a 1968 letter to John Alexander, a fellow geographer who left the field to become national director of the US branch of campus ministry InterVarsity Christian Fellowship:

> Regent College will have two primary purposes. . . . The first is to provide an intensive one-year course to graduates, of both sexes, on an inter-denominational basis, before taking up their secular careers. . . . The second aim is to have a research centre rather on the lines of Tyndale House in Cambridge, U.K., where scholars—not necessarily theologians—can have the facilities to write and publish works of significance to evangelical testimony.[24]

---

[22]McGrath, *J. I. Packer*, 48-50. Like much in the history of Houston and Regent College, the Tyndale Fellowship also had close ties to InterVarsity Christian Fellowship. Tyndale Fellowship was founded in 1938 by a British Inter-Varsity Christian Fellowship committee in an effort to reengage evangelicals intellectually. For Ward Gasque's take on the significance of the Tyndale Fellowship and its study center, see W. Ward Gasque, "Evangelical Theology: The British Example," *Christianity Today*, August 10, 1973.

[23]McGrath, *J. I. Packer*, 50. For more on the Tyndale House program and J. I. Packer's role in it, especially his 1973 speech on the atonement, see Leland Ryken, *J. I. Packer: An Evangelical Life* (Wheaton, IL: Crossway Books, 2015), 55, 137-39.

[24]James M. Houston to John Alexander, August 31, 1968, box 1, folder 41, JHF. By the time Alexander accepted the position of InterVarsity national director in 1964, he had already been ministering for twelve years to college students and faculty at the University of Wisconsin, where he had been chair of the geography department. Keith Hunt and Gladys M. Hunt, *For Christ and the University: The Story of Intervarsity Christian Fellowship-USA, 1940–1990* (Downers Grove, IL: InterVarsity Press, 1992), 238-45.

In one of his earliest published reflections on the need for Regent College, Houston made much the same point: "It is planned that Regent College will provide facilities for an academic community of scholars engaged in the advancement of published work considered to be of importance for Christian witness. Scholars of repute will be granted financial assistance to stay at the College during sabbatical leave from their own Universities."[25] Though implicit, the model of Tyndale House shone through.

In these early years Houston also saw Tyndale House as a model that might prompt established evangelical scholars to relocate to Vancouver. By 1968 he had identified Carl F. H. Henry (1913–2003) as a top prospect. Henry was among the best-known evangelical theologians and public intellectuals in both North America and Europe. Close friend of neo-evangelical organizers such as Harold Ockenga and Billy Graham, Henry served on the original faculty at Fuller Theological Seminary before leaving to become the first editor in chief of *Christianity Today*.[26] Houston spoke of his hope of getting Carl Henry to "throw in his effort with us" to his friend Stacey Woods, founding director of Canadian InterVarsity Christian Fellowship (founded 1929) and then-director of the International Fellowship of Evangelical Students.[27] In Houston's opinion Henry's involvement was especially important because, as he told Woods, "notable scholars are not all that common in evangelical circles."[28] Houston laid out his idea to Henry in January 1969. He hoped that Regent College might "provide a residential centre for Christian scholars that may be considered comparable to Tyndale House, though much broader." Houston then suggested the possibility of merging Henry's recently founded Institute for Advanced Christian Studies (1967–2002) with Regent College if Henry were interested in "being the director of the research centre of Regent College and perhaps Professor of Christian

---

[25]James M. Houston, "Regent College Vancouver: A New Venture in Christian Scholarship," *Thrust* (January 1969): 7.
[26]For more on Carl Henry see Carl F. H. Henry, *Confessions of a Theologian: An Autobiography* (Waco, TX: Word Books, 1986). For Henry's role at Fuller, see George M. Marsden, *Reforming Fundamentalism: Fuller Seminary and the New Evangelicalism* (Grand Rapids: Eerdmans, 1987). For Henry's role at *Christianity Today*, see Elesha J. Coffman, *The Christian Century and the Rise of the Protestant Mainline* (New York: Oxford University Press, 2013).
[27]"History," Canadian Inter-Varsity Christian Fellowship, http://canadianivcf.org/history (accessed February 23, 2016); C. Stacey Woods, *The Growth of a Work of God: The Story of the Early Days of the Inter-Varsity Christian Fellowship of the United States of America as Told by Its First General Secretary* (Downers Grove, IL: InterVarsity Press, 1978).
[28]James M. Houston to C. Stacey Woods, October 17, 1968, box 1, folder 39, JHF.

communication." Houston's high hopes would be disappointed, however. Henry, who perhaps unbeknownst to Houston had been working to found his own "Crusade University" since 1955, turned down the offer.[29]

Henry's decision was one of many disappointments Houston faced in his first years at Regent. Tyndale House only worked as a model if he could get eminent scholars to join the effort. Early in the process Houston's own expansive vision for the school and sense of divine calling made him optimistic that notable scholars in a range of fields would be drawn to Regent. In the end, however, he would only be able to entice one other prominent scholar, W. J. Martin, to Regent's full-time faculty. Martin, a professor in Semitic languages at the University of Liverpool, took early retirement in order to join the venture. The other posts were either part time (Ian Rennie, John A. Toews), short lived (Stanley M. Block, Samuel J. Mikolaski), or held by promising but relatively unproven Brethren scholars (Gasque, Armerding). Furthermore, besides Houston and Block, every one of these early faculty members had fairly traditional seminary credentials.[30] Yet Houston's dream necessitated a superstar faculty with wide-ranging academic backgrounds. In 1969 this scholarly community seemed out of reach. Necessity, however, became the mother of one of Regent's most significant inventions.

In their early planning Houston and the Vancouver committee decided to launch Regent College by hosting a summer school for six weeks (divided into two three-week

Figure 2.1. From right to left, Carl Armerding, James Houston, and W. Ward Gasque in an early faculty meeting.

---

[29]James M. Houston to Carl F. H. Henry, January 6, 1969, box 1, file 24, JHF. For more on Henry's efforts to found an evangelical research university see Owen Strachan, *Awakening the Evangelical Mind: An Intellectual History of the Neo-evangelical Movement* (Grand Rapids: Zondervan, 2015), 127-57; Owen Strachan, "Carl Henry's University Crusade: The Spectacular Promise and Ultimate Failure of Crusade University," *Trinity Journal* 35, no. 2 (2014): 75-92.
[30]This largely follows Armerding's assessment of the situation: Carl E. Armerding to Michael G. Collison, July 22, 1993, folder 4, MCF.

sections) in the summers of 1969 and 1970 before the launch of regular classes in fall 1970. While few established professors were willing to relocate to western Canada and risk their careers at a fledgling school, the opportunity to spend a few weeks of the summer school surrounded by Vancouver's pristine beauty proved much more enticing. From its first year on Regent's summer school regularly hosted some of the biggest names in evangelical scholarship and church life. Within its first six years the summer school brought together a who's who of evangelical figures, most notably Conwell Seminary president S. S. Babbage (1969), Canadian poet Margaret Avison (1969), leading British New Testament scholar F. F. Bruce (1970), Dutch art historian and founder of Dutch L'Abri Hans Rookmaaker (1970, 1974), L'Abri worker and emerging evangelical public intellectual Os Guinness (1971), New Testament scholar R. N. Longnecker (1972), vice president of the Tom Skinner Association William E. Pannell (1973), leading South American evangelical Samuel Escobar (1973), Wheaton College's famous philosopher Arthur Holmes (1973), British theologian and Bible scholar J. I. Packer (1975), general secretary for the Latin American branch of the International Fellowship of Evangelical Students C. Rene Padilla (1975), and leading scholar of church growth Donald A. McGavran (1975).[31] Not only did these scholars attract attention and students (fifty-six students the first summer and hundreds after that), but together they also offered North American evangelicals a much more diverse and cosmopolitan expression of evangelicalism than what one would find in even the best evangelical seminaries at the time. Furthermore, the summer faculty seemed to enjoy their time at Regent, sometimes forming friendships and even scholarly relationships with other scholars they met in Vancouver.[32] F. F. Bruce, though admittedly not an unbiased observer, published glowing reviews of Regent after teaching at the 1970 summer school:

> Those who have been concerned in establishing it have received so much encouragement in unforeseen ways that they are left in no doubt that God has been directing and blessing the enterprise throughout. News of what it intends to do

---

[31] Both Escobar and Padilla played an important role in forcing North American and European evangelicals to consider the concerns of their fellow evangelicals in the Majority World. See David R. Swartz, *Moral Minority: The Evangelical Left in an Age of Conservatism* (Philadelphia: University of Pennsylvania Press, 2012), 113-34.

[32] An example of this can be seen in the scholarly appreciation that grew between F. F. Bruce and Hans Rookmaaker during the summer school of 1970. F. F. Bruce, "Regent College, Vancouver," *The Witness* 100, no. 1199 (October 1970): 419.

has already stimulated one or two other North American schools to that imitation which is the sincerest form of flattery, and if it goes on as it has begun, it will discharge an outstanding ministry for the kingdom of Christ.[33]

That scholars enjoyed Regent's summer school can also be inferred from the fact that in some cases, most notably that of Packer, involvement in summer school became a trial run for relocation to Vancouver. Indeed, for students and professors alike, summer school was one of Regent's best recruiting mechanisms.[34]

Like many of Houston's ideas, Oxford University was an important model for the summer-school project. Prior to his permanent relocation to Vancouver in 1970, Houston had lived in Oxford since he had begun his doctoral studies there in 1945. For Houston, the Oxonian influence on Regent was obvious. As he later noted, "Much of what we introduced [at Regent] was experimented at Oxford." By the time Houston helped launch the 1969 summer school, he already had eighteen years of experience running a similar summer program in Oxford. Along with several concerned professionals and scholars (including F. F. Bruce) in local Open Brethren assemblies, Houston helped develop the Young Men's Bible Study Conference in Oxford. These conferences offered students a chance to study the Bible and interact with Christian experts in the field. According to Houston, the success of these Oxford conferences led directly to the proposal that Regent begin with a summer program. Rather than functioning as a one- or two-year temporary measure, Regent's summer school became one of the most notable, lasting, and, indeed, imitated features of the college. Houston's Oxford experiences and the connections he made there went a long way in helping to make the program a success. More than one of the lecturers at Regent's summer school had previously taught at the Oxford conference.[35]

It was not simply that Houston moved in the right networks; it was also that these earlier schools, located in the heart of historic university towns, offered access to scholars and professionals in a wide variety of fields. Thus Houston was able to work with surgeon Melville Capper as well as with scientists such as Sir Robert Boyd, a pioneering atmospheric physicist, and Donald Mckay, who worked in artificial intelligence. These helped expand the Oxford Bible Conference beyond standard Bible study to include conversations on a wide

---

[33]Bruce, "Regent College, Vancouver," 419.
[34]McGrath, *J. I. Packer*, 233-36.
[35]Botton, "Regent College," 127.

range of topics, each of which was considered in relation to Christian thought. According to Houston, the "integration of faith, theology, and all the professional disciplines," one of Regent's most distinctive if also elusive goals, "emerged from this milieu."[36] Summer school was a means for continuing and expanding this integrative work.

Oxford was not, however, the only stream of influence that pushed Regent toward an engagement with disciplines that frequently moved beyond the standard curriculum of theological schools. Both Gasque and Armerding had been deeply formed by two of North America's foremost evangelical liberal arts colleges (Wheaton and Gordon, respectively). Unlike the Bible institutes that had sprung up in the United States and Canada in the 1920s and 1930s, liberal arts schools such as Wheaton and Gordon attempted to provide students with a well-rounded education that balanced theological aims with instruction in fields ranging from literature and the arts to science, mathematics, and philosophy. This integrative perspective was further enhanced by interaction with Kuyperian theology, especially as adapted in the writing, teaching, and personal influence of Hans Rookmaaker.[37] The combination of Houston's Oxford experience, the influence of leading evangelical liberal arts institutions, and the far-reaching implications of Reformed theology made Regent's summer schools inspiring models of cross-disciplinary study.

As inspiring as this melding of influences may have been for some on the Regent staff, for Houston, Oxford long served as the primary institutional model and relational hub. Indeed, in some ways the second, relational aspect of Houston's Oxonian orientation proved even more lasting than the first. Between 1946 and 1953 Houston shared an apartment in Oxford with Nicolas Zernov, the leader of the Orthodox community in England and lecturer in Eastern Orthodox culture at Oxford.[38] Zernov's academic position combined with his prominent position as the secretary of the Fellowship of St. Alban and St. Sergius, an organization that sought to promote dialogue between Anglicans and Orthodox, made him a prominent figure in the religious landscape of Oxford. That Houston, far outside his Brethren element, gained much from this friendship

---

[36]Botton, "Regent College," 127.
[37]Carl E. Armerding, email to author, March 24, 2018.
[38]James M. Houston and D. Bruce Hindmarsh, *For Christ and His Kingdom: Inspiring a New Generation* (Vancouver: Regent College Publishing, 2012), 49.

is hard to doubt. Even though Houston's deep appreciation for the spiritual writings from Catholic and Orthodox traditions became stronger later in his career, it took root during this time.[39] Yet it was not Zernov himself but one of the many other prominent religious figures who found his way into Houston and Zernov's apartment who exerted the most significant influence on Houston.

Houston met British novelist, scholar, and lay theologian C. S. Lewis during one of the discussion groups Zernov hosted at the apartment. In Lewis, Houston found a professional scholar willing to take the risk of venturing out of his own field and into the realm of theology, all the while emphasizing that he was "a very ordinary layman of the Church of England."[40] Whereas Houston was initially unwilling to deliver papers outside his own field of geography to the group, Lewis was willing to give broadcast talks to the entire nation on theological topics far removed from his work as a literary scholar.[41] Houston and Lewis took part in Zernov's monthly meetings together for six years. Though the two never became close friends—Houston remembers Lewis being quite guarded about his personal life—Lewis made a deep impact on the younger scholar. In Lewis, Houston found a model for the kind of "amateur" theologian he aspired to cultivate in his own life and in the life of his students. For the rest of his life Houston maintained that "a vital need today is to preserve the Christian life's 'amateur status.' For just as family life and friendship are where we live relationally, so is the Christian life. These are the realms of *dilettantes*, literally, those taking 'delight' in God, and as *amateurs* or 'lovers' of each other."[42]

Lewis's rejection of a reductionist, functional view of life also left a lasting mark on Houston. Half a century later, Houston was still noting the significance of the last conversation he had with Lewis, in which he asked Lewis, "What would you say was your central message you were communicating though all your literary works?" Lewis promptly replied, "Against reductionism."[43] For Houston this translated into a growing sense that the modern impulse toward

---

[39]Thomas, "James M. Houston, Pioneering Spiritual Director to Evangelicals," 7.
[40]C. S. Lewis, *Mere Christianity* (Grand Rapids: Zondervan, 2001), viii.
[41]This was a move that came with high costs in the context of Oxford University. See Alister E. McGrath, *C. S. Lewis: A Life; Eccentric Genius, Reluctant Prophet* (Carol Stream, IL: Tyndale House, 2013), 216-18.
[42]Houston's esteem for Lewis's version of amateurism lasted throughout his life. For an example of his concept of this, see James M. Houston, *The Mentored Life: From Individualism to Personhood* (Vancouver: Regent College Publishing, 2012), 30.
[43]Houston and Hindmarsh, *For Christ and His Kingdom*, 49.

isolated, professional identities had to be countered by a turn to the relational. Prior to meeting Lewis, Houston was already disillusioned by the overreach of professionalism. As he watched British architects develop the new profession of "regional planning" during World War II or geographers at Oxford scramble to reestablish their place in the profession in the postwar years, Houston became convinced that one's identity must be rooted in Christ, not a profession.[44]

This shift in Houston's thinking became evident in 1969, when his friend E. M. Blaiklock, a classics professor at the University of Auckland, New Zealand, who was spending a year in Britain, asked Houston to contribute to a collection of essays titled *Why I Am Still a Christian*. The book was designed to be a response to Bertrand Russell's (1870–1972) widely read *Why I Am Not a Christian* (1957).[45] Of the eleven contributors, Houston was the only one to reject an explicit link to his professional identity. Sandwiched between a list of titles ranging from "A Philosopher Examines the Question" to "A Biochemist Shares His Faith" to "A Musician and His God," Houston's "A God-Centered Personality" stood apart. Rather than allowing oneself to be defined by a professional identity, Houston called for a renewed emphasis on the personal and relational elements of the Christian faith in an increasingly fragmented culture:

> Do we not find it so much easier to ask of the stranger, *what* he is? instead of being aware of *who* he is? So much of our secular and materialistic culture is obsessed with our *having*, and ignorant of our *being*. This anxiety is not being dispelled by science and education. Rather our ailment grows with their increase. . . . It is my contention that our society may distinguish individuals as units of the human species, but it is only the Christian faith that has truly recognized *persons*, their real purpose and genuine relationships.[46]

With this essay Houston publicly set his course along what he later termed "the trajectory of the personal." It was a direction from which he never veered.[47]

---

[44]Houston, interview.
[45]Houston and Hindmarsh, *For Christ and His Kingdom*, 51.
[46]James M. Houston, "A God-Centered Personality," in *Why I Am Still a Christian*, ed. E. M Blaiklock (Grand Rapids: Zondervan, 1971), 84-85.
[47]In 2012 Houston was awarded the inaugural Christian Leadership Award in Higher Education by Christian Higher Education Canada. In his remarks Houston affirmed this continuity: "What has given integration and meaning to my whole narrative more than fifty years later has been consistently living 'this trajectory of the personal'" (Houston and Hindmarsh, *For Christ and His Kingdom*, 52-53). See also Thomas, "James M. Houston, Pioneering Spiritual Director to Evangelicals," 7-8.

Houston's Vision for Regent College

The same convictions that inspired his contribution to Blaiklock's book also informed Houston's vision for Regent College, especially his strong emphasis on the theological training of laity. Sheppard and the Vancouver committee had always understood their project as having a lay emphasis. Everything in their Brethren background pointed in this direction. While some among the Brethren did work in full-time ministry as missionaries, local assemblies did not, as a rule, hire professional clergy. Instead, local laymen were expected to share the preaching and teaching roles. Notably, however, for Sheppard and the majority of the early members of the Vancouver committee, these Brethren sensibilities did not preclude the possibility of what Cochrane's 1965 *Calling* article described as "a three-year course for those who believe God may be leading them into full-time ministry."[48] Houston shared these Brethren sensibilities but also harbored a much deeper personal aversion to what he felt was an increasing overemphasis on professionalism in all of life. The latter sensibility eventually pushed Houston to emphasize the education of laity to a degree that sometimes baffled board members and other Regent faculty.[49] For Houston, all professionalism was suspect, but religious professionalism especially so.

In the early years of Regent College, however, Houston did not seem to have a significant problem welcoming both lay Christians and those who were studying for full-time (i.e., professional) ministry. Given the realities of founding (and then funding) a new college, pragmatism had to curtail idealism. There were bills to be paid and friends to be made, so Houston had to tread carefully.[50] Furthermore, he had a committee of highly capable Brethren assemblymen in Vancouver who had already been planning on a three-year course of study that sounded a lot like a bachelor of divinity (the professional ministerial degree that proceeded the development of the master of divinity degree).[51] Facing

---

[48] Cochrane, "Effect of Increased Education," 11.
[49] Laurel Gasque, W. Ward Gasque, and Carl E. Armerding, interview with author, October 23, 2015, Vancouver; Carl E. Armerding, email to author, February 27, 2018.
[50] Reactions to Cochrane's original proposal in Brethren publications demonstrate suspicions within Houston's own denomination. Carl E. Armerding to James M. Houston, January 20, 1968, box 1, folder 11, JHF.
[51] Cochrane, "Effect of Increased Education." Carl Armerding remembers that he and others understood talk of a three-year degree to be synonymous with a bachelor of divinity. See Gasque, Gasque, and Armerding, interview.

these realities, Houston embarked on a tricky balancing act as he emphasized the uniqueness of Regent's focus on lay education while still allowing room for what seemed very much like a professional ministerial degree.

Starting in 1968, Houston went to work laying out the college's vision to potential donors, faculty, students, and allies. Writing to Paul Little of Inter-Varsity Christian Fellowship in June 1968, Houston expressed his hope that Regent "would be more like an institute of Christian Education with a non-professional bias" aimed at "graduates ready to start their secular career" who "would be recruited for a one-year basic course." Houston predicted that the course of study would include "courses in pastoral theology, religious sociology, contemporary arts" in addition to "more traditional subjects such as biblical exegesis, Theology, and Church History." This vision amounted to what soon became Houston's golden standard: Regent College, an institute dedicated to making laypeople more thoroughly Christian in their everyday lives and their secular careers. Notably, however, Houston did not stop there. He followed up these lay-centric goals by opening other doors of possibility, adding, "There might be a minority doing a three year professional course, and a few doing doctorates."[52]

Houston's exchange with Little reflects the ambiguity that marked the divide between lay and professional education for years to come in Houston's vision for the school and, not surprisingly, in the vision of others. In early 1969 founding board member Don Bennett told one inquirer that Regent's program would likely include a "three-year Bachelor of Divinity and Doctoral Studies." Yet Bennett was not entirely sure of himself. That same day he dashed off a worried letter to Houston noting that he had responded in the interest of good public relations but felt that he was "in no position to intelligently reply other than what I have done."[53] What he needed from Houston was a form letter that laid out Regent's vision and goals.

At almost exactly this time Houston published an article in the Evangelical Fellowship of Canada's *Thrust* (founded 1968) that situated Regent's particular mission within the context of the university.[54] Citing examples of international

---

[52]James M. Houston to Paul Little, June 25, 1968, box 1, folder 41, JHF.
[53]Don Bennett to Robert B. Merritt, January 15, 1969, box 1, folder 4, JHF; Don Bennett to James M. Houston, January 15, 1969, box 1, folder 4, JHF.
[54]For more on the Evangelical Fellowship of Canada and *Thrust*, see Stackhouse, *Canadian Evangelicalism in the Twentieth Century*, 165-73.

student unrest, Houston described the modern academy as "adrift" and "confused." In Houston's eyes the state of evangelical attitudes toward scholarship were not much better. Citing Harry Blamires, who in his 1963 book *The Christian Mind* lamented, "There is no longer a Christian mind. . . . The modern Christian has succumbed to secularization," Houston joined in the critique noting that evangelical Christians had forgotten how to "think Christianly." In Houston's view a key part of this "tragedy" was that "many University graduates have well trained minds in secular studies, but a simplistic faith, not much advanced beyond what they learnt in Sunday School." Because of this they tended to be "schizophrenic in thought with separate compartments of mind marked 'secular' and 'religious.'" Counteracting these trends was, to Houston's mind, Regent's primary mission. Noting that the college's "primary purpose is to train laymen," Houston laid out a one-year diploma program for students "who will be willing to sacrifice one year off their careers for an intensive course in Christian thought and life." Though the diploma program was not a professional degree, Houston conveyed a hope that it would be accredited with other colleges and universities. Houston envisioned that the program's "main objective will be the training in Christian maturity so that graduates will leave to be better equipped Christians, ready to enter their careers as engineers, doctors or housewives."[55]

But did Regent's focus on the theological training of the laity exclude professional clerical training? In 1969 even Houston did not seem to think so. In February he wrote to Ian Rennie (1929–2015), a credentialed scholar who was also an influential Presbyterian minister in Vancouver. Perhaps considering Rennie's potential reservations to a lay-oriented graduate school with strong Brethren influences, and undoubtedly aware of the good Rennie's support could do for the fledging venture, Houston laid out a vision for Regent that explicitly included room for a three-year professional degree:

> While we want to make the one-year course for graduate students a distinctive feature of Regent College, I see clearly the need also to establish a full three-year professional course for theological students who will be ministers of the Gospel. Perhaps we can start the latter program a year after we have engaged the first of

---

[55] Harry Blamires, *The Christian Mind: How Should a Christian Think?* (Ann Arbor, MI: Servant Books, 1978), 3; Houston, "Regent College Vancouver: A New Venture," 4; Houston, "Founding Days at Regent." Blamires was also a student of C. S. Lewis.

our staff for the one-year course, to give time to plan carefully a curriculum that will be academically sound and also realistic for full-time Christian ministers.[56]

Houston's letter apparently convinced Rennie that there was room for a professional minister at Regent. Rennie joined Regent's board shortly after this exchange and served on Regent's original faculty as a "special lecturer" in church history from fall 1970 until fall 1972, when he took up a full-time position as an associate professor of church history.[57]

As an ordained Presbyterian minister, Rennie did not see professional training for ministers as something to be avoided, and his presence alone sent a strong message to inquiring students. By hiring Rennie Regent seemed to be saying that individuals in established denominations—even those who were considering ministerial degrees—were welcome at Regent. Yet Rennie bridged the lay-professional divide by more than his presence alone. As the debate about Regent's identity began to heat up in the mid-1970s, when Houston began to publicly downplay his earlier acceptance of professional training at Regent, Rennie emerged as an important commentator on Regent's vision and trajectory. In 1974, he presented a paper titled "Emphases of the Program: Lay vs. Professional" to Regent's first strategic planning conference. Rennie began by laying out the two sides of the debate at Regent. While some claimed that "everyone seems to have been agreed thus far that the training of 'lay' Christians is the exclusive or at least a major part of the task of Regent" and a key part of what made Regent unique, others contended that "the original vision of Regent contained a 'professional' as well as a 'lay' element." While both of these sides could harness evidence to back up their claims, Rennie demonstrated that the most powerful indicator of Regent's key concern was what it was actually doing, not what it claimed as its founding vision. "Whether it was in the original vision or not," the school was now training professional biblical scholars and was seriously considering adding a program for the training of Young Life staff members to its curriculum. For Rennie, and what seemed to be a growing number of Regent faculty and board members, the answer was not *either* lay *or* professional; it was *both* lay *and*

---

[56]James M. Houston to Ian S. Rennie, February 8, 1969, box 1, folder 6, JHF. Houston later stated that at some point early on he realized that Rennie "was very much looking to establish the 'Fuller of the North.'" See Botton, "Regent College," 181.
[57]Brian P. Sutherland, "Are You Keeping Up?," *Calling* (1970).

professional. Regent could retain its distinctive identity by combining both emphases in "its own unique mix."[58]

By focusing on the reality that Regent had already moved decidedly toward granting professional degrees, Rennie likely fueled Houston's own anxiety about the role of professional education at Regent. By spring 1974 Houston and the Regent board and faculty had taken significant steps toward making Regent College a viable institution. In 1972 the college had launched a two-year program leading to a degree—the master of Christian studies. Then in fall 1973 Regent moved toward Houston's original vision by gaining affiliation (though provisional) with the University of British Columbia.[59] Just that spring Houston had successfully lured Clark Pinnock, a rising evangelical star in the field of theology, to Regent's faculty. Moreover, student numbers were promising: 225 students attended the summer school of 1973, and 40 students were set to graduate in spring 1974 with a diploma in Christian studies.[60] Seven more would be graduating with the master of Christian studies degree. Yet even these successes did not assure the college's long-term economic stability. The college may have been on the evangelical map, but it was still renting space from the Vancouver School of Theology, and it looked like there was going to be an operating deficit at the end of the fiscal year on May 31, 1974. Thus, even as Houston affirmed Regent's emphasis on lay education and was hopeful about Regent's future prospects, he was still interested in pursuing new opportunities to serve the people of God and to grow Regent's student body and donor base.

As Rennie noted in his 1974 paper, one of the ways Houston had attempted to do this was by exploring the possibility of developing a curriculum in youth ministry. William Starr, president of Young Life from 1964 to 1977, had approached Houston in summer 1973 with an idea: Perhaps Regent could be the primary training center for Young Life staff workers in Canada?[61] Starr's proposal was worth

---

[58]Ian S. Rennie, "Emphases of the Program: Lay vs. Professional" (paper presented at "Openness to the Future: A Prelude to Planning," 1974), 2-3. The entire program, including all the presented papers, are available in the box 2, folder 12, of the JHF. Houston felt that this conference successfully conveyed Regent's character and had the conference papers published so they could be distributed to incoming board members and faculty. See also Ian S. Rennie, "Regent College: A Reflective View," *Regent Collage* 2, no. 1 (June 1981).

[59]"Ad Hoc Committee on Regent College—Request for Affiliation," UBC Senate Summary, November 14, 1973, 3-4.

[60]"Summer School 1973," *Regent College Bulletin* 3, no. 3 (Summer 1973); "Convocation IV," *Regent College Bulletin* 4, no. 2 (Spring 1974).

[61]William S. Starr to James M. Houston, July 25, 1973, box 3, folder 17, JHF. For Houston's part, he

Figure 2.2. Regent College held classes in the basement of the Vancouver School of Theology from 1970 until 1975.

consideration. If Regent were to become Young Life's Canadian hub, not only would Regent exert a theological influence on student ministry in Canada, but students and funds would also likely be forthcoming. In fall 1973 Houston, himself not entirely convinced of the program's merit, brought the idea to the faculty senate, where it was met with mixed reviews. The faculty were worried about fit. Since Regent's curriculum was not set up as a professional school, it would need new courses were it to undertake the training of Young Life staff members. This, however, raised the question: Would it be inconsistent to adopt this program and still not offer the bachelor of divinity program for church pastors and ministers? Or would this open the way to becoming a fully developed seminary?

By January Houston had warmed to the idea of a Young Life track at Regent. In conversations with Young Life leader Chet Starr, Houston came to believe that a separate master of Christian youth ministries degree geared toward developing Young Life staff members was both "feasible and mutually attractive."[62] With Houston and Starr's backing, the Regent board and faculty senate began moving forward on a program geared to the ministry needs of Young Life staff

---

had been considering some kind of relationship with a student ministry since 1968. See Houston to Woods, October 17, 1968.

[62]James M. Houston to Arthur D. Parker, January 30, 1974, box 3, folder 17, JHF.

members. In addition to a new degree program, the Young Life Training Curriculum for 1974–1975 proposed that students in the second year of the program could choose to take pastoral care classes at the Vancouver School of Theology. By including an option for students to take a course in pastoral care, Regent College was inching toward a seminary degree.

A seminary degree at Regent was not to be, though—at least not on Houston's watch. Following the Young Life experiment of the 1974–1975 academic year, Houston grew more skeptical of what he deemed to be Regent's shift toward training for professional ministry. Houston had found the Young Life curriculum to be somewhat disappointing from the start. The initial class attracted few students, and the second class, which began with seven students, finished with four. Additionally, Houston noted that the courses were "clearly . . . not on the same academic level as other courses in the college."[63] The faculty, however, having gradually come around to see the program's potential, believed it could be improved and was worth the effort.

By 1975 Houston's doubts were growing. Did the Young Life programs and similar professionally oriented programming mesh with his original vision for lay theological education? When Chet Starr moved on from his teaching position at Regent in 1977, Houston was not willing to go to great lengths to replace him. As some on Regent's faculty and board moved further toward the prospect of professional education—even discussing the possibility of a master of divinity program—Houston moved with heightened resolve in the opposite direction by reemphasizing his call for lay theological education. By the second half of the decade, Regent was no longer struggling for life. The school was now attracting the best evangelical scholars in the world as summer lecturers and full-time professors. Furthermore, in 1975 the college had managed to buy a property (and the two large fraternity houses on it; see photo 2.3), which was ideally located near the University of British Columbia—an institution with which Regent gained indefinite affiliation in 1977.[64] Now Houston saw that his fear that the college might grow too big was being realized.[65] To his mind Regent

---

[63]James M. Houston to Gary Bell, January 29, 1975, box 3, folder 17, JHF.
[64]W. Ward Gasque, "The History of Regent College," 11, folder 23: Ward Gasque, MCF.
[65]By the late 1970s Regent was too big in Houston's eyes. See James M. Houston to Doug Coe, September 30, 1974, box 3, folder 1, JHF; James M. Houston to Doug Coe, December 4, 1975, box 3, folder 1, JHF; James M. Houston to Robert and Mary Boyd, January 28, 1976, box 2, folder 4, JHF; James M. Houston to S. Chowdry, August 9, 1977, box 2, folder 4, JHF.

Figure 2.3. In 1975 Regent College obtained its own property, including two former fraternity houses on Wesbrook Mall. This property functioned as the Regent College campus until a new building was built on University Boulevard in 1988.

College did not need more specialty programs to attract new students, especially not specialty programs in professional ministry.

Not everyone at Regent shared Houston's sentiment. By the late 1970s many members of the Regent faculty and board felt that the time had come to offer a formal master of divinity degree. For many longtime Regent faculty, the idea that Regent might offer a master of divinity degree was by no means a new development. The possibility of a three-year professional degree had been a part of the Regent vision from the start. Similar disagreement existed between Houston and the faculty as far as the issue of student enrollment numbers was concerned. While Houston lamented growing student enrollment, other members of the faculty tasked with the practical

Figure 2.4. The current Regent Campus (foreground) set against Vancouver's pristine natural beauty.

operations of the college rejoiced that Regent had *finally* become a financially viable institution—a reality that required tuition-paying students. Furthermore, even if the Regent administration and faculty had wanted Regent to remain small, by the mid-1970s it was becoming increasingly difficult to turn back the tide of applications that accompanied Regent's high-profile faculty and growing reputation. (Within a decade Regent College became the largest graduate school of theology in Canada.)[66] As these conflicts became more pronounced, they pushed Houston and the Regent board and faculty into increasingly polarized positions. When combined with faculty concerns about what some considered Houston's questionable administrative capacities, these issues caused more than a few members of the Regent College faculty and board to worry in 1976 and 1977 that the college—in the very midst of unprecedented success and influence—was actually headed for a crisis.

The Ethos of Regent College in Its First Decade

Growing disputes about the nature and implications of Regent's focus on lay education aside, by 1977 Regent had firmly established a community ethos that many seemed to find both unique and compelling. Throughout the 1970s Regent developed a reputation as a theologically orthodox option for evangelicals seeking an innovative learning community capable of blending academic rigor with evangelical spirituality, personal relationships, and—thanks to its nontraditional goals and methods, relatively young faculty, and emphasis on community— a touch of countercultural allure. In short, Regent College was exciting, and it soon joined L'Abri as a destination for intellectually inclined evangelical pilgrims. For some, Regent became the logical post-L'Abri step.

Time, place, and hospitality. For all their differences, L'Abri and Regent shared several important similarities. Like L'Abri, Regent possessed a charismatic founder-leader who thrived in one-on-one conversation and seemed to understand the deep angst of evangelicals coming of age in the midst of the counterculture and the "technological society" that Jacques Ellul had critiqued a decade before. Houston, however, held several advantages over Schaeffer. Houston had an earned doctorate, taught at Oxford, and had a personal relationship—the depth of the friendship did not much matter—with C. S. Lewis, who was then

---

[66]Stackhouse, *Canadian Evangelicalism in the Twentieth Century*, 161.

fast becoming a heroic figure for American evangelicals. (By the 1970s everything and everyone Lewis had touched was turning to evangelical gold in North America. Houston benefited for the rest of his life from this connection.[67]) Regent also offered a less dogmatic theology than did Schaeffer. Regent was generally Reformed, but it also had strong Plymouth Brethren tendencies and a few Mennonite and Baptist influences as well.

Context mattered too. Like L'Abri, Regent was geographically situated in a picturesque setting, surrounded by expansive mountain ranges *and* access to the sea. Furthermore, like L'Abri and other international evangelical communities, Regent occupied a position that maintained some distance from the rough-and-tumble world of American evangelical infighting. Canada, much like Switzerland, was a country inclined more toward peaceful neutrality and polite sociability than its neighbor to the south. Indeed, as Rennie once noted, "Canada, with its dislike of extremes and polarities, provided a healthy setting for a college that did not want to be aligned with passing fads, but that would strive to affirm the inestimable vision of 'mere Christianity.'" Furthermore, Regent College was positioned to reap benefits secondhand as Canada's star rose on the international scene thanks to events such as the 1967 Montreal Expo, the 1976 Summer Olympics in Montreal, and the 1983 World Council of Churches Assembly in Vancouver.[68]

Even within Canada, Vancouver was a city with a distinctive culture all its own. Houston picked up on the city's unique ethos and strategic value early on.

> Toronto, I sensed, is too nationalistic and self-contained within its culture to want or supply north-south links with the U.S. and Latin America. Montreal has it preoccupation with French-speaking Quebec. An American University campus would not interest Canadian Christian enterprise very significantly apart from

---

[67] Houston's papers contain at least nine papers in manuscript form on C. S. Lewis. The topics of these range from "The Sexuality and Prayer Life of C. S. Lewis" to "The Mythopoetic World of C. S. Lewis" to "Mere Christianity: Lewis's Understanding of the Christian Life." Most of these can be found in box 6, folder 9, JHF. For more on evangelicals' lasting interest in touching someone who touched Lewis see David Graham, *We Remember C. S. Lewis: Essays and Memoirs* (Nashville: Broadman & Holman, 2001); James M. Houston and Bruce Hindmarsh, "An Interview with James Houston About His Friend C. S. Lewis in Honor of the Lewis Anniversary," Titus One Nine: The Weblog of the Rev. Canon Dr. Kendall Harmond, January 14, 2014, http://kendallharmon.net/?p=42056; James M. Houston, "C. S. Lewis as Prophet for Postmodernism," C. S. Lewis Institute, April 22, 2010, www.cslewisinstitute.org/node/1112.

[68] Rennie, "Regent College: A Reflective View"; Carl E. Armerding, "Reflections of a Canadian Theological Educator—A Personal History," in *Studies in Canadian Evangelical Renewal: Essays in Honour of Ian S. Rennie*, ed. Kevin Quast and John Vissers (Markham, ON: FT Publications, 1996), 69.

Wheaton and Dallas, Fuller, etc. For N. American Christian co-operation why not select a Canadian city for the next venture? Vancouver is open fully to U.S. influences and links.[69]

But Vancouver's connective capacity did not only extend north to south; it also stretched east to west. Vancouver was simultaneously the last outpost of the British Empire and the emerging gateway to the East—a fact that Sheppard had long intuited. With an eye on the strategic significance of the Pacific Rim, Sheppard had conveyed his opinion early and often that "Vancouver *is* in the centre of things!"[70] History proved him right. In the ensuing decades Vancouver and the University of British Columbia emerged as a major hub for Chinese students, businesses, and tourism—all trends that positively affected Regent.[71] David Lam from Hong Kong brought in Leung In-Sing to teach the first classes in Cantonese, and Lam went on to financially underwrite Regent's upgraded campus in the late 1980s. Regent's first endowed chair was established as a result of the generosity of a single Chinese family. By 1995 Chinese endowments accounted for over 1.7 million of Regent's total 3.6-million-dollar endowment.[72] Together these factors meant that Regent developed a community ethos that was simultaneously Canadian and international.

In addition to influences outside North America, larger socioreligious trends in the United States and Canada benefited Regent as well. In the late 1960s and early 1970s, the Jesus movement helped evangelical Protestants catch up to the laicizing trends that had moved through mainline denominations and the Catholic Church in the prior decades.[73] The strong charismatic sensibilities of the Jesus movement fostered a belief that the Christian "rank and file" (i.e., the laity) could be filled with the Holy Spirit and his gifts regardless of their lack of credentials or formal training. Jesus people did not see established churches or ecclesiastical hierarchies in the book of Acts; they did, however, see a Holy Spirit–filled community that was perfectly suited to the communal impulse of

---

[69] Houston to Woods, October 17, 1968.
[70] Botton, "Regent College," 83.
[71] Armerding, "Reflections of a Canadian Theological Educator," 73-74.
[72] W. Ward Gasque, "Regent Reflects," 10, MCF; "Regent College: The Annual Report, 1994–1995," MCF.
[73] The reforms of Vatican II are prime examples of this trend: Paul Lakeland, "The Laity," in *From Trent to Vatican II: Historical and Theological Investigations*, ed. Raymond F. Bulman and Frederick J. Parrella (New York: Oxford University Press, 2006), 193-208; Walter M. Abbott and Joseph Gallagher, *The Documents of Vatican II* (London: Chapman, 1966).

the times.[74] These impulses meshed well with Regent's nonclerical, low-church Brethren background and Houston's explicit concern for the laity. Houston's antiestablishment (or at least outside-the-establishment) sensibilities enticed some young people in the generally anti-intellectual Jesus movement to devote themselves to study, but Regent could not have done this without its equally strong emphasis on community. At Regent one could both learn *and* belong.

Community came naturally in Regent's early years. A small student body and the college's close quarters in the basement of the Vancouver School of Theology, where Regent rented classroom space, virtually guaranteed that students would get to know each other well (see photo 2.5).[75] Yet it was more than acquaintance or proximity that gave early students and faculty a sense that they were part of a "family."[76] Informed by Plymouth Brethren practice and inspired by Oxford collegiality and Houston's emphasis on personal relations, students, faculty, and faculty families worked intentionally to build a sense of community at Regent. Hospitality served as an important means of bringing these goals to fruition.

Figure 2.5. An early Regent College class in the Vancouver School of Theology basement.

---

[74]Deryck W. Lovegrove, *The Rise of the Laity in Evangelical Protestantism* (New York: Routledge, 2002), 254-55.
[75]For personal reflections on community life during these years, see, Kit Schinell, "Kit Schindell," *Regent Reflects* (1995): 3-4, MCF; Schindell, "Have You Met Dal Schindell?," *Crux* 50, no. 1 (2014): 46-47.
[76]The title of Regent's first in-house news sheet was *Family Affair*. See "Rita Houston," in James M. Houston to Arthur D. Parker, January 30, 1974, box 3, folder 17, JHF.

For many in Plymouth Brethren circles, personal hospitality was a way of life. Inspired by Scripture, many Brethren homes had special "prophet's chambers," where Brethren leaders or out-of-town guests could stay. Many of those involved in Regent's early history had experienced this type of in-home hospitality firsthand. Following a stint in the US Navy, Carl Armerding spent two years traveling around Europe as an Officers Christian Union Staff member. According to Armerding, "in England you had people with big suburban homes, and you always stayed with them. You never stayed in a hotel. Hospitality in the home was a key." For Ward and Laurel Gasque, too, home hospitality was of high value. Both were the recipients of Brethren home-based hospitality from Vancouver to London.[77] The Gasques also spent time at Schaeffer's L'Abri and hosted Francis and Edith Schaeffer in Manchester while Ward was studying for his PhD.[78]

Houston intentionally cultivated an emphasis on hospitality. He encouraged Regent's early faculty members to buy homes nearby so they could be involved in the life of the college outside working hours.[79] Houston and his wife, Rita, led by example. After purchasing a home in the area, the Houstons began entertaining students each Sunday afternoon.[80] On occasion they also hosted students for longer periods of time. In summer 1974 they hosted several students in their home for the entire six-week summer school. Writing in the pages of the *Regent College Bulletin*, Rita Houston described how her initial hesitancy to host "several strangers" changed to enthusiasm as the students joined the family in meal preparation, long discussions, and prayer. She summed up her experience that summer with a commentary on Regent's community: "Looking back over the summer school, I view it primarily in terms of people rather than lectures or classes."[81]

Houston expected that other faculty would follow his example by opening their homes to students as well.[82] The faculty needed little prompting. According to Armerding, the early faculty were fully united around Houston's emphasis

---

[77]Gasque, Gasque, and Armerding, interview. Ward stayed at the home of prominent London editor C. G. D. Howley (1907–1980) in 1959. Gasque stayed at the home of Marshall Sheppard on his first trip to Vancouver in 1965 (Phillips and Tan, *Serving God's Community*, xvi, xxii).
[78]Phillips and Tan, *Serving God's Community*, xxiv.
[79]Armerding, interview.
[80]James M. Houston and Rita Houston to friends, December 13, 1971, box 2, folder 3, JHF.
[81]Rita Houston, "Summer School Perspective," *Regent College Bulletin* 4, no. 3 (Summer 1974).
[82]Clark H. Pinnock to Michael G. Collison, June 13, 1994, folder 33, MCF.

Figure 2.6. Whether at home or in the library, professors and students engaged in numerous informal meals and get-togethers. Here Ward Gasque and students enjoy tea and cake in the Regent library.

on home-based hospitality. Faculty members opened their homes for discussion groups, meals, and informal conversations. Laurel Gasque remembers "rich wonderful times" full of "communal meals" and interaction that "deepened our commitments." Sometimes famous scholars such as Hans Rookmaaker would take part in informal discussions in a Regent faculty home full of inquisitive students. Larger events such as Christmas parties filled even modest faculty homes with nearly a hundred people. In one instance, a marriage engagement was announced in "a great, warm glowing celebration" in the Houstons' large dining room. Sometimes students were more permanent guests. Nearly every early faculty family rented out rooms to students to help make ends meet or to help a student through a difficult situation.[83]

All of these interactions fostered a sense of community that transcended faculty-student divides. As Armerding later reflected, "If you go back to the early days of Regent and talk to the students . . . no student would ever have gone through Regent without having been repeatedly in a faculty home. Not

---

[83]Gasque, Gasque, and Armerding, interview; Sharon Gallagher, interview with author, December 3, 2015, Berkeley; Linda Mercadante, interview with author, December 16, 2015; Mercadante, *Bloomfield Avenue*, 152-53.

once or occasionally but repeatedly in a faculty home. That was the basis for Regent community."[84] That students *and* faculty were part of a community together made Regent unique. For a student generation turned off by hierarchy and bureaucracy, faculty hospitality mattered.

Whether at faculty homes or in the common room in the Vancouver School of Theology, unique spaces of interaction fostered community at Regent. Early students fondly recall how the cramped classrooms and the common room's role as the central student union, chapel, study area, and cafeteria helped build relational bonds (see photo 2.6).[85] When Regent did finally gain its own geographical home in 1975, place once again played a role in community formation as faculty members and their families joined students painting and scrubbing graffiti off the walls of two former fraternity houses.[86] For the next fourteen years, the buildings housed the college even as student enrollment grew well in excess of two hundred. Physical space—unique and in short supply—helped make Regent a community.

Figure 2.7. From the beginning, the Regent College bookstore, originally located in the Vancouver School of Theology basement, was a centerpiece of community life.

---

[84]Armerding, interview.
[85]Beat Steiner and Barbara Steiner, interview with author, February 28, 2016.
[86]Rita Houston, "Rita Houston," *Regent Reflects*, 21, MCF.

Figure 2.8. The architecture of Regent College's campus demonstrates continuity with the past. The college's main campus building combines classroom and office space with an art gallery (rear second floor), a bookstore and coffee shop (left), and a main lobby (foreground) where students, faculty, and friends can gather to eat, study, and converse.

Gender and lay theological education. Another Plymouth Brethren influence in Regent's cultivation of community came in the form of the college's openness to enrolling female students. Nearly alone among the best-known evangelical theological schools of the day, Regent accepted female students without any limitations. The Brethren emphasis on the ministry of the laity certainly helped in this regard. Regent could easily sidestep questions on the controversial topic of female ordination by arguing that it was a school for the laity, not a seminary. From the start, however, it should be noted that Regent's openness to female students was not thoroughgoing. Even at Regent female students were sure to meet some classmates and even a professor or two (e.g., Bruce Waltke, J. I. Packer) who did not fully endorse equal status for female students and/or the ordination of women. Even with Regent's progressive model, evangelicals' longstanding hermeneutical approaches to Scripture and cultural convictions died hard.

Yet even if Regent was hardly a bastion of feminism, the college was significantly more open to women than many evangelical learning intuitions at the time. The stories of Thena Ayers and Linda Mercadante illustrate both the

Figure 2.9. J. I. Packer was one of the many celebrity professors who helped raise the profile of Regent College among evangelicals in the 1970s.

successes and limits of Regent in comparison with other prominent evangelical learning communities. Both Ayers and Mercadante came to Regent via Swiss L'Abri. For Ayers, who graduated from the University of British Columbia in 1967, involvement with Regent College was a return home. For Linda Mercadante, a New Jerseyan of Jewish and Catholic heritage, it was one more stop on a personal pilgrimage. Both women benefited from the evangelical openness of the Regent community, but both also noticed the limits of this openness.

Even though she was from British Columbia and had moved in InterVarsity circles on the campus of the University of British Columbia, Ayers did not hear about Regent until Jerram Barrs brought it up for prayer during a small group prayer time at L'Abri. Astonished by the revelation, Ayers sought out more information on the new school but did not make immediate plans to return to Vancouver. She had come to L'Abri planning to stay only until she took up graduate studies at Princeton Theological Seminary in the fall. Her experience at L'Abri changed her plans. She turned down her acceptance to Princeton and spent a year as a L'Abri worker and acolyte of Edith Schaeffer. Then, newly alerted to the perils of "liberal" theology, Ayers chose to apply to evangelical graduate schools and seminaries in North America.

It was not long before Ayers encountered evangelical sexism.[87] Because she was a woman, Ayers, who had been awarded a full academic scholarship to study at Princeton Theological Seminary the year before, was accepted "conditionally" at both Fuller Theological Seminary and Trinity Evangelical Divinity School. Furthermore, "on the basis of being a woman" she was informed that she "could not take the homiletics course." Ayers, who was a relatively recent convert to evangelical Christianity, had never considered this possibility. "I was a new Christian at university and the message that women were not gifted of God had not gotten through to me, and I had no idea that I could not do these things, so I was genuinely surprised and a bit taken aback." In the end, Ayers still opted to join seven others from L'Abri who were headed to Covenant Theological Seminary, a Schaeffer-approved seminary in St. Louis.[88]

At Covenant Ayers had much the same experience as she had when looking into Fuller and Trinity. Upon arrival, she learned that she was being placed on academic probation at the seminary even though she had earned first-class marks at the University of British Columbia. It quickly became apparent to her that this was more than a bias against Canadian grading structures. Soon after this experience, one of the seminary's administrators called Ayers into his office and informed her that there were five women in the college and "it was hoped that [she] would act and dress accordingly."[89] Nothing in her L'Abri experience or her Anglican upbringing had prepared her for this.

After her Covenant graduation, Ayers was invited back to Vancouver to join the InterVarsity staff at the University of British Columbia. She was thrilled at the chance to apply her theological education and follow in the footsteps of her college mentor, Cathy Nickle. In Nickle, a prominent female Bible teacher and InterVarsity leader, Ayers found a mentor and an organization open to the ministry of women. Shortly thereafter she also discovered that some at Regent College shared these sympathies. In the early 1970s Ward Gasque made a personal phone call to ask Ayers whether she would consider joining Regent's senate as the InterVarsity Christian Fellowship liaison. This was the beginning of a lifelong relationship with the college. With a large network of InterVarsity

---

[87] Ayers does not recall encountering any sexism at L'Abri (Ayers, interview).
[88] Barry Hankins, *Francis Schaeffer and the Shaping of Evangelical America* (Grand Rapids: Eerdmans, 2008), 52.
[89] Ayers, interview.

contacts, Ayers was from the start an influential recruiter for Regent. In the early 1970s Ayers spread the word about Regent as she traveled across North America in her work with InterVarsity. For Barbara Butler, a young InterVarsity Christian Fellowship worker in northern Colorado who later played a role in founding a study center in Charlottesville, Virginia, Ayers's enthusiasm for Regent was contagious. Butler did not recognize the names of the scholars coming to summer school, but she hungered for solid biblical teaching and respected Ayers's opinion. Ayers went on to earn her doctorate in adult education and eventually returned to Regent as the first permanent female faculty member. As the sole female on the faculty, Ayers worked hard to increase the number of women instructors at Regent. But even as the openness to hire women grew at Regent, she found that "it was very difficult to find women" because there were "not a lot of women who were encouraged by their churches . . . or by other Christians to study theology."[90]

There were a few women, however, who pushed against the evangelical grain toward scholarship. Linda Mercadante was one such individual. After growing up in a Catholic-Jewish family, Mercadante took up a career in journalism and exchanged her Christian faith for feminism before eventually winding up at Swiss L'Abri, where the Schaeffers' hospitality and way of life led her to become a Christian. At L'Abri Mercadante first heard of Regent when a fellow L'Abri student showed her a copy of a paper that offered a compelling theological and biblical argument against women's oppression written by a female graduate student at Regent. Her curiosity piqued, Mercadante applied and was accepted to begin studies in fall 1975. At Regent Mercadante quickly fell in love with the graduate school's unique ethos. "It was informal, intellectual, and sociable. The faculty was very accessible, and students came from many different professional fields and religious backgrounds, all taking time out to explore their faith." Mercadante's mind blossomed at Regent, and so did her feminism. After finding the women's studies reading room at the Vancouver School of Theology's library, Mercadante began reading all she could about feminism. Soon she was hosting talks on the Christian feminism at Regent and as far afield as Pasadena, California, where she addressed the fledgling Evangelical Women's Caucus. Under the supervision of Clark Pinnock, she also finished a thesis on the subject, titled

---

[90]Steiner and Steiner, interview; Ayers, interview.

"From Hierarchy to Equality." Ward Gasque, a strong believer in gender equality, helped her turn the thesis into a book. Her initial print run of five hundred sold out on the day it arrived.[91]

Not everyone was as helpful as Pinnock and Gasque. Mercadante recalls, "Whenever I spoke about my research, many fellow students seemed skeptical of my findings, especially the men who thought my feminist leanings made me a radical." Even Houston, whose experience with his own professionally capable sisters informed his belief in the capacity of women, let Mercadante down. In what may have seemed like a compliment to some, Houston offered Mercadante a position as his secretary.[92] To the aspiring scholar who later earned a PhD from Princeton Theological Seminary and was ordained in the Presbyterian Church (USA), the offer was yet another vestige of evangelical sexism. Still, even if being an ambitious woman was not easy at Regent, it was, unlike many places in North American evangelicalism, at the very least possible.

Regent's Wider Evangelical Openness. Regent's evangelical openness extended beyond issues of gender equality. Unlike most theological schools, Regent never espoused a single theological or eschatological outlook—a surprising feat for a school founded by Plymouth Brethren.[93] Following its Brethren impulse, Sheppard and the first generation of Regent's founders tried to avoid forcing the faculty to sign a yearly statement of faith. Given the concerns of their constituency, however, Sheppard relented. Regent adopted the World Evangelical Fellowship's generic statement of faith, which intentionally avoided dogmatism on issues such as eschatology and variations of inerrancy.[94] Houston himself was a cosmopolitan evangelical who, unlike Francis Schaeffer, R. C. Sproul, or even J. I. Packer, was not willing to get bogged down in the theological swamps of six-day young-earth creationism or the intricacies of inerrancy and the growing evangelical "Battle for the Bible."[95] For some, such as Francis Schaeffer, Houston's evangelical openness came as confirmation of previous

---

[91] This account of Linda Mercadante's experience is drawn from both her published memoir, *Bloomfield Avenue*, and an interview conducted on December 16, 2015.
[92] Mercadante, *Bloomfield Avenue*, 156; Houston, interview; Mercadante, interview.
[93] John Nelson Darby, the founder of the Plymouth Brethren, was also the founder of dispensational eschatology.
[94] Brian Sutherland, "Regent College Opens July 2," *Letters of Interest*, February 19, 1969, 20; Botton, "Regent College," 7.
[95] For a polemical and widely read take on this, see Harold Lindsell *The Battle for the Bible* (Grand Rapids: Zondervan, 1976).

doubts about the orthodoxy of the Vancouver school.[96] When Schaeffer finally consented—after years of requests—to visit Regent, in 1975, he delivered a stark convocation address on the inerrancy of Scripture that kept Regent students talking for months.[97]

It was not that Houston lacked firm evangelical theological convictions. Throughout his life Houston held closely to historic Christian orthodoxy and at times was even willing to put a friendship on the line when he saw a ministry moving in a direction that seemed contrary to evangelical principles.[98] Unlike many influential evangelicals in the 1970s, however, Houston largely avoided polemics. Instead, he worked hard to foster a broadly evangelical openness at Regent. For many this proved a winsome formula. As visiting professor Robert L. F. Boyd observed in 1974, "If I look for a single delightful word to epitomize the varied impressions I get from Regent College, it would be 'openness.'" Boyd encountered a student body and faculty whose openness to friendship almost made him "lose [his] British reserve." "Above all," he reflected, "minds are open, open to the Word of God in Christ and in nature, through scripture and through science."[99]

The last comment is telling. Openness to fields beyond the traditional realms of theology and biblical studies (i.e., interdisciplinary studies) was Houston's goal from the start. A background in geography naturally pushed Houston toward awareness of his environment, and along with a few others, including Francis Schaeffer, Houston pioneered the concept of "biblical ecology" in evangelical circles. These themes dominated *I Believe in the Creator*, the first book Houston published outside the field of geography.[100] Other fields were open too. In the early days of Regent art was especially intriguing for Houston. Writing to Francis Schaeffer in summer 1970, Houston predicted that an openness to art would be among Regent's most distinctive features: "We believe that it is through the encouragement of the creative arts, as well as doing some

---

[96]For one perspective on Schaeffer's take, see Mercadante, *Bloomfield Avenue*, 141-42.
[97]"Convocation," *Regent College Bulletin* 5, no. 2 (n.d.). Schaeffer had already expressed his doubts to Houston in a letter from 1971 (Francis Schaeffer to James Houston, September 7, 1971, box 52, file 26, FSC). See also Linda Mercadante to Francis A. Schaeffer, October 4, 1975, box 51, file 36, FSC.
[98]For example, Houston broke off his support for the 1977 Congress of the Laity at Howard Butt's Laity Lodge because he thought the event had lost its evangelical moorings. See James M. Houston to Sam Fore, August 10, 1977, box 3, folder 15, JHF.
[99]Rita Houston, "Summer School Perspectives," 43.
[100]James M. Houston, *I Believe in the Creator* (Grand Rapids: Eerdmans, 1980).

work in the behavioral sciences, that the distinctive character of the college will be best promoted."[101] Houston was right. Thanks to the work of Laurel Gasque and early Regent diploma of Christian studies graduate Dal Schindell, Regent went on to develop a reputation as one of the most innovative centers for evangelical art on the continent. Eventually Regent dedicated a portion of its new building to function as the Lookout Gallery, a permanent art gallery that hosted work from Regent students and Vancouver-area artists as well as exhibits by widely renowned artists such as John Koerner.[102]

Figure 2.10. Even today artistic expression plays a central role in the ethos and built environment of Regent College.

As innovative as Houston's vision for an interdisciplinary institute was, moving from these grand visions to reality proved more difficult than expected. Notably absent from Houston's description of the "distinctive character of the college" was any mention of traditional theological fields such as biblical studies and theology—fields in which every other individual on Regent's early faculty was trained. As early as 1968 Houston presented Ward Gasque and Armerding— both junior biblical scholars who had been preselected by Sheppard to be

---

[101]James M. Houston to Francis A. Schaeffer, August 7, 1970, box 52, file 26, FSC.
[102]Laurel Gasque and Armerding, interview; Julie Lane Gay, Loren Wilkinson, and Maxine Hancock, "Introduction," *Crux* 50, no. 1 (2014): 2-3.

part of the project—with a list of proposed faculty that did not include even one biblical scholar. In the end it was the work of Sheppard, and the fact that Houston was never able to entice established department heads in nonbiblical fields to Regent, that kept Gasque and Armerding involved in the project.[103] This was not the last time that Houston seemed to downplay the importance of maintaining explicitly theological fields such as biblical studies at Regent. For individuals such as Gasque and Armerding, Houston's attitude was confusing and unsettling. For Regent as a whole, Houston's early ambivalence on the issue of biblical studies, which many of the early Vancouver founders considered a given and assumed Houston did too, foreshadowed deeper divides to come.

Houston's Vision at Regent and Beyond

If many members of the early faculty struggled to interpret Houston's vision in the midst of the practicalities of sustaining a fledgling educational endeavor, the same did not seem to be true for the young evangelicals with less necessity to move from vision to practical implementation. For most outside observers, the most important—if not sole—shaper of Regent's early ethos was Houston himself. Like Schaeffer, Houston possessed a story of faith that inspired young people who were themselves seeking to find God outside the standard, middle-class routine. Houston and other Regent founders such as Armerding initially anticipated that the college would cater to "young professional people, who would 'take time out' for a year of theology." Instead, they "found a good many of the 'lost generation,' hoping to 'find themselves.'"[104]

Houston's unique personality proved appealing for individuals in both groups. In Houston, professionals found someone able to see them as people, beyond their degrees and achievements, while "seeking" students found an individual who blended a deep knowledge of the counterculture and emerging postmodernism with a willingness to engage students personally.[105] According to Don Lewis, an early Regent student who went on to become a professor of church history at the school, "there was a sort of aura around Jim Houston" in the early

---

[103] Carl E. Armerding, email to author, March 8, 2018; Carl E. Armerding, email to author, February 2, 2018.
[104] Carl E. Armerding to Michael G. Collison, July 22, 1993, MCF.
[105] Houston was among the very first evangelicals to identify postmodernism. See Hans Boersma, Craig M. Gay, and D. Bruce Hindmarsh, "Introduction: A Festschrift for James M. Houston," *Crux* 48, no. 3 (September 2012): 4.

days. To students he was "a heroic figure," who at the call of God left his own Ur (i.e., Oxford) and was now "like an Abraham leading into an unknown land."[106] As Armerding later noted, Houston's "Brethren credentials . . . Oxford background . . . genuine 'lay' status . . . eloquent rhetoric" and "remarkable ability to relate to a wide variety of individuals" granted him immediate "credibility for the vision we all embraced." Furthermore, Houston possessed what Armerding describes as "an aura of mystique" and "personal magnetism" that "endeared him to a wide circle of young followers" and seemed to provide the new school with "an early fascination factor." Thus even as Houston benefited greatly from the stability of a board and faculty that preceded his involvement, his leadership and personality were essential aspects of Regent's early identity and public appeal. As Regent grew, so did Houston's status as an evangelical celebrity. Thus, though it may be an overstatement to say that Houston's leadership singlehandedly "made" Regent, it is hardly an exaggeration to say that Regent made Houston—just as the venture made other faculty members such as Gasque and Armerding—in the orbit of North American evangelicalism.[107]

Refreshingly, most students at Regent found that Houston, in spite of his larger-than-life persona, was not distant or unapproachable. Indeed, if anything, board and faculty members thought Houston was too approachable and thus unable to fulfill his administrative duties. Even as principal, he spent huge chunks of his time in one-on-one meetings with students in which he offered counseling and spiritual direction. Eventually Houston filled entire days of the week with these sessions.[108] The roots of this practice stemmed from Houston's own personality as well as his experience as an Oxford tutor. Tutorial instruction stood at the center of Oxford pedagogy. Within the Oxford system, students were permitted to skip Houston's one lecture each week, but tutorial sessions were mandatory. Houston found that students began sharing about their personal problems during these one-on-one sessions. He soon dedicated himself to reading psychology in order to more adequately meet the psychological needs of his students.[109] In light

---

[106] Don Lewis in Botton, "Regent College," 122.
[107] Armerding, "Reflections of a Canadian Theological Educator," 66; Armerding, email, Feb 2, 2018.
[108] In 1993 Houston was providing spiritual direction to students two to three days a week with appointments stretching form 8:30 a.m. until 5:00 p.m. (Thomas, "James M. Houston, Pioneering Spiritual Director to Evangelicals," 2).
[109] All of the material on Houston at Oxford in this paragraph comes from Thomas, "James M. Houston, Pioneering Spiritual Director to Evangelicals," 6.

of these experiences, Houston began to see the multiple ways in which universities had forfeited their prior emphasis on personal relations. The "crisis of the university" that resulted from this severance alienated thought from action and glorified "technological values" above all else.[110] Universities were left with cold scientism: "For the truth divorced from personal relationships can degenerate into another science of human thought."[111]

Houston sought to counter these "technological values" at Regent through a commitment to getting to know students at a personal level. The results were profound. As Bruce Hindmarsh, the James M. Houston Professor of Spiritual Theology at Regent, later observed, "There are countless Christian men and women today whose lives have been changed by a single, never-to-be-forgotten conversation with Jim. Informally and formally, he became a spiritual director and mentor to a whole generation of students, and to hundreds of men and women around the world."[112] Many of the individuals who came under Houston's care during these years became loyal friends of Houston and his personal vision for Regent College. Furthermore, by pioneering spiritual direction among evangelicals in North America, Houston played a key role in altering the landscape of evangelical spirituality on the continent. He also gave Regent yet another claim to innovative distinctiveness.

If Houston's relational emphasis was refreshing to a generation who had lived through the height of the counterculture, his radical penchant for antiestablishment rhetoric—albeit in a reserved British form—also attracted attention. According to Armerding, "the simple fact remains that people came out of his presentations with greatly varying ideas of what was projected, though most were enthusiastic about what they heard. Common to almost every hearer was the following: Jim's vision was in some sense *radical*."[113] In Houston, a generation of students saw an individual who wanted to do away with the trappings of technocracy in favor of personal relations. Furthermore, Houston's transdenominational stance and emphasis on the laity registered well with evangelical baby boomers, many of whom, along with their nonevangelical peers, had come to distrust hierarchies of all kinds. Indeed,

---

[110]James M. Houston, "The Christian Presence in the University," *Crux* 10, no. 4 (Summer 1973): 22. Houston references scientism in C. S. Lewis's *That Hideous Strength* to make this point.
[111]Houston, "Regent College Vancouver: A New Venture," 7.
[112]Boersma, Gay, and Hindmarsh, "Introduction."
[113]Armerding to Collison, July 22, 1993, 1-2, emphasis original.

the surging popularity of C. S. Lewis's *Mere Christianity* among American evangelicals during these years testified to deep desire for basic Christianity devoid of the trappings of religious hierarchy and doctrinal infighting. To at least a few it seemed Houston had achieved this goal. One summer-school student described Regent's "theological atmosphere" as "relaxed and unthreatened, without doctrinaire arrogance. Essentials of Scriptural belief were affirmed and reaffirmed, while secondary matters were left there and differences welcomed and affirmed."[114] It is hard to imagine a more unqualified implicit endorsement of "mere Christianity" than this.

Fueled by these convictions, Houston set his eyes on the university during his first decade at Regent. He sensed that modern students were "not going to be satisfied with University life in a desperate world, if it is only a preparation for a better job, or an institution concerned with learning for its own sake." He also predicted that as the church declined in public esteem the university was destined to "become the central institution of our time." Thus "the Christian presence is vitally needed there now." For a generation of evangelicals who had come too late for the activism of the civil rights movement and who still debated the best approach in Vietnam, the university could stand in as a unifying cause, a battleground worth fighting for. Ready for action, evangelical young people from Berkeley to Charlottesville, Virginia, to Washington, DC, found their own calling in Houston's words. Houston, in his life, his writing, and in his efforts to build Regent College as a lay-centered, university-affiliated graduate school, gave young evangelicals a clarion call: "Do not desert the campus for the church."[115] As it turned out, a good number of them were listening.

---

[114]Rita Houston, "Summer School Perspective."
[115]Houston, "Regent College Vancouver: A New Venture," 4; Houston, "Christian Presence in the University," 23.

PART 2
REPLICATION

THE C. S. LEWIS INSTITUTE

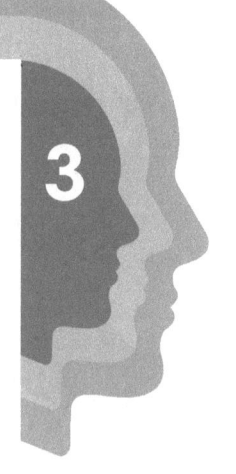

IN MAY 1972 *Christianity Today* carried a proposal that caught Regent College principal James Houston's attention. In one of the periodical's featured articles, Frank C. Nelsen, an assistant professor of history and philosophy at the University of Wisconsin, suggested that "evangelical living and learning centers" be established "on private property near large state universities." In the midst of increasing "economic stresses and strains," Nelsen envisioned that these centers might provide evangelical parents with alternatives to costly private colleges.[1] Nelsen's primary model was Oxford. His American precedent came from universities such as Michigan State and the University of California, Santa Cruz, which each housed smaller state colleges.

In terms of function, Nelsen imagined that these centers would employ a "permanent staff" of "academically qualified evangelical educators" with other "outstanding scholars brought in to lecture for a semester or two." This teaching staff would host group discussions and mandatory seminars but would also "spend time talking informally with students." Nelsen emphasized that these centers "would not replace good Christian liberal-arts colleges," nor would they be in competition with existing student ministries. Rather, he believed that these privately funded centers would complement the work of student ministries

---

[1] Frank C. Nelsen, "Evangelical Living and Learning Centers: A Proposal," *Christianity Today*, May 26, 1972, 7. For an example of the staying power of this argument, see Thomas Albert Howard, "Should I Send My (Christian) Child to a (Secular) State University?," Anxious Bench, February 16, 2014, www.patheos.com/blogs/anxiousbench/2014/02/should-i-send-my-christian-child-to-a-secular-state-university/.

and offer cash-strapped evangelicals a rationale for sending their daughters and sons to a secular university. Nelson's goals for these centers were tailored to this evangelical demographic. According to Nelson, "the objectives of the Center would be to develop in the Christian student both the courage and the skills necessary to make his witness for Christ effective in the classroom and on campus."[2] Maintaining one's faith and evangelism were front and center, but there was room for an intellectual dimension.

In general, Houston liked the idea. In fact, as principal of Regent College, he was already leading a venture very similar to what Nelsen proposed, and he did not want this to be lost on *Christianity Today*'s readers. In a letter to the magazine's editors Houston pointed out that Nelsen's article "describes what in fact has already been established by Regent College since 1970."[3] Regent did, however, differ from the proposal in a few respects. Critiquing Nelsen's proposal, Houston noted that Regent functioned on a graduate level. In Houston's opinion, this made Regent a better fit within the life of a university, "since universities could reasonably object that [undergraduate] students attending the centre may have conflicts of interest, time-tables and subject matter with the courses on campus."

Second, Houston was against Nelsen's recommendation that these centers own their own property. To Houston's mind—at least in 1972, before Regent gained its own property, in 1975—this strategy represented "an unnecessary expense" for the Christian community while simultaneously indulging the deep-seated evangelical tendency toward what Houston termed "the 'ghetto' mentality" and the "holy huddle."[4] For Houston it was "the faith and commitment of their teachers," not the sheltered atmosphere these centers might provide, that would inspire students toward meaningful Christian engagement. Thus, although Houston admitted that it was "exciting to see the growing evidence of emphasis on evangelical scholarship, seeking to re-establish itself on our university campuses and in public life," he was convinced that Regent's example, not an undergraduate study center, provided the best way forward for evangelicals who found themselves at a university.

---

[2]Nelsen, "Evangelical Living and Learning Centers," 7-8.
[3]James M. Houston to *Christianity Today*, June 3, 1972, box 2, folder 3, JHF.
[4]In January 1976 Houston wrote to a Regent College supporter, noting, "It has made a tremendous difference for us to have our own property, though it will now take us some years before we can repay all those to whom we are indebted for the initial purchase" (James M. Houston to Robert and Mary Boyd, January 28, 1976, box 2, folder 4, JHF).

What Houston did not say, however, was that he was already beginning to wonder what it might look like if his model were exported. Could Regent be replicated on other university campuses? By the mid-1970s, Houston was convinced it could be done. For the better part of a decade he worked to convince other evangelicals of the same thing.

Developing Regent College as a Model for University Engagement

The university was central to Houston's early vision for lay theological education. When he first dreamed of an institute for advanced Christian studies in his Winnipeg apartment in 1962, the model was Oxford University, with its embedded colleges, not the autonomous Bible schools or seminaries that characterized evangelical higher education in the United States. By the 1960s Houston was a university man through and through. He had risen through the ranks at Oxford to achieve the influential position of bursar of Hertford College in 1967. The next year the University of Texas offered him a full professorship in geography and the directorship of its prestigious Institute of Latin American Studies.[5] In general, Houston believed in the university's potential for good. But, in an era when science had delivered the atomic bomb to humanity, he also feared its tendency for ill if scientific rationalism were divorced from the moorings of personal relations and Christian belief.[6] Either way he was confident that the second half of the twentieth century would be determined by the academy, not the church.[7]

Upon arrival at Regent College, Houston's first instinct was to foster as close a connection to the University of British Columbia as possible. Beginning in winter 1967, he began seeking out a part-time position in the University of British Columbia's geography department. He encouraged W. J. Martin, formerly a professor of Semitic languages and linguistics at Liverpool University, to do

---

[5]Kenneth V. Botton, "Regent College: An Experiment in Theological Education" (PhD diss., Trinity Evangelical Divinity School, 2004), http://search.proquest.com/pqdtglobal/docview/305080117/abstract/FE2B427B616E4F05PQ/1, 88.

[6]Houston followed his friend C. S. Lewis in this regard. See Lewis, *That Hideous Strength* (New York: Scribner, 1945); C. S Lewis, *The Abolition of Man* (New York: Macmillan, 1947).

[7]The mid-1960s were the highwater mark for church attendance in America. For more on church attendance rates in American history, see Roger Finke and Rodney Stark, *The Churching of America, 1776–2005: Winners and Losers in Our Religious Economy* (New Brunswick, NJ: Rutgers University Press, 2005).

the same in the religious studies department. Of course, an additional source of income was welcomed given Regent's uncertain financial future, but for Houston this was a strategic effort as well. If Regent hoped to significantly influence modern society, it had to do so from within one of society's most influential institutions—the academy. Thus, Houston believed that it was "absolutely essential that we integrate as much as we possibly can with the University." Houston was confident that Regent could successfully achieve this goal if only he could "get the right scholars" to sign on.[8]

For Houston, integration with the University of British Columbia meant one thing—official affiliation. It was not enough to be on the edge of campus. Houston envisioned Regent as an evangelical partner within the University of British Columbia community, not a neighbor across the way. Affiliation came with fringe benefits such as expanded library use, but it also meant that Regent faculty would be permitted to sit on the University of British Columbia senate and vice versa. Affiliation was a top priority for Houston in Regent's early years. He alerted University of British Columbia president Walter Gage of his intent in December 1970. With the help of Robert M. Clark, a University of British Columbia economics professor and the dean of academic planning, Regent successfully won its bid for provisional affiliation in 1973 and indefinite affiliation in 1977.[9] To Houston's mind, affiliation with a major university set Regent College apart from evangelical Bible schools. Convinced that Regent offered a model for cultivating Christian minds while meaningfully engaging the secular university, Houston pondered whether Regent could be reproduced elsewhere.

One of the first people Houston told about his emerging concept of imitation was Francis Schaeffer, whom Houston had spent an enjoyable few hours chatting with in London prior to his move to Vancouver. Both men shared a love for art and a sense of the holistic impact of the gospel across all spheres of society. Writing to Schaeffer in early 1973, Houston conveyed how encouraged he was by the growth of the fledgling college, but he was also beginning to realize what Schaeffer knew well by this time: growth, though exciting, brought a host of new challenges. What had seemed barely possible in fall 1970, when the college

---

[8]James M. Houston to C. Stacey Woods, October 17, 1968, box 1, folder 39, JHF.
[9]"Affiliation," *Regent College Bulletin* 4, no. 1 (Winter 1974); "Ad Hoc Committee on Regent College—Request for Affiliation," UBC Senate Summary, November 14, 1973; Robert M. Clark, "Robert M. Clark," *Regent Reflections* (1995).

kicked off its first full semester of classes with only four full-time students, was on the verge of becoming a reality; Regent was growing too big. Houston expressed his hope to Schaeffer that Regent would "keep our numbers to about 100." Houston's emphasis on personal relations made small numbers a necessity. Because he believed "personal contact is all important," he predicted that Regent would "lose qualitatively" if it grew beyond one hundred full-time students. The solution, Houston insisted, lay in creating Regent-like institutes in other places to help meet a real and understandable demand. "Our real concern," Houston explained, "is not Regent College as such, but to create the possibility of others to do similar ventures on other secular campuses. By being credible and viable on one campus, perhaps we can then be imitated and repeated on many others."[10] This was Houston's major emphasis for the next five years. Regent College, he believed, was poised to start a movement.

Houston was not alone in this conviction. Like L'Abri, Regent's success inspired individuals to approach Houston about the possibility of starting other "Regent Colleges" around the world. One of these inquiries came from Peruvian evangelical leader Samuel Escobar. Less than a year before his famous speech

Figure 3.1. Engaging students in personal conversation was extremely important to James Houston.

---

[10]James M. Houston to Francis A. Schaeffer, February 23, 1973, box 52, file 26, FSC.

at the 1974 Lausanne Congress on Evangelicalism, Escobar wrote to Houston proposing the Acadia region in eastern Canada as a good location for a second Regent College.[11] Escobar was not the only one with a desire to replicate Regent. In summer 1974, the *Regent College Bulletin* reported that Houston's travels revealed the extent to which "Regent's reputation has spread to different parts of the world." Houston reported that in places such as Australia and New Zealand Christians "wish to build up similar work."[12] Individuals in Toronto and in prominent US college towns such as Berkeley and Ann Arbor, Michigan, all made their case for a Regent of their own between 1974 and 1977.[13]

Houston's growing interest in the replication of Regent made a significant impact among Regent's student body as well. At Regent's first long-term planning conference, in spring 1974, Regent student Beat Steiner (b. 1950) presented a paper titled "The Replication of Regent College." Steiner, the son of a Swiss chemist who relocated to New Jersey, had come to faith during his studies at the University of Virginia. While at Virginia, his experiences in a strong campus ministry and his encounters with Francis Schaeffer paved the way for his enrollment in Regent's 1973 summer school and his full-time enrollment in the diploma of Christian studies program. At Regent, Steiner's sharp mind and natural capacity for administration quickly became apparent to Houston, who made Steiner his research assistant for the 1973–1974 academic year. In addition to tracking down obscure journal articles for Houston's *I Believe in the Creator*, Steiner also spent a lot of time with Houston and his family. Houston became one of Steiner's most valued mentors, advising him at critical junctures in life for years to come. Steiner's access to Houston was nearly unparalleled among other students. The Houstons invited a different group of students to their home each Sunday, but only Steiner and one other student had an open invitation every week. The Houstons became like a family to Steiner, and Steiner came to deeply appreciate Houston's mind, heart, and vision for lay education. By the middle of spring semester 1974, Steiner was a staunch advocate of his mentor's vision for Regent's multiplication.[14]

---

[11]Samuel Escobar to James M. Houston, September 10, 1973, box 2, folder 3, JHF.
[12]"Travelers," *Regent College Bulletin* 4, no. 3 (Summer 1974).
[13]Houston spent about a month during summer 1975 at a summer-school startup in Toronto. For other inquiries about starting Regent-esque ventures, see Max De Pree to James M. Houston, May 18, 1977, box 3, folder 13, JHF; David Gill to Carl E. Armerding and James M. Houston, October 25, 1977, box 3, folder 7, JHF.
[14]Unless otherwise noted, all details of Steiner's time in Vancouver that appear in this paragraph are taken from my interview with Beat Steiner and Barbara Steiner, February 28, 2016.

Steiner began his paper on replication by summarizing Regent's mission. After having spent nearly a year at Regent, Steiner was convinced that "Regent was from the start . . . based on a fundamental need in the church for theologically aware laymen and for professionals who could think Christianly about their professional activities." To Steiner the fact that others in "New Zealand, Latin America, and Asia" were beginning to express a desire for the same type of education demonstrated that "the need" was "as broad as it has shown itself to be deep." Regent as a single institute in Vancouver could never hope to meet these needs singlehandedly. Echoing Houston's concern, Steiner noted that Regent was already approaching "what appears to be its maximum size." Replication seemed to be the only way to be faithful to both Regent's own vision and the real needs of the church: "It is thus consistent with, if not integral to, the vision of Regent College, Vancouver, that similar institutions should be developed elsewhere, presumably on the same principles. . . . It is appropriate that the College begin planning for such replication."[15] Houston could not have said it better himself.

After laying out the grand vision, Steiner moved to practicalities. First, he suggested that the replication of Regent would require a local group of Christian leaders capable of giving the new college administrative leadership, raising funds, and building community support. Steiner's second requirement was "a suitable university setting." For Steiner this entailed "library services, a site within the confines of the campus, a group of Christian faculty committed to the vision," and "the possibility of relating to the university in a formal academic manner."[16]

That the idea of replication had taken firm root in Steiner's mind—and by implication the mind of his mentor, Houston—became unmistakably clear in the paper's next section, which went on to list nine locations that were already under consideration. Each suggestion was accompanied by a paragraph description of the merits of the location. In addition to broad considerations (e.g., Latin America, Asia, and Australia and New Zealand), Steiner listed specific locations in North America. In Canada, Kent Garrett, a former InterVarsity regional director, was planning a summer school based on the Regent model for summer 1975 at Stanford Fleming College just outside Toronto. "Regent has been

---

[15]Beat U. Steiner, "The Replication of Regent College" (paper presented at "Openness to the Future: A Prelude to Planning," 1974), 1.
[16]Steiner, "Replication of Regent College," 2.

requested to become involved if not sponsor the summer school," Steiner noted.[17] Steiner noted that Queen's University in Kingston, Ontario, was another possible Canadian site.

In the United States the interest of professors such as Robert Linder and Richard Pierard made Indiana State University a strong possibility. Likewise, several professors at the University of Wisconsin had contacted Regent about their interest in "founding an evangelical learning center." The University of Virginia, where Steiner had just helped campus Christian groups gain access to campus facilities for their meetings, also came up for consideration. Perhaps the most interesting location of all was the University of Maryland, whose "close links with Washington D. C." made the site "a strategic location."[18] Steiner, who as a student at the University of Virginia was involved in the National Prayer Breakfast and knew of powerful evangelical Christians in DC, was not the only one who saw the strategic appeal of the University of Maryland's proximity to the capital.

"Regent College East"

Like other evangelical stars such as John Stott and Schaeffer, Houston spent a lot of time touring the InterVarsity Christian Fellowship circuit in the early 1970s. The parachurch student ministry was one of the biggest promoters of an academically attuned evangelical spirituality in the United Kingdom and North America. More than most campus ministries, InterVarsity Christian Fellowship blended the typical evangelical emphasis on personal piety (i.e., the heart) with intellectual openness (i.e., the head). For Houston, who embodied this combination of head and heart, it was a good match. His connections with InterVarsity were deep, going back at least to his early days in Oxford. There, he had led the local chapter of InterVarsity for some years before his move to Vancouver.[19] In North America, Houston found that InterVarsity connections also proved to be one of Regent's best forms of student recruitment. Thus, his long-term concern for the intellectual and spiritual vitality of students and his new concern

---

[17]Steiner, "Replication of Regent College," 3.
[18]Steiner, "Replication of Regent College," 3.
[19]While in Oxford Houston had tried to get British Inter-Varsity to host C. S. Lewis for a talk. As a testament to the ambiguity with which evangelicals viewed Lewis prior to his death, the group refused Houston's idea. Amazingly, the Oxford chapter of Inter-Varsity never hosted Lewis (Houston, interview).

to see Regent established as a viable college together prompted Houston to speak to InterVarsity groups whenever possible. It was entirely true to form that Houston accepted an invitation to speak to the InterVarsity group at the University of Maryland in fall 1973.[20] The talk was held at Cornerstone, an independent student ministry and community house directed by Jim and Lorraine Hiskey.

By the time Houston arrived at Cornerstone, Hiskey had already been involved in student ministry for about ten years. After a successful career as a professional golfer and a conversion from Mormonism to evangelical Christianity, Hiskey had founded a student ministry in Kansas and worked there until 1964, when Frank Carlson (1893–1987), a US senator from the state, invited him to relocate to the DC area. In Carlson, Hiskey found an advocate with connections to make his emerging study center dream a reality. In 1953 Carlson joined fellow Kansan Dwight D. Eisenhower (1890–1969) and Methodist minister Abraham Vereide (1886–1969) to found the Presidential Prayer Breakfast. (The name was changed to the National Prayer Breakfast in 1970.) Carlson was also connected to the Fellowship, a secretive discipleship group also founded by Vereide that focused on mentoring politicians and key decision makers in DC.[21] The senator saw the Hiskeys' ministry as an outgrowth of the Prayer Breakfast's concern to meet growing student discontent with Christian principles.[22] Further encouragement came from prominent members of the Fellowship such as future Senate chaplain Richard "Dick" Halverson (1916–1995) and an up-and-coming DC socialite and

Figure 3.2. Jim and Lorraine Hiskey in the mid-1980s.

---

[20]Hiskey and Houston met prior to this during a 1971 conference in Jerusalem. In an interview Hiskey dated Houston's visit to 1973.
[21]Jeff Sharlet, *The Family: The Secret Fundamentalism at the Heart of American Power* (New York: HarperCollins, 2008).
[22]Jim Hiskey, interview with author, February 23, 2015.

pastor to presidents, Douglas Coe (1928–2017).[23] Hiskey was impressed by the opportunity. Later that year he and his family moved to College Park, Maryland, a convenient twenty-minute drive from DC.

As Hiskey worked with students, he began to see important connections between his desire to see Christians engage their faith holistically (i.e., intellectually as well as emotionally) and the emphases of Schaeffer's ministry at L'Abri. Furthermore, L'Abri seemed to uphold these twin commitments while simultaneously emphasizing a third trait that was close to Hiskey's heart—hospitality. Desiring to experience L'Abri for himself, Hiskey took his family to L'Abri for six months in 1971. He loved what he found there. Hiskey returned home more determined than ever to help others develop Christian faith marked by Schaeffer's emphasis on "content and community," or as Hiskey would more frequently say, "the head and the heart."[24]

Hiskey's trip to L'Abri seems to also have been motivated by developments within his ministry at the University of Maryland. Just prior to Hiskey's L'Abri pilgrimage, the generosity of local businessman Arthur Seidenspinner allowed Cornerstone to buy a house that had once been the home of former University of Maryland president Curley Byrd. This purchase enabled Cornerstone to transition from a standard campus ministry to a ministry centered in a permanent L'Abri-esque living-and-learning space. The sprawling eight-bedroom brick house on over two acres of land offered proximity to the university and room for practical hospitality and a variety of programs. The basement became a study center, with a library that included a large selection of Schaeffer's tapes. Common rooms on the main floor offered plenty of space for large gatherings. The house also offered living space. The Hiskeys and their children lived communally at the house with a few college students and recent graduates. Both L'Abri and Dietrich Bonhoeffer's description of his underground seminary in *Life Together* informed Hiskey's efforts to nurture a learning *community*. Soon other local Christians began opening their homes as communal living spaces. Around the time Houston arrived in 1973, there were five houses and about forty people involved in Cornerstone's ministry.[25]

---

[23]See D. Michael Lindsay, *Faith in the Halls of Power: How Evangelicals Joined the American Elite* (Oxford: Oxford University Press, 2007), 32, 35-38.

[24]Hiskey, interview. Unless otherwise specified, all information on Cornerstone's ministry to students prior to Houston's 1973 visit comes from my interview with Hiskey.

[25]These details come from my interview with Hiskey. For an example of Cornerstone's activities and ethos, see the ministry's newsletter, *Cornerstone*, June 1975, box 3, folder 10, JHF.

Houston was inspired by what he found when he arrived at the Hiskeys' College Park home and thought Cornerstone—with its large house on the edge of a major university and its proximity to DC—might be just the place for an experiment in replicating Regent College. During the course of his talk that night, Houston explicitly mentioned such a possibility. As Hiskey remembers, "[Houston] . . . saw a vision that we could be something like Regent College. He would call it a 'Regent College East.'" Hiskey, who harbored no ambitions of founding anything more than "a little study center" to "help people love God and love each other . . . and get a solid foundation," was shocked by the suggestion. To his mind, Houston's idea seemed almost irrational.[26]

Figure 3.3. An artist's rendition of Cornerstone in the early 1970s.

Houston, however, was serious. As he sought to establish Regent as a viable institution, he simultaneously mulled the idea of replication. By the 1974–1975 academic year, the concept of Regent's replication loomed larger than ever in Houston's mind. In a contemporary audiocassette geared toward student recruitment, Houston again outlined his vision for the college. Two aspects of Regent's identity shaped his remarks. First, Regent was not a seminary; rather, it had a

---

[26]Hiskey, interview.

special calling to train laypeople. Second, Regent maintained a deep regard for personal relations. As Houston described it, "Regent is not an institution; rather, it is a family." Thus the school needed to remain small. Houston's target was one hundred students. Together Houston's belief in Regent's vision and his concern that the school not grow too large led him to conclude, "Regent must be repeatable."[27]

By 1975 Houston was convinced the best option for such a venture was College Park, Maryland. True to form, Houston decided to pursue the idea by reaching out to his network of friends, many of whom were highly visible evangelical leaders. In 1975 Hiskey received a call from Houston that began with the words, "I'm here with John Stott. Did you want to start this summer study institute?"[28] Hiskey said yes. He could not pass up the opportunity to bring one of his heroes to College Park. From that point on, Cornerstone became Houston's primary experiment in the replication of Regent College.

Regent-Sized Ambitions: From Cornerstone to C. S. Lewis College

From the time Stott committed to lecture at the College Park 1976 summer school, Houston threw himself wholeheartedly into the venture. In addition to his role as Regent's principal, Houston took the unofficial job of primary booster for the new project. College Park became a notable fixture in Houston's correspondence during fall 1975 and spring 1976. Houston knew that to a great degree the success of the venture relied on him. As he had done at the start of Regent's summer school in 1969, Houston reached out to academic friends such as F. F. Bruce for help. This time, however, he also had another group of supporters—Doug Coe and the influential politicians and businesspeople linked to the Fellowship House in Washington, DC.

Houston had first met Coe in 1974. It was not surprising that Coe, who had moved into leadership of the Fellowship in 1969, made a good impression on Houston. In many ways the slightly younger Coe was a man after Houston's own heart. Coe was a sharp, lay Christian who emphasized personal discipleship and Christian witness in professional environments.[29] His access to

---

[27]James M. Houston, *The Aims and Spirit of Regent College in the Early 1970s*, CD, Regent Audio, 1974.
[28]Hiskey, interview.
[29]Lindsay, *Faith in the Halls of Power*, 32, 35-37.

high-ranking US politicians no doubt also endowed him with a sense of mystique and gravitas that helped to catch Houston's attention. Houston and Coe began a correspondence in fall 1974. Over the next several months Houston stayed in touch with Coe and more than once invited him to Regent. He also kept Coe up to date about the upcoming Maryland summer school. In November 1975 Houston laid out his vision for the College Park project to Coe in detail. "I want to be quite clear about my own motive in being at Cornerstone," Houston wrote. "This could have strategic importance, as with the influence of many Christian leaders in Washington, the possibility of breaking through the prejudices concerning Church and State on a secular campus are best faced at College Park." Even though other universities may have offered stronger faculty support or greater name recognition, to Houston proximity to the capital made the University of Maryland the ideal site.[30]

For Houston, Cornerstone, already well established on the edge of a major American university, was appealing for other reasons as well. Its proximity to the University of Maryland offered Houston an opportunity to try out his model for university-embedded graduate institutes in an American context. In order to have any hope of success at penetrating the American university system, Houston knew he had to start at the top. As he told Coe, "I am seeing . . . more and more that a whole new area of approach to leadership must be to the top down administrators and to the university scholars, in order to see this further outreach in Christian faith and witness." Such lofty aims, however, required high-caliber academic leadership. Houston suggested Ken Elzinga (b. 1942), an active evangelical Christian and a promising young economist at the University of Virginia, as a possible choice for the director of the project.[31]

Finally, Houston related a third contributing rationale to Coe: Regent was simply growing too large. Lest Coe think Regent was trying to launch an imperialistic takeover of Cornerstone, Houston emphasized that "we have no ambitions at Regent to do anything else than to encourage brethren, and indicate that what

---

[30]James M. Houston to Doug Coe, September 30, 1974, box 3, folder 1, JHF; James M. Houston to Doug Coe, June 30, 1975, box 3, folder 1, JHF; James M. Houston to Doug Coe, November 12, 1975, box 3, folder 1, JHF; James M. Houston to G. Gutsche, December 18, 1975, box 3, folder 7, JHF.
[31]Houston to Coe, November 12, 1975. Though it "was not an easy decision for me," Elzinga decided to turn down the offer for a variety of personal and professional reasons. He did, however, note that if Houston considered moving the school to Charlottesville, Virginia, he might be inclined to take up the post. Ken Elzinga to James M. Houston, November 20, 1975, box 3, folder 7, JHF.

has been possible in Vancouver is possible again on many other campuses." Regent, in Houston's view, was fighting the trend toward overextension made possible by new "technical and organizational structures." For Houston these structures were "the Trojan horse that penetrates and secularizes our whole life."[32] Replication was the only solution capable of keeping Regent small without compromising the college's mission to help Christians around the world "think Christianly" within their professions and university.[33] Houston wanted to change the evangelical world, but he wanted to change it through myriad small ways.

Houston's support for the College Park venture took multiple forms. In addition to laying out a vision and recruiting faculty for the 1976 summer program, Houston personally coached Hiskey from the other side of the continent. He passed along information on Regent's policy regarding its summer school faculty honorariums and the payment of travel expenses. He sent Hiskey Regent's own East Coast mailing list for promotion purposes. He encouraged Beat Steiner (then back in Charlottesville, Virginia) to help with the venture.[34]

Houston himself traveled to College Park to visit Hiskey and check up on the project's progress in fall 1975. Not entirely convinced that the staff at Cornerstone had the administrative know-how to pull off such a large venture, Houston also offered, "pending board approval," to loan Hiskey the services of Regent College chief administrative assistant and "first class organizer" Marguerite Dunn for two weeks. Houston assured Hiskey that sending Dunn "was not in any way to interfere with your own organization and plans, but rather to simply encourage you that in the most practical way that we saw possible we were really doing all we could to stand by you and back you in this great project."[35] This was no doubt true to a point, but Houston was also far too ideologically and emotionally involved in the idea to stand passively aside.

Even as Houston tried to assure Hiskey that he was not trying to meddle in the Cornerstone venture, he could not hide his concern. Just twelve days after assuring Hiskey of his intent to avoid interfering in the project, Houston wrote

---

[32]Houston to Coe, November 12, 1975.
[33]For Houston's use of this term over the course of the 1970s, see Houston, "Christian Presence in the University"; James M. Houston to Doug Coe and Dick Halverson, July 13, 1978, box 3, folder 1, JHF.
[34]James M. Houston to Jim Hiskey, May 30, 1975, box 3, folder 6, JHF; James M. Houston to Jim Hiskey, March 17, 1976, box 3, folder 6, JHF; James M. Houston and Barbara Steiner, interview.
[35]James M. Houston to Jim Hiskey, October 22, 1975, box 3, folder 6, JHF; James M. Houston to Jim Hiskey, November 26, 1975, box 3, folder 6, JHF.

what he called a "candid" letter about his growing concern for the Maryland project. Houston was worried that perhaps Hiskey was trying to play too many roles and do too much himself. While Houston believed "deeply . . . in the importance of personal relations," in this case Houston urged that Hiskey match his person-centered emphasis with "efficiency and institutional management."[36] Most of all, Houston wanted to be sure that Hiskey understood that the Regent model was distinct from Hiskey's earlier model—L'Abri. By 1975 Houston was convinced that an unhealthy mix of nepotism, dogmatism, and celebrity culture marked Schaeffer's ministry. Houston saw Schaeffer as an intellectually isolated pontificator. He had told Schaeffer nearly as much at least twice, but Schaeffer had seemingly downplayed his advice.[37] Thus, when directing Hiskey, Houston placed distance between the College Park project and L'Abri:

> We need to focus more clearly on the model to follow at College Park—L'Abri or Regent? L'Abri [is] more unstructured, more related to a guru cult, where the leader dominates the structure. . . . The L'Abri model has no chance of success on a university campus. . . . This is exactly what we are struggling to overcome at Regent—the whole culture of evangelical guru-ism. It is unhealthy to be dogmatic without contradiction from one's peers or betters. And it is unrealistic to challenge academic life with this attitude. This is Francis Schaeffer's failing. No man today, in the complexities of our society, can afford to pontificate on so many areas, as he does.

Houston knew that his letter "must sound extremely harsh and judgmental"; therefore he reaffirmed his care for Hiskey and his deep desire "to see this venture succeed." In order to accomplish the latter, Houston recommended that Hiskey delegate the work. Replicating Regent would not be easy. It demanded "a whole new lifestyle."[38]

Throughout spring 1976 Hiskey and Houston worked to make the 1976 College Park summer program a success. Hiskey led the team on the ground, and Houston did what he could while simultaneously attempting to lead a growing graduate school in Vancouver. One thing Houston *could* do was exude vision and charisma through his letters. In spring 1976 he did just that—over and over again. Writing to his friend F. F. Bruce (and once again trying to get him to lend his time and

---

[36]James M. Houston to Jim Hiskey, December 8, 1975, box 3, folder 6, JHF.
[37]James M. Houston to Francis A. Schaeffer, May 1, 1975, box 52, file 26, FSC; Francis A. Schaeffer to James M. Houston, June 19, 1975, box 52, file 26, FSC. Houston and Schaeffer never again corresponded.
[38]James M. Houston to Jim Hiskey, December 8, 1975, box 3, folder 6, JHF.

name to another fledgling venture), Houston gave what was perhaps his most detailed vision. College Park was "a strategic opportunity," he wrote:

> It will link and provide a depth to evangelical scholarship to some of the leaders in American society. There are a number of congressmen and Senators who have recently been won for Christ and they need nurturing and training.... It seemed to me that it was more likely that with the influence of men like Senator Mark Hatfield and other influential Christian politicians we would have a better chance of succeeding in proximity to them, than in a more remote university situation. But once the precedent is established that there is such an institute in the University of Maryland, it can of course then be replicated elsewhere in the country. I really do believe that within the next decade we shall see a number of such institutions on some of the major universities. I have recently returned from a trip to Princeton, Columbia, Pittsburgh and Washington and found on each campus people who were already dreaming such possibilities.[39]

Houston concluded the letter with a personal appeal that framed the venture in heroic proportions. Houston urged Bruce to consider being involved in the project, which was "of real strategic concern for the future of evangelical scholarship."

Bruce turned down Houston's request, but Houston's disappointment did not last long. Overall, the 1976 College Park summer study institute was an encouraging success. With over 150 students and a list of speakers that included Houston, John Stott, J. I. Packer, R. C. Sproul, Senator Mark Hatfield, and Chuck Colson, the institute immediately rivaled Regent's previously unsurpassed summer school.[40] As one summer-study-institute brochure made explicit, the College Park effort was intentionally attempting to follow Regent's example by moving from the "summer program" toward a "school" centered on "biblical studies." Community, too, was a shared emphasis between Vancouver and College Park. "Like Regent College," the first brochure noted, "Cornerstone is convinced that academic objectivity is compatible with Christian commitment, and that Christian community is compatible with Christian scholarship."[41] Regent, it seemed, had been replicated.

---

[39]James M. Houston to F. F. Bruce, April 9, 1976, box 3, folder 7, JHF.
[40]On the number of students (153), see James M. Houston to William S. Starr, June 4, 1976, box 3, folder 17, JHF. Later Houston put the number registered at 165. Regent's summer school, where Stott also spoke, drew in over 450 students (James M. Houston to William S. Starr, July 5, 1976, box 3, folder 17, JHF).
[41]"Background and Development of the Institute," *Summer Study Institute* (1976).

Both Hiskey and Houston were pleased with the first College Park Summer Institute. Writing to Young Life's national director, William S. Starr, just a few weeks after the conclusion of the 1976 institute, Houston enthused, "We were most encouraged at Maryland. We prayed that we might have 100, hoping at least for 50. Instead, there were 165 or more registered in the program. . . . I believe that within the next two or three years another venture like Regent will be established there." Houston's vision was nearly unbounded. He saw the success of the College Park summer study institute as perhaps the beginning of a movement that would sweep through evangelicalism:

> In fact I can see a score or more of informal experimentations on many campuses eventually becoming a number of similar ventures like Regent. There is keen interest at Princeton and there is also the beginnings of a program at Columbia University in New York and also an interest at Oklahoma State University. I believe that within a decade we shall see something that might be comparable to the Cistercian revival of the 12th and 13th centuries developing evangelicals through such cultural centres. How true it is that when we keep things to ourselves the spirit of God cannot operate. That when we scatter like the wind—God's wind—a seed that goes into the ground to die, then there is much fruit.[42]

Houston was beginning to think that by scattering Regent's influence rather than seeking to build an institutional empire he was helping to catalyze a movement that might change the face of North American evangelicalism. This vision stayed with Houston for the better part of six months. By December he was still riding the wave of the idea's potential. Writing to R. T. France at Tyndale House, Houston again expressed his goal: "Our vision . . . is to make Regent a strong prototype that can be replicated elsewhere."[43] Current developments at the University of Maryland, the University of Texas, the University of California, Berkeley, and Columbia led him to believe that replication was already at work. Buoyed up by these examples, Houston predicted "within a decade there may be a number of centres developing on similar lines as Regent."[44]

---

[42]Houston to Starr, July 5, 1976.
[43]James M. Houston to R. T. France, December 10, 1976, box 2, folder 4, JHF. For a similar example, see James M. Houston to Joseph Bayly, December 22, 1976, JHF.
[44]Houston to France, December 10, 1976. Houston noted the work of Earl Palmer, an influential Presbyterian pastor in Berkeley. There was also a L'Abri-like experiment going on in the Bay Area. In 1976 Houston was more interested in working with Stanford than Berkeley (James M. Houston to Jim Hiskey, October 17, 1976, box 3, folder 6, JHF).

The success of the initial summer program had also done much to convince Hiskey that that Houston's vision might be possible. Like his mentor, Hiskey knew the success of such a venture depended on getting the right people—or person—to commit. Sometime in early fall 1976 Hiskey approached Houston about the possibility of his permanently relocating to College Park. Nothing better represented the high hopes Hiskey and many others had for the summer study institute's potential.[45]

That Houston seems to have seriously entertained Hiskey's request demonstrates his deep interest in the College Park project and Washington, DC, more generally. It may also suggest a slight ambivalence about leading Regent through a season of growing pains and highly charged personnel conflicts, which some on the Regent faculty and board attributed to Houston's own failures as an administrator.[46] In a letter to Hiskey that fall, Houston seemed to be holding the option within the realm of the possible, noting that he was "open to the will and ways of the Lord." Houston informed Hiskey that he was praying along with him "that it is His will that I should be involved the way that you suggest for the future of the work at College Park."[47]

Houston's interest was not so great, however, that it precluded his asking others to step into the chief administrative role at College Park. As Houston scanned the horizon for individuals capable of leading a "Regent East," he decided on Peace Corps director John Dellenback.[48] Writing to Dellenback in December 1976, Houston laid out an expansive vision that explicitly moved from the idea of an institute to that of a freestanding college. "I am committed to seeing the replication of Institutes of Christian Studies attached to university campuses," Houston began. Noting how "encouraged" he was by the "progress made at Cornerstone," Houston then laid out his vision that "a full-time college will be established by 1979–80." Houston also ventured the possible name of the hoped-for school—"C. S. Lewis College."[49]

---

[45]Houston refers to Hiskey's suggestion in a letter to Jim Hiskey dated October 7, 1976, box 3, folder 6, JHF.

[46]James M. Houston to Doug Coe, August 4, 1976, box 3, folder 1, JHF; Ian Rennie to Carl Armerding, November 19, 1976, private collection; Brian Sutherland to Carl Armerding, September 27, 1976, private collection.

[47]James M. Houston to Hiskey, March 17, 1976; James M. Houston to Hiskey, October 7, 1976.

[48]Houston had recently spoken with Dellenback at a White House Prayer Breakfast; see John Dellenback to James M. Houston, December 6, 1976, box 3, folder 7, JHF.

[49]James M. Houston to John Dellenback, December 22, 1976, box 3, folder 6, JHF.

Though Houston knew the idea of a C. S. Lewis College might seem "a far-fetched dream," he hoped Dellenback would dream with him. Houston could see "an evangelical academic movement developing" with similar "colleges on university campuses."[50] Even the name of the college demonstrated Houston's high academic and spiritual goals for the institution. Houston later reflected that the mission of the venture was to "create not a lot of fans for C. S. Lewis but to have 10,000 like him."[51] Would Dellenback be willing to serve as the first president of such a college? The answer, it turned out, was no. Like many of the high-caliber leaders Houston approached through the years, Dellenback was not willing to leave an influential and well-established post to commit himself to an unproven project.

Still, that Houston could ask Dellenback to serve as the president of a college and not the director of a summer institute shows how far the idea had progressed within the span of little more than a year. Buoyed up by the success of the 1976 summer institute, Houston and the College Park team moved forward toward their primary goal—the creation of a degree-granting college. Hiskey and his team drafted articles of incorporation for "The C. S. Lewis College for Biblical and Theological Studies" in October 1976.[52]

The first official board meeting was held on November 5, 1976. Hiskey began the meeting by presenting his vision for the college to the three other members present. C. S. Lewis College would offer serious "graduate-level" scholarship to "all men and women" by assisting them as they formulated a "worldview that integrates their academic and professional training with their Christian faith." Hiskey was clear that the school needed to be situated close to the University of Maryland campus in order to ensure that "our programs may have real relevance in the academic marketplace." Last, Hiskey demonstrated his longstanding commitment to discipleship ministry and the formulation of Christian community. "We would like to see the learning that takes place in the college based upon the context of a community of believers studying and worshipping together." Such an emphasis "would allow the current Cornerstone work of training young leaders, concentrated on character building, to take

---

[50]James M. Houston to Dellenback, December 22, 1976, box 3, folder 6, JHF.
[51]J. Edward Glancy and Joel S. Woodruff, "Celebrating Forty Years of Heart and Mind Discipleship: A Brief History of the C. S. Lewis Institute," *Knowing and Doing* (Spring 2016): 2.
[52]Craig H. Johnson, "Articles of Incorporation of the C. S. Lewis College for Biblical and Theological Studies, Inc.," October 1976, box 3, folder 10, JHF.

place in the college programs."[53] When taken together, Hiskey's vision well represented the "content and community" or "head and heart" emphasis he found at L'Abri and in the person of Houston.

Incorporation and the first official board meeting capped off a year filled with excitement for Houston and the folks at College Park. It also signaled the highwater mark of C. S. Lewis College and Houston's replication ideal. With Houston's backing, Cornerstone had been transformed from a small study center and student ministry into C. S. Lewis College, an endeavor with Regent-sized ambitions. Yet even in the halcyon days of 1976 there were reasons for concern. Not only had the college failed to sign on a president by the end of the year; it also faced a context that differed notably from Vancouver. Whereas the federal system of British Columbia, not far removed from its days as a frontier province, made generous provision for the affiliation of smaller colleges with larger institutions, the situation in Maryland was less encouraging—a reality that Hiskey began to realize early on.

Near the conclusion of the first C. S. Lewis College board meeting, Hiskey listed what he termed "major obstacles." These included: "building a library adequate to meet student needs and State requirements for accreditation" and "the obtaining of $500,000 to be spent over a five year period to meet the accreditation requirements of the State of Maryland."[54] Unlike Regent, which had slid through provincial accreditation on the merits of the University of British Columbia library and a shoestring budget, C. S. Lewis College had to stand—or fall—on its own.

Perhaps the greatest obstacle to the founding of a "Regent East," however, had nothing to do with libraries and differing regulations. The Maryland venture never garnered a team like the original Marshall Sheppard–led coalition in Vancouver, where board members such as Brian Sutherland, Dick Richards, and Ken Smith provided vital economic and administrative stability. From the start Regent College was also blessed with an enthusiastic and committed faculty made up of credentialed scholars who were intentional about building the college's reputation through publishing, involvement in academic societies, and extensive letter-writing and networking efforts. Additionally, Regent benefited

---

[53]Craig H. Johnson, "Minutes: Board of Trustees Meeting, C. S. Lewis College for Biblical and Theological Studies, Inc.," November 5, 1976, box 3, folder 10, JHF.
[54]Johnson, "Minutes," 2.

from its connection to the large and largely supportive Plymouth Brethren community both in Vancouver and around the world.[55] Though the school was transdenominational, Brethren took a keener-than-usual interest in the endeavor, sending their dollars and their sons and daughters to the college.

These easily overlooked aspects of Regent's success stood in stark contrast to C. S. Lewis College, which from the start was much more dependent on Houston's personal charisma and administrative leadership. Thus, while the Regent community had the stability to embrace—and sometimes endure—all that accompanied Houston's penchant for heady idealism rather than practical implementation, the DC venture was less prepared to handle these realities. These administrative realities, when combined with the monumental obstacles related to affiliation with the University of Maryland, made replicating Regent difficult, if not impossible.

Trimming the Sails: From C. S. Lewis College to the C. S. Lewis Institute

In addition to C. S. Lewis College's looming difficulties with affiliation, Houston also faced growing dissent in Vancouver. In Houston's mind the unrest stemmed from a conflict of vision. Since at least 1973, Houston had desired to keep Regent small, perhaps no larger than one hundred students. Houston's ideal number, however, did little to convince the rest of the faculty or discourage Regent's increasing popularity and enrollment. Indeed, many at Regent were looking toward the further growth of the institution through increases in enrollment and perhaps even the introduction of a master of divinity program. On top of these curricular decisions, the dismissal of New Testament professor Larry Hurtado, and the attendant controversy, also took a toll on Houston.[56] So, too, had the necessity of raising funds to pay for new buildings and a larger faculty.[57] There were a few encouragements—J. I. Packer had committed to come for the 1979 school year, and the newly acquired properties offered Regent a lasting footprint on prime real estate next to the University of British Columbia—but the discouragements weighed on Houston and the entire Regent board and faculty.

---

[55]Carl E. Armerding, email to author, February 2, 2018.
[56]Ian S. Rennie to Carl E. Armerding, November 19, 1976, private collection; James M. Houston to Doug Coe, August 4, 1976, box 3, folder 1, JHF.
[57]In a letter to Bob Smith, Houston described the financial situation at Regent as "tight" in winter 1977; see James M. Houston to Robert Smith, n.d., box 3, folder 7, JHF.

By early 1977 Houston was frustrated and tired. He and Rita "really need a break," Houston wrote to a friend. Growth had meant more administrative work and less opportunity to know students on a personal level. Each of these changes wore on Houston. Writing to a former student, Houston reflected on the situation, "It is my deep concern that Regent should remain a small college, that we really know our students individually and are able to nurture them in personal contact. To succeed is therefore so often to fail. Succeed perhaps before the eyes of men, but to fail in the needs of the spirit of God."[58] To Houston, Regent's success came at a high cost.

By the mid-1970s Houston was not the only faculty member at Regent who had misgivings about the direction Regent was taking. Though long-term faculty such as Gasque and Armerding had always appreciated Houston's charisma and his ability to create what Armerding once described as an "aura of mystique" around Regent, these sentiments were often balanced by their general bewilderment regarding what they perceived to be Houston's lack of ability to handle the practical aspects of leading an institution and relating to faculty. By 1976, due in part to these persistent concerns—concerns that were no doubt heightened by Houston's growing involvement in the Maryland venture as well as the increasing stress and strain of Regent's burgeoning student body and faculty—members of the Regent faculty were beginning to talk in terms of a crisis at Regent, and one board member worried about the possible large-scale loss of faculty if something was not done.[59] When the efforts of the board's personnel committee and individual members of the faculty failed to convince Houston that changes in his leadership style were needed, the board made a last-ditch effort to reduce Houston's administrative load and quell faculty unease with Houston's leadership by appointing Armerding—who was on sabbatical in Cambridge, England, during the 1976–1977 academic year—to the office of vice principal in spring 1977.[60]

From September 1977, when these changes were introduced, through spring 1978, these circumstances at Regent made a move to College Park an appealing option for Houston. By taking the helm at C. S. Lewis College, Houston would

---

[58]James M. Houston to Patricia Coldman, January 6, 1978, box 2, folder 6, JHF; James M. Houston to S. Chowdry, August 9, 1977, box 2, folder 4, JHF.
[59]Brian Sutherland to Carl E. Armerding, September 27, 1976, private collection.
[60]Carl E. Armerding, email to author, February 2, 2018; Ian Rennie to Carl E. Armerding, May 12, 1977, private collection.

not only have the chance to shape an institution from the ground up, but he would also be able to step out of an increasingly difficult situation at Regent College. Further, the realities on the ground in College Park almost guaranteed that the fledgling venture would remain small, thus ensuring the potential for an emphasis on personal relations. There certainly was much to prompt Houston to act on Hiskey's hopes of seeing Houston himself lead up the venture.

But there were also undeniable downsides. As 1977 wore on, Houston began to realize that replicating Regent would be more difficult than he had ever imagined. The 1977 Maryland summer institute encountered problems from the start. Unlike Regent, which had followed up its first summer school by inviting even bigger names in its second year, it was virtually impossible for the College Park institute to better a first-year roster that included the likes of Stott, Packer, Houston, and Mark Hatfield. Enthusiasm, financial contributions, and student enrollment lagged in 1977. Even Houston's personal efforts to raise money for the venture in spring 1977 were barely enough to keep the summer institute administrators paid. Then, only a few weeks after the 1977 summer institute concluded, Hiskey wrote asking Houston, who was seemingly endlessly raising money for Regent, to raise more much-needed cash for C. S. Lewis College. At about the same time Hiskey confided to Houston that he was beginning to realize that "the college is [a] little big for me."[61]

Still, Houston was convinced that C. S. Lewis College could succeed if given the right leadership. Houston decided to test the waters in Maryland during a four-month sabbatical leave in spring 1978. During this time both Houston and

Figure 3.4. Carl Armerding was named principal of Regent College in 1978.

---

[61]James M. Houston to Charles E. Hummel, April 7, 1977, box 3, folder 16, JHF; Jim Hiskey to James M. Houston, August 26, 1977, box 3, folder 6, JHF; Jim Hiskey to James M. Houston, September 6, 1977, box 3, folder 6, JHF.

his wife, Rita, stayed at the Fellowship House while the Regent principal spent his days organizing C. S. Lewis College and serving as the scholar-in-residence at Richard Halverson's prominent Fourth Presbyterian Church in Bethesda, Maryland.[62] During his time in DC, Houston worked to solidify C. S. Lewis College by compiling another stellar cast of speakers including: Halverson, Hatfield, Edmund P. Clowney, Richard Mouw, Chuck Colson, Armerding, and Earl Palmer—who was at that time also involved in a similar Regent-inspired venture in Berkeley.[63]

Yet the proposed college struggled to pick up enough institutional momentum to surmount the realities of its context. There was no getting away from Maryland's requirements that the school build a suitable library and amass a $500,000 endowment prior to its official accreditation. Neither Hiskey nor anyone else involved in the effort had the heart to take on the kind of fundraising necessary to meet those goals.[64] Thus, even as Houston continued to seek out prominent evangelicals such as Elisabeth Elliot and Michael Green for the 1979 school, he was coming to terms with the fact that C. S. Lewis College would never be "Regent East."

The most decisive blow to C. S. Lewis College came in July 1978, just after the Houstons returned to Vancouver following their sabbatical. In an emotionally charged letter to Coe and Halverson, Houston related that after having "travailed before God" he had decided to remain in Vancouver. "I wanted to come to Washington D. C.," Houston wrote. "It made such good sense. The call fitted my temperament and gifts, hand to glove." Yet Houston had others to consider. First there were "Rita and the children." Houston knew Rita would come if he wanted, but he was afraid that "she might also die within herself." During their time in DC Houston had sensed his wife's needs deeply. He told Coe and Halverson that he had pledged "myself to be her help-meet as I had not been before. The family is the unit of Christian witness, not public Christian activities."[65]

For better or worse, Houston was also "married" to something else—Regent College. Even though Houston had returned from his sabbatical to find what

---

[62]James M. Houston to Sam Fore, April 12, 1978, box 3, folder 15, JHF; James M. Houston to Jim Hiskey, February 18, 1977, box 3, folder 6, JHF.
[63]"Summer Study Institute: June 5-23, 1978 at the University of Maryland," spring 1978, box 3, folder 9, JHF.
[64]Hiskey, interview.
[65]Houston to Coe and Halverson, July 13, 1978.

THE C. S. LEWIS INSTITUTE   115

he described as "a palace revolution" replete with "talk of removing me from the principalship, etc.," Regent still held a special place in his heart. "I am not indispensable [at Regent]," Houston told his friends, "but the central struggle of . . . Regent that gives it its uniqueness is inter-disciplinary study. I have not been able to give as much emphasis to this, as the college needs, to be established in its vision." Houston knew his work was not done at Regent. He also seemed to sense that he had been overextending himself for the last few years. In a particularly introspective moment, Houston asked himself the same question he had posed to other enterprising evangelicals such as Schaeffer. "Perhaps," Houston pondered, "a servant of God can only do one thing properly for a life-work of radical change in one's society. This is mine: not to have more professional theologians, more seminaries, but men and women who learn to think Christianly in all their professions."[66] Houston was ready to commit himself to this work at Regent for the long haul.

New Directions

By 1980, C. S. Lewis College had changed its name, its style, and its ambitions.[67] The C. S. Lewis Institute (no longer C. S. Lewis College) moved it courses into downtown Washington, DC, where it was hosted by places such as National Presbyterian Church and the Brookings Institution. This move had major implications for student demographics and the institute's mission.[68] The C. S. Lewis Institute continued to work toward wedding the head and the heart, but it no longer specifically targeted a college-aged constituency.[69] On a programming level, the institute developed a twin focus. The continuing involvement of individuals such as Hiskey and Houston (who served for a time as board chair) ensured that the C. S. Lewis Institute would be known for blending scholarship and personal discipleship (i.e., the head and the heart). Some in the organization, however, desired that the institute move in the direction of public policy or a think tank.[70] Discussions between these two camps grew increasingly

---

[66]Houston to Coe and Halverson, July 13, 1978.
[67]The name change took place in fall 1979. "Core Community Meeting," November 4, 1979, box 3, folder 10, JHF.
[68]"C. S. Lewis Institute: Summer 1980," box 3, folder 9, JHF; Hiskey, interview.
[69]This changed to some degree in 1999, when the institute introduced the C. S. Lewis fellows program, which was primarily geared to recent college graduates. See "C. S. Lewis Institute Vision, Mission, Strategies, and Projects," circa 2009, box 3, folder 10, JHF.
[70]Glancy and Woodruff, "Celebrating Forty Years," 3.

polemical through the early 1980s and reached a crescendo in 1985. Those who desired that the institute focus more heavily on public policy went their own way, leaving the C. S. Lewis Institute to those who favored an emphasis on discipleship. In significant ways, this was a return to the institute's Fellowship House roots. The C. S. Lewis Institute had come full circle.

For his part, Houston maintained close association with the C. S. Lewis Institute for the rest of his life.[71] The institute became an outlet and a place of reprieve for him as he encountered personal disappointments at Regent, which began soon after his return in summer 1978 and extended through the early 1980s. To some extent, Houston was right when he told his friends that a palace revolution awaited him. In 1978, years of faculty and board unrest and Houston's own preoccupation with the idea of replicating his personal version of Regent in places such as College Park culminated in an effort to remove Houston from the principalship of Regent.[72]

Figure 3.5. Hiskey and Houston in 2016 at the C. S. Lewis Institute's fortieth-anniversary celebration.

---

[71]Houston did not miss a C. S. Lewis Institute summer program until 1992; see James M. Houston to Ernst van Eeghan, April 16, 1992, box 3, folder 11, JHF.

[72]Houston later described these years as a desert experience. See Arthur Dicken Thomas, "James M. Houston, Pioneering Spiritual Director to Evangelicals," *Crux* 29, no. 4 (December 1993): 17-27. By mid-July 1978 Houston was prepared "to resign as Principal an[d] stay on as lecturer in Christian Inter-Disciplinary Studies." Houston chose this title, saying, "I do not think I am worthy of being called a Professor in a field that does not exist academically" (Houston to Coe and Halverson, July 13, 1978).

Throughout the rest of the decade, Houston found solace in the friendships he had made in Washington, DC. In addition to Coe and Halverson, Houston also poured out his heart to Chuck Colson, another DC insider with deep ties to the Fellowship and the C. S. Lewis Institute. After listing several possible reasons why public opinion among Regent's board and senate seemed to have turned against him, Houston outlined what he felt was a new, more appropriate strategy at Regent:

> The decision, therefore, to stay at Regent seems to be necessary. At the same time, the only way in which I can seek to see expressed more clearly the need to have training and wisdom for Christian persons [rather] than simply professional scholarship for its own sake means that I may have to take another strategy other than the use of power as Principal. I am therefore offering my resignation to the Board of Regent and to step down to be lecturer in Christian studies at the College. It may be that the Board wish to also call me Chancellor or some other title that would indicate a continuing advisory role in the College, but this is merely a cloak of conventionality to hide the radicalism of spirit that I believe is necessary to continue to serve here. As a lecturer I shall be academically at the bottom, not only now but indefinitely. For I also see that when we get caught up in the traps of academia, that creates its own in-built professionalism too.[73]

Using power from below, Houston hoped to accomplish at Regent College what he could not accomplish as principal. He also demonstrated a subtle shift that was occurring in his thinking. By relinquishing (or being stripped of) his title as principal, Houston moved further from the mainstream of academic life. More than that, his proposed position, lecturer in cross-disciplinary studies, had no attachment to a professional field of scholarship. By stepping away from the principalship, Houston, who had once been a member of a recognized guild (geography), moved further into the margins of the academy. How could he penetrate the modern secular university as a "lecturer" in an unrecognized field? It seems even Houston—whose capacity for scholarship and charisma had opened many academic doors—knew this was the end of a chapter.

Together, the loss of his principalship and the reality that the College Park endeavor would not be able to raise the $500,000 necessary to set up a library and form "Regent East," when combined with the excitement of Houston's

---

[73] James M. Houston to Chuck Colson, July 27, 1978, box 3, folder 18, JHF.

business and political connections in Washington, DC, helped shift his attention away from the university—a sphere of society he had been working to reform for years. In future decades it was discipleship in the "marketplace" (i.e., the business world, politics, etc.), not the academy, that most captured Houston's attention.

Close observers such as Armerding, Houston's successor as principal at Regent College, noticed a change in Houston's approach. As Armerding later reflected, "A significant shift occurred sometime in the late seventies when [Houston] apparently lost interest in the university as a change agent, and shifted his extracurricular interest to the business community."[74] Within the business community, personal spirituality and relational connection held more allure than rigorous academics. As Houston sought to nurture his own spirit in the deep wells of Christian spirituality through the ages, he was well prepared to bring perspective and discipleship to business communities in Washington, DC, Vancouver, and around the world. As time went on, Houston channeled more of his energy into this sphere of society in part by organizing and leading businessmen prayer breakfasts modeled loosely on the National Prayer Breakfast movement in the United States.[75]

Houston turned his academic pursuits in a similar direction. In fall 1978 he began teaching his first course in "spiritual theology."[76] Not only was the course a good fit with his longstanding emphasis on personal relations, but Houston also found that evangelicals were hungry for personal soul care and theological learning that brought out the best from the classics of Christian devotion. In the face of this need, he took on more students for spiritual direction and developed more courses related to the topic. Practically speaking, Houston was indeed living out his strategy—influencing the course of Regent from below. Houston countered the college's decision to offer the master of divinity in 1979—the year after Houston's title was changed to chancellor—by almost singlehandedly developing Regent's reputation as the evangelical world's leader in spiritual theology.

---

[74]Carl E. Armerding to Michael G. Collison, July 22, 1993, folder 4, MCF. Armerding was not alone in his assessment. Alister McGrath noted in 1997 that "Houston gradually shifted his interests from the university to the business community, reflecting a growing conviction that the best interests of Regent would be served by stressing the links between theology and everyday life." See McGrath, *J. I. Packer: A Biography* (Grand Rapids: Baker Books, 1997), 231.

[75]Hans Boersma, Craig M. Gay, and D. Bruce Hindmarsh, "Introduction: A Festschrift for James M. Houston," *Crux* 48, no. 3 (September 2012): 4.

[76]Boersma, Gay, and Hindmarsh, "Introduction," 4.

By 1984 Houston's interest in the field of spiritual theology and his continuing desire to develop other Regent-inspired efforts internationally led him to resign from his position as chancellor. Freed from all administrative duties, Houston had two specific goals: to increase his involvement in "the furtherance of lay training in other parts of the world" and be "the facilitator of the heart in others, in personal counseling."[77] Together these goals—lay education and spiritual direction—shaped the legacy of Houston, Regent College, and those institutions that sought to replicate Regent's success. By the beginning of the twenty-first century, few had done as much as Houston to raise the awareness of these two emphases within North American evangelicalism.

Conclusion

For the next several decades, Houston maintained his emphasis on lay theological education and spiritual theology even as his primary target shifted from shaping the university to forming evangelical hearts. While Houston never again became intricately involved in the creation of a North American effort to re-create Regent's initial goal of providing university-embedded lay theological education, throughout the 1970s no one had been more of an international voice for university-embedded lay theological education than Houston. As Houston drew prominent evangelical businessmen and scholars into his summer school at Regent College and the summer study institute at College Park, he exposed them—and his students, many of whom came to care for him deeply—to his vision for replicating Regent College on university campuses across North America and the globe.

Thus, even as Houston's own direction changed and his focus shifted away from replicating Regent College on the campus of other North American universities, there were some among his students and admirers who, emboldened by the scope of his early vision and the example of Regent College, worked to launch their own innovative learning communities on university campuses across America. In the process this new generation of educational entrepreneurs did much to shape the future of the study center movement to which they belonged.

---

[77]James M. Houston, "Chancellor's Report," November 8, 1984, KSGC; James M. Houston, "Chancellor's Report," October 24, 1984, KSGC.

THE LIGONIER VALLEY STUDY CENTER

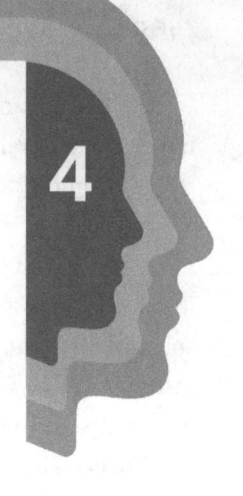

THE SUCCESS OF PLACES such as L'Abri and Regent College inspired other enterprising evangelicals to attempt similar ventures. Throughout much of the 1970s and early 1980s, one of the most significant attempts to build on the legacy of these earlier ventures was R. C. Sproul's Ligonier Valley Study Center. Founded in rural Stahlstown, Pennsylvania, in 1971, Ligonier Valley experimented with place-based lay theological education before becoming an early evangelical pioneer in the mass production and distribution of videotaped lectures. The latter emphasis helped propel Sproul and his blend of staunchly Reformed theology and everyman, grassroots appeal into national celebrity. Though Ligonier Valley was conceived as a residential study center in the mold of L'Abri, Sproul and his team gradually and intentionally shifted their focus away from a residential study center, opting instead for a video-based ministry headquartered in a small office complex located just outside Orlando. Leaving the Rust Belt for the Sun Belt, Sproul and his team built Ligonier Ministries into one of American evangelicalism's most recognized distributors of Reformed lay theological education.

R. C. Sproul and the Shaping of a Reformed Mind

Robert Charles "R. C." Sproul (1939–2017) was born in Pittsburgh in 1939. After graduating with a BA in philosophy from nearby Westminster College, Sproul enrolled at Pittsburgh Theological Seminary in fall 1961.[1] While there he came under the teaching of renowned Jonathan Edwards scholar John H. Gerstner (1914–1996). Gerstner was a fellow Westminster College alum who went on to earn multiple degrees at Westminster Theological Seminary before eventually joining other "Cambridge evangelicals" for doctoral studies at Harvard University during the World War II years.[2] After earning his PhD in 1945, Gerstner joined the staff of Pittsburgh Xenia Seminary (later Pittsburgh Theological Seminary) as a professor of church history in 1950.

Gerstner encouraged Sproul's natural proclivity for both scholarship and traditional Reformed theology. Following his 1964 graduation, Sproul continued to build on these two interests by enrolling as a doctoral student in systematic theology under noted Reformed theologian G. C. Berkouwer (1903–1996), then teaching at Abraham Kuyper's Free University in Amsterdam. Sproul's time at the Free University was cut short, however, due to the extended illness and death of his mother, dwindling finances, and complications related to the birth of his son, R. C. Sproul Jr., the next year. Forced to return to the States, Sproul was granted a waiver from the faculty at Free University and took a temporary teaching position at his alma mater, Westminster College. Sproul and his wife, Vesta, soon developed an informal ministry to college students that combined education and hospitality. Both traits eventually marked the Sprouls' work at Ligonier Valley Study Center. In addition to R. C.'s educational duties at the college, the Sprouls invited students to their home nearly every evening for times of Bible study and prayer. Sproul recalls that these meetings typically lasted until midnight, though "on a couple of occasions, it went all night."[3]

---

[1] The biographical details of Sproul's earlier life that appear in this chapter are almost universally taken from an oral-history interview with Sproul; see R. C. Sproul, interview with author, February 12, 2016. The best biographical treatment is R. C. Sproul and R. C. Sproul Jr., *After Darkness, Light: Distinctives of Reformed Theology; Essays in Honor of R. C. Sproul* (Phillipsburg, NJ: P&R, 2003). Other short biographical treatments of Sproul include "Meet the Staff: The Sprouls," *Tabletalk* 2, no. 2 (April 1978): 5; Dick Staub, "R. C. Sproul's Testimony: The Theologian and Author of Five Things Every Christian Needs to Grow Talks About How He Met Jesus and Why Playing the Violin Is like Reading the Bible," ChristianityToday.com, December 1, 2002, www.christianitytoday.com/ct/2002/decemberweb-only/12-30-21.0.html; Burk Parsons, "R. C. Sproul: A Man Called by God," Ligonier Ministries, www.ligonier.org/learn/articles/r-c-sproul-man-called-god/ (accessed May 27, 2016).

[2] The term "Cambridge evangelicals" comes from the work of Owen Strachan; see *Awakening the Evangelical Mind: An Intellectual History of the Neo-evangelical Movement* (Grand Rapids: Zondervan, 2015), especially 23, 96.

[3] Sproul, interview.

The Sprouls continued to foster close relationships with students through home-based hospitality and prayer the next year when R. C. Sproul took a teaching job at Gordon College just outside Boston. Sproul's move to Gordon was also a strategic move for his own education. Berkouwer had worked behind the scenes to help Sproul transfer his academic work to Harvard University, where he would be working with Dutch scholar Heiko Oberman (1930–2001). Once again, however, Sproul was forced to change plans. Shortly after Sproul took up his teaching duties at Gordon, Oberman left Harvard for a position in Germany. Berkouwer again worked on behalf of his student, eventually organizing a plan that would allow Sproul to commute to the Netherlands while continuing to teach in the United States. Under this agreement Sproul earned a doctorandus (drs) degree in 1969.[4]

Without an academic rationale for being in New England, Sproul accepted a call in fall 1968 to teach philosophical and systematic theology at Temple University's Conwell School of Theology. The move offered Sproul a chance to develop a personal affinity for lay theological education. In addition to his responsibilities at Conwell School of Theology, Sproul worked part time for Orland Evangelical Presbyterian Church, near Westminster Theological Seminary. As he taught adult education classes composed of "doctors, lawyers, and housewives and farmers" the young theologian acquired what he later described as his "taste for lay education."[5]

An affinity for lay education was not the only thing Sproul discovered during his year in Philadelphia. During his time at Conwell School of Theology, Sproul encountered a personality that deeply informed the shape—if not entirely the content—of his future work. In the late 1960s Francis Schaeffer was a relatively new player on the American evangelical stage. Schaeffer's rise in prominence during these years was largely due to the publication of his first books, *Escape from Reason* and *The God Who Is There*, in 1968. Schaeffer had previously held little interest for Sproul, but at Conwell Sproul found that his students' interest in the Swiss phenomenon necessitated engagement with Schaeffer's work. "I had hardly even heard of Francis Schaeffer," Sproul remembers, "but many of my students had listened to

---

[4]Sproul, interview; Parsons, "R. C. Sproul: A Man Called by God." Justin Taylor, "R. C. Sproul (1939–2017), The Gospel Coalition, December 14, 2017, www.thegospelcoalition.org/blogs/justin-taylor/r-c-sproul-1939-2017/ (accessed, September 10, 2019). The drs degree was the equivalent of a masters. Sproul later received a PhD from the unaccredited Whitefield Theological Seminary.
[5]Sproul, interview.

his tapes. Some of them had gone to Switzerland, to Huemoz, and had been students at L'Abri. So all of a sudden students were asking me questions about Francis Schaeffer, about whom I did not know anything." Sproul "started reading all his material, so I would be able to interact with the questions the students were raising."[6]

Just as Sproul was getting used to a new position, he encountered another unexpected obstacle. In 1969, only one year after he began teaching at Conwell, the school moved to Hamilton, Massachusetts, as part of a merger with Gordon Divinity School. Though invited to move to Boston, Sproul decided against returning to New England. Instead, in a move that demonstrated his growing appreciation for lay theological education, Sproul considered several options outside the academy. Eventually he took a position as associate pastor at College Hill Presbyterian Church in Cincinnati.

At College Hill the young pastor came into his own as a lay educator.[7] Through his Evangelism Explosion courses and Wednesday and Sunday evening Bible studies, Sproul developed a large following in Cincinnati.[8] Soon his Sunday night teachings were being attended by hundreds of people representing twenty-five Protestant and Catholic churches.[9] One of those attracted to Sproul's teaching during this time was Jack Rowley, a young videographer at General Electric's Cincinnati facility. Rowley, like so many others, was inspired by what he describes as Sproul's "brilliant mind" and ability to explain theology at a "lay level."[10] Sproul's keen insight and everyman appeal won over listeners to his teaching style and the version of Reformed theology that he advocated. Many of the students who took part in his ministry at College Hill found themselves seeking out Sproul's teaching—whether on audiocassette or in person at Ligonier Valley Study Center—in the years ahead.

Wider Influence: Sproul and the Pittsburgh Offensive

Sproul's success at College Hill soon drew the attention of individuals beyond the Cincinnati area. One group that took an especially keen interest in his

---

[6]Sproul, interview.
[7]"Meet the Staff: The Sprouls."
[8]Evangelism Explosion was developed in 1962 by D. James Kennedy. See "History," Evangelism Explosion International, http://evangelismexplosion.org/about-us/history/ (accessed June 13, 2016); James Davison Hunter, *American Evangelicalism: Conservative Religion and the Quandary of Modernity* (New Brunswick, NJ: Rutgers University Press, 1983), 80-83.
[9]Sproul, interview.
[10]Jack Rowley, interview with author, April 4, 2016.

abilities as a teacher was the Pittsburgh Offensive, a coalition of Christian leaders in the greater Pittsburgh area. The makeup of the Pittsburgh Offensive shows the degree of cross-pollination that existed among Pittsburgh's evangelicals during these years.[11] Reid M. Carpenter, the city's Young Life director and a friend of Pittsburgh Experiment director Don James, headed up the ambitious venture. Other local parachurch leaders such as John Guest, founding director of the Pittsburgh-based college ministry Coalition of Christian Outreach, and former University of Pittsburgh football standout Bob Long (who replaced Guest as executive director of the Coalition of Christian Outreach in 1972), joined Carpenter in the venture. Another individual who exerted significant influence within this coalition was Dora Hillman, widow of industrial tycoon J. Hartwell Hillman. Dora Hillman took a keen interest in the group and hosted the meetings of the Pittsburgh Offensive in her home.[12]

By 1970 members of the Pittsburgh Offensive had decided that the region needed a study center dedicated to educating campus ministry staffers who usually had neither the time nor the desire to attend a traditional seminary. Originally the group had considered founding this study center in Pittsburgh's Oakland district.[13] Oakland was a natural choice. Located adjacent to both the University of Pittsburgh and Carnegie Mellon University, Oakland was the intellectual center of life in the city. Hillman had other ideas. She agreed with fellow Pittsburgh Offensive members that the region needed a study center, and she was willing to back the venture on one condition—the study center would be located not in Oakland but in Stahlstown, Pennsylvania, a rural area an hour to the east, near Ligonier. Ligonier and the surrounding mountains had historically been a favorite haunt of Pittsburgh's most wealthy class, and Hillman had constructed a mansion on top of one of the area's highest peaks.[14]

Though Hillman's motive for insisting on the study center's Stahlstown location is not known, it seems likely that her desire to exercise personal influence and oversight in the center's development motivated the move.

---

[11] For more on Christian activity in Pittsburgh during this time, see Gary Scott Smith, *A History of Christianity in Pittsburgh* (Charleston, SC: History Press, 2019), 61-89.

[12] Jack Rowley, "The Ligonier Valley Study Center Early Years," Ligonier Ministries, June 20, 2010, www.ligonier.org/blog/ligonier-valley-study-center-early-years/.

[13] Sproul, interview.

[14] Because the Carnegie and Mellon families often spent time in the area, the region surrounding Ligonier was sometime referred to as "the Mellons' playground." Sproul, interview; R. C. Sproul Jr., interview with author, May 24, 2016.

Furthermore, by keeping her favorite Bible teacher close, she joined many powerful evangelicals who opted to align themselves with an individual pastor or teacher rather than a local church.[15] Speculation aside, from the start Hillman took charge of the study center's development and personally traveled to Cincinnati to discuss the concept with the Sprouls. During her visit she offered fifty-two acres and help in building accommodations for the study center if the group was willing to locate the center in Stahlstown.[16] For his part, Sproul was interested in the idea but still unsure. The concept of a study center caught his attention, but before he launched into such an uncertain and relatively unproven venture, he wanted to talk with someone who knew the ins and outs of starting and sustaining this type of ministry, and there was one obvious choice—Francis Schaeffer.

By the early 1970s Swiss L'Abri was packed throughout much of the year, and Schaeffer was receiving a growing number of invitations for speaking engagements in North America. One of the invites Schaeffer accepted was to a March 1971 conference at Covenant College in Lookout Mountain, Tennessee. For Sproul, Schaeffer's visit was a chance to ask Schaeffer about what it might take to start a L'Abri-type ministry somewhere else, somewhere like Stahlstown. With the help of Covenant College president Marion Barnes, who hosted a meeting between Sproul and Schaeffer in his home, Sproul was able to spend "several hours" with Schaeffer. During this time Schaeffer offered "words of encouragement and strategy for starting the Ligonier Valley Study Center."[17]

Sproul came away from the meeting impressed with Schaeffer and convinced that it might be possible to start a L'Abri-esque study center in western Pennsylvania. In early 1971 the Sproul family spent a week at Hillman's Stahlstown estate. When they left, they had decided to take part in the venture. By the end of that summer Sproul and his family, along with the Thompson family from College Hill, moved to Stahlstown. The Ligonier Valley Study Center was born.

---

[15]D. Michael Lindsay, *Faith in the Halls of Power: How Evangelicals Joined the American Elite* (New York: Oxford University Press, 2007).
[16]Sproul, interview; Parsons, "R. C. Sproul: A Man Called by God."
[17]R. C. Sproul, "In Memoriam: Francis Schaeffer, 1912–1984," *Tabletalk* 8, no. 4 (September 1984): 12; R. C. Sproul to Francis A. Schaeffer, March 18, 1971, box 56, file 6, FSC. For his part, Schaeffer encouraged the venture; see Francis A. Schaeffer to R. C. Sproul, March 22, 1971, box 56, file 6, FSC.

The Ligonier Valley Study Center: Early Years and Ethos

When the Sprouls and Thompsons arrived in Stahlstown in summer 1971, they began building the ministry from the ground up. Sproul moved his family into a newly constructed house—the first of many tangible testaments to Hillman's generosity and penchant for underwriting new building projects.[18] The Sprouls' large living room, which could seat over forty people comfortably, became the study center's primary teaching space. This home-centered ministry represented one of many undeniable carryovers from L'Abri.[19] According Jack Rowley, who joined the ministry in the mid-1970s, "It was L'Abri that inspired the way we did things at Ligonier. We kind of patterned ourselves pretty much after L'Abri."[20] As at L'Abri, community and home-based hospitality stood near the center of what Sproul envisioned for the ministry.

Hospitality was *near* the center but not *at* the center of Sproul's initial hopes for his study center. It was lay theological education that most shaped Sproul's vision. With the backing of parachurch ministries and a few prominent churches in the Pittsburgh area, the Ligonier Valley Study Center emerged in its early years as a ministry that was for churched people and parachurch ministers what L'Abri was for seekers and those who had perhaps grown up in the church and then drifted away. Ligonier Valley emphasized lay theological education that included a L'Abri-like emphasis on apologetics alongside a rigorous commitment to educating evangelicals in systematic theology.

Another disposition built into the ethos of Ligonier Valley was the characteristic evangelical emphasis on growth and "reaching" larger numbers of people.[21] To some extent, growth and survival were necessarily linked in Ligonier Valley's early years. From 1971, when Sproul moved to Ligonier with his family and the Thompsons through the middle of the decade, it was apparent that the ministry needed to grow in order to survive. Through a series of

---

[18] Rowley, interview.
[19] Many of those who frequented Ligonier Valley brought L'Abri connections with them; see, e.g., "A British Scholar at Ligonier," *Tabletalk* 1, no. 2 (July 1, 1977); "Student Life," *Tabletalk* 1, no. 3 (August 1977).
[20] Rowley, interview.
[21] Eventually Ligonier Valley's newsletter, *Tabletalk*, carried a regular feature titled "Reaching" that drew attention to the ways in which the footprint of Sproul's ministry was growing. For examples, see Esther DiQuattro, "Reaching," *Tabletalk* 7, no. 1 (February 1983): 5; DiQuattro, "Reaching," *Tabletalk* 7, no. 2 (April 1983): 5; DiQuattro, "Reaching," *Tabletalk* 7, no. 4 (September 1983): 5, 14; R. C. Sproul, "Reaching," *Tabletalk* 7, no. 5 (December 1983): 5.

planned and unplanned occurrences Sproul and the study center board made strategic decisions starting in 1977 that were meant to dramatically increase the ministry's influence. For the next seven years this emphasis on growth helped to make Sproul a celebrity among American evangelicals. It also played a key role in the study center's shift from a relationally based ministry centered on a geographical place to an idea-based ministry focused on mass media.

Community and place. Perhaps nothing better demonstrated the influence of L'Abri on Ligonier Valley than the Sprouls' emphasis on home-based hospitality. In his 1970 book *The Church at the End of the Twentieth Century*, Schaeffer called American Christians to open up their homes to what he described as "unantiseptic situation[s]."[22] To some extent the Sprouls had been doing just that since the mid-1960s as they welcomed people, usually college students, into their home. At first these efforts were limited to their own personal decisions as a family. With the founding of Ligonier Valley, however, the Sprouls intentionally made their personal convictions regarding home-based hospitality a distinctive of the entire ministry. At Ligonier Valley the Sprouls worked to ensure that not only *their* home but *all* staff homes were places of hospitality and community.

Staff homes at Ligonier were both public and private spaces. While serving the needs of staff families, which often included young children, staff homes also played a central role in the life of the study center, and staff families often hosted students in their homes overnight.[23] By the time the first dormitory was completed in summer 1978, 3,624 people had spent the night in staff homes at the study center.[24] Throughout much of the 1970s staff families also hosted students several times each week for evening meals. As former Ligonier Valley executive director Stu Boehmig remembers,

> We would have, say, two people staying with us. . . . If there were eight homes available who were doing this, then two of those homes would host a dinner for them. If we were hosting a dinner that night we might have twelve people for dinner. We were told what to have. . . . They would come to dinner at our house

---

[22]Francis A. Schaeffer, *The Church at the End of the Twentieth Century*, in *Complete Works of Francis A. Schaeffer: A Christian Worldview*, vol. 4, *A Christian View of the Church* (Westchester, IL: Crossway Books, 1982), 93.
[23]I've drawn these details from my interviews with early Ligonier Valley staff members, including R. C. Sproul, Jackie Shelton Griffith, Stuart Boehmig, Jack Rowley, and R. C. Sproul Jr.
[24]"Cedarwood Housing Facility Now Ready," *Tabletalk* 2, no. 4 (June 1978): 1.

and somebody else's house. The next night they would go to two other people's houses. Then we would gather for an evening singing and lecture time.[25]

In these informal settings Ligonier students were offered an opportunity to develop close ties with staff members, and the study center's ministry seemed as much relational as it was educational. For students and the staff members working to market the study center, these relational connections were among the most frequently emphasized aspects of the Ligonier program. As one student noted, "What I like most is having time with the staff families. I've been so aware of their acceptance of me. There's a real feeling of welcomeness in the homes."[26] The only aspect of the study center's ministry referenced with more frequency was Sproul's capabilities as a teacher.

Beyond ministry ideals, geographical realities made community formation among the Ligonier staff a necessity. The study center's rural location meant that the study center was a campus virtually unto itself. In the 1970s, when many Christians were intrigued by the idea of Christian community, the communal aspect of Ligonier was appealing. A desire to be part of this community prompted individuals to move to the area simply to be part of what was going on. Sometimes individuals who began spending time at the study center eventually became staff members, such as the Rowley family. In other cases, people who moved to the area never joined staff but were simply a part of the general Ligonier community. As early Ligonier staff member Jackie Shelton Griffith remembers, "People just came and lived in Ligonier and Stahlstown to be part of what was going on there. . . . There was something bigger than just R. C. and his teaching going on."[27]

A sense of community spirit was also forged through activities that occurred away from the dinner table and outside the classroom. With few options for entertainment off campus, staff and students alike were forced to create their own activities. Sports were a cheap and easy way to kill time and engage a student population that in the early and mid-1970s still skewed young due to

---

[25]Stuart Boehmig, interview with author, May 23, 2016. Boehmig and his wife, Kathy, served on the Ligonier staff until May 1979; see "The Field Mouse," *Tabletalk* 3, no. 4 (May 1979).

[26]For student takes on home-based hospitality, see "The Challenge," *Tabletalk* 2, no. 8 (October 1978): 1; Robert Michael Coho, "Why I Give to Ligonier," *Tabletalk* 2, no. 8 (October 1978). Hospitality was also used to market the study center: "Table Talk," *Tabletalk* 1, no. 5 (October 1977); "Cold Winter, Warm Hearts," *Tabletalk* 1, no. 8 (February 1978); "Ligonier—A Place for You," *Table Talk* 2, no. 5 (n.d.): 3.

[27]Jackie Shelton Griffith, interview with author, May 31, 2016.

Sproul's emphasis on college ministry. Harking back to the experiences of many staff members (Sproul included) who participated in sports through high school and college, Ligonier staff emphasized athletic competition and fun throughout the week. In Bill White's Leaping Ahead in Your Life program, physical activities such as jogging and weightlifting were incorporated into a curriculum that also included coursework. This and similar programs represented the Reformed conviction that all of life was spiritual while also reflecting national fitness trends and the so-called jogging revolution.[28] At other times sporting events were less formal. For many years a highlight of the summer months was the Wednesday night hot-dog roast and picnic, which was always followed by a softball or volleyball game and a campfire replete with singing and a marshmallow roast.[29]

As was the case with L'Abri, the net effect of Ligonier's rural setting was not entirely negative. Pennsylvania's Appalachian Mountains were not the Alps, but they were still a source of natural beauty and solitude. Indeed, not infrequently individuals came to Ligonier specifically seeking a slower, more relaxed pace. One student at the study center noted how Ligonier's "relaxed, casual atmosphere" with opportunities "to rest and relax while studying" compared favorably to the stricter regimen of normal seminary life.

Figure 4.1. R. C. Sproul teaching at Ligonier Valley circa 1977.

Not all time away from the classroom was strictly leisure. Following the L'Abri model, Sproul initially required that resident students offset the cost of their stay by working twelve hours a week at the study center.[30] Still, even as students worked and studied, the study center and the surrounding mountains offered

---

[28]Griffith, interview. The unrivaled success among how-to videos of *Jane Fonda's Workout* in 1982 symbolized the increasing attention Americans were paying to physical fitness. See Frederick Wasser, *Veni, Vidi, Video: The Hollywood Empire and the VCR* (Austin: University of Texas Press, 2001), 125-26.
[29]"Meet the Staff: Pat Erickson," *Tabletalk* 1, no. 2 (July 1977); "The Field Mouse," *Tabletalk* 1, no. 3 (August 31, 1977). L'Abri also hosted a weekly hot-dog roast for years; see Frank Schaeffer, *Crazy for God: How I Grew Up as One of the Elect, Helped Found the Religious Right, and Lived to Take All (or Almost All) of It Back* (New York: Carroll & Graf, 2007), 145.
[30]Andrew J. Trotter, interview with author, April 6, 2016, Charlottesville, VA; "Student Life"; "Ligonier Is for Learning," *Tabletalk* 1, no. 3 (August 1977).

plenty of time and space for leisure pursuits such as hiking and trout fishing.

The function of Ligonier as a retreat center was especially appealing to high-profile individuals such as Nixon hatchet man and rising evangelical celebrity Chuck Colson (1931–2012).[31] In summer 1978 Colson visited the study center, where he enjoyed "the quiet and lovely atmosphere" and noted that he would "love to come back."[32] In the years to come this desire became reality. Colson joined the Ligonier board in 1980 and helped facilitate a close connection between Ligonier and his parachurch ministry, Prison Fellowship.[33]

As new Ligonier staff members soon discovered, not all was pastoral bliss, however. Life lived in such close proximity was not without trials. For many Ligonier staff members, the relational demands of the study center, especially the continuing cycle of house and dinner guests, became a strain. Eventually, the limited space and the intense obligations related to housing students in family homes led Sproul to push for the building of the Cedar Lodge dormitory in 1978 (see photo 4.2).[34] According to Rowley, this was a necessary step away from the L'Abri model because housing students in staff homes "was burning staff families out because it was so demanding on the families," especially those with children at home. Staff families still continued to feed students in their homes for several years after the completion of the dormitory; eventually, however, this practice was also eliminated.[35]

Figure 4.2. Cedar Lodge, built in 1978.

Lay theological education at Ligonier. A desire to expand the theological education of the laity formed the center of Ligonier's mission. Indeed, it

---

[31]Charles W. Colson, *Born Again* (Old Tappan, NJ: Chosen Books, 1976).
[32]Kent Schoffstall, "Christ Last Hope for U.S.—Colson," *Tabletalk* 2, no. 7 (September 1978), 1; "Prison Fellowship Attends Seminar," *Tabletalk* 3, no. 3 (April 1979): 1.
[33]Esther DiQuattro, "Reaching," *Tabletalk* (September 1983). See also "Remember Those Who Are in Prison," *Tabletalk* 4, no. 4 (n.d.): 9; "Prison Ministry Seminar," *Tabletalk* 4, no. 3 (March 1980): 1.
[34]Boehmig, interview; "Decisions for Christ," *Newsweek*, October 25, 1976.
[35]Rowley, interview; Sproul Jr., interview.

was the study center's emphasis on education—as opposed to evangelism—that in Sproul's mind most distinguished his study center from Schaeffer's efforts at L'Abri. According to Sproul, "the central difference between the LVSC and L'Abri was that L'Abri was founded basically as an outreach in evangelism to non-Christian students . . . whereas the vision for the LVSC was for nurture and for grounding in theological education principally for para-ministry workers and church people." To a large extent this educational emphasis was the original motivating factor for the members of the Pittsburgh Offensive when the group originally contacted Sproul in 1971 about training for lay workers in parachurch campus ministries such as the Pittsburgh-based Coalition for Christian Outreach. Through most of the 1970s Sproul catered the ministry of Ligonier to the needs of these groups by hosting yearly training sessions for incoming Pittsburgh-area campus ministers.[36]

While college students and young campus ministers made up a large portion of those who studied at Ligonier in the early and mid-1970s, Sproul worked to diversify the study center's student base along the lines of gender and age through efforts such as the long-running Wednesday Morning Bible Study, which began in August of 1971, when a group of women from a local church asked Sproul to lead a month-long Bible study. Within a few weeks women from as far as sixty miles away were making the weekly trip to Stahlstown for the study, which demonstrated the local desire for Sproul's down-to-earth yet intellectually stimulating teaching style. Between August 1971 and July 1978, the Bible study that was originally supposed to last a few weeks had garnered a total attendance of more than sixteen thousand.[37]

Another weekly meeting that frequently drew large crowds was Sproul's Monday Night Summer Lecture Series. Like only the Wednesday Morning Bible Study, Monday night lectures were open to both paying resident students and the general public. A typical Monday night included two lectures, the first by a Ligonier staff member at 7:30 and the second by Sproul at 8:45. Many weeks these lectures drew large crowds to the Sprouls' living room. Attendees frequently spilled onto the floor, where they sometimes sat within inches of the lecturer's

---

[36]Sproul, interview. For example, in fall 1977 thirty-eight members of the Coalition for Christian Outreach came to Ligonier for training; see "Ligonier Trains Campus Leaders," *Tabletalk* 1, no. 5 (October 1977): 1.
[37]"Wednesday Study Rolls On—Rain or Shine," *Tabletalk* 2, no. 5 (July 1978): 1. The exact number given by Ligonier was 16,466.

feet. "We would get one hundred or two hundred people coming out once a week from Pittsburgh in buses or private cars," Sproul remembered. "We would have people occupying every square inch."[38] At times overflow crowds flowed out of the house and onto the porch, where they listened through open windows. Lectures were followed by what Sproul referred to as gab fests, which were similar to Schaeffer's Saturday night free-flowing question-and-answer sessions. Gab fests were designed to be times of "informal discussion" where individuals could "ask your most troublesome questions" and then receive an answer "in a secure and healthy atmosphere."[39]

Many of those who made their way to weekly Ligonier gab fests and the study center's programming in general were college students. Six years into the study center's history, college students made up about 40 percent of the over eighteen thousand visitors who found their way to Stahlstown.[40] One of the ways in which the study center attracted a large number of college students was by hosting courses for college credit in January and May. Sproul typically taught courses in the field of apologetics or theology, and attendance ranged from the teens to nearly forty. One of the study center's most ambitious undertakings involving courses for college credit was the Leaping Ahead program, in which students could earn a full term of college credit by "completing four weeks of work at home in addition to participating in the ten weeks residence at Ligonier." By the end of the 1970s over forty colleges and universities had awarded credit for courses taught at the study center.[41]

Gender at Ligonier. In addition to the theological "what" of the lectures and coursework at Sproul's study center, the "who" of the student body was also significant for evangelicals who were striving to think Christianly. At Ligonier, as at virtually every study center, the emphasis on cultivating a student body that was primarily made up of laypeople meant that at places such as L'Abri and Ligonier women were explicitly encouraged to develop theologically attuned minds. Thus, while lay education mattered for all evangelicals, it mattered most

---

[38]Sproul, interview; "Ligonier Packs Them In on Monday Night," *Tabletalk* 2, no. 7 (September 1978): 9.
[39]"Monday Night Summer Lecture Series," *Tabletalk* (July 1978).
[40]Of the eighteen thousand who studied at Ligonier Valley, only eight hundred were resident students; see "Ligonier Celebrates Sixth Year," *Tabletalk* 1, no. 4 (September 1977): 1.
[41]"New Year Starts Big," *Tabletalk* 3, no. 1 (February 1979): 1; R. C. Sproul, "The Year in Review," *Tabletalk* 3, no. 8 (September 1979): 1-3; "Leaping Ahead Program for College Credit," *Tabletalk* 4, no. 2 (February 1980): 1; "January Term," *Tabletalk* 2, no. 7 (September 1978): 5.

THE LIGONIER VALLEY STUDY CENTER   133

Figure 4.3. "A Beautiful Place to Grow," advertisement in a 1979 issue of *Tabletalk*.

for evangelical women, who were still excluded from or marginalized at most evangelical seminaries.[42] From the beginning women were welcomed at Ligonier.

This did not mean, however, that Sproul and the Ligonier staff advocated a thoroughgoing egalitarianism. Part of the reason Sproul left the United

---

[42]Numerous female interviewees noted how difficult it was for a woman to gain entrance to or study at most evangelical seminaries during this time (e.g., Thena Ayers, Linda Mercadante, Jackie Shelton Griffith), but the female interviewees I spoke with did not sense any disparity in the treatment of female students at Ligonier Valley. See Jackie Shelton Griffith, interview; Margaret Cullen, interview with author, July 27, 2018.

Presbyterian Church in the United States of America in 1975 and joined the Presbyterian Church in America was his conviction that the former denomination's acceptance of women's ordination underscored a deeper failure to uphold biblical authority.[43] Sproul's caught-in-the-middle stance between a desire (and perhaps logistical need) to have women in the classroom was balanced by his practice of making sure that if women were in the classroom they were in student's desk rather than at the teacher's lectern. In general, female staff members at Ligonier were most often confined to domestic duties such as childcare and meal preparation rather than teaching and preaching.

There was one exception, however, to the otherwise consistent Ligonier staff norm of male teachers and female domestic workers. Jackie Shelton first came to the study center in 1975 after being directed to Ligonier by a Young Life leader whom she had asked, "Where can I go to just learn about God?" He responded by laying out three options—L'Abri, Regent College, or Sproul's Ligonier Valley Study Center. After listening to Sproul teach at the initial Philadelphia Conference on Reformed Theology in 1975, Shelton chose Ligonier. "I just knew that I could learn from this man the very thing that I was seeking, just to know God," Shelton later remembered.[44] Shelton quit her job at the National Audio Visual Center in Washington, DC, and became a long-term resident student at Ligonier.

Shelton loved the Christian community and learning that she found at the study center. She "devoured" the tape library, and soon found that she had listened to every available tape. Throughout her time at the study center, one pressing need stood out to her: the lack of a female staff member dedicated to counseling and advising courses of study for female students. Even though hundreds of women studied at Ligonier, "there was no one on staff if you think about the teaching staff—not including the wives of the people on staff—that was dealing with the women students." To Shelton the need for a female staff member was obvious. At the end of three months of study at Ligonier, Shelton made a proposal: she offered to stay on at the study center "to help the women students come up with a study program when they come." To her surprise,

---

[43]Sproul, interview; "Pressure in Pittsburgh," *Christianity Today*, January 4, 1974, 53-55. Sproul's contemporary reflections on the situation as well as Francis Schaeffer's response can be found in FSC; see R. C. Sproul to Francis A. Schaeffer, September 3, 1975, box 56, file 6, FSC; Francis A. Schaeffer to R. C. Sproul, September 14, 1975, box 56, file 6, FSC.

[44]Griffith, interview. A short biographical treatment of Griffith can be found in an early *Tabletalk* article; see "Meet the Staff: Jackie Shelton," *Tabletalk* 1, no. 4 (September 1977).

Ligonier staff unanimously supported her proposal on one condition—that she also draw on her previous media experience and teach a course on Christianity and twentieth-century culture.[45]

For the next three years Shelton took part in teaching and community life at the study center. Shelton remembers Sproul's kindness and support of her role as a female teacher throughout this time. Once she specifically asked Sproul, "Where are the women in [church] history?" She remembers him responding by calling the absence of women's stories "a failure of history." Because "it wasn't [her] mission to have some kind of radical impact," Shelton did not press the point. In truth, she felt "privileged to be where I was and learn what I was learning from so many great teachers and just have the opportunity to do something." Her own theological and biblical study had convinced her that women were perfectly justified to teach men outside of the ordained offices of the church. That was good enough for her and, so it seemed, for Sproul. When she eventually left Ligonier in fall 1978 to pursue a master's and then a PhD in counseling at the University of Pittsburgh, she received a warm Ligonier sendoff.[46] In the end, Shelton's time at the study center was an anomaly. No other woman ever held a teaching role at Ligonier.

A New Reformation

From the beginning, Reformed theology defined the ethos of Ligonier. Sproul attributed his deep affection for Reformed theology to the influence of Gerstner. As R. C. Sproul Jr. later noted, it was Gerstner who transformed his father into "a zealot for the Reformed faith."[47] Sproul's entire graduate education, from his time with Gerstner to his time with G. C. Berkouwer at the Free University, helped deepen and clarify this theological stance. Unlike many American evangelicals, who peddled a theologically nondescript "born-againism," Sproul wore his specific brand of theology on his sleeve. From his teaching, writing, and institutional involvement (e.g., the Philadelphia Conference on Reformed Theology), Sproul emphasized a staunchly Reformed message that influenced

---

[45]Griffith, interview. This emphasis on cultural media fit well with the typical way in which a handful of women found their way into evangelical organizations. During these years women could gain a foothold when they focused on literature, art, or media, whereas they could never have entered as lecturers in biblical studies or theology.

[46]Griffith, interview. See also "The Field Mouse," *Tabletalk* 2, no. 7 (September 1978).

[47]Sproul and Sproul, *After Darkness, Light*, 5.

thousands of lay Christians to see their faith through the lens of John Calvin. Together with a handful of high-profile, staunchly Reformed pastors including John F. MacArthur (b. 1939) and D. James Kennedy (1930–2007), Sproul worked to raise the profile of Reformed theology.[48]

Sproul's appreciation for the Reformers and the principles they espoused exerted a seemingly constant influence in his ministry. In addition to the magisterial Reformers' emphasis on theological principles such as *sola Scriptura*, *sola fide*, *sola gratia*, *solus Christus*, and *soli Deo gloria*, Sproul frequently cited the Reformers' willingness to take theological learning to the masses (i.e., the laity).[49] Describing the Reformers in a 1979 issue of Ligonier's periodical *Tabletalk* (whose title was itself a testament to Luther's practice of talking theology with students around his kitchen table), Sproul noted that the Reformers "were not interested merely in publishing technical works for the applause of the scholarly world." Instead, they "were willing to risk their academic reputations in order to minister to the people"—a trait Sproul likely recognized in himself. Based on this assessment, Sproul emphasized a path toward this "new reformation" that essentially called for widespread adoption and replication of his own efforts at Ligonier. "We need scholars today who have a burden for the education of Christians everywhere. . . . The real effort of reformation in our day must be met head-on by the finest scholars that the Church has produced. They should spend at least a portion of their time communicating, writing, and preparing materials for the laity."[50]

For Sproul, the task of reaching the multitudes with quality educational materials was urgent. In his mind education followed close on the heels of grace as God's main tool in the process of transformation. As Sproul noted in his widely read 1985 book *The Holiness of God*, "the renewal of the mind" is "the key method Paul underscores as the means to the transformed life." For Sproul,

---

[48]On Kennedy's influence, see William C. Martin, *With God on Our Side: The Rise of the Religious Right in America* (New York: Broadway Books, 1996), 198-200.

[49]Schaeffer saw the Reformers as men who could appreciate art and as people who, "standing under the teaching of Scripture[,] had freedom and yet at the same time compelling absolute values." See Francis A. Schaeffer, *How Should We Then Live?*, in *The Complete Works of Francis A Schaeffer: A Christian Worldview*, vol. 5, *A Christian View of the West* (Westchester, IL: Crossway Books, 1982), 134. The chapters in a festschrift dedicated to Sproul in 2003 testify to Sproul's appreciation for these Reformation principles. The chapters of the book follow the five *solas* of the Reformation and the five points of Calvinism; see Sproul and Sproul, *After Darkness, Light*.

[50]R. C. Sproul, "Right Now Counts Forever: My People Perish," *Tabletalk* 3, no. 7 (August 1979): 1. For more on the rationale for the name *Tabletalk*, see "Table Talk" (1977).

Paul's emphasis was clear. Renewal of the mind meant "nothing more and nothing less than education. Serious education. In-depth education. Disciplined education in the things of God. It calls for a mastery of the Word of God. We need people whose lives have changed because our minds have changed."[51]

With Paul and the Reformers behind him, Sproul hoped that Ligonier might "contribute to the cause of spiritual renewal and reformation" through an expanding program of lay theological education.[52] Indeed, the need for "a modern reformation" had been on Sproul's mind since at least fall 1977, when he unveiled an ambitious set of goals for the Ligonier staff. In the face of "rising secularism and the instability it brings," Sproul laid out an expansive vision: "What do we need? We need a new Reformation. Nothing less than a Reformation comparable to the 16th century Protestant Reformation will do. I am convinced that the future of Western Civilization is at stake. Reformation is not an option. It is a necessity." Drawing on the example of the Reformers, who met the challenge of their age by cultivating leaders who were "great scholars" but "not ivory tower scholars" and who were willing and able to "make full use of the most advanced methods of communication available," Sproul challenged the Ligonier staff to a similar level of engagement that was "bold, yet disciplined and responsible."[53] In so doing he harnessed his ambitions for the future of Ligonier to a Reformation past.

Ambition for Growth and Wider Influence

While Sproul's call for a new Reformation was a cry of the heart for theological instruction that was intellectually robust and yet widely accessible at the same time, the talk he gave on the topic and the following article also served as a pragmatic way to frame his desire to expand the study center's ministry—a goal that became central to Sproul's thinking by fall 1977. After over six years of work, the study center was still struggling to pay bills and expand beyond its primary identity as a regional training center. The lack of national prominence was not

---

[51] R. C. Sproul, *The Holiness of God* (Wheaton, IL: Tyndale House, 1998), 164.
[52] "The Mission of Ligonier," *Tabletalk* 5, no. 7 (October 1981): 1. The full mission statement read: "To contribute to the cause of spiritual renewal and reformation through a teaching ministry designed to inform masses of people with Biblical content and to train key church and para-ministry leaders in Biblical truth including doctrine, practice, and cultural interpretation (theology, ethics, practical theology, and apologetics)."
[53] R. C. Sproul, "A Modern Reformation: Ligonier's Vision," *Tabletalk* 1, no. 6 (November 1977).

entirely for lack of trying. Sproul had attempted to raise the profile of Ligonier and build a larger coalition of Reformed scholars before 1977. In 1974 the study center hosted leading evangelical scholars such as Gerstner, J. I. Packer, Clark Pinnock, John Warwick Montgomery, and others for what *Christianity Today* described as "a top-level conference on the inspiration and authority of Scripture." As a result of this conference the study center published *God's Inerrant Word: An International Symposium on the Trustworthiness of Scripture*.[54] Edited by lawyer and Christian apologist John Warwick Montgomery (b. 1931), these essays spoke to American evangelicalism's greatest internal controversy and paved the way for Sproul to become the first president of the International Council on Biblical Inerrancy (founded 1977).[55] Framed as "a ten-year effort to study and defend the doctrine of biblical inerrancy," the International Council on Biblical Inerrancy brought many of evangelicalism's leading voices together around the issue of scriptural authority. The organization's influential 1978 Chicago Statement on Biblical Inerrancy owed much to the work of the earlier conference at Ligonier.[56]

Sproul's involvement in these conferences and the networks they represented helped to enlarge the scope of Ligonier's ministries, but the study center's greatest catalyst for growth came not through these large organizations but through the work of a consultant named Bobb Biehl (b. 1943). After working for several years on World Vision's executive team, Biehl founded Masterplanning Group in 1976. Over the next four decades, Biehl became a key behind-the-scenes shaper of American evangelicalism as he advised "large, fast growing, churches," nonprofit and for-profit organizations and served on boards as diverse as Duane Pederson's Jesus People USA (twenty-five years) and James Dobson's Focus on the Family (thirty-one years).[57]

---

[54]K. Eric Perrin, "Back to Basics," *Christianity Today*, November 23, 1973, 56-57; Conference on the Inspiration and Authority of Scripture, John Warwick Montgomery, and Ligonier Valley Study Center, eds., *God's Inerrant Word: An International Symposium on the Trustworthiness of Scripture* (Minneapolis: Bethany Fellowship, 1974).

[55]Sproul served for a short time as president of the International Council on Biblical Inerrancy. R. C. Sproul to Francis A. Schaeffer, June 21, 1979, box 56, file 6, FSC.

[56]"A Campaign for Inerrancy," *Christianity Today*, November 4, 1977, 51-52; Donald Tinder, "Pro-inerrancy Forces Draft Their Platform," *Christianity Today*, November 17, 1978, 36-37; David P. Scaer, "International Council on Biblical Inerrancy: Summit II," *Concordia Theological Quarterly* 47, no. 2 (April 1983): 153-58. For the full text of the Chicago Statement on Biblical Inerrancy, see International Council on Biblical Inerrancy, "Chicago Statement on Biblical Inerrancy," *Journal of the Evangelical Theological Society* 21, no. 4 (December 1978): 289-96.

[57]Bobb Biehl, "Would You Like to Know a Bit About Me?," Bobbbiehl.com, http://bobbbiehl.com/about/ (accessed June 13, 2016).

Sproul contacted Biehl in 1976 after Archie Parrish, the executive director of Evangelism Explosion and mutual friend of Sproul and Biehl, "challenged R. C. to expand his outreach and contact his chief consultant—Bobb Biehl." At first Sproul hesitated, telling his friend, "I'm not a visionary, I am just a teacher." Over time, however, Sproul warmed to Parrish's advice. By fall 1977 Sproul had hired Biehl to consult with Ligonier. The implications of this relationship soon became apparent in Sproul's own sense of the study center's unrealized potential. Addressing his staff at their annual meeting, he put forth a vision whose scope was immense. "I've caught Archie's vision and I pass it on to you," Sproul told his staff. "Here is where the Ligonier Valley Study Center is headed. Here is our game plan. Here are our goals. Here is what I'm giving myself to for the next five years, God willing. Our goal is to have 100,000 people using our materials for education and encouragement on a regular basis by January 1, 1982." For Sproul these projections symbolized his decision to lead Ligonier in a gear up for "maximum ministry"—a prerequisite if the study center staff hoped to "contribute to Reformation."[58]

By the time Sproul addressed his staff in fall 1977, they were already well aware of some of the changes that came with Sproul and Biehl's lofty goals. Changes designed to help Ligonier meet these new expectations had already led to what Sproul himself described as "a time of enormous stress, anxiety, and work-load for all of us" as "the security of our established patterns was upset and uncertainty of where we all fit in has been keenly felt." In addition to concerns about staffing and programming, this shift in scope if not in emphasis was also accompanied by financial hardships, as the study center raised its original 1977 budget from $185,000 to $250,000 over the course of one year. "That's not boldness, that's brinkmanship," Sproul reflected. "We took enormous risks by putting together the kind of organizing

Figure 4.4. Stu Boehmig leading Monday night Bible study in the Sprouls' living room in 1978.

---

[58]Sproul, "Modern Reformation."

and staff I've needed to reach our goals. I feel the weight of those risks everyday. The winter was a disaster and we were pushed to the wall. . . . But we will end the year meeting this greatly increased budget."[59]

Of the many staffing changes that accompanied the study center's structural overhaul, one of the more significant was the decision to name Stuart Boehmig executive director. This shift in responsibility came at the direct suggestion of Biehl. According to Boehmig, "Bobb came in from California *a lot*, and spent days and days at the study center interviewing people [and] talking to people." In the end Boehmig remembers that Biehl told Sproul, "You need to be teaching and you need to be directing, but you need somebody to run it for you." In Biehl's estimation, Boehmig was the man for the job. Soon the recent seminary graduate moved from a basic teaching role into what he describes as "a management role of implementing the new direction of LVSC." If, as Biehl emphasized, Sproul was "the goose that lays the golden eggs," Boehmig's job was to take those eggs and get them out to people in a way that was going to generate more resources and greater ministry.[60]

Under Boehmig's oversight, Ligonier expanded its institutional reach by launching a monthly in-house newsletter, *Tabletalk*, in May 1977. The publication was meant to embody the study center's "conviction that the things of God should be regularly discussed in the course of everyday life."[61] Early on the newsletter was filled with a number of regular columns written by Sproul, Boehmig, and other Ligonier staff members. These regular columns were usually devoted to theological or biblical teaching, though Sproul used his "Right Now Counts Forever" column to reflect on contemporary issues ranging from a discussion of "the Pepsi Generation" to the prescient topic of violence in professional football and political articles with titles such as "Theology and 'Reaganomics.'"[62]

As important as these teaching articles were, *Tabletalk*'s greatest contribution to the study center's mission was likely the publication's ability to market the

---

[59]Sproul, "Modern Reformation."
[60]Boehmig, interview.
[61]This text was printed for a time on the *Tabletalk* masthead; see "The Mission of Ligonier," *Tabletalk* 5, no. 8 (November 1981): 1.
[62]Boehmig called *Tabletalk* "our primary teaching platform"; Boehmig, interview. See R. C. Sproul, "Right Now Counts Forever: Roots in the Pepsi Generation," *Tabletalk* 1, no. 1 (May 6, 1977); Sproul, "Right Now Counts Forever: God, Violence, Pro Football," *Tabletalk* 1, no. 4 (September 1977); Sproul, "Right Now Counts Forever: Theology and 'Reaganomics,'" *Tabletalk* 6, no. 1 (February 1982).

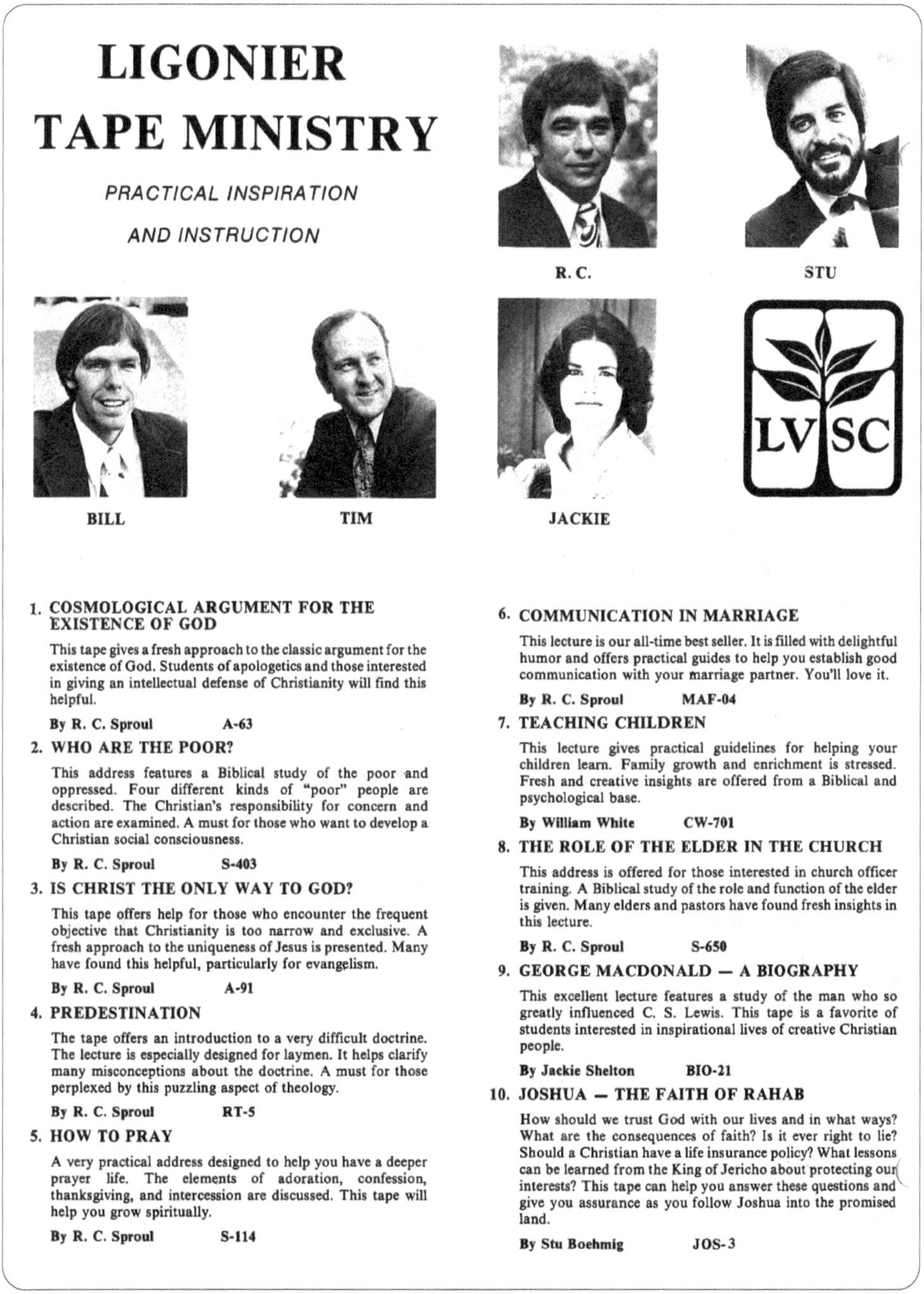

LIGONIER TAPE MINISTRY

PRACTICAL INSPIRATION AND INSTRUCTION

R. C.

STU

BILL

TIM

JACKIE

LVSC

1. **COSMOLOGICAL ARGUMENT FOR THE EXISTENCE OF GOD**

   This tape gives a fresh approach to the classic argument for the existence of God. Students of apologetics and those interested in giving an intellectual defense of Christianity will find this helpful.

   By R. C. Sproul   A-63

2. **WHO ARE THE POOR?**

   This address features a Biblical study of the poor and oppressed. Four different kinds of "poor" people are described. The Christian's responsibility for concern and action are examined. A must for those who want to develop a Christian social consciousness.

   By R. C. Sproul   S-403

3. **IS CHRIST THE ONLY WAY TO GOD?**

   This tape offers help for those who encounter the frequent objective that Christianity is too narrow and exclusive. A fresh approach to the uniqueness of Jesus is presented. Many have found this helpful, particularly for evangelism.

   By R. C. Sproul   A-91

4. **PREDESTINATION**

   The tape offers an introduction to a very difficult doctrine. The lecture is especially designed for laymen. It helps clarify many misconceptions about the doctrine. A must for those perplexed by this puzzling aspect of theology.

   By R. C. Sproul   RT-5

5. **HOW TO PRAY**

   A very practical address designed to help you have a deeper prayer life. The elements of adoration, confession, thanksgiving, and intercession are discussed. This tape will help you grow spiritually.

   By R. C. Sproul   S-114

6. **COMMUNICATION IN MARRIAGE**

   This lecture is our all-time best seller. It is filled with delightful humor and offers practical guides to help you establish good communication with your marriage partner. You'll love it.

   By R. C. Sproul   MAF-04

7. **TEACHING CHILDREN**

   This lecture gives practical guidelines for helping your children learn. Family growth and enrichment is stressed. Fresh and creative insights are offered from a Biblical and psychological base.

   By William White   CW-701

8. **THE ROLE OF THE ELDER IN THE CHURCH**

   This address is offered for those interested in church officer training. A Biblical study of the role and function of the elder is given. Many elders and pastors have found fresh insights in this lecture.

   By R. C. Sproul   S-650

9. **GEORGE MACDONALD — A BIOGRAPHY**

   This excellent lecture features a study of the man who so greatly influenced C. S. Lewis. This tape is a favorite of students interested in inspirational lives of creative Christian people.

   By Jackie Shelton   BIO-21

10. **JOSHUA — THE FAITH OF RAHAB**

    How should we trust God with our lives and in what ways? What are the consequences of faith? Is it ever right to lie? Should a Christian have a life insurance policy? What lessons can be learned from the King of Jericho about protecting our interests? This tape can help you answer these questions and give you assurance as you follow Joshua into the promised land.

    By Stu Boehmig   JOS-3

Figure 4.5. This early advertisement in *Tabletalk* demonstrates the range of topics covered by Ligonier Valley staff members and provides a visible reminder of gender underrepresentation among teachers at the study center.

materials Sproul and his staff were producing in ever-increasing quantities. While early issues of *Tabletalk* included a number of substantive articles, the average reader could be forgiven for mistaking the publication for a Christian book supplier's mail-order catalog. In the magazine's first year of publication (May 1977–April 1978) just under half of its total pages were devoted to either appeals for support or to advertising the study center's programs and products.[63] Three years later (May 1980–April 1981) over 50 percent of the pages in *Tabletalk* were devoted to advertising products ranging from the Ligonier cookbook (*Our Favorite Recipes*) and "Christian Education Audits" to new residence programs and videotapes.[64] Unlike many other Christian and secular periodicals, *Tabletalk* took no paid advertisements. All marketing within the magazine was directed back into the study center or back into the publication and teaching ministry of Sproul himself.

In addition to the publication of *Tabletalk*, two other decisions that traced back at least in part to Biehl's recommendations also dramatically influenced the future course of Sproul's ministry. The first of these decisions concerned an overhaul of the Ligonier board of directors. In early 1979 the board voted "to expand from 7 members to a maximum of 21 members."[65] Soon the original in-house board made up of Ligonier staff had expanded to include numerous executives and nationally known figures such as Chuck Colson. The new board had less direct connection to the everyday rhythm of life at the study center and the sense of place that the study center represented. The implementation of a new board model at Ligonier and the corresponding loss of geographic rootedness marked a subtle but significant departure from the study center's first seven years of ministry. It was a change made possible—even preferable to some—by the study center's success in the relatively new field of videotaped ministry. In the years to come Sproul's decision to invest heavily in the new technology of video enabled his transformation from a local star to a national evangelical celebrity.

---

[63] Between May 1977 and April 1978, 53 (or 46 percent) of *Tabletalk*'s 115 pages were devoted to advertisements or fundraising.
[64] Sixty-two of *Tabletalk*'s 118 pages during this twelve-month period were devoted explicitly or implicitly to marketing or fundraising. This does not count the ten-page "Ligonier Valley Study Center Audio/Video Tape Catalogue" that appeared in the April 1981 issue. If this supplement is counted, the amount of *Tabletalk*'s pages devoted to marketing or self-promotion rises to 59 percent.
[65] "New Directors Join Board," *Tabletalk* 3, no. 6 (July 1979): 1.

The Video Revolution Comes to Stahlstown

The timing could hardly have been better for Sproul's transition from a ministry of place and presence to one defined by videotape and technology. While magnetic video recording was first developed in the United States in the early 1950s, it was only in the late 1970s, when Japanese engineers developed video technology such as Sony's Betamax (1975) and Matsushita's VHS (1977), that video became affordable for a mass market. By 1978 the VHS format—with a four-hour recording time that was intentionally long enough to record an American football game—had become dominant in the United States.[66] As production rose and prices fell, the VCR became a standard feature of American society. By 1984 nearly fifteen million Americans owned a VCR, and *Newsweek* declared a "Video Revolution," while major film companies, cable networks, and a small army of video-rental store owners sprang into action in an attempt to grab a portion of the new medium's revenue.[67]

Evangelical Christians were not far behind their secular peers in the appropriation of video. Among the most famous evangelicals to make use of video in the late 1970s was James Dobson, a child psychologist turned evangelical family guru. Dobson discovered not only the power of video but also the usefulness of coupling video with the marketing savvy of a Christian publishing house. In 1978 the Texas-based Word, Inc., approached Dobson about videotaping and marketing his seminars on Christian parenting. The success of this symbiotic relationship soon inspired what has been termed the "Dobson effect," as numerous other publishing houses and "megacommunicators" sought to cash in on the phenomenon.[68]

The vast potential of video technology did not go unnoticed in Stahlstown. Thanks to the effort and foresight of a young videographer named Jack Rowley, the video revolution was transforming Sproul's ministry at Ligonier years

---

[66] Wasser, *Veni, Vidi, Video*, 53-60; Michael Z. Newman, *Video Revolutions: On the History of a Medium* (New York: Columbia University Press, 2014), 21-22, 72, 91.

[67] Eric Gelman et al., "The Video Revolution: How the VCR Is Changing What You Watch"; Wasser, *Veni, Vidi, Video*, 81-136.

[68] Eithne Johnson, "The Emergence of Christian Video and the Cultivation of Videoevangelism," in *Media, Culture, and the Religious Right*, ed. Linda Kintz and Julia Lesage (Minneapolis: University of Minnesota Press, 1998), 197. The Dobson effect seems to have been recognized first in a 1987 *Christianity Today* special advertising piece, "An Industry on the Move," *Christianity Today*, April 1987, 50, 54-55, but the magazine had started emphasizing video earlier, when it devoted its full November 1981 issue to the topic of video.

before the Dobson effect took effect. In mid-1974 Jack Rowley, a former student of Sproul's in Cincinnati and a videographer who made educational videos for companies such as General Electric and Kroger, wrote to Sproul offering to videotape some of his lectures at no charge over the 1974 Thanksgiving holiday. Sproul gave his assent to the trip, and the video revolution came to Stahlstown a few weeks later in the Rowley motorhome. It was the beginning of Sproul's most influential and long-lasting professional partnership.[69] Over the course of the next year Rowley made twelve trips to Ligonier to videotape Sproul and showed Sproul's taped lectures in ten Cincinnati churches and numerous video Bible studies. These efforts culminated in Sproul's decision to bring Rowley on Ligonier staff as media director in August 1977. The move signaled Sproul's decision to follow the trajectory of expanded ministry, which Biehl had outlined the year before. As Rowley noted in a 1982 *Tabletalk* article on video, "To reach our goal of helping 100,000 students by 1982 . . . every means of mass communication will be necessary."[70]

Figure 4.6. Jack Rowley in the Ligonier Valley recording studio in 1982

Creating a National Market for Video-Based Theological Education

By the early 1980s the study center's videotape ministry was fast garnering national attention. In some cases individuals such as John MacArthur, prominent pastor of Grace Community Church in Los Angeles, sent representatives to Ligonier to learn more about developing a video ministry of their own.[71] Through better production and increased marketing, Sproul's influence grew within American

---

[69] Unless otherwise noted, the details of Rowley's early involvement at the study center are all taken from a 2016 interview with Jack Rowley. Rowley joined the Ligonier Valley staff in 1977 and remained on the Ligonier Ministry staff throughout the entirety of Sproul's career. He was the only individual to do this.
[70] Jack Rowley, "Video Revolution Begins," *Tabletalk* 3, no. 3 (April 1979): 12. See also Rowley, "Video Education: A Reality for You," *Tabletalk* 3, no. 4 (May 1979): 12; Rowley, "What to Consider Before Starting a Video Ministry," *Tabletalk* 3, no. 5 (June 1979): 12; Rowley, "How Many Can You Reach with a Video Ministry?," *Tabletalk* 3, no. 6 (n.d.): 12.
[71] Rowley, interview. Rowley dates this visit to 1983.

THE LIGONIER VALLEY STUDY CENTER 145

evangelicalism, especially among evangelicals in Reformed circles. The biggest boost to Sproul's profile came in 1982—a year Rowley described at the time as "the breakthrough year for video." During that year Dora Hillman and an anonymous donor financed the construction of a new state-of-the-art production studio. At the same time Sproul, with a plan for distributing his tapes, decided to partner with Tyndale for video marketing and distribution.[72]

The partnership aligned well with Ligonier's reshaped mission to "contribute to the cause of spiritual renewal and reformation" by educating "masses of people."[73] To Sproul and Ligonier staff, the growth of Sproul's ministry was an important contributor to the needed modern reformation. As Rowley noted in 1980, "in order to have sufficient impact upon a culture which seems to be running out of time, it would seem reasonable to make use of every means of mass communication possible."[74] Ligonier spared no energy in seeking to do just that.

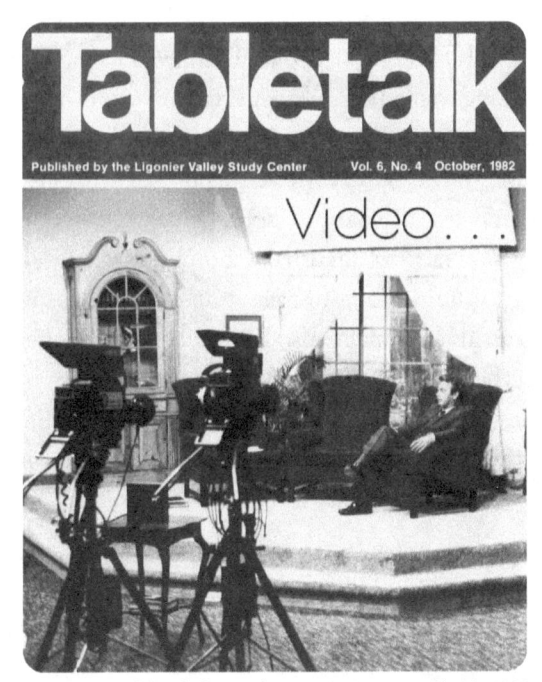

Figure 4.7. *Tabletalk* devoted an entire issue to video in 1982.

---

[72] Jack Rowley, "LVSC Video: Small Beginnings ... New Horizons," *Tabletalk* 6, no. 4 (October 1982).
[73] This quotation comes from "The Mission of Ligonier," which was published on the masthead of *Tabletalk* in October 1981.
[74] Jack Rowley, "Audio/Video: Video Equipment," *Tabletalk* 4, no. 1 (January 1980).

The Impact of Video on the Study Center

As important as video was to the expanding ministry of Ligonier, the video revolution did not affect everyone on the study center staff uniformly. Together, the partnership with Tyndale and the fact that it was predominantly Sproul's tapes that were marketed gave much greater visibility to Sproul as a "widely acclaimed communicator" and master teacher.[75] This pointed to a larger trend at Ligonier. From at least the early 1980s and possibly from the time of Biehl's involvement, the work of Ligonier moved away from a team-based, residential ministry toward a ministry increasingly focused on Sproul's individual abilities. Whereas early visitors to Ligonier experienced a relaxed, extended family setting, by 1982 even personal interaction with Sproul carried a price tag. In addition to purchasing general Ligonier materials, *Tabletalk* readers could also support Sproul's individual radio teaching ministry directly through the Luke Club, or even buy a membership in the Romans Club, which *Tabletalk* billed as "a special fellowship of people with whom R. C. will stay in regular contact" and will "share new insights."[76]

Furthermore, as Sproul's strategy pivoted toward video-based mass communication, the entire ministry had to adapt to the time constraints that video demanded. In the study center's early years, Sproul's sermons ranged in their duration, sometimes lasting nearly an hour. Once video became a key emphasis, however, Sproul's teaching was usually shortened to twenty-minute chunks of time in order to afford room for follow-up discussions in Sunday school classrooms.[77] Consumer demand also meant that Sproul often felt forced to teach on subjects he saw as of secondary importance. In a 1981 *Tabletalk* piece titled "Frustrations of a Christian Educator," Sproul noted that while a need existed for "heavier" teaching because "content changes lives," most Christians who purchased materials from Ligonier voted with dollars for lighter subjects.

> When we spend money to advertise or promote series like the Holiness of God or other "non-practical" teaching tapes we lose our collective shirts. They are a disaster at the "box office." I know, for example, that if we advertise a lecture series that speaks directly to a *felt* need, such as improving marriages, dealing

---

[75] "Dr. R. C. Sproul, Noted Theologian and Widely Acclaimed Communicator Will Be Speaking at Grace Presbyterian Church."

[76] For more on the Luke Club, see "The Luke Club," *Tabletalk* 6, no. 2 (April 1982); "Join R. C. in an LVSC Club Today!," *Tabletalk* 7, no. 1 (February 1983). For more on the Romans Club, see "The Romans Club," *Tabletalk* 6, no. 4 (October 1982): 13.

[77] Rowley, "How Many Can You Reach with a Video Ministry?"

with teenage sexual problems, and the like, we will almost certainly break even in our expenses and perhaps do a little better. But if we attempt to promote something like The Holiness of God, I know going in, we are going to incur a serious deficit.[78]

Even as video opened up new doors of influence for Sproul and the study center, the new medium and the consumer's will proved difficult to contain.

In the end, as much as Rowley and Sproul shaped the content and distribution of Ligonier videos, the videos also shaped them and the study center community. More than standardized lecture times and more national speaking tours for Sproul, video technology began to make the difficulties of sustaining a physical study center less necessary—perhaps even less desirable. As video transformed Sproul into a national evangelical figure, it also marked the beginning of the end for the study center.

Leaving Residential Learning Behind: From Study Center to Ligonier Ministries

By late 1985 the Ligonier Valley Study Center had ceased to exist. Ligonier Ministries, an Orlando-based ministry dedicated to the production of Sproul's teaching via large conferences, publishing, and various forms of mass media, had taken its place. Rather than a residential study center, Sproul's ministry was now primarily a videotape-based teaching ministry that could fit easily within a small office complex in the Orlando suburbs. It was a change that had been a long time coming. The study center's transition from a regional, residential training center to a national and international producer of materials for lay theological education had shaped Sproul's vision for his own ministry, and with it life at Ligonier.[79]

While the publication of *Tabletalk* and the development of a well-honed video production and marketing team had helped to facilitate this transition, two major changes in the study center's leadership structure also made the shift from a relational, multifaceted ministry toward a mass-produced ministry possible. The first of these was a Biehl-inspired reorganization of the Ligonier board in 1979. It was this board, made up of ministry and business leaders from

---

[78]R. C. Sproul, "Right Now Counts Forever: Frustrations of a Christian Educator," *Tabletalk* 5, no. 4 (April 1981): 2.
[79]As individuals such as Boehmig and Sproul Jr. attest, these changes, while perhaps right for the success of the ministry, were not easy on Ligonier staff and family members; Boehmig, interview; Sproul Jr., interview.

Figure 4.8. With the video camera prominent in the foreground, this 1983 *Tabletalk* cover shows Sproul moving toward a more professional mode of dress and instruction.

across the nation, who eventually decided without Sproul's knowledge that Sproul's gifts would be best utilized if the ministry left behind its taxing and costly residential emphasis and focused instead on conducting a national ministry headquartered in a major metropolitan area.

Of course, this change could never have taken place when Dora Hillman was alive. Throughout the study center's first decade, no one had been as firm a supporter of Sproul or as generous with finances as Hillman. The study center's very location had been moved from Pittsburgh's Oakland district to its bucolic setting in Stahlstown because Hillman—"a thundering paradox of a woman," whom Sproul described as both an "exuberant Christian" and "willful"—had deemed the rural site appropriate.[80] It would have been extremely difficult for

---

[80] Sproul remarked in his eulogy for Hillman, "Only God knows the intensity of her will." See "A Thundering Paradox of a Woman," *Tabletalk* 6, no. 4 (October 1982): 2-3.

Sproul to leave Stahlstown while his principal benefactor was still alive. In the end he did not have to make such a difficult choice. Hillman died in late summer 1982. Shortly thereafter, the Ligonier board began moving ahead with plans for relocation to the Sun Belt city of Orlando.

Orlando was a strategic site not only for the thousands of tourists Disney World was attracting each year but also because it was relatively virgin territory for national ministries in the early 1980s. Originally, Sproul described the launch of his Orlando office not as a relocation, but as an expansion: "We are opening a new office in Orlando designed to have a base to reach people from a metropolitan center," he told readers of Ligonier's yearly update letter. Sproul noted the obvious, that "our remote location has been a serious detriment to outreach," but he assured his readers that in spite of the geographic shift and the downsizing of Ligonier staff "summer sessions will continue at our Ligonier campus."[81]

By August 1984, however, Sproul's trajectory was moving further and further from its former orbit. The Sproul family moved to Orlando with another Ligonier family and two single Ligonier staff members in November 1984. With the exception of the Rowleys, the rest of the Ligonier staff either found jobs in Stahlstown or dispersed to other ministry positions. Because the study center had already scheduled programming through summer 1985, Rowley stayed in Stahlstown for one more year before moving his family to Orlando in late summer 1985. In spite of Sproul's insistence that summer sessions would continue in Stahlstown, the 1985 session was the last to be held at Ligonier. The property was sold in late 1985 to a Christian drug rehabilitation ministry.[82]

In some ways Sproul remade himself (and his renamed Ligonier Ministries) in Orlando. Gone was the countercultural appeal as his plaid pants, turtlenecks, sunglasses, and long hair disappeared along with his relational, community-centered ministry. A well-oiled professional ministry took its place as together Sproul and Rowley built an evangelical media miniempire and developed R. C. Sproul and Ligonier Ministries into a marketable brand. In Orlando, Rowley sold off his increasingly outdated video equipment and rented space from the

---

[81] R. C. Sproul to LVSC friend, August 1984, box "Archives—Programs, 1985–1989," folder "Brochures," CCSA.

[82] This ministry closed in the mid-1990s, and the property was sold to a private businessman. The buildings have now been renovated into a lodge, bed and breakfast, and restaurant called Foggy Mountain Lodge.

local CBS station, whose crew handled all the filming.[83] From that point on Sproul was filmed most frequently on a specially made set at the front of an audience composed not of resident students but of local friends of the ministry with time to stop by the studio during recording. The move to Florida also crystallized a demographic shift in Sproul's target and actual audiences—now mostly middle-aged and middle-class professionals with little time for extended stays at a residential study center but with money to purchase Ligonier products.[84]

Fittingly, Sproul's videotaped sermons provide some of the best demonstrations of the ministry's transition away from its original countercultural appeal and collegiate emphasis toward a more formal, traditional, and mass-marketable teaching ministry. Watching a young, somewhat eccentric Sproul describe the holiness of God from behind the Ligonier pulpit in 1975 and watching the suit-and-tie-clad, nicely tanned Sproul deliver a lecture titled "Man, the Supreme Paradox" from Orlando's CBS studio in 1986 offers vastly different visual aesthetics and relational appeal.[85] In the latter lecture Sproul seems the consummate professional, far removed from the raw, sunglasses-bespectacled teacher of former years. The audience, unseen in the earlier tape but comfortable enough to blurt into Sproul's teaching with an unscripted question, becomes a part of the set in the latter video, functioning as a well-dressed, perfectly behaved studio audience. Ironically, it was video that made these changes clear. If one simply listens to the message, the same passionate voice and sharp logic can be heard in 1975 and 1986. As much as things had changed, continuities remained.

Throughout the rest of his ministry Sproul ranked among the leading American advocates of Reformed theology and lay theological education. Through his numerous books, videos, radio programs, and addresses at conferences and in his independent St. Andrew's Chapel in Sanford, Florida, Sproul arguably did as much as any popular evangelical preacher or media personality of his generation to bring theological education to the masses. His impact on the Christian study center movement, however, was less lasting. Originally one of

---

[83]Rowley, interview. Rowley described the transition in detail during his interview: "The studio, the CBS station, would supply all the equipment, the personnel to operate the equipment, and all of the lighting. And then I would go back and we would later edit the masters, put the titles on, develop a set of masters we would use for duplicating purposes. We were cranking them out."

[84]Sproul Jr. commented on a noticeable shift toward an older, more established demographic during his interview.

[85]My thanks to Jack Rowley for supplying me with these early Sproul videos.

the most sought-out voices in the American study center movement, Sproul's influence in the sphere declined as he gradually replaced a ministry rooted in place and hospitable presence with a ministry that increasingly favored ideas detached from relationship. It was a reductionism that both reflected and foreshadowed evangelicals' growing affinity for talking-head videos in which solitary teachers and self-proclaimed experts waxed eloquent on any number of theological themes. While this form of education was still lay theological education of a kind, it was no longer lay theological education rooted in a study center or in the larger Christian study center movement. Thus even as Sproul expanded his national reach through technology, his growing platform as a video-centric teacher was inversely related to his influence on the Christian study center movement he had once represented so compellingly. Ironically, his mantle was to some extent taken up by a group of radical Christians in Berkeley who took an intentional stand for place and people rather than the efficiency-driven ethos of a technological society.

5

NEW COLLEGE BERKELEY

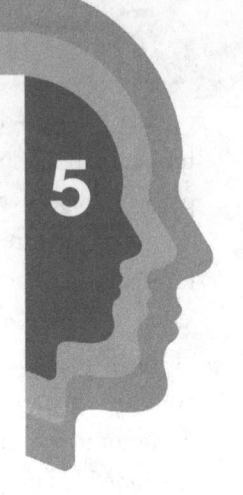

IN THE LATE 1960S and early 1970s Berkeley was about as far from the hills of Stahlstown, Pennsylvania, as one could get. Long a key shaper of countercultural trends in wider American culture, by 1969 Berkeley was also home to one of the continent's most ambitious and influential communities of countercultural Christians. Berkeley's Christian World Liberation Front (founded 1969)—a name inspired by Berkeley's revolutionary Third World Liberation Front (founded 1968)—represented Jesus people with an intellectual edge.[1] Efforts such as *Right On*, a street paper that became one of the Jesus movement's most significant and long-running publications, and its own free university, the Crucible, stood as intellectually informed models to which many other Jesus movement efforts aspired.

Both initiatives demonstrate the degree to which the Christian World Liberation Front benefited from the combination of intellectual vitality and countercultural activity that marked the university town. This context helped the community avoid the anti-intellectualism that marked much of the Jesus movement. Instead, Christian World Liberation Front leaders drew on the example of thinking evangelicals such as Francis Schaeffer and James Houston, whose learning communities were emerging as baby boomers' most compelling examples of culturally engaged and thinking evangelicalism. With these models

---

[1] Donald Heinz, "The Christian World Liberation Front," in *The New Religious Consciousness*, ed. Charles Y. Glock (Berkeley: University of California Press, 1976), 144; David W. Gill, interview with author, December 15, 2015.

in view, individuals in the Christian World Liberation Front launched a number of initiatives aimed at deepening the intellectual and cultural engagement of North American evangelicals. Eventually, some with Christian World Liberation Front ties moved on to develop an even more ambitious venture, New College Berkeley, a graduate school of theological and biblical studies for lay Christians. Founded in 1977, New College Berkeley, like its model, Regent College, sought to take graduate theological education to laypeople in innovative ways. The result of these efforts was an educational experiment, at times exciting, at times unwieldy, that offered North American evangelical laypeople a chance to experience graduate theological education Berkeley-style.

Hippies, Jesus, and Berkeley in the late 1960s

If the American counterculture had an epicenter in the late 1960s, it was Berkeley and the larger San Francisco Bay Area. In the years following the free speech protests of 1964, the University of California, Berkeley's Sproul Plaza and nearby Peoples Park and Telegraph Avenue joined other Bay Area locations such as the Haight-Ashbury District as hippie strongholds and countercultural seedbeds. In the face of an escalating conflict in Vietnam, the 1967 "summer of love" drew an estimated seventy-five thousand people to San Francisco in search of alternative lifestyles, trips, and gurus to those offered by parents and mainstream culture.[2]

The hoped-for utopia never materialized. As hundreds of thousands poured into the Haight, the summer of love began to deteriorate in the face of overcrowding, rampant drug use, venereal diseases, a predatory sexual culture, and organized crime. As a famous Haight-Ashbury broadsheet put it, "Rape is as common as bullshit on Haight Street." As the idealism of the counterculture faded, a handful of evangelical Christians began to experiment with forms of evangelistic outreach geared toward the physical and spiritual needs and bohemian sensibilities of their hippie neighbors. In late summer 1967 Ted and Liz Wise began reaching out to hippies and street people through the Living Room, an innovative coffeehouse ministry located on Page Street about a block from the intersection of Haight and Ashbury.[3]

---

[2]Charles Perry, *The Haight-Ashbury: A History* (New York: Random House, 1984), 229.
[3]See Larry Eskridge, *God's Forever Family: The Jesus People Movement in America* (New York: Oxford University Press, 2013), 29-33. For more on drug use, violence, and organized crime in the Haight-Ashbury District, see Perry, *Haight-Ashbury*; Robert Houriet, *Getting Back Together* (New York: Coward, McCann & Geoghegen, 1971), xix-xx.

Within two years an array of similarly contextualized ministries began popping up, first in California and then across the country. In summer 1968 two Christian coffeehouses and nightclubs were launched in Hollywood alone, while David Berg's Light Club began attracting a sizable following in Huntington Beach, and Chuck Smith's Calvary Chapel in Costa Mesa transitioned from stuffy fundamentalism to the nation's premier hippie church. In 1969 ministries with a countercultural bent spread to Seattle, Chicago, and Atlanta, among other places. Soon participants and observers alike began talking about Jesus people and a Jesus movement.[4] By the early 1970s the shift in America's spiritual landscape was undeniable. In March 1971 both *Newsweek* and the *Wall Street Journal* covered the new movement in front-page articles. In June *Time* followed suit, and by the end of 1971 the Jesus movement had been named the top religious news story of the year.[5] The Christian press was not to be left behind. Though the Jesus movement barely caught the attention of evangelical publishers in 1970, in 1971 evangelicalism's leading periodical, *Christianity Today*, published more than three dozen feature stories on the phenomenon. Even Billy Graham got in on the act. His 1971 book *The Jesus Generation* sold over half a million copies.[6]

Among the early Jesus people—or Jesus freaks, as they were often called—few were as truly countercultural as those who made up Berkeley's ambitiously named Christian World Liberation Front.[7] As an organization, the Christian World Liberation Front was part Jesus freak commune, part countercultural campus ministry, and part social-justice advocacy group. Its founder, Jack Sparks, was

---

[4]For a full treatment of these individuals and the ministries they launched, see Eskridge, *God's Forever Family*.

[5]Earl C. Gottschalk Jr., "Hip Culture Discovers a New Trip: Fervent, Foot-Stompin' Religion," *Wall Street Journal*, March 2, 1971; "The Jesus People," *Newsweek*, March 22, 1971; "The New Rebel Cry: Jesus Is Coming!," *Time*, June 21, 1971. See also Heinz, "Christian World Liberation Front," 143; Eskridge, *God's Forever Family*, 130-32.

[6]Eskridge, *God's Forever Family*, 132, 137-39, 335n44; Billy Graham, *The Jesus Generation* (Grand Rapids: Zondervan, 1971).

[7]The best early treatments of the Christian World Liberation Front include Don Heinz's unpublished PhD dissertation "Jesus in Berkeley" (Graduate Theological Union, 1976), along with his chapter, "The Christian World Liberation Front," in Charles Y. Glock's *The New Religious Consciousness* (Berkeley: University of California Press, 1976), 143-61; and Richard Quebedeaux, *The Young Evangelicals: Revolution in Orthodoxy* (New York: Harper & Row, 1974), 94-98. For Sparks's autobiographical take on the Christian World Liberation Front, see Jack N. Sparks, *God's Forever Family* (Grand Rapids: Zondervan, 1974). The best recent work on the Christian World Liberation Front can be found in David R. Swartz, *Moral Minority: The Evangelical Left in an Age of Conservatism* (Philadelphia: University of Pennsylvania Press, 2012), 86-110.

personal contact with African Americans during his weekly trips to Alameda County Juvenile Hall. Beginning in 1966, Gill and a friend preached and witnessed weekly to crowds of up to three hundred people at the juvenile center. In addition to leading weekend meetings and weeknight Bible studies, Gill also began publishing a weekly paper, *Straight to You*, for inmates.[18]

After his graduation from the University of California, Berkeley, in 1968, Gill continued his ministry at the juvenile hall for three years while he taught history to high school and junior high students during the day and studied part time for a master's in history at San Francisco State. During this time he first came into contact with the work of Francis Schaeffer. Gill had been interested in apologetics since high school. By 1969 he was already a fan of the writings of John Warwick Montgomery and was working Montgomery's historical apologetics into his master's thesis, but it was his 1969 discovery of Schaeffer's *The God Who Is There* that most shaped him.[19]

Gill was inspired by Schaeffer's "swashbuckling writings," which attempted to unite theology, art, and the history of philosophy under a biblically inspired worldview. Revealing both his esteem for Schaeffer and a visionary bent, Gill went on to ask whether the Swiss guru had "ever considered a sort of 'Farel House West' in Berkeley?" To the high school history teacher, evangelist, and budding religious entrepreneur, Berkeley seemed to offer "an ideal place to take over an old fraternity house and use it to confront modern men ... with the person of Jesus Christ."[20]

That Schaeffer responded to Gill's inquiry by offering him use of the L'Abri tape list and the names of a few L'Abri-friendly folks in the Bay Area rather than sustaining any discussion about the likelihood of establishing a L'Abri branch in Berkeley did not quell Gill's enthusiasm for Schaeffer or the work of L'Abri. Though Gill had had negative reactions to campus ministries such as Campus Crusade and Jesus movement ministries such as Linda Meissner's Jesus People Army (founded 1969) in Seattle, the allure of hearing L'Abri's Os Guinness speak was enticing enough to draw him to his first Christian World Liberation Front meeting in spring 1971. At the lecture Gill met Guinness and started a lifelong friendship, but he also discovered that Sparks and the Christian World Liberation Front were

---

[18]Gill, "Chapters in My Life," 5; Heinz, "Jesus in Berkeley," 123; Gill, "Autobiography."
[19]Gill, interview; Gill, "Chapters in My Life."
[20]David W. Gill to Francis A. Schaeffer, 1970, box 56, file 6, FSC. In his autobiography Gill uses the term *swashbuckling* to describe Schaeffer's writings.

a different breed of Jesus people. "These were not your normal Jesus freaks. These people were really thoughtful about life and politics, and yet they loved studying the Bible, and they really did love Jesus." To Gill, "the whole atmosphere" brimmed with "so much life, so much love."[21] He was hooked.

Gill soon became involved in a number of Christian World Liberation Front projects, but it was his work as a contributor for *Right On* that was especially significant. Biblically literate, energetic, well educated, and fluent in the student scene at University of California, Berkeley, Gill was exactly the type of person Sparks needed to bring better content, greater professionalism, and a degree of stability to the paper. Within six months Sparks offered Gill the position of editor. Gill accepted the editorship of *Right On* on the condition that the Christian World Liberation Front break its pattern of all-male leadership by appointing Sharon Gallagher coeditor.[22]

Figure 5.1. David Gill speaking on the steps of University of California, Berkeley's Sproul Plaza circa 1972.

Sharon Gallagher, from L'Abri to Berkeley

Gallagher was a natural choice for the position. By 1971 she had been working with *Right On* three months longer than Gill and had proven herself as a writer and film critic. Her résumé was further enhanced by her connections to significant figures in the evangelical world. As a teenager in a Los Angeles–area Plymouth Brethren assembly, she had been mentored by Laurel and Ward Gasque during the years Ward studied at Fuller Theological Seminary.[23] Following high school, Gallagher went on to study at Westmont College, where she came into contact with Schaeffer, Guinness, and other members of the L'Abri Fellowship when they

---

[21] Gill, interview. For Gill's assessment of Campus Crusade and Meissner's ministry, see Heinz, "Jesus in Berkeley," 123-24.
[22] Heinz, "Jesus in Berkeley," 125; Gill, interview.
[23] Gill, interview; see also, "Sharon Gallagher and the Politics of Spiritual Community," in Swartz, *Moral Minority*, 86-110.

visited Westmont in fall 1968. Gallagher began reading Schaeffer's books, and in 1970 she and a friend from Westmont celebrated their college graduation by spending four weeks at Swiss L'Abri. For Gallagher, L'Abri provided an "exciting" and "intellectually stimulating" setting in which she could finally engage topics in art and movies that her church had designated as beyond the pale of Christian pursuit and analysis. "Coming from a fundamentalist background where a lot of the things that I loved were verboten," Gallagher was thrilled "to have somebody, you know, very Christian, talk about movies, talk about art, talk about books." For Gallagher, the entire experience was "very liberating."[24]

L'Abri also gave her what she describes as "a taste for Christian community." Inspired to further explore all of these new trajectories, Gallagher decided to defer her acceptance to a PhD program in counseling psychology at the University of Southern California and further explore Christian community. "I had been so profoundly affected not just by what I had been taught at L'Abri, but by a sense of Christian community in the countercultural setting, that I wanted more of that. . . . So I thought, *I've been in school my whole life. I'm going to take a year off and do something else.*" During her junior year of college Gallagher had visited the Christian World Liberation Front and left impressed with the group's work and spirit. Following her visit to L'Abri, she again visited Berkeley. This time she decided to stay.[25] When her talents as a writer became known in the Christian World Liberation Front, she "was quickly put to work for *Right On*."[26] Drawing on the techniques she learned at L'Abri, Gallagher began writing film reviews and articles that covered current events with an explicitly

Figure 5.2. The staff of *Right On* in 1971: Gallagher, front left; Gill, center.

---

[24]Sharon Gallagher, interview with author, December 3, 2015, Berkeley; Laurel Gasque, W. Ward Gasque, and Carl E. Armerding, interview with author, October 23, 2015, Vancouver.
[25]Unless otherwise stated, all quotations and details in this paragraph are drawn from my interview with Gallagher.
[26]Sharon Gallagher, "From Right On to Radix: A Short History," *Radix* 11, no. 1 (August 1979): 3.

evangelistic twist. The quality of her work caught the attention of fellow *Right On* staffers and made her selection as coeditor seem natural to Gill.

Lay Theological Education in Print

The 1971 appointment of Gill and Gallagher as coeditors marked an important shift in the history of the fledgling publication. Beginning in late 1970 and growing more pronounced under the editorship of Gill and Gallagher, *Right On* gradually transitioned from a street paper into a more professional and nuanced publication. Observers of the paper began to notice "more articles which were an intellectual presentation and defense of the Christian faith," many of which followed "the kind of reasoning one might find at L'Abri or Wheaton College." The paper's layout also shifted, from a loose amalgam of stories and graphics to a tighter layout by May 1971.[27] The September 1971 edition provided the names of the *Right On* staff for the first time and listed Gill and Gallagher as coeditors.

Under Gallagher and Gill's leadership, the staff at *Right On* began to conceive of its audience not as street people or anti-intellectual Jesus freaks but as literate and thoughtful Christians and curious non-Christians. Under the direction of Gill and Gallagher, *Right On* attempted to highlight the work of individuals and movements that could function as models for a generation of countercultural Christians who had left Billy Graham and "establishment evangelicalism" behind.[28] Bonhoeffer's *Life Together* came in for a positive review, as did other books on communal living such as Dave and Neta Jackson's *Living Together in a World Falling Apart*, which described life in several Christian communes. Sparks himself reviewed E. F. Schumacher's *Small Is Beautiful* and urged his readers to "Get this one and *read* it."[29]

Like many evangelicals, the *Right On* staff showed a special appreciation for C. S. Lewis, the Inklings (a group of writers headed by Lewis and J. R. R. Tolkien), and Lewis's friend and writer Dorothy Sayers. *Right On* devoted nearly four full pages of its April 1972 issue to C. S. Lewis and his fellow Oxford Christian intellectuals. In addition to articles such as "The Inklings of Oxford: An Introduction" and "Dorothy Sayers an Artist for All Seasons," the issue also included an interview

---

[27]Heinz, "Jesus in Berkeley," 283-84.
[28]Heinz, "Jesus in Berkeley," 291, 293; Quebedeaux, *Young Evangelicals*, 28-36.
[29]Jack Buckley, "Media: Life Together," *Right On* 6, no. 1 (August 1974): 4; Jack Sparks, "Small Is Beautiful," *Right On* (July–August 1974): 4.

with Regent College principal James Houston. Because Houston had been personally acquainted with Lewis, the interview offered readers the sense of having personal access to Lewis. Over the course of the next decade, articles such as *Right On*'s tribute to "J. R. R. Tolkien: Man of Another Age" or Presbyterian minister Earl Palmer's five-page discussion titled "Theological Themes in C. S. Lewis' Fiction" kept Lewis and others among the Inklings before the eyes of the publication's readers.[30] The attention the paper devoted to Lewis throughout these years demonstrates the Cambridge professor's enduring power to inspire American evangelicals who were looking for models capable of blending a winsome and orthodox faith with intellectual curiosity and scholarly proficiency.

Another individual who frequently came in for positive treatment in the pages of *Right On* during the early to mid-1970s was Schaeffer. While L'Abri was mentioned in passing as early as 1970, it was not until May 1972 that Schaeffer received extensive treatment in *Right On*.[31] In a review of Schaeffer's recent book *The Church at the End of the Twentieth Century* (1970) Gill endorsed Schaeffer with only a small caveat. While he admitted that he differed with Schaeffer "on some points of his thinking," Gill poured on high praise: "I can say that his works are among the very most insightful, perceptive, creative, and stimulating that I have ever read. They are all highly recommended."[32] In 1974 *Right On* gave three full pages to an interview with Schaeffer in which the American expatriate rehearsed many of his most popular themes. Three months later the publication gave similar treatment to Schaeffer's son, Frank, in a conversation that examined the possibility of Christian art.[33] It was only in 1977, following the publication of Schaeffer's book and film project *How Should We Then Live?*, that members of the publication's staff began to voice discontent with the direction of Schaeffer's work.[34]

---

[30]Jack Buckley, "The Inklings of Oxford: An Introduction," *Right On* 3, no. 10 (April 1972): 5; Donna Dong, "Dorothy Sayers an Artist for All Seasons," *Right On* 3, no. 10 (April 1972): 6; James Houston, "Reflections on C. S. Lewis," *Right On* 3, no. 10 (April 1972): 5; "J. R. R. Tolkien: Man of Another Age," *Right On* 5, no. 3 (October 1973): 9; Earl Palmer, "Theological Themes in C. S. Lewis' Fiction," *Radix* 9, no. 1 (August 1977): 12-16.
[31]Heinz, "Jesus in Berkeley," 281.
[32]David W. Gill, "Schaeffer!," *Right On* 3, no. 11 (May 1972): 7.
[33]Danny Smith with Francis A. Schaeffer, "A Conversation with Francis Schaeffer," *Right On* 5, no. 10 (April 1974): 1, 2, 10; Dale A. Johnson and Franky Schaeffer, "A Conversation with Franky Schaeffer," *Right On* 6, no. 1 (August 1974): 3, 8. Notably, the younger Schaeffer's cynicism, which became a characteristic feature of his later speaking and writing career both within and outside evangelicalism, was on full display during the conversation.
[34]Sharon Gallagher, "How Should We Then Live?," *Radix* 8, no. 4 (April 1977): 12.

While Schaeffer and Lewis were both common heroes within American evangelicalism, *Right On* was notable for its efforts to open evangelicals up to outside voices. From their first involvement with the paper, Gallagher and Gill attempted to get their readers—and by implication the larger evangelical world—to wrestle with the work of countercultural voices such as Theodore Roszak, and new movements within evangelicalism such as the socially conscious 1973 Chicago Declaration and feminist voices from the Evangelical Women's Caucus (founded 1974), including Berkeley's own Virginia Hearn. While Gill supported all these efforts, he most frequently used his regular "Radical Christian" column and various other book reviews and articles as a means of introducing American evangelicals to the work of Jacques Ellul, a French philosopher and ethicist who emphasized the dehumanizing impact of the current political system and the "technological society" that undergirded it. For Gill, understanding and disseminating Ellul's thought became a lifelong educational passion. In addition to writing his 1979 PhD dissertation, "The Word of God in the Ethics of Jacques Ellul," on Ellul, he spent his first sabbatical year (1984–1985) with Ellul in France and organized the founding of the International Jacques Ellul Society in 2000.[35]

Throughout the 1970s *Right On* continued to function as one of the foremost educational arms of the evangelical left—a loosely connected network of evangelicals who maintained traditional orthodoxy while adopting some of the most prominent causes (social justice, withdrawal from Vietnam, mutual disarmament, etc.) of liberal politics.[36] Its staying power was a testament to both its unique place within American evangelicalism

Figure 5.3. Gill had the chance to visit Jacques Ellul at his home in Bordeaux, France, in summer 1982.

---

[35]David W. Gill, "The Word of God in the Ethics of Jacques Ellul" (PhD diss., University of Southern California, 1979), http://search.proquest.com.proxy.its.virginia.edu/pqdtglobal/docview/1655602495/citation/99EB195A1B284C39PQ/1. For more on Gill's appreciation for Ellul and the International Jacques Ellul Society, see Gill, "Autobiography"; International Jacques Ellul Society, https://ellul.org (accessed July 20, 2016).
[36]Swartz, *Moral Minority*.

and the dedication and capacity of its editorial team—especially Gallagher, who became sole editor in fall 1973 when Gill left Berkeley to pursue doctoral study at the University of Southern California in Los Angeles.

Right On survived the breakup of the Christian World Liberation Front in summer 1975, when Sparks left the organization, taking a third of God's forever family, and the Christian World Liberation Front mailing list, with him.[37] When the Berkeley Christian Coalition was founded in fall 1975 to replace the Christian World Liberation Front, *Right On* took its place along with four other former Christian World Liberation Front ministries under the coalition's umbrella.[38] Within the coalition, *Right On* continued to mature. By the end of the decade the publication, like all Berkeley Christian Coalition ministries, became an independent entity responsible for financing its own budget.[39]

Maturation also meant a shift away from the counterculture and student revolution. In summer 1976 "after some years of feeling uncomfortable with the name *Right On*," Gallagher and the publication's staff adopted a new name—*Radix*, Latin for "root/base." Under this new moniker, which pointed to the longtime emphasis of individuals such as Gill to inspire "radical" (i.e., root-based) Christianity, the publication continued working to serve what Gallagher called its "dual purpose: evangelism for non-believers and education for the Christian community."[40]

The Crucible: A Forum for Radical Christian Studies

In the early 1970s Gill had more energy, vision, and ambition than any one Christian World Liberation Front project could contain. By mid-1972 he was ready to build on the platform his position as coeditor of *Right On* and Christian World Liberation Front elder afforded him by expanding his educational efforts beyond the printed word. For some time individuals in the Christian

---

[37]Heinz, "Jesus in Berkeley," 477-78. Sparks had become a bishop in what would become the Evangelical Orthodox Church (founded 1979). The Evangelical Orthodox Church was admitted into the North American Antiochian Orthodox Church in 1987. For more on Sparks's transition, see Christian World Liberation Front, "From the Very Beginning," 1975, box 1, folder 51, "CWLF-Member Outreach Correspondence, 1975–1977," CWLFC; Eskridge, *God's Forever Family*, 262-63.
[38]"Berkeley Christian Coalition," circa 1976, box 1, folder 13, "The Crucible," CWLFC.
[39]This shift occurred early in 1979. See "Berkeley Christian Coalition Restructured," February 1979, box 1, folder 4, "BCC," CWLFC.
[40]Sharon Gallagher to people, July 1976, box 1, folder 56, "Right On/Radix," CWLFC; Gallagher, "From Right On to Radix: Notes on Our Purpose, Vision, and Name," *Right On* 8, no. 1 (August 1976): 2; Gallagher, "From Right On to Radix: A Short History." Gill began emphasizing "radical" Christianity in 1972 ("Berkeley Christian Coalition Restructured").

World Liberation Front had discussed the possibility of founding a Christian educational alternative modeled on the free universities that popped up across the nation in the wake of the 1964 Berkeley Free Speech Movement and the founding of the Free University of Berkeley in 1965.[41] In direct contrast to the hierarchies and bureaucratic mazes that defined the nation's traditional universities, free universities were dedicated to maintaining an alternate educational forum where "anyone can teach and anyone can learn" with little or no financial constraints or bureaucratic overhead. Tens of thousands of individuals of all ages took part in courses at one of the nation's nearly fifty different free universities before the initial phase of the free university movement peaked in 1971.[42]

The Christian World Liberation Front's push for a Christian Liberation University of Berkeley, or CLUB, as it was often referred to, fit well within this framework and quickly became one of the foremost examples of a Christian free university. Initially, the fledgling educational venture was led by Ron Roper, a Christian World Liberation Front member with an affinity for philosophy and Reformed theology.[43] In early 1972 Christian Liberation University of Berkeley members met at Christian World Liberation Front's Dwight House "several times a week for prayer, lecture, question-answer, discussion, and tape listening" around the theme "On the Nature of Academic Witness." The theme for the Christian Liberation University of Berkeley's spring quarter, "Towards a Radically Christian Education Enterprise," demonstrated the group's desire to develop an educational environment that was simultaneously countercultural and thoroughly Christian. Roper and other leaders of the Christian Liberation University of Berkeley looked optimistically toward the future. Perceiving "the great desirability of living and studying more intimately and identifiably as God's People in Berkeley," Christian Liberation University of Berkeley organizers hoped for "the liberation of a Fraternity House for just this purpose."[44]

---

[41]The first three free universities were all located in the Bay Area. See William A. Draves, *The Free University: A Model for Lifelong Learning* (Chicago: Association Press, 1980). See also Jane Lichtman, *Bring Your Own Bag: A Report on Free Universities* (Washington, DC: American Association for Higher Education, 1973).

[42]Draves, *Free University*, 16, 47-48, 93-97. In spring 1966 the Free University of Berkeley enrolled 750 students. When the movement picked up again in 1978, enrollment in the sixteen largest free universities ranged from 6,000 to 28,000 (pp. 50, 81).

[43]David W. Gill email to author, "Christian Liberation University Question," July 21, 2016; Hearn and Hearn, interview.

[44]CWLF, "Christian Liberation University: CWLF Newsletter," 1972, box 1, folder 51, "CWLF-Member Outreach Correspondence, 1975–1977," CWLFC.

Before the 1972 academic year started, however, Roper left Berkeley in order to study at the Toronto Institute for Christian Studies, an effort that he believed provided a working model for what the Berkeley group was considering. Gill stepped in to fill the leadership vacuum by calling a meeting at his home and organizing a steering committee that soon included Sparks, Gallagher, Virginia and Walter Hearn, Jack Buckley, Don Heinz, and several others.[45] Together Gill and his group of countercultural friends rebranded the Christian Liberation University of Berkeley as the Crucible.

Almost to a person the individuals who were present at the founding of the Crucible were among the best-educated members of the Christian World Liberation Front. Both Buckley and Heinz were ordained ministers with seminary degrees and an interest in communal living and alternative education.[46] Buckley was the director of the Covenant House, a small Christian community with a L'Abri-like emphasis on reasoned faith that was affiliated with a Presbyterian church in Berkeley, and Heinz, a Lutheran minister, was a PhD candidate at Berkeley's Graduate Theological Union, the largest affiliation of seminaries in the country. The steering committee also included two earned PhDs (Sparks, statistics; Walter Hearn, biochemistry). Hearn had worked for years as a tenured professor at Iowa State University before "dropping out" in spring 1972 when he and his wife, Virginia, moved to Berkeley in search of Christian community and simple living. In line with his self-described "experimentalist" personality, Hearn relished the chance to escape the academic rat race in favor of an experiment in countercultural living, which for Hearn included foraging in dumpsters for unspoiled food and other usable items. An emphasis on simple living did not imply simple thinking, however. Both Walter and Virginia Hearn stayed abreast of current trends within science and the evangelical world through their combined work as freelance editors and Walter's involvement in the American Scientific Association.[47]

---

[45]Hearn and Hearn, interview; "The Crucible: A Forum for Radical Christian Studies, Winter Quarter, Jan-Mar 1973," Fall 1972, box 1, folder 13, "The Crucible," CWLFC.

[46]In an interview Earl Palmer referred to Buckley as "a brilliant young man." Buckley later joined Palmer's staff at First Presbyterian Church of Berkeley. See Earl Palmer, interview with author, August 17, 2016.

[47]Hearn and Hearn, interview; Walter Hearn, "Somewhere Between: A Journey Toward Simplicity," *Radix* 8, no. 4 (April 1977): 10-11, 16-17. Before leaving academia, Hearn contributed a chapter to E. M. Blaiklock's *Why I Am Still a Christian* (Grand Rapids: Zondervan, 1971). In 2016 the Hearns estimated that they had edited over two hundred books since moving to Berkeley.

Though neither Virginia Hearn nor Sharon Gallagher had graduate degrees, both had supplemented their undergraduate education through extensive reading, interviewing, travel, editing, writing, and seminar and coursework at L'Abri, Regent College, and elsewhere. By fall 1972 Virginia Hearn had worked for years as an editor, most notably for InterVarsity's *His* magazine, and Gallagher had nearly two years under her belt at *Right On* in addition to her experiences at L'Abri and participation in the 1971 and 1972 summer schools at Regent College. Both women had felt the sharp edge of sexism within the evangelical community and were intent on bringing biblically rooted egalitarianism to the fledgling educational institution.[48] Unlike most evangelical ventures at the time, including the 1973 Evangelicals for Social Action conference, where Gallagher "felt a little intimidated, as if she had walked into an eastern men's club," the Crucible was an egalitarian learning community from the start. Well before the Evangelical Women's Caucus was formed in 1974—after the few women who attended the original Evangelicals for Social Action conference noticed that it seemed easier for evangelical men to openly discuss the problems of racism than sexism—the Crucible was offering courses that addressed sexism head-on. When the Crucible launched its first full term in fall 1972, one of its four courses was Gallagher's Women's Liberation in the Context of Radical Christianity. The following term the budding feminist followed up her original offering with a course titled Liberation and the Christian Brothers and Sisters.[49]

Gill's own intellectual development also shaped the Crucible's progressive stance regarding gender roles and the role of women teachers. As the director of the Crucible, Gill's growing interest in the radical church tradition exerted a strong influence within the Christian World Liberation Front's free university. In the history of radical Christian sects, Gill saw "recurring emphases on peacemaking, community, simplicity, a working priesthood of all believers" and, significantly for the future of the Crucible, "a better record on the 'women's issue.'" Inspired by this radical tradition, Gill subtitled the Crucible "A Forum

---

[48]Sharon Gallagher, "Radical Evangelicalism: A Conference Report," *Radical Religion* 1, nos. 3 & 4 (Summer-Fall 1974): 61-64; Sharon Gallagher and Robert L. Burt, "A Conversation with Sharon Gallagher," *New Conversations* (Winter/Spring 1976); Gallagher, "How Should We Then Live?"; Virginia Hearn, "Women's Place in the Evangelical Milieu: Is Progress Possible?," *Radix* 8, no. 4 (April 1977): 18-19; Virginia Hearn, *Our Struggle to Serve: The Stories of 15 Evangelical Women* (Waco, TX: Word Books, 1979).

[49]Gallagher, "Radical Evangelicalism," 64; Quebedeaux, *Young Evangelicals*, 95; "The Crucible: A Forum for Radical Christian Studies, Winter Quarter, Jan–Mar 1973."

for Radical Christian Studies." For Gill the use of the word *radical* was strategic. "By 'radical Christianity' we mean that we are not institution oriented or tradition oriented but rather are determined to uncover the *roots* of the Christian faith and explore the ramifications of our position in as many areas as possible."[50]

By spring semester 1973 the number and diversity of Crucible courses, students, and instructors led Gill (a bit tongue-in-cheek) to declare the Crucible to be "the fastest growing free university in Berkeley." For only $10 a course—or half that if one purchased a $10 Crucible membership, which also granted access to the Crucible's small book and tape library at Dwight House— students could take part in "courses specializing in open-eyed realism and based on the kind of radical Christian commitment that stands up to both analysis and experience."[51] On a practical level, the latter emphasis was a key aspect of the Crucible's draw. For individuals educated within the confines of established institutions, the Crucible offered more than just knowledge; it offered intimacy and a holistic experience. Initially, classes were usually composed of about ten people and were informal affairs where people were free to sit on the floor, enter into discussion with the instructor, or in some instances bring their infant to class.[52]

As students and teachers at the Crucible dedicated themselves to creating a space where "the pursuit of truth in all areas of life" could take place, they were, with varying degrees of intentionality, bringing the emphases of learning communities such as L'Abri and Regent College to bear in a form contextualized to Berkeley.[53] As the Crucible grew into one of the largest and most intellectually rigorous free universities within the Jesus movement, its momentum flowed into the Christian World Liberation Front and wider Christian community as individuals involved in the free university also took part in the Christian World Liberation Front's Spiritual Counterfeits Project and "book raps" on authors

---

[50]Gill, "Chapters in My Life: David Gill," 5; "The Crucible: A Forum for Radical Christian Studies, Winter Quarter, Jan–Mar 1973."

[51]"The Crucible: A Forum for Radical Christian Studies, Winter Quarter, Jan–Mar 1973"; "The Crucible: A Forum for Radical Christian Studies, Spring Quarter, Apr–Jun 1973."

[52]Numerous written summaries and photos of early Crucible classes can be found in box 1, folder 13, "The Crucible," CWLFC.

[53]Swartz, *Moral Minority*, 106. Later in the decade, the impulse for education within the heirs of the Jesus movement spawned "discipleship schools" rather than free universities. One of the most notable of these was the Vineyard School of Discipleship, founded by Kenn Gullikson as part of the Vineyard Christian Fellowship of Beverly Hills in 1975.

such as Schaeffer, Dorothy Sayers, and John Warwick Montgomery at Logos, an independent Christian bookstore at the corner of Channing and Telegraph.[54]

Yet the Crucible's initial success was not enough to quell looming uncertainty about its future. Gill's departure in summer 1973 for graduate study in Southern California left the Crucible without its founding director and most compelling voice. Gill's replacement as Crucible director was Don Heinz, who was writing a PhD dissertation at Berkeley's Graduate Theological Union based on his experiences as a participant-observer at the Christian World Liberation Front. Heinz shared Gill's commitment to alternative education but supplemented it with a stronger emphasis on communal living. Over summer 1973 Heinz used a series of planning meetings and potlucks at the Hearns's "Troll House" to put forth "A Modest Proposal for Crucible: A Community for Life-Style and Learning." Heinz's proposal stemmed from his sense that "the most popular [Crucible] courses seemed to be those dealing with life-style" rather than the more theoretical or biblical courses. Looking back to a model that Gill was already beginning to move away from, Heinz posed the question, "Can there be a Berkeley L'Abri?"[55]

Over the course of the 1973–1974 academic year, Heinz worked to make his vision for a L'Abri-style work-study community a reality in Berkeley. As before, the Crucible offered an array of courses ranging from Fran and Emmanuel Osseo-Asare's Inter-Racial Marriage to Walt and Virginia Hearn's Writers' Workshop to Carole Craig's course On Death, Dying, and Grief along with The Lifestyle of the Single Woman, which Craig cotaught with Judith Sanderson. Keith Craig's course Gourmet Cooking for the Single Person was yet another example of the strong lifestyle emphasis that Heinz brought to the Crucible.[56] During the winter quarter Heinz cut the length of the courses to two weeks, complementing the Crucible's standard program with what he described as "a separate work-study community" that was "coming into being as a second Crucible focus." Throughout the 1973–1974 academic year, Heinz threw most of his energy into this residential branch of the Crucible by organizing discussions of Benjamin Zablocki's *The Joyful Community* and often devoting the

---

[54] Christian World Liberation Front, "Summer of 1973 Newsletter"; "The Crucible: A Forum for Radical Christian Studies, Spring Quarter, Apr–Jun 1973."

[55] Donald Heinz, "A Modest Proposal for Crucible: A Community for Life-Style and Learning," July 17, 1973, box 1, folder 13, "The Crucible," CWLFC.

[56] "Crucible," Fall 1973, box 1, folder 13, "The Crucible," CWLFC.

better part of his letters to Crucible supporters to descriptions of the development of the work-study community rather than its standard courses.[57]

By May 1974 the Crucible as a free university was on the verge of collapse. Writing from Southern California, Gill took to the pages of *Right On* to comment on the Crucible's uncertain future. Gill noted that "rumors" had reached him that "'The Crucible: A Forum for Radical Christian Studies' in Berkeley is about to cease." Reflecting on the Crucible's short history, Gill stated that he would be "very disappointed if The Crucible dies in its childhood." Though Gill was "well aware of the very relative value of education institutions as compared with educational experiences themselves," he still insisted that "institutions have value." Educational institutions "help to structure and order ... learning experience" and possessed the potential to "make visible for a large group what was previously a blessing only for the privileged initiates." To Gill's mind this was exactly what the Crucible, as originally conceived, promised to do: "The Crucible made public some processes that many of us were enjoying privately. There was some sacrifice involved to be sure, but it seemed worth it in view of the sterility of secular education."[58]

In the end the rumors of the Crucible's death turned out to be exaggerated. At the conclusion of the 1974 academic year, Heinz left the directorship of the Crucible, and the decision was made to hire a director from outside. Sparks and the Crucible steering committee decided on Bernard "Bernie" Adeney (later Adeney-Risakotta). From the start Adeney-Risakotta, the long-haired son of lifelong missionaries to China, proved to be a good fit for the program. Over the next four years Adeney-Risakotta led the Crucible out of its unstable infancy and through the upheaval surrounding the departure of Jack Sparks and the breakup of the Christian World Liberation Front and formation of the Berkeley Christian Coalition. Under the Berkeley Christian Coalition, the Crucible gained greater independence, though it continued to make use of coalition buildings, especially Dwight House, for its courses. Under Adeney-Risakotta, the Crucible pivoted away from the counterculture sensibilities that drove it in its early years. In fall 1974 the Crucible's staff began referring to the

---

[57]Donald Heinz to Crucible people, January 9, 1974, CWLFC; Donald Heinz to people, September 22, 1973, CWLFC.
[58]David W. Gill, "The Radical Christian: Education," *Right On* 5, no. 11 (May 1974): 7. Gill maintained his "Radical Christian" column throughout his time in Southern California.

program as "A Forum for *Radically* Christian Studies" rather than "A Forum for *Radical* Christian Studies."[59] Less noticeable but more significant was an accompanying shift in the content and style of the Crucible's course offerings.

In Adeney-Risakotta's first year, Crucible course offerings took the form of slightly expanded Sunday school lessons. Sparks offered a Sunday morning "Bible Study on Exodus" and Jack Buckley led "Discussions from a Reformed Perspective." A course in New Testament Greek and the "regular meetings of Inter-Varsity Christian Fellowship" rounded out the stripped-down and Christianized course offering.[60] By 1975 the Crucible had once again developed the capacity to offer a high number of courses, but the shift in focus from an emphasis on integrating Christianity with lifestyle and the counterculture was mostly gone. Courses now fell into three primary categories—biblical studies, theology, and Christian perspectives—and a greater percentage of Crucible courses seemed to be aimed at Christian students who wanted to grow deeper in their faith. Occasionally, however, courses still appeared that would have had a hard time gaining the acceptance of most evangelical Sunday school superintendents. In fall 1976 Crucible students could sign up for Ecology: The Crisis and the Christian, and the next spring Gallagher taught Biblical Feminism, a course whose less strident title reflected the cultural shifts that were changing America, even in places such as Berkeley, as the radical sixties mellowed through the seventies.[61]

New College Berkeley: The Crucible Grows Up

By the time Gallagher gave her 1977 variation on her favorite theme, the Crucible was no longer the sole venture in evangelical lay education in Berkeley. Since he had left Berkeley in summer 1973, Gill had held on to his dream of being part of an alternative educational community in the Bay Area. By 1976, perhaps emboldened by his academic success at the University of Southern California, where he was nearing the final stages of a PhD program, Gill realized the time had come to act on his dream by writing to Earl Palmer. Palmer, well known in the Berkeley area and beyond as an excellent preacher, had earned

---

[59]"The Crucible: A Forum for Radically Christian Studies," Fall 1974, box 1, folder 13, "The Crucible," CWLFC; Gill, interview.
[60]Bernard Adeney, "The Crucible Sprouts Anew in Berkeley," Summer 1974, box 1, folder 13, "The Crucible," CWLFC.
[61]Todd Gitlin, *The Sixties: Years of Hope, Days of Rage* (New York: Bantam, 1993), 427-33.

an undergraduate degree from Berkeley before going on to graduate work at Princeton Theological Seminary. Since 1970 he had served as senior pastor of Berkeley's historic two-thousand-member First Presbyterian Church, which was two blocks from the Berkeley campus.[62]

In Palmer, Gill saw a potential partner with intellectual sensibilities and the establishment connections he desperately needed. Writing to Palmer in March 1976, Gill laid out his conviction regarding "the great need and potential" for what he now described as "a 'Regent College-style' ministry in Berkeley." In Gill's mind launching a version of Regent College in Berkeley made sense. Gill believed that a lay-oriented school would avoid coming into direct competition with the established seminaries that made up the Graduate Theological Union. Furthermore, he counted on the city itself to be a major draw for students. "The least worry of all, I am convinced, would be students. Berkeley would be a natural, an ideal location." Palmer, who was familiar with Gill through the young scholar's work in the Christian World Liberation Front and his articles in *Right On*, wrote back with a positive response a few days later. "I fully share your vision that a Regent type College is right for Berkeley, and I believe it could have a very significant ministry with wide implications," Palmer opined.[63]

Gill and Palmer decided to host two informational meetings in 1976, one at San Francisco's Menlo Park Presbyterian Church (near Stanford University) and another at Palmer's church in Berkeley. Approximately fifty of Palmer's and Gill's friends attended the first informational meeting in Berkeley, and around thirty attended the Menlo Park meeting. Many of those who attended demonstrated enthusiasm for the venture. Ten of the roughly eighty individuals offered to serve on a monthly study committee to further explore the feasibility of the new school. This study committee, chaired by Gill, included Earl Palmer along with Crucible faithfuls such as Walt and Virginia Hearn and Sharon Gallagher as well as newcomers such as Cal Farnham, Craig Anderson, Robert Schoon, Bev Schmidt, and Bob Baylis. After six months of planning, the study committee became a board of directors when the New College for Advanced Christian Studies was officially founded on April 7, 1977.[64]

---

[62]Gill, email to author, December 1, 2016.
[63]David W. Gill to Earl Palmer, March 15, 1976, private collection; Earl Palmer to David W. Gill, March 24, 1976, private collection.
[64]Earl Palmer, foreword to David W. Gill, *The Opening of the Christian Mind: Taking Every Thought Captive to Christ* (Downers Grove, IL: Inter Varsity Press, 1989), 9-12.

From its inception, the New College for Advanced Christian Studies's lay emphasis was born out of the radical discipleship of the Anabaptist tradition, the Brethren rejection of a two-class ecclesial framework that distinguished between clergy and the laity, and a rich Reformed theology culled in part from Francis Schaeffer but also from European Reformed thinkers such as Karl Barth and Jacques Ellul.[65] Gill's desire to make New College a degree-granting graduate institution on the order of Regent College, rather than a free university or independent study center, also developed out of his own experiences. Gill was familiar with the lengths to which the Christian World Liberation Front and leaders at the Crucible had gone to try to influence the culture of the University of California, Berkeley. As early as 1974, he had urged Christians to counter modern education's "lack of a coherent and consistent world-view" by forming "new educational institutions to serve the people . . . at all levels" and by working to found "institutes . . . planted right next to the secular school or university." In regard to the latter need, Gill held up Regent College as "an example at which all Christians can rejoice."[66]

By the time Gill penned these reflections in spring 1974, Regent College had replaced L'Abri as his primary educational model. Gill, with his eyes set on a PhD (an educational choice inspired by the example of Regent), was already moving away from Schaeffer's more intellectually isolated model. Furthermore, with the benefit of hindsight, he was now able to take better stock of his own experiences at the Crucible. These reflections led Gill to believe that Christians would "never . . . penetrate the University of California and the academy" through "self-accredited study centers."[67] Instead, he was coming to see that Christians needed a more "muscled up" means by which they could approach the academy as academic insiders and peers rather than outsiders. Regent's "first-class faculty" and continuing ability to demonstrate what Gill described as "the progressive spirit for which we have long been looking" became his gold standard.[68]

Gill's interest in Regent College did not go unnoticed in Vancouver. By fall 1976 word of the proposed Berkeley venture had reached Regent principal James Houston. During a 1976 trip to Stanford, Houston learned of a group working "to have something more like the L'Abri experiment" in the Bay Area and Earl

---

[65]Gill, email, December 1, 2016.
[66]Gill, "Radical Christian: Education."
[67]Gill, interview.
[68]Gill, "Radical Christian: Education."

Palmer's efforts to "organize something at Berkeley." Houston—then vigorously promoting the replication of Regent in places such as College Park, Maryland—saw in Palmer's efforts a clear example of Regent's success. Writing to Jim Hiskey in Maryland, Houston observed, "Now the church leaders have suddenly realised the tremendous potential there is in the whole of the area and they are all scrambling to do something. They see the success of what's happening at Regent and already they understand clearly what is going forward at College Park campus, and so this is obviously the motive behind Earl Palmer's rallying letter."[69]

Houston had already urged Palmer and Gill to "collaborate with other leaders in the area" before going forward with the project. To Houston's mind, the best scenario for Gill, and potentially Houston's own efforts to replicate Regent in the Bay Area, was a slower process that would allow Gill to spend "two or three years with us before going back to the Bay Area." Postponement of the Berkeley venture, however, was not an option that Gill and Palmer were ready to consider. Rather than spending several years learning the ropes at Regent College, Gill jumped directly into work as the project director of New College Berkeley.

Gill's decision not to follow Houston's timeline did not mean that he distanced himself from Houston and Regent College. Gill worked intentionally to develop close ties with Houston and other Regent College veterans such as Carl Armerding and Ward Gasque—a task made easier by Gill and Gallagher's Plymouth Brethren roots and Gallagher's longstanding friendship with the Gasques. From the start, the significance of Regent's role as New College's primary model was undeniable. New College adopted Regent's original strategy by planning to launch its new institution with a summer school in 1978 before beginning a full-fledged academic program in fall 1979, and it advertised itself in language that harked back directly to Regent College's publicity rather than previous Crucible advertisements or the language with which people described L'Abri. In fall 1977 Gill echoed early Regent College publicity materials verbatim by describing New College Berkeley as "an idea whose time has come." Like Houston before him, Gill promoted his educational venture as a remedy to the educational gap that existed between the growing educational attainment of Christian laity and the minimal theological education programs that were offered to lay professionals at most churches:

---

[69]James M. Houston to Jim Hiskey, October 19, 1976, box 3, folder 6, JHF.

> It is clear that, on the broad view, most . . . confessed Christians have little sense of what it means to "be Christian" in their vocations and in "secular life." And that is altogether understandable. Most Christians are educated (as doctors, business administrators, lawyers, educators, etc.) in institutions that do not (or cannot) help individuals to question the non- or sub-Christian values, ways and means, the goals typical of those professions. Thus, we have a fairly large group of professed Christians who, consciously or not, are living divided lives where the confession of Christ is not worked out into all areas of life.

Gill desired to meet this false dichotomy with a graduate program that would "specialize in the situation of the 'laity,' living, thinking, and working in the sub-Christian world of today."[70]

Another indication of New College's conceptual debt to Regent College can be seen in the effort Gill put into understanding the minutiae of Regent's business and organizational structure.[71] In early 1978 Gill traveled to Vancouver for a crash course in replicating the Vancouver experiment. Gill hoped the trip might give him a chance to "spend time looking at and listening to Regent College from top to bottom." He wanted to "look over: Regent's . . . office procedures, record keeping systems, know more about your board governance, your library relationships, etc."[72]

As important as Houston's influence was, the most important link between New College and Regent came in the person of Ward Gasque. The longtime Regent College faculty member joined New College as the institution's first president in the summer 1979, just before the college embarked on its inaugural fall semester. Though Gasque only came to New College on a two-year loan from Regent, his hire was an indication of the direction Gill and New College's board of directors desired to take their fledgling institution.[73] Gasque had served as one of the most significant organizers and networkers during the founding years of Regent College just over a decade before. Since that time he had further distinguished himself as

---

[70]David Gill, "New College Berkeley: An Idea Whose Time Has Come," *New College Berkeley Notes* (Fall 1977). For Houston's earlier use of this phrase, see James M. Houston, "An Idea Whose Time Has Come," *Regent College Bulletin* 2, no. 1 (Winter 1972).

[71]While Regent attempted to encourage the fledgling venture over the years, it never offered New College Berkeley any financial assistance (Susan Phillips and Steve Phillips, interview with author, December 2, 2015, Berkeley).

[72]David Gill to Carl E. Armerding and James M. Houston, October 25, 1977, box 3, folder 7, JHF.

[73]David Gill, "The President: Ward Gasque," *New College Berkeley Notes* (Fall 1978); Gasque, Gasque, and Armerding, interview; Susan S. Phillips and Soo-Inn Tan, *Serving God's Community: Studies in Honor of W. Ward Gasque* (Vancouver: Regent College Publishing, 2015), xxviii-xxix.

both a capable scholar and academic administrator. On top of this, Gasque's far-ranging connections instantly raised the profile of the college.

Theologically, Gasque shared Gill and Gallagher's Plymouth Brethren heritage and thus carried a longstanding commitment to lay theological education. Gasque also came to New College with the strong conviction that the Bible authorized women to participate in all aspects of the life of the church, a view he shared with Palmer, Gallagher, Gill, and others in Berkeley, though not with all his colleagues at Regent. Not surprisingly given these views, Gasque held a commitment to egalitarian education that was not merely theoretical. When he came to New College Berkeley, he and his wife, Laurel, had just spent the better part of a year apart while Laurel studied for a master of letters in art history at the University of Edinburgh.

Figure 5.4. New College Berkeley 1979 board of directors meeting. Founding principal Ward Gasque is seated at the corner of the table on the far left.

Under Gasque's leadership, New College expanded from a summer program into a full-time graduate institution beginning in fall 1979. From the start, Gasque and Gill worked to bring many aspects of the Regent College experience to New College Berkeley. Summer school courses at New College provided the opportunity for students to interact with cosmopolitan evangelical superstars while also offering the "warm" and "personal atmosphere" that defined Regent's summer schools.[74] With an enrollment of ninety-eight, the 1978 New College summer

---

[74]"Summer School Revisited," *New College Berkeley Notes* (Fall 1978).

school provided the boost of momentum its organizers had hoped for prior to the start of the fall 1979 semester. That September New College also benefited from the consolidation of energy and resources within the Berkeley Christian community when the leaders of the Crucible decided to merge their ministry—including their financial resources and library—with New College. As the 1970s came to a close, lay theological education had a new face in Berkeley.

Searching for Sustainable Lay Theological Education in Berkeley

The 1980s proved to be a whirlwind of successes and disappointments for Gill and the New College community. The foremost American experiment in graduate lay theological education began the decade with hope and a sense of promise, but by 1990 serious questions about the sustainability of the venture had emerged. The uncertainty with which New College Berkeley entered the 1990s came as a result of both internal and external factors, only some of which were avoidable.

The New College community spent the majority of the 1980s building up what they hoped would be a theological graduate school for the laity comparable in size and influence to Regent College. In addition to its summer school faculties, which were loaded with familiar evangelical names ranging from John Stott and Carl Henry to James Houston and Madeleine L'Engle, Gasque and his successor, William A. Dyrness, worked to build a first-rate full-time and adjunct faculty at New College. In addition to standard courses in biblical studies and church history, the college demonstrated its explicit emphasis on the laity by offering courses such as Theology of the Laity. Furthermore, because New College had access to a large and diverse pool of adjunct and visiting professors, students encountered a surprising array of course options ranging from Laurel Gasque's course on the life and music of Johann Sebastian Bach to a course on Christian writing and journal keeping taught by Walter and Virginia Hearn.[75]

While Gasque's task was one of establishing New College, the task of building New College into a school on the level of Regent fell to Dyrness, a graduate of Fuller Theological Seminary who had found his way to Hans Rookmaaker and a theology of aesthetics via Francis Schaeffer.[76] New College experienced

---

[75]"Be Challenged . . . Be Fed . . . New College, Berkeley . . . Courses for the First Fall," *New College Berkeley Notes* 2, no. 4 (Summer 1979).
[76]On the influence of Francis Schaeffer and Hans Rookmaaker on Dyrness, see Laurel Gasque, *Art*

significant growth and operational expense under Dyrness. In fall 1982 the college was given the chance to acquire a geographical footprint by buying Dwight House from the Berkeley Christian Coalition. By winter 1983 the former Christian World Liberation Front and Berkeley Christian Coalition building had become an important part of New College life. In addition to providing student residences, Dwight House also offered space for building community among New College students. The large house functioned as a community hub where students could meet together for meals, birthday celebrations, group sharing, and prayer.[77]

Dwight House was not the only demonstration of New College's expanding presence in the Berkeley educational scene. In September of 1982 the state of California approved New College's master of Christian studies, master of theology, and master of arts degrees, and New College transitioned away from its Regent-inspired, nine-month diploma in Christian studies program toward a greater emphasis on its one- and two-year master's degree programs. With state approval of New College degrees, Dyrness began his term as the school's second president by putting the college on a path that he hoped would lead to accreditation from the Western Association of Schools and Colleges and full membership in the Graduate Theological Union.[78]

Both of these emphases took money, however, and money was one thing New College had in short supply. The need to attract a faculty who were up for the challenge of teaching graduate courses was a significant expense.[79] Between 1979 and 1985 the college hired a full-time staff that included seasoned scholars such as Ward Gasque, Francis Andersen, Don Tinder, and Dyrness alongside promising new scholars such as Adeney-Risakotta and Joel Green (1985). Throughout the 1980s, New College was committed to paying these scholars a livable salary and promoting their professional health and scholarly writing by offering sabbatical leave on a schedule comparable to peer institutions.

---

and the Christian Mind: The Life and Work of H. R. Rookmaaker (Wheaton, IL: Crossway Books, 2005), 164. Bernard Adeney-Risakotta, in an interview on August 16, 2016, addressed Dyrness's vision for New College Berkeley to grow into a larger graduate school of theology.

[77]"Dwight House Serving as Student Residence," *New College Berkeley Notes* 5, no. 2 (Fall–Winter 1982).

[78]"College News: New College Degrees Approved," *New College Berkeley Notes* 5, no. 2 (Fall–Winter 1982); William Dyrness, "President's Column: End of Year Countdown!," *New College Berkeley Notes* 8, no. 1 (Fall 1985).

[79]"College News: New College Degrees Approved."

Faculty salaries were not the only part of the college's growing ambitions that far outdistanced what the school's existing budget could handle. In order to gain accreditation, Dyrness and the New College board and faculty knew that they would have to either develop a better library or find a way to become a part of the Graduate Theological Union's excellent library system. Eventually they decided on the second option. In 1985 New College applied for and was accepted unanimously as the tenth member school within the Graduate Theological Union common library agreement. While Dyrness was right to note that the agreement signified "a great step forward in our quest for accreditation," it also came with significant price tag—an annual membership fee of over $100,000.[80]

Having secured suitable library resources, New College pressed forward in its quest for Western Association of Schools and Colleges accreditation. In 1986 the newly appointed New College dean, Joel Green, compiled and submitted an extensive accreditation candidacy report that was to be voted on by association officials in February 1987.[81] By this time significant changes were taking place at the college as the need for increased fundraising became unavoidable. After reflecting on his "vision and gifts and the particular needs of the college," Dyrness decided to resign as New College president, effective August 1, 1986. In his place the New College board hired Gill as the college's third president not only to maintain the school's "vision for lay ministry" but also to "keep New College 'on target' and growing in the years to come."[82] What the latter goals essentially translated to was fundraising. More than any president before him, Gill was hired to make connections with donors who could right an institution whose income had fallen far short of its expenses.

Over the next four years Gill worked to help New College achieve financial solvency without compromising its mission to provide quality graduate education aimed specifically at the laity. The task proved titanic. Even though New College was pulling in some of its largest summer school enrollments ever—

---

[80] Dyrness, "President's Column: End of Year Countdown!"; Adeney-Risakotta, interview. As part of the agreement, New College Berkeley also gave its entire library to the Graduate Theological Union (Phillips and Phillips, interview).
[81] "Accreditation Update," *New College Berkeley Notes* (Fall 1986), NCBA.
[82] William Dyrness, "President's Column: Change," *New College Berkeley Notes* 7, no. 3 (Summer 1986); "David W. Gill Appointed President of New College Berkeley," *New College Berkeley Notes* 8, no. 4 (August 1986).

sometimes as many as three hundred students—New College's full-time degree programs were still underenrolled. Graduating classes of twenty to thirty students was simply not enough. The quality of the students was excellent by all accounts, but New College needed *quantity*, not just quality, to fund its ambitious accreditation goals and faculty. The extent to which New College's lack of financial resources had hamstrung the school's earlier idealism became unavoidable in spring 1987, when the Western Association of Schools and Colleges committee rejected New College's petition to become an official candidate for accreditation until the school demonstrated that it had enough financial reserves to guarantee its long-term sustainability.[83]

While the decision to pursue an ambitious plan of growth certainly gave New College's financial woes a homegrown dimension, internal decisions were only part of what kept New College from developing into the educational behemoth that Regent College had become by the late 1980s. Whereas Regent College had benefited from its geographic and chronological location, New College found both to be impediments more than catalysts to growth. The American landscape was far more dotted with evangelical options for graduate theological study than was western Canada. For clergy and increasingly laity alike, Fuller Theological Seminary in Southern California held a lion's share of the graduate theological market. For individuals who sought specifically lay-oriented instruction, Regent was still the more enticing option for those willing to travel for study.

On top of this, Berkeley itself had changed. Once a destination city for thousands, Berkeley held less allure as the counterculture drifted from America's consciousness. By the late 1980s Gill's earlier claim that "the least worry of all, I am convinced, would be students" rang with irony. If anything was in shorter supply at New College than money, it was students. "We always had a few who were willing to take the time and put in the effort and energy and money to do serious graduate studies relating their faith to their profession, their academic discipline," former New College professor Adeney-Risakotta remembered, "but there were always too few of them. We had some really great students, but we didn't have enough."[84]

---

[83]Gill, interview; Adeney-Risakotta, interview; Palmer, interview; "Accreditation Update," *New College Berkeley Notes* (Spring 1987).
[84]David W. Gill to Earl Palmer, March 15, 1976, private collection; Adeney-Risakotta, interview.

New College's failure to attract a critical mass of students was also a product of its time. Whereas the first generation of institutions in evangelical study centers benefited enormously from cultural forces that spurred a generation of young people to "drop out" or at least delay professional obligations in favor of a peripatetic search for community, meaning, and personal edification at places such as L'Abri and Regent College, New College emerged at a cultural pivot point when economic scarcity was replacing postwar abundance and when a generation of baby boomers were starting families and being forced to settle into the jobs they had once rejected.

Furthermore, as long-term studies of American collegiate freshman indicate, student motivations for attending college and choosing a degree program were undergoing a marked shift during these years. According to one prominent study, in the late 1960s nearly 80 percent of American freshmen endorsed "developing a meaningful life philosophy" as an "essential" or "very important" value, while only 45 percent of entering American freshman gave the same value to "being very well-off financially." By the time New College Berkeley was founded, in 1977, college freshmen afforded the two competing values virtually the same importance in their decision-making process. By the next year the motivation for financial gain had overtaken the desire to develop a meaningful life philosophy in the minds of a majority of students. This shift in values continued until it stabilized in 1988 at levels almost exactly inverse of the 1966 findings. Financial gain, not personal development, motivated the vast majority of college students for years to come.[85]

These trends ran counter to the very ethos of New College's emphasis on lay theological education. Whereas Regent College adopted the master of divinity—a professional degree oriented toward those seeking employment in the church—in 1978, just as these trends were shifting, the board, faculty, and administration of New College made a principled decision to avoid taking a similar route. Regent was their model, but it was an earlier Regent—a Regent reflected perhaps primarily in James Houston's description of the school than in the school's actual practice—that provided the framework for replication in Berkeley. In addition to these educational and theological convictions, there were significant

---

[85]Alexander W. Astin et al., *The American Freshman: Thirty Year Trends, 1966-1996* (Los Angeles: Higher Education Research Institute, Graduate School of Education & Information Studies, University of California, Los Angeles, 1997), 12-15.

practical considerations in Berkeley that also prompted the New College board to lean away from considering the launching of a master of divinity program. For interested evangelicals, Fuller already had a large extension campus in the Bay Area. For mainline Christians, the Berkeley Graduate Theological Union staunchly opposed the launching of new master of divinity programs in the area. Gill and others at New College had assured Fuller and the Graduate Theological Union for years that New College would not offer competing professional degrees.[86] Given all of these considerations, many in the New College community chose to press on in the institution's current lay-centric trajectory, hoping that at some point the tide would turn.

But there were some among the New College faculty and administration who were beginning to have doubts. Among them was New College's president, David Gill. By 1988 he was convinced him that it was time to seriously reevaluate and restructure New College. Gill found that together "the cost of being in the Graduate Theological Union Library, the doubling overnight of our facility's rent, the growing cost of living, especially housing through the 1980s" was overwhelming. "We just could not make it work despite a monumental effort," Gill remembered years later. Convinced that the New College model was unsustainable, Gill and a handful of New College board members began fishing for mergers or partnerships with both Fuller and Regent College. Neither school bit. The financial uncertainty that marked New College made both institutions unwilling to adopt the college into their existing programs.[87]

When partnerships failed to materialize, Gill began working with a couple of likeminded New College board members to develop what he described as "a radical new educational model for our target lay audiences." Gill's proposal included "decentralized, mostly noncredit" instruction "based in marketplace and church more than [in an] academic setting." The core faculty opposed these changes, and the New College board demonstrated an understandable hesitancy to terminate the positions of faculty members who were as much friends and colleagues as employees. Burned out after fourteen years at New College and wanting to give the institution plenty of time to choose a successor, Gill had turned in his resignation even before the outcome of this future of New College

---

[86]Gill, email, December 1, 2016.
[87]Gill, interview; Gill, email, December 1, 2016.

study was known.[88] After nearly three decades of leadership, Gill was no longer a driving force in Berkeley's Christian community.

Following Gill's departure, the situation at New College continued to deteriorate. Unwilling to make drastic changes to New College's organizational structure and unable to attract enough students to make New College a viable full-time institution, the next two New College presidents fought a losing battle. Under the interim presidency of Richard Benner, the New College faculty and board decided to sell Dwight House in order to raise enough capital to right the ship. The decision backfired. When the New College board hired Steve Pattie to replace Benner in 1993, the funds from the sale were nearly gone, and the college was on the edge of insolvency. Furthermore, the college's long-running effort to gain Western Association of Schools and Colleges accreditation had come to an end when the college's candidacy for accreditation expired in 1993. In summer 1994 the New College board recommended that the corporation of New College Berkeley be dissolved, effective August 31, 1994.[89]

To some members of the New College community, such drastic measures seemed unwarranted and unnecessary. Leading the charge was New College's academic dean, Susan Phillips. Phillips, a Berkeley-trained sociologist who studied for her PhD under renowned sociologist Robert Bellah, had been teaching at New College since 1985.[90] Together with longtime New College friend and board member Sharon Gallagher, Phillips drafted "A Proposal for the Continued Ministry of New College Berkeley" in July 1994. Arguing that the programs of New College "can be sustained for significantly less money," Phillips and Gallagher outlined a plan in which New College could cut its overhead by eliminating full-time faculty positions and partnering with the Graduate Theological Union as an affiliate, non-degree-granting institution. This last step was among the most important of Phillips and Gallagher's proposal. As a full, degree-granting member of the Graduate Theological Union, New College was obligated to maintain its membership in the Graduate Theological Union library at a cost of over $100,000 a year. As an affiliate member New College could offer courses within the Graduate Theological Union and use the library without paying annual membership fees.

---

[88]Gill, interview; Phillips and Phillips, interview; Gill, email, December 1, 2016.
[89]Susan Phillips to Sharon Gallagher and Ranon, "NCB WASC Candidacy Information," October 12, 2005; Susan Phillips and Sharon Gallagher, "A Proposal for the Continued Ministry of New College Berkeley," July 1994, NCBA, 1.
[90]Bellah served on New College Berkeley's advisory board from 1994 until his death in 2013.

With the help of board pledges, grants, and conference fees from the multiple national conferences New College was already scheduled to host in the upcoming year, Phillips and Gallagher believed that the legacy and ministry of New College could be continued for at least another year or two in order to see whether the proposed financial restructuring would succeed. Writing from Easton, Pennsylvania, where her husband was serving as provost of Eastern College, Laurel Gasque gave her support to Phillips and Gallagher's proposal in "A Passionate and Practical Plea." For Gasque, New College's "unique place in the history of Christianity in America" and role as an evangelical voice in the Graduate Theological Union was significant and worth maintaining if at all possible. Rather than dissolving New College or letting it lie dormant, Gasque believed that New College could be sustained if the board chose to act on Phillips and Gallagher's proposal.[91]

In the end, the board found the argument of Phillips, Gallagher, and Gasque convincing. Rather than close the school, the New College board named Phillips executive director—a title she chose over president in order to identify with the study center model rather than a traditional seminary—and Gallagher associate director. Phillips immediately went to work to make New College financially sustainable. She streamlined New College's budget by using a part-time staff and opting for a modest but comfortable rented office space.[92] In addition, Phillips took a significant step in ensuring New College's financial viability by following through on her earlier proposal to shift the college's status in the Graduate Theological Union to that of an affiliate, non-degree-granting institution. This shift allowed Phillips and the faculty of New College to teach and maintain an evangelical presence within the Graduate Theological Union without forcing the college to pay the library fee.

To some observers, the transition away from full-time faculty, permanent space, and independent degree programs was disappointing, but to Phillips and many of those closest to New College, these changes, far from being disappointments, proved liberating. No longer under a cloud of debt or a set program of studies, the college began functioning with an institutional

---

[91]Laurel Gasque to Board of New College Berkeley, "A Passionate and Practical Plea," July 30, 1994, folder "WASC Candidacy Extension Report," NCBA, 1-2, 4.
[92]For teaching purposes New College Berkeley faculty use shared classrooms at the Graduate Theological Union and the University of California as well as space in local churches (Susan Phillips, email to author, December 20, 2017).

nimbleness that enabled Phillips and other instructors to fit course offerings to the ever-shifting needs of students. The significance of this organizational structure increased over time as seminary leaders facing declining enrollment and unused seminary buildings began approaching Phillips to learn about the New College model.[93]

The benefits of institutional nimbleness can also be seen on the curricular level, especially in the college's ability to respond to increasing interest in Christian spirituality and spiritual formation. In 1976, long before most evangelicals in North America had even heard of spiritual formation, the Graduate Theological Union, following conversations with Bellah, among others, launched a doctoral program in Christian spirituality. In the next decades Berkeley, long a hub of interest in spirituality more generally defined, emerged as an important center for studies of Christian spirituality. This became even more significant after 1992, when the American Academy of Religion acknowledged Christian spirituality as an academic discipline. The next year the discipline launched its own peer-reviewed journal, *Christian Spirituality Bulletin*. Fittingly, the new journal was published in Berkeley.

Given her academic background, close ties to Bellah, and longstanding interest in spiritual formation, Phillips was well positioned to emerge as a leading voice within the new discipline. When the Association of Theological Schools began a partnership with the Lilly Endowment in the early years of the twenty-first century to assist Association of Theological Schools–accredited schools in better cultivating and assessing spiritual formation in their students, Phillips and New College were ready to shift programming toward this new need. As Phillips's scholarly interests turned more in the direction of spiritual formation, so did her writing. In 2008 Phillips published *Candlelight: The Art of Spiritual Direction* and followed it up in 2015 with *The Cultivated Life: From Ceaseless Striving to Receiving Joy*.[94] Both books addressed aspects of spiritual formation while simultaneously raising the profile of Phillips and New College as a place for those interested in spiritual formation and Christian spirituality more generally.

---

[93]Susan Phillips, email to author, December 20, 2017.
[94]Susan S. Phillips, *Candlelight: Illuminating the Art of Spiritual Direction* (Harrisburg, PA: Moorehouse, 2008); Susan S. Phillips, *The Cultivated Life: From Ceaseless Striving to Receiving Joy* (Downers Grove, IL: InterVarsity Press, 2015).

Figure 5.5. New College Berkeley executive director Susan Phillips.

In all of this Phillips and the New College board sought to stay true to the values that had shaped the college from the beginning. While New College failed to match Regent in terms of size and influence, the Berkeley venture managed to hold on to its core emphasis—providing graduate theological education for the laity—with a focus that was second to none. In the process New College helped thousands of everyday Christians better understand their faith and its implications in their vocations and life. Perhaps more importantly in terms of its uniqueness within the North America study center movement, since 1994 New College has done all this while being led at the highest level by a woman—something that even in 2019 only three other study centers in the Consortium of Christian Study Centers could claim.[95] Long after the counterculture had passed, the egalitarian legacy that marked Berkeley's evangelical community continued to bear fruit.

---

[95]In 2019 only four of thirty member study centers of the Consortium of Christian Study Centers had female directors. In addition to New College Berkeley, these included Missy DeRegibus's Cogito ministry at Hampden-Sydney; Theological Horizons, a collegiate ministry that has thrived for decades at the University of Virginia under the leadership of Karen Wright Marsh; and the Christian Study Center of Champaign-Urbana, which is headed by Melody Green. See "Member Study Centers," Consortium of Christian Study Centers, https://studycentersonline.org/membership/member-study-centers/ (accessed July 3, 2019).

While New College may have been alone in the intensity of its commitment to graduate lay theological education and its willingness to hire a female executive director at a time when almost no other evangelical study centers challenged accepted evangelical gender norms, the Berkeley experiment was hardly unique in its passion to help individuals think Christianly on the campuses of major North American universities. Indeed, even before Gill and his Bay Area cohort officially launched New College, another group of individuals who also looked to Houston and Schaeffer for inspiration were already experimenting with a university-based study center thousands of miles away from Berkeley at a university that regularly vied with Berkeley for the title of the nation's top public university. Unlike virtually all study center efforts before them, this group eventually found ready-made communities of students and wider pools of donors by rooting their ambitions for lay theological education in the fertile, constantly renewing soil of a large undergraduate student body.

THE CENTER FOR CHRISTIAN STUDY

IN SUMMER 1974 Beat Steiner returned to Charlottesville, Virginia, with a new Regent College diploma in hand and a wedding on the horizon.[1] As a student, Steiner had been a vocal advocate for Houston's pet project—the replication of Regent College on university campuses in North America and around the world. What Steiner could hardly have realized when he presented his paper "The Replication of Regent College" at Regent's first long-range planning conference in spring 1974 was that through his work in Charlottesville he would play a major role in bringing his mentor's hopes to fruition.

When Steiner returned to Charlottesville following his graduation from Regent College, it was with markedly less ambitious goals than replicating a graduate school for laypeople. Steiner moved back to Virginia in order to join the staff of Daryl Richman's Action Ministries (founded 1968), a campus ministry focused on evangelism and discipleship that was led by Richman and University of Virginia economics professor Ken Elzinga. It was not long, however, before Steiner found himself being pulled in a new direction—the creation of an independent study center adjacent to the grounds of his alma mater. Birthed out of a hybridized evangelical and cultural milieu that blended aspects of the counterculture and the Jesus movement with the intellectual rigor of a major university and the learning-in-community emphases of L'Abri and Regent College, the Charlottesville-based Center for Christian Study eventually grew

---

[1] Steiner married fellow Regent College alum Barbara Butler. Center for Christian Study, "A Beat with a Different Drum," *Praxis* 2, no. 1 (Spring 1998).

from its roots in the campus ministry of Steiner, Richman, and Elzinga to become one of the most significant North American models for university-embedded Christian study centers.

Establishing an Evangelical Presence: Daryl Richman and Action Ministries

Though the Center for Christian Study was officially founded in 1975, it was the earlier ministry of Daryl Richman (1934–2019), an evangelical pastor turned campus minister, that made the project possible in Charlottesville. By all accounts Richman was an unlikely candidate to pioneer a new student ministry at the University of Virginia.[2] Richman, the third of nine children, was born into a farming family in the small town of Tower City, North Dakota. After graduating from high school in 1952, Richman went on to Concordia College, where he earned a bachelor's in English in 1956. By 1957 he had scraped together enough money to follow the radio preaching of Charles Fuller to Fuller Theological Seminary in Pasadena, California.[3] Upon graduation, Richman followed up on a connection he had made with a pastor the previous summer while working with the Billy Graham Evangelistic Association in Virginia. Soon Richman was pastoring two small Baptist churches in rural Fluvanna County, just outside Charlottesville.[4]

In fall 1967 Richman's trajectory began to shift after a chance meeting in the University of Virginia's Memorial Gym. Richman had initially begun making the ten-mile trip to the campus in order to use the university's library. Before long, he was also taking full advantage of the university's decision to grant community members free access to the weight room located in the gym. One day, as Richman was working out, he struck up a conversation with a third-year commerce student named Bob Bissell. Though Richman had not come to the gym specifically to evangelize, he found himself asking Bissell, "What do you make of the claims of Christ?" A conversation ensued, and the two men agreed to meet within the week to discuss matters of faith at greater length. Richman and Bissell hit it off. In a matter of weeks their meetings expanded to include

---

[2]"A Friend for All Seasons," *Praxis* 2, no. 2 (Summer 1998).
[3]For the Fuller Seminary story, see George M. Marsden, *Reforming Fundamentalism: Fuller Seminary and the New Evangelicalism* (Grand Rapids: Eerdmans, 1987).
[4]Daryl Richman, interview with author, May 27, 2014.

Bissell's roommate, some of his friends, and several female students at the nursing school.[5] Sensing a call to this growing community of university students, Richman decided to step away from his pastorates in Fluvanna County and become an independent faith missionary to the university community. Shortly thereafter, Richman moved to Charlottesville with his wife, Allayne, and their three young daughters.

Once in Charlottesville, Richman sought out a young, newly appointed economics professor named Ken Elzinga (b. 1941). Elzinga, who joined the University of Virginia faculty in 1967, was almost as new to his faith as to his position at the university. He had experienced a conversion to Christianity only a few years earlier during his time as a graduate student at Michigan State University. By spring 1968, Richman had convinced Elzinga to join him as he followed up on an invitation to speak at the St. Anthony's Hall fraternity.[6] This engagement marked the beginning of a team ministry to the university's fraternities (and eventually sororities). It also marked the beginning of Elzinga's preaching career. The economist soon became one of the most influential members of the evangelical community in Charlottesville, even as he was simultaneously gaining a reputation in the classroom for excellence in teaching and research. He went on to become one of the university's most popular and celebrated professors. Over the course of his career he taught over forty-five thousand students—more than any other professor in the history of the University of Virginia.[7] From his first outreach with Richman, Elzinga became a linchpin of evangelicalism at the university. His status as a respected academic gave much-needed credibility to the ministry of Daryl Richman, an academic outsider.

In spring 1969 Richman began referring to his ministry as College Life. Two weeks later, after some pushback from another parachurch group that was already using that title, the name was changed to Action Ministries.[8] For the next decade Action Ministries served the university community as the foremost

---

[5]Richman, interview; Daryl Richman, interview with founders at the Center for Christian Study, DVD, September 2012. The nursing school and the education school opened to women students before the College of Arts and Sciences. Women were not admitted to the college until 1970.
[6]David Turner, interview with founders at the Center for Christian Study, DVD, September 2012.
[7]Lauren Jones and Mitchell Powers, "After Teaching 45,000 Students, Elzinga in a Class by Himself," UVA Today, January 27, 2015, https://news.virginia.edu/content/after-teaching-45000-students-elzinga-class-himself; "Professor Hoo: Ken Elzinga," The Cavalier Daily, February 10, 2013, www.youtube.com/watch?v=hXMTk4MBTqI.
[8]Andrew Trotter, interview with founders at the Center for Christian Study, DVD, September 2012.

evangelical group on the grounds. Weekly "action meetings" formed the center of Richman's burgeoning ministry. Even though these meetings were composed mostly of students, the logistics of carrying out the Sunday night meetings required substantial involvement from the Christian community in Charlottesville. Action meetings were usually held at the homes of local Christians. Each Sunday afternoon, a caravan of cars would leave the Memorial Gym parking lot and travel to the designated meeting spot for that week.

Community involvement was important during the early years because, throughout most of the 1960s and into the early 1970s, the University of Virginia enforced, though somewhat unevenly, a policy that largely prohibited religious groups from meeting on university grounds. This did not mean that there were no student ministries at the university. Most of the city's larger churches and established denominations had collegiate ministries, but these were usually housed in the church or in an off-grounds building located adjacent to the university. Unlike denominational ministries with local churches or long-established off-grounds property, evangelical parachurch groups such as Campus Crusade for Christ, InterVarsity Christian Fellowship, and Navigators did not own property and struggled to find meeting spaces. This logistical problem helps to explain why there were only two small evangelical ministries (InterVarsity and Navigators) at the University of Virginia in 1968, when Richman and Elzinga began holding action meetings. Without local infrastructure and access to university meeting spaces, parachurch ministries were at a distinct disadvantage.

Figure 6.1. Daryl Richman speaking to a group of students at an Action Ministries meeting in spring 1974.

As Elzinga later noted, finding space off-grounds for weekly meetings "was a huge obstacle" to the work of Action Ministries. The necessity of community involvement did have a silver lining, however. According to Richman, holding the weekly meetings off-grounds gave entrée to a lot of people. "The mothers and fathers who were living in those homes saw what was going on, and they all liked it because they were the ones who were volunteering their homes to us." As the influence of Action Ministries grew, a network of student leaders and committed community members expanded with it. Soon religious life at the University of Virginia began to look much different. The spiritual soil of the university, which had proved infertile for two different efforts to establish Campus Crusade for Christ in the past, began to sprout a number of new Christian groups. Many of these efforts were launched (or relaunched) by student-focused parachurch organizations such as Crusade, Fellowship of Christian Athletes, and InterVarsity.[9]

Evangelical Parachurch Ministry Moves onto University Grounds

As evangelical Christianity gained momentum in Charlottesville, some of Action Ministry's student leaders began to envision a more public outreach at Thomas Jefferson's university. In spring 1972 Beat Steiner and other evangelical students tapped into the anti-institutional ethos of the Jesus movement to plan a three-day Jesus Christ Versus Christianity conference at the university. Organizers scheduled both teaching seminars and outreach events during the weekend-long event and lined up local Christian leaders as well as professors such as William Lane and Richard Lovelace from Boston's Gordon-Conwell Theological Seminary to teach. The Charlottesville event also featured prominent campus evangelist Leighton Ford (b. 1930), brother-in-law of Billy Graham, and Tom Skinner (1942–1994), an African American evangelist who had once been the leader of a notorious gang in New York City. Both men had played significant roles in InterVarsity's Urbana 1970, an event that had challenged evangelicals to rise against the racial and class status quo.[10]

As far as Steiner knew, the University of Virginia had never hosted a large-scale evangelistic effort like this before. Furthermore, there were some—even some Christians—in the Charlottesville community who were not enthusiastic

---

[9]Ken Elzinga, interview with founders at the Center for Christian Study, DVD, September 2012; Richman, interview with founders; Trotter, interview with founders.
[10]For more on the influence of Ford and Skinner on a generation of young evangelicals during these years, see Richard Quebedeaux, *The Young Evangelicals: Revolution in Orthodoxy* (New York: Harper & Row, 1974), 86-94. For more on Urbana 1970, see Quebedeaux, *Young Evangelicals*, 90-94; David R. Swartz, *Moral Minority: The Evangelical Left in an Age of Conservatism* (Philadelphia: University of Pennsylvania Press, 2012), 33-38, 191.

about changing the pattern. On the Wednesday before the weekend event, seven prominent Charlottesville pastors penned a short letter to the *Cavalier Daily*, the university's student newspaper, explaining their "reservations about the style" of the planned evangelistic event. While they admitted that "an evangelistic crusade" might be one way to help people grow in the faith, they were quick to add, "it would be dishonest if we were to pretend that it reflected our understanding of what it means to preach the Gospel or build Christian community."[11]

For Steiner, the letter called to mind the seven churches reprimanded by Christ in the first chapters of Revelation.[12] For administrators at the university, the letter was all the impetus they needed to forestall the event. They immediately called into effect a somewhat selective no-use policy for religious events that developed in the 1960s, likely in the wake of monumental *Abington v. Schempp* Supreme Court decision of 1963, which outlawed Bible reading in public schools and stressed the divide between church and state institutions.[13] Just days before the event was set to be held, they informed Steiner that evangelistic meetings could not be held on university grounds, even though Steiner had successfully reserved the auditorium in Old Cabell Hall through the standard procedure. Through the help of Elzinga—who reminded university officials that decisions regarding the support of student groups held political implications during a budget year—the event was saved at the last moment, but university officials on the facilities committee insisted that future events of this kind would not be tolerated at the university.[14]

As noted above, the university's policies were not opposed to religion per se. At times various individuals at the university made religious options at local churches known to students by publishing pamphlets such as "Religious Affairs in the University of Virginia Community, 1970–1971." The 1970 pamphlet, seemingly intended for distribution to students at the beginning of the new academic year,

---

[11] "Community Members Explain Crusade Stance," *Cavalier Daily*, March 15, 1972.
[12] Beat Steiner, interview with author, March 25, 2014, Charlottesville, VA.
[13] For more on the Supreme Court ruling, see "School District of Abington Township, Pennsylvania v. Schempp," Legal Information Institute, www.law.cornell.edu/supremecourt/text/374/203 (accessed April 22, 2016). It is unclear why university administrators did not enforce this policy initially. It seems that members of evangelical parachurch groups were affected by university policies more than established denominational ministries, in part because of parachurch groups' lack of off-campus buildings but also likely because of their lack of cultural clout. From the time of Jefferson and throughout the life of the University of Virginia, religion had been a part of the life of the university.
[14] Steiner, interview.

listed most of the nearby churches and provided a map pinpointing their locations. It also listed "University Religious Organizations, Programs, Committees, and Offices," which included addresses and brief descriptions of fifteen religious ministries. These ministries ranged from "The University Chapel Committee" and the "Baptist Student Union" to The "B'Nai B'Rith Hillel Foundation" and less traditional opportunities such as "The Prism-Coffee House." Most of these groups met in buildings located just off university grounds, but Madison Hall was "an official agency of the university for volunteer student involvement in local social needs."[15] It also housed the University's Office of Religious Affairs, which was responsible for sponsoring and coordinating religious activities on grounds. If the university was opposed to religion on grounds, efforts such as Madison Hall made it hard for many to tell. For evangelicals who lacked the cultural clout and religious institutions needed to fit the university's system, the policy seemed starkly opposed to faith-based ministries. Evangelicals such as Steiner and Richman and the parachurch groups they represented noticed the way the university's policies seemed to perpetuate the virtual absence of an evangelical presence at the university.[16]

In this context, the Ford-Skinner crusade functioned as a watershed event for evangelical parachurch ministry at the University of Virginia. On one level, the event was a large success in its own right. The presence of two prominent leaders, one a white preacher and relative of Billy Graham and the other an African American and former gang leader from Harlem, helped demonstrate the egalitarian power of the gospel in the midst of a university community not far removed from Jim Crow segregation. The sessions were well attended, and multiple students made professions of faith in response to the messages.[17] Furthermore, the inclusion of professors from one of evangelicalism's top

---

[15] "Religious Affairs in the University of Virginia Community, 1970–1971," clippings file "Religion at UVA," Alderman Library, University of Virginia. In 1858 the first college YMCA in the world was established at the university, and in 1905 the YMCA established Madison Hall, which grew in the early 1970s into one of the largest Christian and philanthropic student organizations in the country. For more on religion at the University of Virginia in the first three-quarters of the twentieth century, see S. Vernon McCasland, *The John B. Cary Memorial School of Religion of the University of Virginia* (Indianapolis: United Christian Missionary Society, 1944).

[16] The story of the university's seemingly total and complete repudiation of religion on the grounds became a standard founding myth of the study center.

[17] Andrew Trotter, interview with author, March 6, 2014, Charlottesville, VA. The University of Virginia began accepting African American undergraduates in 1956. In 1958 Leroy Willis transferred from the university's School of Engineering into the university's crown jewel, the College of Arts and Sciences; see Lauren F. Winner, "From Mass Evangelist to Soul Friend," ChristianityToday.com, October 2, 2000, www.christianitytoday.com/ct/2000/october2/7.56.html.

seminaries demonstrated the appeal reasoned Christianity held for some students even if the pull of the Jesus movement was often in the other direction. In short, the 1972 conference tapped the equalitarian and experiential impulse of the Jesus movement without surrendering the intellectual component that an environment such as the University of Virginia demanded.

In spite of all of this positive momentum, however, one thing remained unchanged after the event. Though university administrators had relented and allowed the event to proceed, they made clear that it was an anomaly and that religious groups would still be prohibited from meeting on university grounds in the future. Steiner was determined to find a solution to this impasse. In a meeting with Dean D. Alan Williams, Steiner learned that university administrators saw the exclusionary policy as in keeping with Thomas Jefferson's own principles. Williams informed Steiner that the University of Virginia had always maintained a strict policy restricting religious groups from the use of university buildings. Furthermore, Williams went on to assert that this policy complied with recent Supreme Court rulings supporting the separation of church and state.[18] Steiner was not easily persuaded. In the weeks after the event he teamed up with Jim Keim, a PhD student in the Department of Politics, to investigate Williams's claims. What they found changed the face of student ministry at the University of Virginia. After six months of research, Steiner and Keim presented their case to Ralph Eisenberg, the chairman of the Calendar and Scheduling Committee.

According to Steiner and Keim, the university's policy impinged on "the right of student religious groups to freedom of speech, press, assembly and religion." For legal precedent they looked to a previous circuit court case, *The Police Department of the City of Chicago v. Mosely*, in which the court ruled that once a public forum is opened to the public it must remain open to speech of all types. A second facet of their appeal hinged on academic freedom as represented by Thomas Jefferson's oft-quoted remark that the University of Virginia should be "an institution of higher learning in which we are free to follow truth wherever and so far as reason and evidence shall lead."[19] While these two

---

[18] Steiner, interview. Williams was also vice president of student affairs at the time; see "D. Alan Williams," University of Virginia Library, http://search.lib.virginia.edu/catalog/uva-lib:2166698 (accessed March 7, 2017).

[19] Beat Steiner and Jim Keim to Ralph Eisenberg, November 13, 1972, private collection. See "Police Dept. of Chicago v. Mosely," Oyez, www.oyez.org/cases/1970-1979/1971/1971_70_87 (accessed June 10, 2014); *Presbyterian Journal*, January 16, 1974, 3.

arguments were strong, the most important aspect of their argument came in their appeal to Jefferson himself. Steiner and Keim noted:

> Mr. Jefferson himself expressed the concern that the religious life of the students not be "precluded by the public authorities" (Minutes of the Board of Visitors, October 7, 1822). On the contrary he himself designated a room in the Rotunda for religious worship subject to a neutral policy. . . . The Rotunda rooms were used for religious worship and Sunday School, a chaplaincy system was established based on voluntary contributions of students and faculty, and the University itself entered a special relationship with the Young Men's Christian Association in 1858. These all indicate an early cooperation with voluntary religious life.[20]

Unable to argue with Jefferson's own policies and a long history of religious practice at the university, University of Virginia administrators changed their policy regarding religious meetings on university property.[21] For the first time in over a decade, Christian groups of all kinds were permitted to use university space for their meetings.

One of the first major events following this change in policy was a five-day conference in March 1973 titled the L'Abri Lectures in Modern Religion and Culture. Once again Steiner played a large role in bringing sought-after speakers to university grounds. Steiner, along with Myron Augsburger, president of nearby Eastern Mennonite University, had been attempting to bring Francis Schaeffer and other speakers from L'Abri to central Virginia since summer 1971. For Steiner, Schaeffer's blend of head and heart religion was something Christians in his community needed to experience for themselves: "We feel that College students and the churches in this area are in great need of a ministry which will further coalesce the community and minister to the hearts and minds of students and others in this area and throughout the country."[22] In the end Steiner was unable to get the increasingly sought-after

---

[20]Steiner and Keim to Eisenberg, November 13, 1972.

[21]Larry J. Sabato to Edgar R. Shannon Jr., February 27, 1973, private collection. In light of the fact that Steiner reserved space in Newcomb Hall for the March 4-8 L'Abri Lectures in Modern Religion and Culture, this change must have been largely underway prior to President Shannon's formal acceptance of the recommendation.

[22]Beat Steiner to Francis Schaeffer, July 27, 1971, private collection. Augsburger was one of the most important Anabaptist voices in the emerging evangelical left during these years. He played a role in drafting the 1973 Chicago Declaration (Swartz, *Moral Minority*, 168-69).

The conference ran from Sunday, March 4, through Thursday, March 8. See Marion Ritter and Rosemary Cooney, "Visiting L'Abri Fellows Present 'The New Inferno' Lecture Series," *The Cavalier Daily*, March 2, 1973.

evangelical star to commit to an engagement at the university, but his efforts resulted in an on-grounds lecture series featuring some of Schaeffer's top protégés.[23] The 1973 L'Abri lecture series included talks by Hurvey Woodson, the director of L'Abri in Italy; Ranald Macaulay, the director of the British L'Abri; and Hans Rookmaaker, professor at the Free University of Amsterdam. These presentations were hosted in the heart of the university, with afternoon and evening lectures held each day.

By making use of multiple university buildings, the L'Abri lectures demonstrated the significance of Steiner and Keim's efforts. In just under a year, the university had been compelled to alter its policy regarding the assembly of Christian groups on the grounds. From that time on, religious groups were allowed to apply for the reservation of university facilities on equal footing with other student groups. The impact of this shift was enormous. With new access to university facilities, parachurch collegiate ministries such as InterVarsity and Campus Crusade gained new momentum at the University of Virginia. As evangelical campus ministries began to find a warmer reception at the university, the number of students interested in learning more about their faith grew. The stage was set for the development of more lasting evangelical institutions.

Founding a Study Center in Charlottesville, 1975-1976

Evangelical efforts in Charlottesville were buoyed during the 1970s by a general rise in the number and influence of evangelicals, both in American society and in the nation's universities, that resulted from the Jesus movement's emphasis on evangelism and growing evangelical affluence and prestige.[24] Yet even as the number of evangelical Christians in America grew, the ethos of the movement changed with American culture. As the hippie counterculture faded in the 1970s, many in American society underwent a reactionary turn toward conservatism. The evangelical converts of the Jesus movement were not immune to this trend. By the middle of the decade many of them had turned in their hippie dress for more standard middle-class styles.[25] The Jesus movement had given American

---

[23]Francis A. Schaeffer to Beat Steiner, September 6, 1971, private collection.
[24]See D. Michael Lindsay, *Faith in the Halls of Power: How Evangelicals Joined the American Elite* (New York: Oxford University Press, 2007).
[25]As Donald Critchlow notes, the 1970s were a paradox, both an age of liberation and an age of reaction. See Critchlow, *Phyllis Schlafly and Grassroots Conservatism: A Woman's Crusade* (Princeton, NJ: Princeton University Press, 2005), 214-21. See also Larry Eskridge, *God's Forever Family: The Jesus People Movement in America* (New York: Oxford University Press, 2013), 242-84.

evangelicalism a fresh wave of converts; now American political and cultural currents were offering evangelicals a degree of social prominence and respectability they had not experienced at any other point in the twentieth century.

When presidential candidate Jimmy Carter announced that he was a born-again Christian, the prominence of American evangelicalism became unavoidable. In a cover story appearing a few weeks before the 1976 election, Newsweek declared 1976 "The Year of the Evangelical." According to the article's authors, "the emergence of evangelical Christianity into a position of respect and power" was "the most significant—and overlooked—religious phenomenon of the '70s."[26] As evangelicals readied themselves to move into the halls of power in the next decades, prominent universities such as the University of Virginia served as important entry points to greater influence across the political, cultural, and educational spectrum.[27] In the wake of this shift, Jesus movement–era ministries such as Charlottesville's Action Ministries and Berkeley's *Right On* took more dignified names such as University Christian Ministries and *Radix*. Within university towns, evangelicals still longed for spiritual and intellectual communities, but increasingly they turned their efforts toward ventures that better represented their upwardly mobile ambitions. In a few places, study centers, offering a blend of community living and hospitality in addition to a more intellectual educational aim, emerged as a means of bridging these competing desires.

In Charlottesville general trends in evangelical and American culture combined with the influence of Francis Schaeffer and Jim Houston to produce a version of evangelicalism well suited to life in the shadow of a major research university. From the mid-1970s on, evangelicals in Charlottesville founded a variety of institutions that sought to further their rising intellectual and social ambitions without compromising their faith. Nothing better represented this impulse than the Center for Christian Study. From the beginning the Center for Christian Study was designed to be a place where community members and University of Virginia students could combine the best of evangelicalism's emphasis on heartfelt, experiential faith with the community emphasis and

---

[26]Kenneth L. Woodward, John Barnes, and Laurie Lisle, "Born Again!," *Newsweek*, October 25, 1976, 68-78. The magazine also carried a one-page insert titled "Decisions for Christ," in which the conversions of notable figures such as Chuck Colson and Eldridge Cleaver were described.

[27]For the rising social prominence of evangelicals following Carter's election, see Lindsay, *Faith in the Halls of Power*; D. Michael Lindsay, "Evangelicals in the Power Elite: Elite Cohesion Advancing a Movement," *American Sociological Review* 73, no. 1 (February 2008): 60-82.

intellectual sensitivity of Schaeffer's L'Abri or Houston's Regent College.[28] Once again, it was Daryl Richman, Ken Elzinga, and Beat Steiner who led the way.

When Steiner returned to Charlottesville in summer 1974 after spending a year at Regent College, he found Action Ministries little changed. But jumping back into ministry alongside Daryl Richman as a support-funded minister proved more difficult than Steiner had expected. He was eager to be involved in meaningful ministry, but he found it difficult to know exactly where to begin. Furthermore, though his time with Houston had convinced him of the importance of theological education for all Christians, Steiner did not readily see an outlet for his passion for theological education in Charlottesville. Fresh from the intellectual heights of graduate theological study at Regent, Steiner found that the first year in Charlottesville was a "humbling" and "soul-searching" struggle. Perhaps sensing Steiner's struggles, Richman suggested that Steiner head up a new ministry. One day, as the two men were walking up Chancellor Street, Richman declared, "Beat . . . what we need in Charlottesville is a study center."[29]

The words resonated with Steiner. Following his conversation with Richman, Steiner threw himself into the development of a center where Christian commitment and scholarly dedication could go hand in hand. In order to make this dream a reality, Steiner needed two things—relational connections and a physical space for the center. As Steiner began seeking out other individuals with a similar vision, Houston directed him to Jim Hiskey and the folks involved in Cornerstone's Regent-style summer school just off the University of Maryland campus. Hiskey soon became an important resource for Steiner and the development of the Charlottesville study center.[30]

The search for a suitable place to house the new endeavor played out in stages. In spring 1975 Steiner leased a former boarding house, which was located just off university grounds on Elliewood Avenue. Though the building needed extensive renovation and was only available on a month-to-month lease, its proximity to the Corner (a popular student haunt full of retail shops and restaurants just off university grounds) made it an ideal location for the fledgling effort. With a physical space in hand, Steiner went to work organizing a team of volunteers,

---

[28]Jane Spencer Bopp, interview with author, April 11, 2014, Charlottesville, VA; Steiner, interview.
[29]Center for Christian Study, "Beat with a Different Drum"; Steiner, interview. It is unclear where the exact terminology "study center" originated, but there is a good chance that it was popularized the most by R. C. Sproul's early and widely known Ligonier Valley Study Center.
[30]This paragraph is based primarily on my conversation with Beat Steiner and Barb Steiner.

who devoted time and financial resources to the project.[31] Foremost among these volunteers was Preston Locher, a businessman and future Center for Christian Study board member who had made his fortune on the Alaska oil fields before relocating to Farmington, Virginia. With Locher's financial assistance and the sweat of local volunteers, the building was successfully renovated into a L'Abri-esque study center. In summer 1975 Beat and Barb Steiner, newly married, settled into the second floor of the house. The study center, with a library and reading room downstairs, officially opened to students in the fall.

It was not long before the Charlottesville community began to take notice. In late September Charlottesville's *The Daily Progress* ran an article featuring an interview with Richman and Steiner and a photograph of the building. The article detailed the day-to-day rhythm of life at the center. Only a month into its first semester of operation, the center was already buzzing with activity. Some students had "come to research the historical background to the book of Job" or to ask "questions about Genesis." Others took part in the Bible studies. On Thursday evenings, "a score or more of law students and their friends" gathered "in the cavernous, freshly painted living room" to "read from the book of Luke and discuss and analyze how the words of the apostle relate to their lives."[32]

Figure 6.2. Daryl Richman and Beat Steiner sit in the newly founded Charlottesville study center in fall 1975.

In addition to spaces for group meetings, the Elliewood building provided students with access to Christian materials that they could not get through the university's library. The building's ground floor housed "a library filled with tapes, books and periodicals on all aspects of Christianity."[33] By 1977 the library included approximately twelve hundred volumes and over one thousand taped lectures. In the early years one of the library's most prized holdings was a complete collection of Francis Schaeffer's taped lectures,

---

[31] Steiner, interview; Ken Elzinga, interview with author, February 28, 2014, Charlottesville, VA.
[32] Charles Hite, "Charlottesville's Center for Christian Study," *The Daily Progress*, September 27, 1975. See also "Charlottesville's Center for Christian Study," fall 1975, CCSA.
[33] Hite, "Charlottesville's Center for Christian Study."

which were donated by Bill and Betty Weldon. Like the Lochers, the Weldons were people of means who became acquainted with the project through Richman's pastoral work in Farmington. Previous to their involvement in the Charlottesville study center, Bill Weldon had also spent time at Swiss L'Abri, where he came to greatly appreciate the work of Francis Schaeffer.[34]

Contributing the entire collection of reel-to-reel L'Abri tapes to the fledgling study center came as a natural outflow of these relationships. It also represented notable developments within evangelicalism. By the mid-1970s Schaeffer was well established as a leading spokesperson for intellectually engaged evangelical Christianity. Furthermore, in addition to expanding the minds and aspirations of North American evangelicals, Schaeffer's methods—be it community-based-learning or his use of technology (e.g., taped lectures, documentary videos)—foreshadowed evangelicalism's move into new methods of mass producing the work of its celebrities. L'Abri's massive effort to develop a broad mail-order tape ministry is a notable example of this trend. Beginning with L'Abri, no self-respecting study center during these years was without a tape library. In places such as L'Abri, Regent College, or the Ligonier Valley Study Center, tapes were made in-house. For smaller efforts such as the Crucible, Cornerstone, and the Charlottesville study center, tape ministries began with tape libraries composed of purchased tapes. These tapes were a significant draw. In the first Center for Christian Study brochure in fall 1975, special attention was given to its tape library, which included taped lectures from individuals such as Schaeffer, Sproul, John Stott, and Regent's Bruce Waltke.[35]

While the extent of their collection of Schaeffer's tapes may have indicated the large ambitions some held for the Charlottesville venture, other realities demonstrated how uncertain the future of Steiner's study center really was. Foremost among these was the building's precarious lease agreement. In December 1975 the building's property manager notified Steiner that the building was going up for sale. A month later the Steiners received their week's notice. Faced with the imminent loss of their residence, the young couple spent the rest of the morning searching for alternative housing. Thanks to a connection Barb

---

[34] Daryl Richman to William Camp Jr., June 27, 1977, box "Archives—Programs, 1985–1989," folder "Fundraising Appeal Letters, 1976–1986," CCSA; Daryl Richman to friends of the Gustafsons, June 5, 1976, box "Archives—Programs, 1985–1989," folder "Fundraising Appeal Letters, 1976–1986," CCSA. Betty Weldon was a member of Richman's Farmington Bible study; Steiner, interview.

[35] "Charlottesville's Center for Christian Study," fall 1975.

had made through her position as a teacher at a local school, they managed to find an apartment by noon that day. Upon returning to the Elliewood building, the Steiners checked their mailbox. Inside they found a letter from Saint Paul's Episcopal Church. The letter informed them that after nearly two years of analysis the church had decided to end its housing ministry. As a result the church was looking to sell its Koinonia House at 128 Chancellor Street—which sat only a block from university grounds. The Steiners could hardly believe their eyes. They had found an apartment for themselves and a potential home for the study center only hours after they had received their week's notice on the Elliewood property.[36]

The timing of these events was momentous for the development of the Charlottesville Center for Christian Study. The sale of the Elliewood building meant that the study center would have to close for the spring 1976 semester; however, the chance to purchase the house on Chancellor Street played a vital role in Steiner's efforts to keep the concept of a study center alive in the minds of students and donors. With a physical location secured and allowed, Steiner, Richman, and Elzinga immediately launched a new fundraising effort. Together the friends of Action Ministries and the study center raised enough money to cover the down payment on the Chancellor Street house by June 1976.

In order to purchase the building, Richman and Steiner incorporated the work of Action Ministries and the Center for Christian Study under University Christian Ministries. University Christian Ministries officially gained possession of the property on June 25. Within a week, a group of enthusiastic volunteers began renovating the building. At the end of the summer Richman quantified the scope of the undertaking:

> Over 2,000 hours of volunteer labor have been put into the house. We are close to completing a total renovation of the Study Center, which has included the construction of an apartment on the ground floor, new porches and a face lifting for each of the eighteen rooms of the house. Five full-time workers were the mainstay of the project. A parade of plumbers, electricians, roofers, and carpenters were supplemented by dozens of volunteers who scraped, sanded and painted.[37]

---

[36] Beat Steiner still refers to this as "the miracle of the study center." This paragraph is taken exclusively from my conversation with the Steiners.

[37] Daryl Richman, Beat U. Steiner, and Rob Gustafson to Virginia graduate, September 1, 1976, box "Archives—Programs, 1985-1989," folder "Fundraising Appeal Letters, 1976-1986," CCSA; Steiner, interview.

Richman reported that $38,500 had been raised toward the total cost ($57,000) of the building. The relocated and freshly incorporated Center for Christian Study was dedicated during a service at the University of Virginia Chapel on November 21, 1976.[38]

Over the course of the next two years, the house on Chancellor Street emerged as a resource for students and community members who wanted to pursue a more intellectually robust version of Christianity than the Christian education programs their churches could offer. Furthermore, beyond the center's own programming, the house on Chancellor Street soon became the primary hub for evangelical student ministry at the University of Virginia. Undergraduate groups such as Fellowship of Christian Athletes and Young Life began making routine use of the building, as did groups of professional and graduate students such as the Christian Law Fellowship and the Medical Fellowship.[39] The center provided free photocopying for the Christian ministries at the university and hosted biweekly meetings that brought together representatives from nearly all of the university's recognized campus ministries. These meetings proved to be a lasting and unique part of the center's ministry. More than one observer over the years has commented on the abnormal degree of unity among parachurch campus ministries at the University of Virginia thanks in large part to these regular meetings.[40]

Building an Evangelical Network in Charlottesville: Trinity Presbyterian Church

The impulse toward spiritual entrepreneurship among Charlottesville's evangelical population during these years was not limited to the development of the Center for Christian Study. Closely related to the study center was the development of another, more traditional evangelical institution—Trinity Presbyterian Church, which aligned itself with the Presbyterian Church in America. From the start, Trinity functioned as an essential ally of the Charlottesville study center. To a significant degree the center's ability to survive and thrive throughout the

---

[38] Board of Directors of University Christian Fellowship, "Dedication Service of the Center for Christian Study," November 1976, private collection.
[39] Daryl Richman to Scott Bauman, May 2, 1977, box "Archives—Programs, 1985–1989," folder "Fundraising Appeal Letters 1976–1986," CCSA; Daryl Richman to Hovey Dabney, June 15, 1977, box "Archives—Programs, 1985–1989," folder "Fundraising Appeal Letters 1976–1986," CCSA.
[40] Andrew Trotter, interview with author, April 6, 2016, Charlottesville, VA.

late 1970s and 1980s even as similar efforts in other places failed to gain or keep momentum is in part attributable to the multifaceted and longstanding support of Trinity Presbyterian Church.

Trinity was founded in summer 1976, when Daryl Richman (himself a Baptist minister), Elzinga, and members of the University Christian Ministries and Center for Christian Study board decided to try to rectify what they felt to be a lack of evangelical presence in the town's churches.[41] The new congregation's growth testified to the newfound vitality of the evangelical community in Charlottesville. When the church met for the first time on August 1, 1976, in the Baptist Student Center just off university grounds, 110 people were in attendance. By November the number had risen to 250. By 1977 the church was meeting at St. Anne's Belfield school and holding two services to accommodate nearly four hundred worshipers. By 1979 the church numbered six hundred and had moved to another local school building.[42] In 1982 Trinity dedicated its own building and began holding two services in its new one-thousand-seat sanctuary.

As a member of the newly founded Presbyterian Church in America, Trinity emphasized a Reformed theology and biblical inerrancy akin to that espoused by Schaeffer and Sproul, both of whom also had close Presbyterian Church in America ties. For Richman, Elzinga, and the church's other founders, Trinity emerged as a remedy to Charlottesville's lack of church options for thinking evangelicals. Trinity aimed to fit the growing evangelical demographic of well-educated professionals by espousing a theology rooted in traditional evangelical orthodoxy without catering to the seeming excesses of emotionalism or anti-intellectualism that had defined many evangelical churches touched by the Jesus movement. From the start Trinity was expected to serve both the university and the greater Charlottesville community as a "town and gown" church.

Even more than the Center for Christian Study, Trinity demonstrated the rising social and intellectual ambitions of Charlottesville evangelicals. Joseph

---

[41] For information on the founding of Trinity, see Dinah Adkins, "The Revival of Religion," *The Daily Progress*, April 10, 1977, private collection; "Young Congregation Outgrows Its Quarters," *The Daily Progress*, January 20, 1979, private collection; Trinity Presbyterian Church, "Special Anniversary Edition," *ACTS 29* (August 1979), private collection; "In the Shadow of Mr. Jefferson," *Continuing: Presbyterian Church in America* 3, no. 9 (1976): 7-8; Sharon Kraemer, "After a Lot of Prayer and Spade Work," June 1, 1989, private collection.

[42] "Young Congregation Outgrows Its Quarters"; Joseph F. Ryan to Francis A. Schaeffer, April 14, 1982, box "Lectures and Programs '80s, '90s," folder "Francis Schaeffer," CCSA.

"Skip" Ryan, Trinity's founding pastor, was a graduate of Harvard University who had spent six months with the Schaeffers at L'Abri, worked as a Young Life staff member in Richmond, Virginia, and studied for a master's of divinity at Westminster Theological Seminary. Westminster was a staunchly Reformed seminary that had a history of conservatism dating back to its founding in 1929 by polemical biblical scholar J. Gresham Machen. In the early stages of Trinity's development, Elzinga contacted longtime Westminster Theological Seminary president Edmund Clowney (1917–2005) looking for a pastoral recommendation. Clowney handpicked Ryan for the Charlottesville position.[43] Together Ryan's ties to Schaeffer and his connection to Clowney helped shape Trinity in the ensuing years. Later in life, Clowney served as a theologian-in-residence at Trinity, and Schaeffer visited the church in 1982, when Ryan invited him to give a talk titled "On Being a Christian in the 1980s" to commemorate the church's move to its newly constructed worship space (see photo 6.3).

Figure 6.3. Francis Schaeffer and David Turner at Trinity Presbyterian Church in November 1982.

In addition to its connection to influential evangelicals, Trinity quickly became the epicenter of evangelical financial and social capital in Charlottesville.[44] By early 1982 Ryan reported to Schaeffer that nearly eight hundred people worshiped at Trinity each week. "A substantial number of these are University related," Ryan noted. "Many are on the faculty (three professors are on our session). 250 or more of our morning congregation are students." Many of these were students affected by what Ryan called "a considerable explosion in Christian ministries here [at the University of Virginia] in the last years." He reported,

---

[43]Trotter, interview; Andrew Trotter, "Ed Clowney: A Personal Remembrance," *Praxis* 9, no. 2 (Summer 2005).
[44]Even today, Trinity's congregation is full of lawyers, medical professionals, and successful businesspeople. Notable evangelical leaders ranging from sociologist James Davison Hunter to University of Virginia men's basketball coach Tony Bennett have also called Trinity home in recent years.

"Inter-Varsity, Campus Crusade and FCA are all strong. Their staff people are in our church and most of their student participants attend our church as well."[45] In addition to Trinity's influence on undergraduate ministries, the church also emerged as the worshiping community of choice for evangelicals in Charlottesville's professional class. Ryan inferred this reality when he noted that many graduate students in the university's prestigious law, business, and medical schools who had ties to the Center for Christian Study's graduate fellowships also attended Trinity. Ryan, an early board member of the Center for Christian Study, had even met his wife, Barbara, a 1980 graduate of the University of Virginia's law school and a lawyer in Charlottesville, in part through her involvement in the study center's Law Fellowship.

The relationship between the Center for Christian Study and Trinity Presbyterian Church continued to deepen over the years. While Trinity's strong educational ministries eventually cut into the study center's community-based enrollment, the center's relationship with Trinity was still extremely beneficial for it. For most of the study center's first decade, the vast majority of its board members, community supporters, and program constituency were also members of Trinity. (Over the last forty-five years every Center for Christian Study director had been a member of Trinity, and many secondary study center staff members also worshiped regularly there.) Ryan was himself a University Christian Ministries board member and went out of his way to boost the study center by writing invitations to speakers such as Schaeffer and Os Guinness. Occasionally, as in the case of the study center's summer program, Ryan also wrote to every pastor in the Presbyterian Church in America on behalf of the program and made the Trinity mailing list available to the Center for Christian Study.[46] More indirectly, Trinity became a stable means of support—spiritually and relationally even more than financially—for the Center for Christian Study. As Trinity's social and financial affluence grew along with its influence within the entire denomination, the connection between the study center and the church it helped birth continued to be of immense importance.

---

[45] Joseph F. Ryan to Francis A. Schaeffer, April 14, 1982, box "Lectures and Programs '80s, '90s," folder "Francis Schaeffer," CCSA.
[46] Joseph F. Ryan to PCA ministers, March 27, 1987, folder "Summer Program 1987," CCSA; Skip Ryan to Trinity member or friend, October 20, 1982, folder "Center for Christian Study," CCSA.

Between L'Abri and Regent College: The Center for Christian Study in Its First Decade, 1977-1985

As at Trinity, the procurement of a permanent geographical location also made a significant difference in the life of the study center. Once the Center for Christian Study had a permanent home, Steiner and other University Christian Ministries leaders wasted no time in solidifying the study center's programming. In fall 1976 the center brought in Dr. Edwin Yamauchi (b. 1937) for the inaugural Staley Distinguished Christian Scholar Lecture Series. Yamauchi was a professor of history at Miami University of Ohio and a frequent contributor to *Christianity Today* who had been raised Buddhist and then studied the Qur'an and hadith in Arabic before converting to Christianity.

The next year the Center for Christian Study hosted C. Everett Koop (1916–2013) and Harold O. J. Brown (1933–2007) for the Staley Lectures. Their presentation, "The Right to Live, the Right to Die: Where Will the Decision Lead Us?" pointed toward future evangelical political impulses.[47] Already by 1977 Koop and Brown had helped catalyze the evangelical charge against abortion by cofounding the Christian Action Council (now CareNet) in 1975.[48] Both men were also close friends with Schaeffer, who, reflecting the political propensity of Reformed theology, was also moving into a politicized prolife stance at the same time. In 1979 Koop and Schaeffer published *Whatever Happened to the Human Race?* along with a companion video series. Both detailed the issues of abortion and euthanasia in graphic detail.[49] In 1982 the pediatric surgeon achieved even more prominence when Ronald Reagan appointed him surgeon general, a post Koop held until 1989.

In addition to special speakers and events, the Center for Christian Study also hosted a regular program of courses meant "to offer interested Christians the chance to study their faith in a more disciplined and deeper way" through four-week and eight-week courses that primarily focused on the Bible and

---

[47]"The Staley Distinguished Christian Scholar Lecture Series," October 1976, private collection. Yamauchi was also elected vice president of the evangelical Conference on Faith and History in 1972; see "Personalia," *Christianity Today*, August 11, 1972, 41.

[48]Susan Wunderink, "Theologian Harold O. J. Brown Dies at 74" ChristianityToday.com, July 9, 2007, www.christianitytoday.com/ct/2007/julyweb-only/128-13.0.html (accessed September 11, 2019).

[49]Francis A. Schaeffer and C. Everett Koop, *Whatever Happened to the Human Race?*, in *Complete Works of Francis A. Schaeffer: A Christian Worldview*, vol. 5, *A Christian View of the West* (Westchester, IL: Crossway Books, 1982), 281-416. On Koop, see William C. Martin, *With God on Our Side: The Rise of the Religious Right in America* (New York: Broadway Books, 1996), 231, 238-57.

evangelism. In what stood for nearly a decade as the center's best-attended course, Don Lemons, an assistant dean at the university's law school, blended self-help with Christian commitment in a course titled Managing Your Time—An Exercise in Stewardship.[50] These courses were affordable—$3 plus books for the four-week course and $5 plus books for the eight-week course—and were "open to anyone in the Charlottesville community." These courses, along with the study center's other programs (e.g., the development of a library and the organization of lecture series) supported the center's larger efforts "to give expression to the principle that academic objectivity is compatible with Christian belief and that Christian community is the appropriate setting for Christian scholarship."[51] Like L'Abri and Regent, the Center for Christian Study was developing a learning *community* that sought to develop both the heart *and* the mind.

Even amid success, however, growth did not come without growing pains. Although University Christian Ministries was still squarely in the hands of Richman throughout the late 1970s, leadership at the study center fluctuated in the years following the purchase of the Chancellor Street residence. At the time of the purchase, Steiner was raising his own support to minister alongside Richman. Additionally, another young couple, Rob and Beth Gustafson, both University of Virginia graduates, had agreed to serve as resident directors of the new study center.[52] Within a year, however, both Steiner and the Gustafsons had moved on to different ventures. For Steiner, the move was vocational, not geographical. After conferring with Houston and Schaeffer, he enrolled in the University of Virginia's law school for fall 1977.[53] In a letter informing his

---

[50] Lemon's course garnered an enrollment of eighty-five. The second-most highly attended course at that point was the Center for Christian Studies' 1980 showing of the film *Whatever Happened to the Human Race?*, which had an enrollment of seventy-three. For more on evening course enrollment, see Chris D. Stanley, "The Study Center Evening Program: Where Do We Go from Here?," November 30, 1984, box "Old CCS Notes, Pre-1987," CCSA.

[51] "Courses: The Center for Christian Study," circa fall 1976, CCSA; "The Center for Christian Study," University Christian Ministries, circa fall 1977, box "Archives—Programs, 1985–1989," folder "Brochures," CCSA.

[52] Daryl Richman to [friends of the Gustafsons], June 5, 1976, box "Archives—Programs, 1985–1989," folder, "Fundraising Appeal Letters 1976–1986," CCSA.

[53] In a letter to friends Beat Steiner noted that during summer 1977 he and Barbara had visited Schaeffer at Swiss L'Abri. Steiner reported, "[The Schaeffers] are excited about what they hear about Charlottesville and reminded me once again of the tremendous potential the study center has." Steiner to family and friends, September 8, 1977, box "Archives—Programs, 1985–1989," folder "Fundraising Appeal Letters 1976–1986," CCSA.

friends, family, and financial supporters of his decision to attend law school, Steiner described the rationale for his decision at length. Noting that he was "leaving the Study Center at the end of its first phase—its establishment physically and organizationally," Steiner went on to state that he was "entrusting [the study center] to Janet Bash and Bob Cochran," a 1976 graduate of the law school. By this point Rob Gustafson had accepted a teaching job at Westminster, a prestigious preparatory school in Atlanta.[54] It was not until 1978, when University Christian Ministry board members hired David Turner from among their own ranks, that the Center for Christian Study had a long-term director.

Like Steiner, Turner came to the Center for Christian Study with strong ties to Action Ministries, Schaeffer, and Houston. As an undergraduate at the University of Virginia, Turner had begun to deepen his largely dormant faith in Christ after hearing Richman and Elzinga preach during the 1968–1969 school year. In the weeks following the sermon, Elzinga checked in on Turner and offered him one of Schaeffer's first books. Upon receiving the book, Turner realized that he knew its author. Turner's family was an influential part of the business and Christian community in Roanoke, Virginia, and was family friends with Jane Stuart Smith, a Roanoke-born opera singer turned L'Abri worker. As a result of the Turners' friendship with the Smith family, the Schaeffers had sent their daughter Debby to live with the Turners for several years while she attended Hollins College in Roanoke, Virginia.[55]

In fall 1970, following his graduation from the University of Virginia, Turner and his wife, Ellen, spent time with Francis and Edith Schaeffer at L'Abri. The experience was extremely significant for the newly married couple. Like so many others, the Turners found L'Abri to be "an extraordinary place" where one could pursue both intellectual and spiritual formation within Christian community. Turner later reflected, "It was at L'Abri, shortly after graduating from UVA, that I came out of the 'spiritual wastelands' of my own life."[56] By the end of his time in Europe, Turner was convinced that he needed to attend seminary rather than business school as he had previously planned. On the

---

[54]Steiner to family and friends, September 8, 1977; David Turner, interview with author, April 22, 2014, Charlottesville, VA.
[55]Turner, interview; Joseph F. Ryan to Francis A. Schaeffer, April 14, 1982, box "Lectures and Programs '80s, '90s," folder "Francis Schaeffer," CCSA.
[56]Turner, interview; David Turner, "University Christian Ministries: Winter, 1983," University Christian Ministries Newsletter (Winter 1983), folder "Newsletter Blurbs," CCSA.

advice of Os Guinness, Turner decided to attend Trinity Evangelical Divinity School, near Chicago. At Trinity, Turner energetically immersed himself in his studies but did not develop a sense of call to traditional pastoral ministry. After earning a master's of divinity in spring 1974, he returned to Roanoke to work as the treasurer for his family's large construction company.

Through each of these transitions Turner kept in touch with Richman. Turner's theological education, when combined with his business acumen and continuing interest in the work of Richman and Action Ministries at the university, made him a natural fit for the newly formed University Christian Ministries board. When he was offered an invitation to join the board shortly after the Center for Christian Studies was founded, Turner accepted. Then, during a routine University Christian Ministries board meeting, Turner was tapped to lead the Center for Christian Study.[57]

Following the brief tenure of Rob Gustafson, the University Christian Ministries board was tasked with finding a new director. Turner was heavily involved in the process. As time passed and the board continued to make little progress, some board members began to think that Turner himself might be the best candidate for the job. During one meeting Skip Ryan, University Christian Ministries board member and pastor of Trinity Presbyterian Church, asked Turner to consider the position. When Ryan suggested the move, Turner responded by asking for six months to consider what he should do. During this period Turner sought council from Regent College principal Jim Houston.[58] Through several long conversations with Houston, Turner's sense of call to the study center and its built-in emphasis on theological education geared toward laypeople was confirmed. In August 1978, he and his family moved to Charlottesville, and he began serving as Center for Christian Study director, a position he maintained through 1985.

Turner's hiring marked a significant period of growth and maturation for the study center. Under Turner, the daily operations moved in a Houstonian direction toward a greater emphasis on theological education of the laity. During these years, the educational work of the study center revolved around an intensive

---

[57]Turner, interview.
[58]Turner, interview. Turner was introduced to Houston by Bob Cochran. Houston spent a number of hours with Turner thinking through the possibility of Turner's involvement as the director of the study center.

one-year internship that emphasized "structured Christian learning and discipleship surrounded by an atmosphere of Christian community."[59] Though the internship program predated Turner, it was Turner who transformed this loosely defined program into something that maintained a personal feel while still adhering to a set schedule of study.[60] Under Turner the intern program blossomed and took a central role at the study center.

Turner saw the intern program as a means of lay theological education that was "more intense than one's Sunday school program but more accessible than a full seminary course." Over the first six years of Turner's tenure, intern cohorts ranged from six to fourteen people.[61] Unlike at L'Abri, most participants in the program did not live at the study center. By and large, the vast majority of those who participated in the program already lived in Charlottesville and attended Trinity Presbyterian Church. Usually classes of interns were composed of fewer than ten individuals, but in some cases a cohort might be as large as fourteen.[62] Interns attended lectures from 9:00 a.m. to 12:30 p.m. every Monday through Thursday. When not studying, each intern worked various part-time jobs in the community. Like Regent College's program of study, Turner's intern program revolved around a traditional course of seminary study aimed specifically at laypeople. There were courses on the principles of biblical interpretation, surveys of the Old and New Testaments, apologetics and evangelism, church history, and practical Christian living.

The Center for Christian Study never conceived of its goals in purely intellectual terms. Rather, Turner and the study center staff emphasized that along with this "growth in knowledge" interns would also encounter "a corresponding stress on personal spiritual growth" as "participants are continually challenged to apply what they are learning to their own lives, that they might not only think, but also live 'Christianly' on a daily basis."[63] Still, like almost

---

[59] "The Center for Christian Study," circa 1984, CCSA.
[60] Ken Elzinga to Christian student, spring 1976, box "Archives—Programs, 1985–1989," folder "Fundraising Appeal Letters, 1976–1986," CCSA. See also Richman to Dabney, June 15, 1977.
[61] Joseph R. Ryan Jr. to friends of the Christian Study Center, October 5, 1984, box "Archives—Programs, 1985–1989," folder "Fundraising Appeal Letters, 1976–1986," CCSA.
[62] In 1980 Turner lists the names of six interns in the University Christian Ministries Newsletter. See David Turner, "University Christian Ministries," 5, private collection. See also "The Center for Christian Study: Interns, 1983–1984," circa fall 1983, box "Archives—Programs, 1985–1989," CCSA; Center for Christian Study, "The Intern Program of the Center for Christian Study," 1984, box "Archives—Programs, 1985–1989," folder "Correspondence," CCSA.
[63] Center for Christian Study, "Intern Program of the Center for Christian Study."

every venture inspired by Schaeffer, Turner's program failed to reproduce Schaeffer's broad-ranging familiarity with topics such as art history and philosophy. Schaeffer, as it turned out, was hard to reproduce. Turner and the study center staff contented themselves with imitating some of Schaeffer's method (e.g., community-based learning) and his general appreciation for the intellect.

During Turner's tenure interns were often, though not always, recent graduates of the university who were looking for "a quality 'lay' educational program that will better equip them to serve Christ both in their vocations and in their home churches."[64] On the whole, participants in the program were usually divided fairly evenly between men and women. Racially, most participants were white; however, there were some notable exceptions. The 1983–1984 cohort of thirteen included internationally known Jamaican jazz pianist Monty Alexander (b. 1944).[65] In many cases the nature of the yearlong program, which required one to step away from full-time employment, virtually necessitated that interns be people with either time or money (or both) to spare.

In addition to the intern program, the study center's educational programming also included evening courses and, beginning in 1983, a weeklong summer program. Both of these efforts primarily catered to Charlottesville's evangelical community, though the summer program, with its condensed schedule and well-known cast of lecturers, did attract out-of-town students. Over 250 students enrolled in the initial summer program. In Elzinga's estimation the 1983 summer program "was a significant step for the Center," and he anticipated that the program would continue to succeed for years to come. For Elzinga, the Center for Christian Study filled a void left when Cornerstone and the C. S. Lewis Institute moved away from its successful College Park summer school in the late 1970s. "We are more and more persuaded," Elzinga noted, "that an event like this east of Vancouver, B. C. is much needed, to the end that we might carry out, in our own mode, what Regent College is doing so many miles west of us."[66]

---

[64]Center for Christian Study, "Intern Program of the Center for Christian Study."
[65]On Alexander, see Jeff Zeldman, "Monty Alexander: New Looks at Old Standards," *Washington Post*, January 12, 1984; Michael Dolan, "The Piano's Jazz Master of Mechanics," *Washington Times*, January 12, 1984; "Center for Christian Study: Interns, 1983–1984." Following his time in the intern program, Alexander continued his illustrious career as a jazz musician. In 2005 he was named among the top five jazz pianists of all time; see Gene Rizzo, *The Fifty Greatest Jazz Piano Players of All Time: Ranking, Analysis and Photos* (Milwaukee: Hal Leonard, 2005), 19-21.
[66]Elzinga to friends of the study center, November 7, 1983; Skip Ryan to Trinity member or friend, October 20, 1982.

Perhaps the most notable similarity between the Center for Christian Study summer program and Regent's summer school was the Charlottesville program's ability to harness a celebrity-filled cast of instructors. By bringing "the leading figures in evangelical Christianity," such as Houston (1983, 1985, 1987), Packer (1983, 1989), Tom Skinner (1985), Bruce Waltke (1985), Os Guinness (1985), Ed Clowney (1985), John Stott (1986), R. C. Sproul (1987), Gordon Fee (1988), David Wells (1988), Richard Neuhaus (1989), Becky Pippert (1989), Philip Yancey (1990), and David Gill (1991), among others, to Charlottesville as lecturers, the summer program offered hundreds of evangelicals in Charlottesville and beyond the opportunity to interact in a personal way with some of the evangelical world's brightest minds.[67]

Furthermore, like both L'Abri and Regent College, the Charlottesville summer program also tapped into the evangelical penchant to combine leisure and Christian education that had defined the camp meeting and Bible conference circuit since the nineteenth century.[68] As one endorsement of the summer program noted, "I don't know of a better way to combine good teaching, a relaxing atmosphere, a beautiful vacation spot and a wonderful opportunity to

---

[67] A nearly complete inventory of summer program brochures can be found in the CCSA: box "Archives—Programs, 1985-1989," folder "Brochures." For information on the later programs, I am drawing on Andrew Trotter's Center for Christian Study newsletters.

[68] Perhaps the most famous of these conferences were the prophecy conferences that emerged in the late nineteenth century at places such as the famous Niagara Bible Conference for prophetic study (founded 1876), D. L. Moody's Northfield conference, and the Winona Lake Bible Conference, which flourished in the early twentieth century. As Marsden notes, "The extended summer Bible conference with a series of famous speakers as the main attraction" was "one of the principal means of evangelical expression" when Billy Sunday made Winona Lake his home in 1911. See George M. Marsden, *Fundamentalism and American Culture: The Shaping of Twentieth-Century Evangelicalism, 1870-1925*, 2nd ed. (New York: Oxford University Press, 2006), 46, 132-33. For a good treatment of the Bible conference movement, see Ernest Robert Sandeen, *The Roots of Fundamentalism: British and American Millenarianism, 1800-1930* (Chicago: University of Chicago Press, 1970), 132-61. For a recent treatment of the Winona conferences, see Terry D. White and Stephen Grill, *Winona at 100: Third Wave Rising! The Remarkable History of Winona Lake, Indiana* (Winona Lake, IN: BMH Books, 2013). In Wesleyan circles camp meetings had served a similar function since at least the early nineteenth century. For examples of this combination of leisure and learning, see Paul Keith Conkin, *Cane Ridge, America's Pentecost* (Madison: University of Wisconsin Press, 1990), 86-87; John H. Wigger, *Taking Heaven by Storm: Methodism and the Rise of Popular Christianity in America* (New York: Oxford University Press, 1998), 185; Terry M. Heisey et al., *Evangelical from the Beginning: A History of the Evangelical Congregational Church and Its Predecessors—the Evangelical Association and the United Evangelical Church* (Lexington, KY: Emeth, 2006), 67-69, 132-33, 201-2, 316-17. The impulse to combine leisure and education was not limited to Christian groups. The highly successful summer Chautauqua Institute in New York provides one notable example; see Theodore Morrison, *Chautauqua: A Center for Education, Religion, and the Arts in America* (Chicago: University of Chicago Press, 1974); Jeffrey Simpson, *Chautauqua: An American Utopia* (New York: Harry N. Abrams, 1999).

spend time with friends than our Summer Program."[69] As at Regent and L'Abri, home-based hospitality and community were also a significant draw. Many local Christians opened up their homes for out-of-town guests, pool parties, and cookouts. The combination of these factors made the study center's summer program an enjoyable, content-rich experience that doubled as a Christian vacation and significant evangelical networking opportunity.

When the Center for Christian Study launched its summer program in 1983, the study center's longstanding evening program was already on the decline. This was a significant change at the Center for Christian Study. Like the intern program, the study center's evening program was initially a large and successful part of the ministry. Over time, however, the success of the evening program began to wane. By 1984 Turner and his staff were forced to seriously reconsider their efforts. From the launch of the evening program in spring 1977 through spring 1981, an average of eighty students attended evening courses each semester. Then, in fall 1981, enrollment started to fall. Between spring 1981 and fall 1984 the average total evening program enrollment dropped to forty-two students per semester. In a report addressing the issue, evening program director Chris Stanley, hired in early 1983 after his graduation from Regent College, pondered the future of the program at length. "It goes without saying," Stanley said, "that our Evening Program is not in the best of health. . . . It is difficult to see how the program can continue in its present form with the current level of attendance."[70] Stanley pointed to several possible reasons for the decline in numbers. In several cases publicity had been late or courses had changed at the last moment. Sometimes instructors were not able to present the material in an engaging way.

Surprisingly, however, Stanley found that the primary reasons for decline stemmed in large part from the growth of vibrant evangelical ministry options in Charlottesville—a trend the work of Richman and University Christian

---

[69]Andrew Trotter to friends, April 1990, box, Archives; folder, Newsletters 1990, CCSA; Trotter, interview; "University Christian Ministries: Spring/Summer 1983: Special Supplement, Summer Program 1983," Spring/Summer 1983, folder "Newsletter Blurbs," CCSA. With the exception of summer 1984 (when no summer program was offered), the study center summer program continued to function as a vital aspect of the study center's ministry until 1991, when poor attendance seemed to show that the summer program had run its course. Andrew Trotter to friends, February 1991, box "Archives," folder "Newsletters 1991," CCSA.
[70]Chris Stanley, "The Study Center Evening Program: Where Do We Go from Here?," November 30, 1984, box "Old CCS Notes, Pre-1987," CCSA; Center for Christian Study, "Intern Program of the Center for Christian Study."

Ministries had helped to catalyze. Stanley pointed out that "the students of today have a much broader range of options for Christian education around the University than they did even a few years ago." In the wake of flourishing student ministries, "most students already have all the Christian growth opportunities that their schedules (and their appetites?) can handle." Students were not the only Christians in Charlottesville with a host of new evangelical options. Surveying the drop-off in adult attendance, Stanley noted, "Many of the more 'evangelical' churches in town have taken steps in recent years to better provide for the educational needs of their people. In particular, both Trinity and Oakleigh, major sources of students in past years, now have their own adult education programs."[71] Ironically, Trinity's success now seemed to be hurting the Center for Christian Study.

In response to these trends, Stanley included a final section of his paper titled "What to Do?" In his opinion there were four possible paths forward. One path involved canceling "all lay education programs directed toward the community" and focusing instead "on student ministry, the Intern Program, and the Summer Program." The other three options involved tweaking the existing program in the hope that the evening program in some version of its current form could be salvaged.

The Study Center's Uncertain Future, 1985-1986

Though Stanley cast his hope in the direction of the final three suggestions, reality voted in favor of the first approach. By 1985 attendance and enthusiasm for evening program were flagging, and University Christian Ministries was struggling to pay the bills. Writing in July 1984, Turner informed supporters that the study center's finances were "critical." "We are operating with a monthly deficit of approximately $2,000," and the study center had closed out its fiscal year on June 31, 1984, "over $12,000 in debt."[72] Turner and other staff members had seen this financial crisis coming. As early as January 1985 they had already been planning to cut costs by trimming the staff at the end of June. For Turner it was time not only to evaluate the study center's programming but also to consider whether his employment at the study center—or even the educational mission of the study center itself—was viable.

---

[71] Stanley, "Study Center Evening Program."
[72] David Turner to friends of the center, July 12, 1984, folder, Newsletters, CCSA.

In a May letter to the University Christian Ministries board, Turner described the previous year's intern program as "disheartening." "Students in general seem to be less interested in issues that one might describe as developing a Christian world-life view," Turner noted. With the corresponding decline in the evening program and the drying up of University Christian Ministries funds, Turner felt that perhaps "ministry in the eighties" required "new wineskins." Noting that "the educational dimensions" of the study center did not "seem to be growing," Turner recommended that the board return the ministry to the emphasis on evangelism and discipleship that had defined Richman's original ministry. He posited two ideas for the future of University Christian Ministries. First, he recommended that the ministry should end the intern program and "find a new director whose strengths would be outreach and discipleship." His second recommendation, likely a response to University Christian Ministries's desperate financial situation, was to "link the Study Center to Trinity Church," thus sharing staff and costs.[73]

In the face of financial pressure, a seeming lack of community interest, and without a director, the University Christian Ministries board gave serious consideration to Turner's suggested revision of the study center's mission. Notably, this proposed shift in focus came at nearly the same time that other second-generation study centers such as the C. S. Lewis Institute and the Ligonier Valley Study Center were also shifting their focus away from the study center models of Schaeffer and Houston as they too adjusted to a changing culture and new financial realities. Although the Center for Christian Study had existed since 1975 with a dual focus on campus ministry and Christian education, by fall 1985 the board was prepared to follow Turner's suggestions and drop the study center's educational emphasis in favor of a campus ministry focus. As Turner noted in one of his last Center for Christian Study letters, the board was "increasingly . . . sensing the need to expand the evangelistic outreach and de-emphasize the educational programs."[74] In order to do this the board opted not to immediately replace Turner, but rather to hand the responsibility for the Chancellor Street house over to Elizabeth Brown, formerly Turner's administrative assistant. Brown had been involved in University Christian Ministries' thriving Fraternity-Sorority Fellowship since she was hired in summer 1983.

---

[73]This paragraph is entirely drawn from David Turner to fellow board members, May 17, 1985, Board Minutes, CCSA.
[74]David Turner to friends, November 18, 1985, folder "Newsletters," CCSA.

Under Brown's leadership, the Chancellor Street house functioned as a center for Christian outreach, including University Christian Ministries' multiple graduate ministries and the undergraduate Fraternity-Sorority Fellowship. The board also decided to keep the successful summer program, which continued to draw an audience thanks to its cast of well-known speakers. All regular educational programming, however, was discontinued, and giving to the center decreased substantially. It appeared that the Chancellor Street house's identity as a center for Christian *study* had come to an end.

PART 3
MULTIPLICATION

THE CONSORTIUM OF CHRISTIAN STUDY CENTERS

IN 1986 DREW TROTTER (b. 1950) received a letter that changed his life. As an ordained minister in the Presbyterian Church in America, Trotter was one of hundreds of ministers to receive a form letter in spring 1986 from Joseph "Skip" Ryan, pastor of Trinity Presbyterian Church in Charlottesville, Virginia, and a board member of the Center for Christian Study. Since 1975 the Center for Christian Study, located just off the grounds of the University of Virginia, had attempted to nurture the minds and the hearts of students and Charlottesville community members through a range of programming designed to develop students' hearts and minds in a way that would help them think and then live Christianly. Ryan's letter, written on behalf of the Center for Christian Study, advertised the study center's upcoming summer program as an educational opportunity for both clergy and their parishioners. For Trotter, the letter inspired nostalgia and piqued his curiosity. In short order he drafted a personal response to reestablish contact with Ryan and gain an up-to-date understanding of what was happening at the Charlottesville study center.[1]

Trotter's interest in developments within the Christian community in Charlottesville was to some extent the natural extension of his own Christian and

---

[1] This is all based on an interview with Andrew Trotter conducted on April 6, 2016. The actual 1986 letter does not remain, but a similar letter from 1987 is extant: Joseph F. Ryan to PCA ministers, March 27, 1987, folder "Summer Program 1987," CCSA. It is notable that this letter is written on Trinity letterhead, not on the letterhead of University Christian Ministries.

intellectual journey. As a student at the University of Virginia (1968–1972), Trotter had been a leader in Richman and Elzinga's Action Ministries—the parachurch ministry that birthed the Center for Christian Study—and was familiar with the later development of the study center and many of those who came to occupy prominent roles in its ministry.[2] Following his graduation from the University of Virginia in 1972, Trotter had first gone on to study for a master of divinity at Gordon-Conwell Theological Seminary before spending three years as a Bible teacher and chaplain at the Westminster Schools, one of Atlanta's most elite preparatory schools. Throughout all this time Trotter desired to take up academics at the highest level. In 1979 he was able to do just that when he and his family moved to England, where he began studying for a PhD in New Testament studies at Cambridge University.

As a student at Cambridge, Trotter sensed the time was right to follow up on a connection he had made years earlier with British-American pastor Stuart Briscoe (b. 1930). In a sixteen-page letter to Briscoe, Trotter outlined a vision for a study center at Elmbrook Church, Briscoe's independent Milwaukee megachurch. Briscoe soon asked Trotter to move to Milwaukee to head up the venture, which Trotter did in 1981. In Milwaukee, Trotter built a program from scratch and developed his ability to teach courses in fields ranging from biblical studies and theology to ethics and church history. The program thrived and soon established a partnership with Trinity Evangelical Divinity School.

Thanks to his experience at the Elmbrook Study Center and his wider educational experiences, Trotter knew a good deal about running a successful study center when Ryan's 1986 letter reached him. What he did not realize at that time, however, was how ready he was to move on to a different venture. This realization came a few weeks later when he received a second letter from Ryan. In his reply Ryan mentioned that the Charlottesville study center had been without a director since David Turner had stepped down in summer 1985. Ryan wondered whether Trotter would be interested in filling the position. Trotter instantly knew the answer. By the next November, he was in Charlottesville for an interview. After a few weeks of deliberation, Trotter was hired as director of the Center for Christian Study.[3]

---

[2] The biographical details of Trotter's life between his graduation from the University of Virginia and his hiring at the Center for Christian Study are drawn almost exclusively from interviews with the author in 2014 and 2016.

[3] Trotter, interview; David Turner to friends, November 18, 1985, folder "Newsletters," CCSA; David Turner to fellow board members, May 17, 1985, Board Minutes, CCSA.

Trotter officially joined the study center on April 1, 1987. Over the course of what would be a nearly twenty-two-year tenure at the study center, Trotter consistently worked to solidify the Center for Christian Study's original dual emphasis on discipleship training and theological education for laity. Not surprisingly, Trotter's greatest programmatic expansion came in the area of the study center's educational ministries. Not content to follow the path away from educational ministry that Turner and the board had begun to chart in 1985, Trotter sought to revamp the Center for Christian Study with a program he called the diploma in Christian studies. He also introduced a Seminary in the Summer program, which, like the Elmbrook Study Center, gave students the opportunity to earn seminary credit through Trinity Evangelical Divinity School (and later Westminster Theological Seminary and then Reformed Theological Seminary in Washington, DC) during a condensed two-week course in Charlottesville.

Expansion during Trotter's tenure at the Center for Christian Study was not limited to programs. In the mid-1990s Trotter also spearheaded a $900,000 expansion of the study center's building that more than doubled available meeting space in the Chancellor Street house. He also helped raise the study center's operating budget from approximately $27,000 in 1986 to over $900,000 during his last year at the study center.[4] All of these activities helped to solidify the study center's institutional identity while also raising its prominence. By the first decade of the twenty-first century, the Charlottesville Center for Christian Study had emerged as one of the foremost models of a university-based study center, and Trotter had moved on to a position of national influence within a study center movement that, thanks in part to the work of the Charlottesville study center, was experiencing a fresh wave of interest and growth.

Expanding the Center for Christian Study's Educational Goals

When he arrived at the Center for Christian Study in April 1987, Trotter inherited a set of Center for Christian Study programs that consisted of several graduate Christian fellowships and the undergraduate Fraternity-Sorority Fellowship. Turner's intern program and evening courses at the study center had both ended in 1985. The only explicitly educational program still hosted by the study center in 1987 was the summer program the Center for Christian

---

[4] Trotter, interview; Shelly Pellish, "Fundraising Update," *Praxis* 13, no. 2 (Summer 2009).

Study had continued to organize even in Turner's absence. When Trotter arrived in spring 1987, he also inherited a fully planned 1987 summer program, featuring famous missionary Elisabeth Elliot, R. C. Sproul, and James Houston.

This was the third time in the summer program's five-year history that Houston, the founding principal of Regent College and his era's most prominent evangelical advocate of lay theological education, was scheduled to speak at the event.[5] Houston's frequent presence symbolized the many connections between Regent and the Center for Christian Study. These were not lost on Trotter. From the start Trotter emphasized the study center's shared origins in both Schaeffer's L'Abri and Houston's Regent College.[6] Trotter had spent time at L'Abri during his college years, so he knew that Schaeffer's Swiss retreat offered a model for the reasoned evangelism and hospitality that to some extent characterized the study center's undergraduate and graduate ministries. It was Regent College, however, that offered Trotter a model for a formal educational program that combined an emphasis on lay theological education with a desire to be a Christian presence on the campus of a secular university.

In no small part Trotter's appreciation for Regent stood behind his decision shortly after his arrival at the study center to revamp the Center for Christian Study's defunct intern program as a more academically rigorous diploma in Christian studies program. From its name—the exact name of Regent's original one-year academic program—to its methodology, the Center for Christian Study's diploma program owed much to its Canadian predecessor. At the center of this instruction was an emphasis on the theological education of the laity. Trotter observed that even at a national level there were "few programs that are geared specifically toward teaching lay people in their language and seeking to meet their need to develop a Christian mind; this is virtually the *raison d'etre* of the Diploma program."[7]

Trotter also planned to include events that would give his diploma program a more L'Abri-esque ethos by seeking to combine classroom learning with outside activities ranging from local service projects to a Fridays in Washington program, which included trips to museums and Capitol Hill, in order to

---

[5] Houston spoke at the Charlottesville summer program in 1983, 1985, and 1987.
[6] In a 2014 conversation Trotter noted, "The study center became a cross between L'Abri and Regent College. . . . That's something I've said a million times between 1987 and now."
[7] Andrew Trotter, "CCS Newsletter: December 1987," box "Archives," folder "Newsletters 1987," CCSA.

Figure 7.1. Drew Trotter leading a discussion with students in the diploma of Christian studies program at the Center for Christian Study in the early 1990s.

"develop each other spiritually, physically, emotionally and intellectually."[8] Thus like Turner's program before it and other study centers deeply inspired by L'Abri and Reformed theology (e.g., the Ligonier Valley Study Center), Trotter planned for learning to take place on a holistic dimension that involved the head, heart, and hands.

One of the things that set Trotter's program apart from both L'Abri and Turner's earlier intern program—while also reinforcing gradually emerging trends in the Christian study center movement—was that Trotter, unlike either Turner or Schaeffer, possessed an earned doctorate. In September 1987, nearly a decade after beginning doctoral studies at Cambridge University, Trotter was granted a PhD in New Testament studies. As Trotter informed the readers of his newsletter, his degree had the potential to open "some exciting doors" at the study center, because "we can now offer graduate credit for the courses we will teach." By December 1987 Trotter had made arrangements with Trinity Evangelical Divinity School to partner with the Center for Christian Study by sending professors to teach courses at the center and by accepting credit for the courses Trotter taught. Like Regent, the Center for Christian Study was

---

[8] Andrew Trotter, "CCS Newsletter: March 1993," box "Archives," folder "Newsletters 1993," CCSA.

moving into the formal graduate instruction of laypeople while maintaining an emphasis on personal relationships since, as Trotter noted, "the tutorial," an essential and individualized aspect of British university education, remained "a staple of instruction."[9]

When the program officially began in fall 1988, Trotter was optimistic. Six students had registered for full-time study, four were taking courses for credit, and approximately twenty-five others were auditing the course. The numbers nearly mirrored Regent's first year of full-time courses. Trotter was encouraged that the group contained "people who are just shortly out of college and some who are over fifty. There are males and females, blacks and whites, people who look to be in business, medicine, academics, ministry." The program's first weekend seminar kicked off with an address by theologian and former *Christianity Today* editor in chief Carl F. H. Henry, who spoke on the history and future of evangelicalism in the United States.[10] The formula seemed right for success.

Yet for all its promise, Trotter's diploma program never really took off. Like most other evangelical efforts to train laypeople after the mid-1970s, Trotter found that there were few people who were willing to take a year off for a diploma program. In July 1989 three of the original four diploma students graduated. Unlike Regent, which had seen the number of full-time students shoot up from four to forty-four during its second year, by September 1992 Trotter's program only had six full-time students.[11]

Trotter was still committed to the program, however, and was convinced that it could continue to expand as the key focus of the Center for Christian Study's ministry to students and laypeople. In June 1993 Trotter informed his readers that the diploma program, which "had never been full before," now had a waiting list. By the next fall Trotter was writing to supporters of the study center regarding what he described as "an exciting new direction we believe Divine providence is leading us in regard to the *Diploma in Christian Studies* program." Describing the diploma program as "a very important part of the answer to the problem of lay theological education in America today," Trotter

---

[9]Trotter, "CCS Newsletter: October, 1987." Trotter's 1986 dissertation was titled "Understanding and Stumbling: A Study of the Disciples' Understanding of Jesus and His Teaching in the Gospel of Matthew."

[10]Andrew Trotter, "CCS Newsletter: October 1988," box "Archives," folder "Newsletters 1988," CCSA.

[11]Andrew Trotter, "CCS Newsletter: September 1992," box, Archives; folder, Newsletters 1992, CCSA; Andrew Trotter, "CCS Newsletter: July 1989," box "Archives," folder "Newsletters 1989," CCSA.

outlined an ambitious plan. Noting that "over half of our graduates over the last six years have no degree from UVa, i.e. are coming to us *not* because they have been students here, we believe there is a market out there for the 30-40 students we would eventually like to have in the program." Such a shift meant that Trotter would have to spend more time traveling and recruiting students. He also planned to "hire the faculty necessary for us to retain the small group focus of our program." In order to meet the second of these needs Trotter entered into conversation with Jeffrey Greenman, a PhD candidate in religious studies at the University of Virginia who had earned a master of divinity at Regent College. The young scholar had taught a class on the Old Testament in the fall, was currently teaching a class on the New Testament for spring semester, and, Trotter wrote in his August 1994 newsletter, "will, God willing, be joining us this coming fall as a second teacher in the *Diploma* program."[12]

This was the high point of Trotter's hopes for a yearlong diploma in Christian studies program based on the Regent model. In spite of his optimism during fall 1994 and early spring 1995, the diploma program never attracted the thirty to forty students Trotter had hoped, and Greenman, whom Trotter had predicted would stay on to teach in fall 1994, opted not to join the Center for Christian Study staff. Instead he launched into a successful academic and administrative career that in fall 2015 saw him come full circle to serve as the fifth president of Regent College. In the end, Trotter and the Center for Christian Study board determined that the program was not a good use of the study center's resources. By May 1997 Trotter's take on the diploma program had changed, and he reported to readers of his newsletter on the "the scaling down and re-thinking" of the diploma program.[13]

Like the study center's summer program, which gradually lost momentum before its final year in 1991, the diploma in Christian studies program, like other efforts in lay education at places such as the Ligonier Valley Study Center and New College Berkeley, ran headlong into a changing evangelical and American culture. Unlike the early 1970s, when places such as L'Abri and Regent thrived,

---

[12] Andrew Trotter, "CCS Newsletter: August 1994," box "Archives," folder "Newsletters 1994," CCSA, emphasis original.
[13] Trotter, interview; Andrew Trotter, "CCS Newsletter: May 1997," box "Archives," folder "Newsletters 1997," CCSA. On Greenman, see "A Historic Moment: The Installation of Jeffrey P. Greenman as President," Regent College, November 2, 2015, www.regent-college.edu/about-us/news/2015/a-historic-moment-the-installation-of-jeffrey-p-greenman-as-regents-fifth-president.

in the 1980s and 1990s Americans often seemed less willing to take time off from their careers to spend a year studying for a diploma, which was not even a formal academic degree. In addition to its Canadian location, which offered less competition in the area of evangelical graduate education, Regent College survived these cultural shifts reasonably well because it had the benefit of a head start during the coming of age of both the baby boomers and the evangelical counterculture. On top of this, the Vancouver college offered accredited academic and professional degrees. By the 1980s and early 1990s American students were often interested more in the financial payoff of a degree than in the experience and content of learning.[14] Both Turner's intern program and Trotter's diploma in Christian studies program had come onto the scene after this shift and had failed to secure high enough enrollment or financial vitality. Thus, even in places such as Charlottesville that was home to an affluent evangelical community that valued education, the 1980s and 1990s were difficult decades for long-term lay education programs.

In the face of these changes, all but the most well-established institutions of lay education had to curtail or completely eliminate long, celebrity-driven summer programs and yearlong diploma programs in favor of a variety of educational programs that either (1) offered seminary credit, (2) were based on one-time lectures and weekend conferences, or (3) tapped into an already present audience (e.g., college students, listeners and viewers at home). The Center for Christian Study adapted to this new reality late, but it did eventually adapt. The result was an educational approach that was more sustainable than anything the study center had previously tried.

As the Center for Christian Study moved away from extensive summer programs and the diploma program, Trotter continued to emphasize the importance of study at the *study* center. One way in which he did this was to turn the Center for Christian Study's educational opportunities increasingly in the direction of courses offered on a no-credit basis. Such courses had been a part of the study center's original programming but had ended with Turner's tenure. Trotter revived them, and even in the midst of the diploma program's most demanding years he conducted open lecture series and one-off talks,

---

[14]For shifts in student motivation during these decades, see Eric L. Dey, Alexander W. Astin, and William S. Korn, *The American Freshman: Twenty-Five-Year Trends* (Los Angeles: Higher Education Research Institute. Graduate School of Education UCLA, 1991).

and at times he worked with departments at the University of Virginia to cosponsor lectures such as the two lectures by novelist Frederick Buechner in March 1992.[15] In 1997 the Center for Christian Study began offering what Trotter called the "long course" and "short course" options as part of a revamped diploma program.[16] In reality this new structure was the beginning of a shift in the Center for Christian Study's regular educational ministry. Trotter hoped the condensed format would meet "the needs of those who cannot take a whole week off (or more)."[17]

By the late 1990s few of the Center for Christian Study's not-for-credit discussion groups were as popular as Trotter's Third Fridays program, a monthly movie discussion that started in fall 1996. For Trotter, the goal was to get people to "think Christianly about movies," a media form he described as "one of the great cultural barometers of our times."[18] Trotter's interest in movies as an art form and cultural commentary spanned the length of his tenure at the Center for Christian Study and is perhaps traceable to the influence of Francis Schaeffer, who delighted in analyzing films with evangelical young people who had been told their entire lives to avoid the perils of Hollywood. Other Schaeffer-inspired evangelicals such as Sharon Gallagher of *Radix* magazine had cultivated similar interests in film criticism following extended interactions with Schaeffer. Trotter had lectured on movies at the Center for Christian Study since at least February 1991, when he and fellow Charlottesville resident Ken Myers, author of *All God's Children and Blue Suede Shoes: Christians and Popular Culture* and later founder of Mars Hill Audio, teamed up to present a weekend seminar titled "Show and Tell: Movies and Television in Contemporary America."[19]

---

[15] Andrew Trotter, "CCS Newsletter: August 1991," box "Archives," folder "Newsletters 1991," CCSA; Andrew Trotter, "CCS Newsletter: March 1992," box "Archives," folder "Newsletters 1992," CCSA.
[16] This was one of the last times Trotter used the terminology "diploma program." The diploma program had not graduated any students since 1995 (Trotter, interview).
[17] For Trotter's discussion of long and short courses, see Andrew Trotter, "CCS Newsletter: June 1997," box "Archives," folder "Newsletters 1997," CCSA.
[18] Writing in winter 1997, Trotter reflected on his interest in movies: "I have written and spoken extensively on film for years now, and seen come into the realm of serious Christian calling what was once simply a hobby of mine." See Andrew Trotter, "From the Executive Director," *Praxis* 1, no. 2 (Winter 1997).
[19] Ken Myers, *All God's Children and Blue Suede Shoes: Christians and Popular Culture* (Westchester, IL: Crossway Books, 1989); Andrew Trotter, "CCS Newsletter: November 1990," box, Archives; folder, Newsletters 1990, CCSA.

Trotter's emphasis on engaging film as a medium represented the ethos that he was trying to bring to the ministry of the Center for Christian Study. Trotter hoped that those who passed through the doors of the Chancellor Street house might be better prepared to think Christianly about all areas of life, learning, and culture, not just the explicitly religious ones. Like Schaeffer before him, such a view did not always win Trotter the approval of his evangelical constituency. In fall 2002 Trotter noted that "twice recently" he had "heard charges against the position the Center for Christian Study has taken on the validity—no let's put it clearly with all the starkness it was put to me—on the rightness of going to some movies." Critiques alleged that when the Center for Christian Study sponsored viewings of movies such as the Academy Award–winning Best Picture of 1999, *American Beauty*, it risked doing harm to the hearts and minds of evangelicals in the audience. While Trotter admitted that "these charges have some merit in their assumptions both that movies are a powerful medium and that they can be harmful to the spirit," he offered a full-throated appeal for evangelical engagement with film. This impulse only grew with Trotter's continued engagement with the medium. For Trotter, a Christian's responsibility was clear: "At whatever level you can you should be watching movies and discussing them with others in light of the gospel."[20]

Over time Trotter's reputation as an evangelical who could analyze film opened the door to a variety of speaking engagements and ministries across the country. Of these opportunities, none had more significance for the future of the Center for Christian Study than his being invited to co-lead a workshop titled "Media, Film, and the Image" at the November 1994 Harvard Veritas Forum. Founded in 1992 by Harvard University chaplain Kelly Monroe (later Kullberg), the Veritas Forum sought "to raise the hardest questions of the university, society, and the human heart to explore the possible relevance of Jesus Christ to all of life."[21] In so doing, Veritas Forum events functioned like condensed and hybridized versions of Regent's summer school and an evening talk around the L'Abri fire with Schaeffer. Veritas Forum weekend conferences were always educational, apologetic, and star-studded affairs that offered Christian

---

[20] Andrew Trotter, "From the President: Signs . . . and Sometimes Wonders," *Praxis* 6, no. 3 (Fall 2002); Andrew Trotter, "Responsibility," *Praxis* 12, no. 4 (Winter 2009).

[21] David McGaw coled the workshop with Trotter and Elisabeth Overman; Bruce Herman and Bill Edgar contributed. See Kelly Monroe, "The Harvard Veritas Forum," November 1994, folder "Harvard Veritas," CCSA.

students a chance to interact with some of the brightest Christian minds of the day while simultaneously reassuring them that orthodox Christian faith and a rigorous pursuit of the intellect were not mutually exclusive. From the start, Veritas Forum events shared many affinities with study centers, none more than a desire to nurture college students in vibrant, intellectually robust faithfulness to Christ, and the partnership was symbiotic. Veritas events provided star power and publicity for geographically rooted study centers, while study centers provided a built-in network and an emphasis on hospitality that made a difference both during and after a Veritas Forum event. Furthermore, as sociologist Michael Lindsay notes, events such as these also played a key role in fostering evangelical networks across various university campuses, a trend especially evident at elite schools.[22]

By the time Trotter traveled to Cambridge, Massachusetts, in November 1994, he was well acquainted with the Veritas Forum. Since first hearing about the program, Trotter had been intent on bringing a Veritas Forum to the University of Virginia. Thanks in large part to the longstanding campus ministry meeting, which brought the ministry heads of various campus ministries together at the Center for Christian Study twice a month, Trotter was able to secure the required invitation signed by over 80 percent of campus ministry heads at the university.[23] In his June 1994 Center for Christian Study newsletter Trotter noted that, "though spear-headed by the Center for Christian Study," the upcoming Veritas Forum "is being actively promoted and co-sponsored by virtually every Christian group on the grounds of the University." As such, he saw it as "a wonderful testimony to the unity that we do have here in Christ that so many groups could come together so quickly in order to pull off something of this magnitude." Only a few months later, in October 1994, the University of Virginia became the third university in the United States to host a Veritas Forum.[24]

---

[22] D. Michael Lindsay, *Faith in the Halls of Power: How Evangelicals Joined the American Elite* (New York: Oxford University Press, 2007), 90-91.

[23] Trotter, interview. The process usually took much longer. Trotter remembers encountering disbelief from the folks at Veritas when he claimed to be able to deliver the signed invitation within a few weeks. Andrew Trotter, "CCS Newsletter: September 1993," box "Archives," folder "Newsletters 1993," CCSA.

[24] Trotter, "CCS Newsletter: August 1994." Only Harvard and Ohio State University hosted events earlier. Both had direct ties to Monroe, who was a campus minister at Harvard and was originally from Columbus, Ohio.

Building on this promising start, the Veritas Forum became a staple of Christian ministry at the University of Virginia and the Center for Christian Study. After experimenting with the idea of an annual Veritas Forum, Trotter and the leaders of campus ministries opted to host the event on a biannual basis. The 1996 Veritas Forum at the University of Virginia was an even bigger success than the first event. Over sixteen hundred people came to hear talks by leading Christian scholars such as John Polkinghorne, George Marsden, Alvin Plantiga, and Edwin Yamauchi. The forum's numerical success continued well into the next decade. It was not uncommon for Veritas Forum speakers such as Os Guinness to fill the university's five-hundred-seat Chemistry Auditorium to capacity for several nights in a row.[25] By the mid-2000s, however, interest among campus groups began to flag, and forum events drew much smaller crowds. In 2013 the Center for Christian Study and other ministry groups decided against continuing the program on a regular basis.

In some ways the study center's participation in the Veritas Forum represented an updated version of the once-successful summer program. Like the earlier program, the Veritas Forum offered everyday evangelicals an educational event that harnessed interaction with celebrity speakers and fascinating discussions on a host of academic topics. Just as the study center's diploma program was being reassessed and only a few years after the last summer program in 1991, the Veritas Forum provided Trotter and the Center for Christian Study with a large event that managed to hit several of the points of emphasis in these earlier programs while also uniting campus ministries and reaching far more individuals. Perhaps more significantly, the Veritas Forum was aimed primarily at an audience of students and professors at the University of Virginia. In so doing it hinted at the study center's move in a similar direction. Whereas early study center educational programs usually aimed for community involvement and attracted at least as many nonstudents as students, during the 1990s the study center began to move gradually in a more student-centric direction. As it did, it charted a course that helped ensure not only its own viability but also the viability of the evangelical study center movement in general.

---

[25] Andrew Trotter, "CCS Newsletter: May 1997," box "Archives," folder "Newsletters 1997," CCSA; Trotter, interview; Andrew Trotter, "Engaging Issues of Truth, Meaning and Purpose," *Praxis* 6, no. 4 (Winter 2002). Guinness returned for the 2009 forum: Wes Zell, "Living Sanely When Life Is Fired Point-Blank: Os Guinness Addresses Students at Veritas Forum 2009," *Praxis* 13, no. 2 (Summer 2009).

Making Room: Hospitality and Place at the CCS

From the start the Chancellor Street house itself had been the epicenter of the Center for Christian Study's student outreach, especially its outreach to undergraduates. Located directly across from the university's sorority row and just a block from Thomas Jefferson's rotunda and the heavily trafficked corner, the house at 128 Chancellor Street was an easily accessible feature of university life. It was a place where students could stop in anytime to study or to enjoy a study break. The building regularly hosted meetings for campus ministers, a wide variety of Bible studies and small group gatherings related to other parachurch organizations, and many of the Center for Christian Study's own ministries, such as Fraternity-Sorority Fellowship and Graduate Christian Fellowship. Learning happened both in the house's meeting rooms and "in the door," where impromptu conversations between students or between a student and Trotter (or one of the four part-time staff members who joined him by December 1988) were common.[26]

In addition to the draw of the building's study spaces, meeting rooms, and staff, the Chancellor Street house was also a magnet for students thanks in part to Trotter's commitment to provide technology—in the form of public computers and a copier—for student use. Shortly after being hired at the study center, Trotter had purchased the Center for Christian Study's first two computers with the help of a grant from the Maclellan Foundation in Chattanooga, Tennessee. The study center's technology was an immediate draw. "We have experienced a tremendous increase in the usage of our equipment and building, too," Trotter noted in late 1991. "Our copier and computers are being used regularly for the ministries of InterVarsity, Campus Crusade, International Students, Inc."[27] By providing the use of free technology to Christian groups at the university, the study center further established itself as the hub of Christian activity at the school.

As the number of students frequenting the Chancellor Street house grew, so did the Center for Christian Study's prominence. Much of the study center's publicity came through word of mouth as former students informed incoming students and as visiting speakers informed their colleagues, though the study

---

[26]Trotter, "CCS Newsletter: October 1988"; Andrew Trotter, "CCS Newsletter: December 1988," box "Archives," folder "Newsletters 1988," CCSA.

[27]Andrew Trotter, "CCS Newsletter: December 1991," box "Archives," folder "Newsletters 1991," CCSA. Trotter was a Tennessean and had connections to individuals involved in this foundation.

center did gain national exposure in 1994 and 1995 when the US Supreme Court chose to hear a religious liberties case surrounding University of Virginia student Ron Rosenberger, who had published a Christian magazine called *Wide Awake* on the study center's computers. Rosenberger and his team of lawyers from the newly formed Center for Individual Rights eventually won a five-to-four decision at the Supreme Court in June 1995. The case of *Ronald Rosenberger et al. v. Rector and Visitors of the University of Virginia et al.* provided a new precedent for state funding of religiously oriented organizations based on the right of free speech.[28]

Though it is difficult to ascertain the extent to which the Rosenberger case benefited the study center by raising its national exposure, it is worth noting that by the time the case was decided in June 1995, giving to the Center for Christian Study had increased to the point that Trotter was able to inform friends of the ministry that the study center was "better off than we have been for some time because of your generosity throughout the year."[29] In Trotter's estimation other areas of the study center's ministry were poised to grow too. Expansion, whether in terms of the success of the Veritas Forum, hoped-for developments in the diploma program, the study center's budget, or simply the growing use of

Figure 7.2. The 1997 expansion (shown in the bottom right) more than doubled the size of the Center for Christian Study.

---

[28] Matthew E. K. Hall, *The Nature of Supreme Court Power* (New York: Cambridge University Press, 2010), 118. The case and the justices' decisions can be found at "Rosenberger v. Rector & Visitors of the University of Virginia," Cornell University Law School: Legal Information Institute, www.law.cornell.edu/supremecourt/text/515/819 (accessed April 28, 2016). For the Center for Individual Rights' take on the case, see "Rosenberger v. University of Virginia," Center for Individual Rights, www.cir-usa.org/cases/rosenberger-v-university-of-virginia/ (accessed April 28, 2016).

[29] Andrew Trotter, "CCS Newsletter: June 1995," box "Archives," folder "Newsletters 1995," CCSA.

the Center for Christian Study building by students, was unmistakable on Chancellor Street. Whether for Bible studies, ministry meetings, or the use of the study center's resources, more students than ever before were making use of the house on Chancellor Street.

The situation posed by a growing budget and a shrinking space soon resulted in plans for a building campaign at the student center. Trotter had been alluding to a need for more space since the early 1990s, but by the mid-nineties the need for expansion could be delayed no longer. Beginning in 1993 the Center for Christian Study board began considering options to expand the study center's physical space, eventually settling on a design by Bruce Wardell, a local architect who had previously taught an evening course at the study center. Wardell's projected five-thousand-square-foot addition would more than double the size of the Chancellor Street house and cost nearly a million dollars. Earlier in the Center for Christian Study's history, such a large undertaking would have been unthinkable. By 1996, however, the study center's Rosenberger bump in publicity, its growing pool of alumni, and the practical appeal of donating toward a building enlarged and energized the study center's pool of donors. Writing in December of that year, Trotter summarized "the building situation" by announcing that "we have raised all but about $100,000 of our needs, and we *can* cover that figure with projected new revenue from the apartment in our plan."[30]

By fall 1997 the Center for Christian Study was ready to welcome students to a building whose appeal had greatly increased. While much of the old section of the house still retained the charm of small, cozy rooms (although the kitchen had been significantly expanded and improved), it was the added sections of the building that set the tone for a new paradigm of ministry at the study center. From a spacious meeting room that could hold upward of one hundred people to a new third-floor library with room for ten thousand volumes—more than double that of the Center for Christian Study's previous library space—the study center's addition offered space for larger events, a better-stocked and better-situated library, and more nooks, crannies, desks, and chairs for study.

It was not simply that the Center for Christian Study was *bigger*; in terms of both utility and aesthetics, the renovated study center building was significantly *better*. From the start Trotter and the board had sought to create spaces

---

[30] "University Christian Ministries: Spring/Summer 1983," folder "Newsletter Blurbs," CCSA; Trotter, interview.

Figure 7.3. The Center for Christian Study library fills with students each semester during exam week.

"that were very beneficial to the academic project" while still allowing the study center "to feel like a home." The expanded library and meeting room helped the Center for Christian Study achieve the first of these goals. So, too, did the newly expanded and relocated Splintered Light Bookstore (founded 1994). The building's larger new meeting rooms were also planned with an eye toward creating an inviting, not just useful, space. Trotter worked with Wardell to ensure that both the large-group meeting room and the new library were centered on fireplaces. Furthermore, with walls all but filled with large windows, both the new meeting room and library were brightly lit spaces that offered panoramic views of the city and outlying mountains from the study center's location on Charlottesville's third-highest point. All of this demonstrated that the Center for Christian Study, following the path of institutions such as Regent College, had matured in its aesthetic self-consciousness. Space became not just functional but also theological. As a later staff member wrote, "One of our theological convictions here at the Center is that while earthly institutions and spaces are not themselves ultimate, they matter greatly because they help point us towards that which actually is. Institutions and spaces are so important because they shape the sort of human life that can happen within them."[31]

---

[31] Wes Zell, "Study Center Spaces: A Site That Supports Kingdom Work of All Kinds," *Praxis* 11, no. 2 (Summer 2007); Trotter, interview; "Splintered Light Adds a New Perspective," *Praxis* 1, no. 2 (Winter 1997); "Center Expansion Makes Room for a Familiar Vision," *Praxis* 1, no. 1 (Fall 1997). The library became a prime study spot for both graduate and undergraduate students; see Eric Vettel, "A Place for Study, a Place for Living," *Praxis* 7, no. 3 (Fall 2003).

Increased space also served the seemingly paradoxical function of making the study center both more autonomous and more connected. The new addition included a basement apartment that could house up to eleven undergraduate men. Not only did this initiate a new residential element in the study center's life that eventually grew into the Faith and Life Residential Year (renamed the Elzinga Residential Scholars in 2010), but the inclusion of apartments also afforded the Center for Christian Study a means of income apart from fundraising.[32] The opportunity to generate additional income in the building helped pay off the mortgage on the new addition and further ensured the study center's financial sustainability. More space also increased the ministry's autonomy in that it had less need to procure space from local churches or the university for midsize events.

With income, space, and a larger-than-ever profile on university grounds, the Center for Christian Study was prepared to enter a new phase of ministry. As a sign of the study center's increasing sense of institutional identity and rising ambitions, the ministry replaced Trotter's regular newsletters with its own quarterly journal, *Praxis*, in fall 1997—just as the renovated building opened its doors to students. *Praxis* featured a number of stories on the newly constructed building and the Center for Christian Study's expanded programming. By its second year *Praxis* was also offering the first published accounts of the study center's history.[33] Trotter and the board had decided they had a story worth preserving—and sharing.

In the midst of change, however, many former elements of the Center for Christian Study's ministry remained. The new building continued to host its traditional fellowship meetings and its bimonthly campus ministers meetings. While the new space afforded greater autonomy, it also allowed the Center for Christian Study to better connect with and serve other parachurch ministries at the university. When the new building opened, Trotter counted "eight to 10 student ministries that call the Study Center 'home' for everything from large

---

[32] "Receiving and Walking: The Faith and Life Residential Year," *Praxis* 12, no. 1 (Spring 2008); Trotter, interview. In fall 2008 the study center began hosting an analogous community consisting of twelve women in the house next door to the study center. See Kathy Schneider, "Chancellor Street House Gives Faith New Meaning," *The Cavalier Daily*, circa 1998, 5.

[33] Articles on the study center's history include "A Beat with a Different Drum," *Praxis* 2, no. 1 (Spring 1998); "A Friend for All Seasons," *Praxis* 2, no. 2 (Summer 1998); "Moving Beyond the Margins," *Praxis* 2, no. 3 (Fall 1998); "Of the Stacking of Many Books," *Praxis* 2, no. 3 (Fall 1998); "A Celebration of Spiritual Roots: Center for Christian Study's 30th Anniversary," *Praxis* 2, no. 4 (Winter 1998).

group meetings to photocopying."[34] In addition to regular leaders' meetings, the Center for Christian Study also fostered collegiality among campus ministers by offering them the use of office space in the study center. In fall 1997 the area director of Young Life and the Virginia director of the Christian Medical and Dental Society shared office spaces with Center for Christian Study staff members. In the years to come the center also hosted the staff members of the University of Virginia's InterVarsity chapter. More than ever, the study center was a hub of Christian activity at the university. Its influence had grown with its building.

Before long, Center for Christian Study staff members began referring to the building as the ninth member of the staff. As a place, the expanded building became what Elzinga described the year after the completion of the renovation as "a geographic locus of identity" for Christian students. Over time the importance of the actual study center only grew in the minds of study center staff and students alike. More than fifteen years after the renovation, longtime Center for Christian Study staff member Bill Wilder noted, "In the minds of most students, our ministry is inseparable from (and unimaginable without) our building on Chancellor Street."[35]

Feeding Hearts, Minds, and Stomachs

From the start the renovated and redesigned kitchen became an especially important feature of the new building as "hospitality came to play an increasingly

Figure 7.4. A student studies in the stacks of the Center for Christian Study library.

---

[34]"Beat with a Different Drum,"; "Friend for All Seasons"; "Moving Beyond the Margins," *Praxis* 2, no. 3 (Fall 1998); "Of the Stacking of Many Books"; "Celebration of Spiritual Roots."

[35]William Wilder, "Strategic Plan, Section I" (unpublished document, Center for Christian Study, Charlottesville, VA, 2012), 14-15; Trotter, interview; "Celebration of Spiritual Roots." Wilder went on to note that the house's importance to the ministry was "a reality also clearly reflected in the prominence of our house in both the older and newer Study Center logos."

important role at the study center."[36] In fall 1999 a few parents decided to meet up at the study center for lunch on first-year-student move-in day with some of their friends who were also dropping new students off at the university. What started as a small group of parents quickly grew into an official Center for Christian Study event. By 2003, move-in-day lunch was a fixture of the study center's regular programming, with 175 students, parents, and siblings in attendance that year to eat and hear talks from prominent University of Virginia professors Ken Elzinga and James Davison Hunter. Elzinga's involvement in the lunch was especially significant. As an esteemed faculty member, Elzinga's presence and support sent an implicit message to incoming students: if one of the university's most prominent faculty members could balance the Christian faith and the demands of the academy, students could too. As attendance at these luncheons grew rapidly to 250 people in 2004 to over 400 people in 2006, the event socialized Christian students into the university's Christian community before their feet even hit the grounds.[37] Describing the lunch, one study center staff member noted:

> [Students are] greeted by veterans of the lunch and their fellow classmates. Conversations happen, and in the course of these conversations they begin to realize they are not in this alone. Friendships form at Move-In Day with classmates who will become future roommates, sorority sisters/fraternity brothers, study partners, small group leaders . . . even future spouses. During the lunch they also hear from Center staff, Grounds Ministry partners, and University Professor Ken Elzinga about the wider believing community at work at UVa.[38]

With parents, upperclassmen, professors, and the leadership of various campus ministries at the University participating, move-in-day lunches functioned as a symbol of the Center for Christian Study's ability to foster unity among Christian groups and as a method for ushering incoming Christian students into the community of Christians at the university.

---

[36]Wilder, "Strategic Plan," 10. It seems to have been with the addition of the new portion of the house and the renovation of the kitchen that hospitality moved into a more central place in the study center's mission. By 2012 Wilder listed hospitality among the study center's four major goals: "The Center for Christian Study seeks to promote Christian formation . . . *Through* the communication of Biblical truth, *For* the good of the University community, *With* hospitality and care, *In* unity with other Grounds ministries" (1).

[37]"175 Attend Luncheon," *Praxis* 7, no. 3 (Fall 2003); Wes Zell, "Hospitality and the Move-In Day Crowd," *Praxis* 8, no. 2 (Summer 2004); Zell, "Move-In Day Lunch Draws 400," *Praxis* 10, no. 3 (Fall 2006).

[38]Shelly Pellish, "Center Welcomes Class of 2011 Families," *Praxis* 11, no. 3 (Fall 2007).

Figure 7.5. The 2013 move-in-day lunch at the Center for Christian Study.

Over time the Center for Christian Study continued to capitalize on its building and its location by expanding its range of hospitality-focused events. The study center's location adjacent to the university's sorority houses afforded it the opportunity to offer coffee, hot chocolate, or simply a chair and a warm room to hundreds of female students during winter rush week. Looking for ways to get parents and alumni more involved, the study center also began hosting a yearly football tailgate and events during parents' week and near graduation. Eventually, the study center also began hosting exam snacks. The program included breakfast, lunch, and dinner every day during fall and spring exam weeks. Like the move-in-day lunch, exam snacks only became a part of the Center for Christian Study program after concerned parents began providing food during exam week. Before long hundreds of students were assembling at the study center, filling the building, its porches, and sometimes Chancellor Street itself, three times a day.[39]

To some extent hospitality-focused events flowed naturally out of the study center's roots in L'Abri. As the Schaeffers demonstrated radical hospitality, their open arms not only drew people to L'Abri but also helped soften people's hearts to the gospel. Reflective of the study center's ties to L'Abri, hospitality had to some

---

[39]By 2019 between two hundred and three hundred students a day were taking part in these meals. The study center hosted these meals over the course of seven days from May 5 to 12. Meals were offered each day except Sunday. See "Exam Snacks," Center for Christian Study, www.studycenter.net/exam-snacks (accessed September, 12, 2019).

degree always been part of the Center for Christian Study's appeal. A shift occurred, however, with the new building and the increasing parental involvement as earlier generations of study center students grew up and as the study center's reputation expanded. With the help of parents and the space afforded by the new building, the Center for Christian Study made hospitality one of its most defining features. Hospitality served two purposes at the study center. As more and more Christian and non-Christian students began to take part in events such as exam snacks, hospitality became both a way for the Center for Christian Study to bless the university community and a means of getting non-Christians through its doors.

The overall effect of this turn toward hospitality was a gradual reorientation toward programming geared for the university's undergraduate community. Throughout his tenure at the Center for Christian Study, Trotter had emphasized that while many observers "may have thought that our programs are only for students," the study center, even after the completion of the addition, was still "in the business of seeing laypeople take the faith seriously enough to study it with the rigor it deserves."[40] Trotter was right; the study center continued to offer plenty of public lectures and opportunities for community involvement. Yet as much as Trotter emphasized that "the study center is for lay people as well as students," the ministry's momentum—aided in no small part by the

Figure 7.6. Exam snacks at the Center for Christian Study.

---

[40]Trotter, "From the Executive Director."

presence of its building, which functioned as "a magnet for students"—was increasingly toward an emphasis on graduate and especially undergraduate students.[41] Of course, even this shift did not necessarily compromise the center's emphasis on laity that directors from Steiner to Turner and Trotter had implemented. The vast majority of the students who took part in Center for Christian Study events were, and did remain, members of the laity.

The Center for Christian Study as Shelter

As the study center expanded its range of hospitality and invited more students to spend greater amounts time in its inviting building, it also tapped into another element of L'Abri, which some in the university community found unsettling. The study center, for all its efforts to engage the university community, was often prone toward functioning more as a shelter or safe house for Christian students than as a true partner in the university's life. While some students who regularly took part in the life of the Center for Christian Study emphasized that they were not "just living in a Christian bubble where we surround ourselves with Christian people and involve ourselves in Christian activities," the study center could aid in the development of bubble-wrapped lives.[42] Not surprisingly, the concept of the study center as a kind of safe haven was best demonstrated in the way parents came to view the study center. The increasing prominence of parents in the study center's life after 1999 both demonstrated and probably facilitated the Center for Christian Study's shift toward undergraduate ministry while at the same time signifying that parents saw the study center as a safeguard against what they felt to be the perils of the secular academy.

From Frank Nelson's 1972 *Christianity Today* article "Evangelical Living and Learning Centers" to Gordon College professor Thomas Albert Howard's 2014 Anxious Bench blog post "Should I Send My (Christian) Child to a (Secular) State University?," evangelical commentators had long advised parents who had to choose schools other than Christian institutions to consider selecting schools based on whether the institution had a Christian study center.[43] As the Center

---

[41]Wilder noted this transition in his 2012 "Strategic Plan."
[42]Schneider, "Chancellor Street House Gives Faith New Meaning."
[43]Frank C. Nelsen, "Evangelical Living and Learning Centers: A Proposal," *Christianity Today*, May 26, 1972, 7; Thomas Albert Howard, "Should I Send My (Christian) Child to a (Secular) State University?," Anxious Bench, February 16, 2014, www.patheos.com/blogs/anxiousbench/2014/02/should-i-send-my-christian-child-to-a-secular-state-university/.

for Christian Study rose in prominence and implemented more programs such as its Parents' Council (founded 2007) and regional outreach gatherings in places such as northern Virginia, Atlanta, Charlotte, and Richmond, larger numbers of Christian parents discovered the Center for Christian Study before their students even matriculated at the university. As longtime study center staff member Shelley Pellish observed, by 2007 "prospective students" were "stopping by the building in increasing numbers during their university tours." The Center for Christian Study was emerging as a key aspect of the college-selection process in the minds of many Christian students and their parents.

Expanding the Movement: Early Efforts Toward Collaboration

As exciting as events at the Charlottesville study center were, however, Trotter and the staff at the Center for Christian Study were not only concerned with forging better relationships with students and parents at the University of Virginia. By the early 2000s they were also working to forge relationships with other study centers. From the time evangelicals began trying to imitate Schaeffer's L'Abri or Houston's Regent College, there had been various efforts to develop connections among the mélange of study centers. Members of the Charlottesville study center took part in a number of early gatherings meant to solidify a study center movement. In 1977 Daryl Richman of the Center for Christian Study joined R. C. Sproul and thirty-four others for a conference on study centers held at Westminster Theological Seminary. These individuals represented nine study centers ranging from those that were church-based to others that were university-based or standalone organizations. The 1977 conference was one of a handful of similar conferences that sprang up during these years.[44]

In spite of these early efforts, however, study centers without direct ties to organizations such as L'Abri or Regent College existed throughout the 1980s and 1990s in a state of friendly independence if not relative isolation. While a study center may have occasionally received a brochure or updates from other study centers, there were few unitive events and no umbrella organization designed specifically to draw study centers and their leaders together for mutual support and relationship. For instance, in the early eighties Turner received pamphlets at the Center for Christian Study from other study centers, including Sproul's

---

[44] A 1980 Christian Study Centers Conference had a mailing list consisting of twenty-eight centers. For a full list, see "Christian Study Centers Conference Pack," June 21, 1980, box 3, folder 10, JHF.

Ligonier Valley Study Center, painter Wes Hurd's Eugune, Oregon, McKenzie Study Center (founded 1979), and the Christian Study Center, which was founded in 1983 in New Haven, Connecticut, by Yale Divinity School graduate Randy Thompson.[45] However, no greater partnership was ever pursued even though these centers were marked by similar influences and emphases. Individual leaders and students within a study center may have had personal connections to other individuals at a different study center, but for the vast majority of study centers there were not avenues available for any kind of formal network or movement on an institutional level. As the Charlottesville Center for Christian Study grew into its new building in the late 1990s, Trotter began thinking in terms of a wider influence among individuals and organizations that shared the Center for Christian Study's motivations and ethos.

By the late 1990s Trotter and other Center for Christian Study leaders had begun to realize that the Charlottesville study center was attracting national attention. The nationally publicized Rosenberger Supreme Court case in 1995 had certainly raised the prominence of the Center for Christian Study, but it was the construction of the new addition and, to a lesser extent, the publication of *Praxis* in 1997 that most caught the attention of other like-minded evangelicals. In a 1999 interview with the relaunched student magazine *Wide Awake,* Trotter noted that while "a lot of people have come and have wanted to know how to start a center," there were still "not very many" other universities that had study centers comparable to the Center for Christian Study. He was hopeful, however, that this might be changing. The previous fall he had attended what he described as "the first annual conference for Christian Study Centers in the country." While Trotter noted that the Center for Christian Study, with its "own building, mailing list, etc.," was "rare" among those study centers represented at the event, he still found it exciting "to see these ideas spreading throughout the country."[46]

---

[45]Thompson, a pastor by training and profession, directed the Christian Study Center in New Haven for five years. He went on to pastor churches and serve with his wife as the hosts of Forest Haven, "a Christian organization that provides a rural, quiet place of healing hospitality and spiritual refreshment for Christian ministers and missionaries." See Tara R. Alemany, "Your Hosts," Forest Haven, New Hampshire, July 9, 2012, http://foresthavennh.org/about/your-hosts/. The McKenzie Study Center eventually founded Gutenberg College, which offered students a Great Books curriculum. See "The History of the McKenzie Study Center," Gutenberg College, http://msc.gutenberg.edu/about/history/ (accessed April 29, 2016).

[46]Astari Daenuwy and Andrew Trotter, "Opening the Center Doors: Astari Daenuwy Interviews Drew Trotter, Director of the Center for Christian Studies," *Wide Awake* (Spring 1999).

The conference Trotter was referring to was the 1998 Francis Schaeffer Lectures, a lecture series hosted annually by Covenant Theological Seminary's Francis Schaeffer Institute. Wade Bradshaw, the executive director of the institute at the time, had spent time at Swiss L'Abri and had served for several years as the director of the English L'Abri before coming to St. Louis. Bradshaw invited Trotter and L'Abri alum and C. S. Lewis Institute staff member Steve Garber (who in 2005 went on to found the Washington Institute for Faith, Vocation, and Culture before joining the faculty of Regent College in 2018) as the principal speakers for the conference. Trotter was slated to lecture on film during the evening, but because both he and Garber were interested in study centers more generally, Bradshaw planned for an independent day session tailored specifically for individuals who were working in similar ministries. Scanning his Rolodex, Bradshaw began inviting "anyone I knew who was evangelical and doing anything like a Christian study center" to attend. In the end he was able to contact individuals at about fifty institutions. The response was heartening. "We had something close to 100 percent acceptance," Bradshaw later remembered, noting that of those who responded, "all of them mentioned that they owed a debt to Francis Schaeffer."[47]

By bringing together study center directors from across the country and by helping individuals invested in these ministries think through the differences between L'Abri-style residential study centers and university-based study centers such as the Charlottesville Center for Christian Study, the 1998 conference marked the unofficial beginning of what eventually became the Consortium of Christian Study Centers. Through the conference Trotter and others who worked in various study centers were alerted to the large number and wide array of similar ministries. "We were all amazed at each other's experiences," Trotter remembers. "We had no idea that there were that many [study centers]." Filled with a new sense of camaraderie, Trotter and five other conference attendees began holding occasional meetings filled with discussions of best practices,

---

[47]Wade Bradshaw, interview with author, September 16, 2015, Charlottesville, VA; Trotter, interview; Daenuwy and Trotter, "Opening the Center Doors," 15. For more on Garber and the Washington Institute for Faith, Vocation, and Culture, see https://washingtoninst.org/ (accessed September 12, 2019). For more on Garber see his semi-autobiographical book *The Fabric of Faithfulness: Weaving Together Belief and Behavior* (Downers Grove, IL: InterVarsity Press, 2007). For more on Bradshaw see Wade Bradshaw, *By Demonstration, God: Fifty Years and a Week at L'Abri* (Carlisle, UK: Piquant Editions, 2005); "Wade Bradshaw," Trinity Church, www.trinitycville.org/Wade-Bradshaw (accessed May 2, 2016).

encouragement, and prayer. In addition to Trotter, the group included the directors of three other prominent university-based student centers: Randy Bare of Westminster House, the student ministry of First Presbyterian Church in Berkeley; David Mahan of the Rivendell Institute (founded 1995), a graduate student–focused study center in New Haven, Connecticut; and Robert Osburn, director of the MacLaurin Institute (now Anselm House), which was founded in 1982 by InterVarsity staff member William Monsma at the University of Minnesota. Others such as Richard Howe, the founder of Christian Study Centers International and longtime director of the Day Spring Institute (founded 1983) at the University of Colorado in Boulder, soon joined. By 2007 the group had grown to fourteen.[48]

It was during the 2007 gathering—while the group was snowed in at Chesterton House in Ithaca, New York—that Karl Johnson, a three-time alum of Cornell and founder of Chesterton House, challenged those assembled to consider developing a more formal organization. A little more than a year later, in July 2008, representatives from university-based study centers in Berkeley, Boulder, Ithaca, New Haven, Minneapolis, and Charlottesville met in Minneapolis to officially form the Consortium of Christian Study Centers.[49] The group appointed Drew Trotter as full-time executive director of the Consortium of Christian Study Centers beginning January 1, 2009. It was determined that the new consortium would function as a subsidiary of Rick Howe's Christian Study Centers International while retaining its own elected board of directors.[50] In addition to serving as the executive director of the Consortium of Christian Study Centers, Trotter was also named the national director of Howe's Christian Study Centers International.

---

[48]Trotter, interview; "Our History," Consortium of Christian Study Centers, https://studycentersonline.org/about/history/ (accessed May 2, 2016). The other individuals represented at the first meeting were Steve Webb of Centers for Christian Study International and Luke Bobo of Covenant Theological Seminary (Bryan Bademan, email to author, June 7, 2016). According to Bademan, the MacLaurin Institute changed its name to Anselm House in 2016 "in an attempt to make Catholics feel more at home in its community and leadership."

[49]"Our History." The meeting, which was hosted by the MacLaurin Institute, was held at Northwestern College (Bademan, email, June 7, 2018).

[50]This is how Trotter described Christian Study Centers International in fall 2008 for interested friends of the Center for Christian Study. See "History," Rivendell Institute, www.rivendellinstitute.org/about/history/ (accessed May 2, 2016). For more on Christian Study Centers International, see "Our History"; "About Study Centers," Centers for Christian Study International, http://studycenters.org/about/study-centers/ (accessed May 2, 2016).

Trotter was a natural choice. Over the course of his career, his involvement in evangelical study centers had spanned the first generation (L'Abri) while moving beyond Schaeffer in important ways, not the least of which was the fact that Trotter held academic credentials. By 2008 he also had well over two decades of experience as the director of leading church-based and university-based study centers. During the late 1990s and early 2000s the Charlottesville Center for Christian Study had emerged as perhaps the foremost US example of a university-based study center. In a trend that only increased over the next decades, the Center for Christian Study increasingly functioned as an essential stopping point on the pilgrimage of those hoping to found a study center. The early history of Chesterton House provides an insight into how this mentoring process worked.

Chesterton House at Cornell University

By the mid-1990s Karl Johnson's experiences as both a student at Cornell and a Christian who struggled to find versions of the faith that were spiritually and intellectually rigorous had given him a desire for a ministry that exposed members of the university community to the best of Christian thought and cultural commentary. Beginning his own doctoral studies in the mid-1990s, Johnson benefited from an evangelical milieu in which resources such as Mars Hill Audio (1993) and *Christianity Today*'s more scholarly *Books and Culture* (1995) joined books such as Mark Noll's *The Scandal of the Evangelical Mind* (1994) and George Marsden's *The Outrageous Idea of Christian Scholarship* (1998) in calling for evangelicals to engage scholarship and the life of the mind more deeply and intentionally.[51] Together with friends and local pastors, Johnson and other members of the Christian community in Ithaca began working to develop programs that would help Christians in their community better think through the contours of faith, life, and learning.

As Johnson began to consider starting a new ministry that would help meet the need for an intellectually engaged Christian presence at the university, a friend referred him to Trotter and the Charlottesville Center for Christian Study. Johnson wrote to Trotter and was amazed by what he found. To Johnson, the Center for Christian Study materials seemed "an intellectual feast." Paraphrasing

---

[51] Karl Johnson, "About Chesterton House: For Charlie Cotherman," March 7, 2016, author's possession; Karl Johnson, "Our Story," Chesterton House, http://chestertonhouse.org/about/our-story (accessed May 2, 2016).

Cornell cofounder and inaugural president A. D. White, who had discovered a model for his new educational venture in Ithaca by looking to the University of Berlin, Johnson found that the Charlottesville study center was his "ideal of a [study center] not only realized—but extended and glorified." Of the few other study centers that Johnson consulted in the lead-up to founding Chesterton House in 2000, it was the Charlottesville Center for Christian Study that most shaped the development of Johnson's work at Cornell.[52]

Figure 7.7. The Chesterton House at Cornell University. In 2017 the ministry expanded from its original building (left) by purchasing an adjacent building (right).

Coming alongside other study centers with experience, encouragement, and counsel was exactly what Trotter hoped his new position as executive director of the Consortium of Christian Study Centers would allow him to do. Trotter described his new position and his hopes in an open letter to friends of the Charlottesville study center in fall 2008. While Christian Study Centers International had what Trotter described as "a passion for seeing study centers planted across the nation and . . . beyond its borders," Trotter wrote that his

---

[52]Johnson, "Our Story." Johnson also spoke with Bob Osborn, director of the MacLaurin Institute, but it was Trotter and the Center for Christian Study that emerged as his principal model. Today Chesterton House is one of the most influential study centers in the consortium. Johnson was a founding member of the Consortium for Christian Study Centers. At the time of this writing Johnson was also the president of the consortium's board of directors.

Figure 7.8. A group of students at Chesterton House.

task as national director "will not be so much in the 'planting' area of things, though, as it will be in the strengthening of centers that already exist alongside a number of universities."[53] Trotter also saw his role as a promoter of what he identified for the first time in print as "the study center movement," a phenomenon in which, he noted, "our Center here in Charlottesville has always been a leader." Trotter's role as executive director of the consortium was closely related to his position at Christian Study Centers International, though different in that the consortium was a collaborative effort that drew on the resources of existing study centers to fill positions on its own independent board of directors.

As good as all this sounded in a Center for Christian Study newsletter, in practice working through the nuts and bolts of formal partnership proved difficult. Almost from the start Trotter found that his relationship to Howe's organization was fraught with uncertainty and miscommunication. In part this stemmed from the lingering effects of the financial crisis of 2008. As Howe's organization struggled to find a way forward in the new financial climate, funding for Trotter's position dried up. On April 1, 2009, after having worked for three months without receiving a paycheck from Howe's Christian Study

---

[53] Andrew Trotter, "An Open Letter to Our Friends," *Praxis* 12, no. 3 (Fall 2008).

Centers International, Trotter cut ties with the organization and filed for 501(c)(3) status for an independent Consortium of Christian Study Centers.[54]

The Consortium of Christian Study Centers

Over the course of the next two years Trotter devoted himself to fundraising, developing the consortium's infrastructure, and visiting numerous churches and sites where study centers were already established or where there was a desire to found a new study center. In the process he further solidified a network of study centers and interested individuals that stretched from coast to coast and from the edge of the Caribbean into Canada. He also developed a four-part taxonomy of study centers that helped further define the mission of the consortium and the study center movement in general. While the Consortium of Christian Study Centers was concerned with what Trotter described as university-based study centers, other models had existed from the start. Destination study centers such as L'Abri, Schloss Mittersill in Europe, and Sproul's Ligonier Valley in the mountains of central Pennsylvania all required that students come to them as destinations in and of themselves.[55] In order to attract students, these study centers usually relied on exquisite natural beauty or a celebrity director. Remote locations, often far from hotels, also meant that destination study centers were usually residential.[56] From his own experience at the Elmbrook Study Center, Trotter was also aware of a significant subgroup of church-based study centers, which were usually but not exclusively found in either megachurches or in churches of a distinctly Reformed cast. A fourth and harder-to-define subset of study centers is what Trotter identifies as city-focused study centers. These study centers focus more on a region than on a particular university community or narrow demographic and include groups such as the C. S. Lewis Institute of Washington, DC.

In 2011, after a series of fits and starts, the Consortium of Christian Study Centers launched its website and moved into a more public role. The transition from dream and development to tangible impact was signified by the consortium's first author symposium. The event, hosted by the Charlottesville Center for

---

[54]Trotter, interview; "Our History." Once again, it was the McClellan Foundation that offered Trotter an initial path toward financial viability.

[55]"Our History"; Trotter, interview.

[56]The lack of nearby hotels and passable roads in the winter played a significant role in the development of programming at Sproul's Ligonier Valley Study Center. These factors also made a move to Orlando appealing.

Christian Study and attended by over twenty representatives from various study centers and partner organizations, offered a taste of the movement's history while also denoting a new direction in the development of the lay evangelical mind and the evangelical presence within America's pluralistic universities. In addition to a panel discussion featuring Trotter, Mahan, and Johnson, the program also dedicated time to an author-led discussion of James Davison Hunter's book *To Change the World*. The book, with its emphasis on the importance of lasting institutions and "faithful presence," exerted what Trotter described as "a strong influence on the study center movement" in the years ahead.[57] For Hunter, "a theology of faithful presence first calls Christians to attend to the people and places that they experience directly.... The call of faithful presence gives priority to what is right in front of us—the community, the neighborhood, and the city, and the people of which these are constituted." This meant that rather than focusing on evangelical standbys such as "slick packaging," "high production values," and an emphasis on a handful of celebrity leaders, Christians and Christian organizations should work to cultivate "a preference for stability, locality, and particularity of place and its needs."[58]

Because Hunter's concept stressed both faithfulness to Christ and presence in one's immediate context, it was a good fit for the fledgling consortium and the study centers that made up its constituency. An emphasis on faithful presences was an especially powerful and fitting tool for study centers and Christians desiring to think Christianly because it held within itself a proactive response to the two opposing temptations—syncretism and isolationism—that Christians frequently encountered on university campuses. Faithfulness entailed a commitment first to the triune God and then to historic Christian orthodoxy, while a call to presence directly opposed the isolationist and sheltered responses that had plagued evangelical efforts in North America for a century.

Trotter's choice of Hunter was both practical (Hunter lived in Charlottesville) and strategic. To a certain extent Hunter's emphasis on living faithfully as a Christian presence was one Trotter had been implementing at the Center for

---

[57]Trotter, interview. For more on faithful presence, see James Davison Hunter, *To Change the World: The Irony, Tragedy, and Possibility of Christianity in the Late Modern World* (New York: Oxford University Press, 2010), 238-54. The consortium also caught the eye of notable historian and evangelical commentator Mark Noll, who described it favorably in his 2011 book *Jesus Christ and the Life of the Mind* (Grand Rapids: Eerdmans, 2011), 157.
[58]Hunter, *To Change the World*, 253.

Christian Study for years. Whereas providing an alternative to the University of Virginia's secular Religious Studies Department was the Charlottesville Center for Christian Study's original raison d'être, by 2011 the emphasis of the Charlottesville study center had shifted, a shift Trotter worked to solidify for the movement in general by choosing to launch the Consortium of Christian Study Centers with an emphasis on constructive engagement with the university community. The change was subtle but significant. By 2011 many of the individuals leading study centers represented by the consortium were similarly convinced that the path forward was more a matter of faithful presence through deeply rooted, engaged, and hospitable relationships and institutions than it was about the apologetics or cultural bluster that had defined some aspects of the movement in its early years. Deeply informed by Hunter's ideas and the practical outworkings of the theological concept of common grace—which noted that God was at work in and through *all* people, Christian and non-Christian alike—Trotter and members of the consortium, already emerging as the leading edge of the evangelical study center movement, were beginning to emphasize the university less as a front in the culture wars and more as a friend, though, as Trotter notes, "a friend with whom we sometimes have great differences."[59]

The emphases that marked the consortium's first symposium, in 2011, demonstrated the change and continuity that shaped an emerging group of study centers such as the Charlottesville Center for Christian Study. The consortium's description of a study center's purpose continued to feature a familiar emphasis on Christian discipleship and Christian community, but it also encompassed a new vision that promoted study centers as "servants to the thought-life itself of the university" and partners with the university who could "participate fully" in its life, all sentiments it is hard to imagine Schaeffer or other first-generation leaders conveying to a similar degree.[60] Less about protecting evangelicals or providing a sheltered space for them as cultural outsiders, these two Consortium of Christian Study Centers emphases demonstrated that evangelicals—at least those directing consortium member centers, if not always the parents who promoted and financed them—had developed a new methodology and a new level of confidence since Schaeffer first began welcoming folks with questions to Chalet les Melezes in 1955. By the end of the first decade of

---

[59]Trotter, interview. Trotter uses this phrase frequently. He believes he first heard it from Os Guinness.
[60]"What Is a Study Center?," Consortium of Christian Study Centers, https://studycentersonline.org/about/what-is-a-study-center/ (accessed May 2, 2016).

the twenty-first century, a new generation of lay evangelicals had created new, financially sustainable study center models marked more by intellectual curiosity and hospitality than by a reactionary fear of the secular academy.

Yet even as study centers moved toward faithful and constructive engagement with the wider university, the study center model itself, with its highly independent nature, continued to possess a reactionary and isolationist strain. The model of freestanding, privately funded study centers allowed each study center to chart a trajectory autonomous of prevailing university policies, and the possibilities of this independence were not lost on the wider evangelical community. During the second decade of the new millennium, models such as Chesterton House and the Center for Christian Study drew increased attention, especially as Christian parachurch ministries began to fall afoul of new university antibias policies mandating that all university-sanctioned groups and ministries remain open to the participation and leadership of all students, even students who might not hold a ministry's key commitments (e.g., Christian sexual ethics, even Christian faith itself). Even as the study center movement moved into a new phase with the launching of the Consortium of Christian Study Centers and its focus on faithful presence and positive engagement with the university, forces were at work that would boost new interest in the movement as a means of maintaining university ministry without forfeiting Christian beliefs and institutional autonomy. As it turned out, the image of a shelter, so essential in the study center movement's early years, was difficult to entirely leave behind.

The McKean Study Center and the Complexities of Faithful Presence

In June 2014 Bowdoin Christian Fellowship made the front page of the *New York Times*. It was a distinction the members of the Bowdoin College campus ministry would have rather avoided. After forty years as an evangelical presence on the campus of the Brunswick, Maine, liberal arts college, the group received notice that Bowdoin would no longer recognize its chapter of InterVarsity Christian Fellowship as an official campus ministry.[61] The college's decision

---

[61]Michael Paulson, "Colleges and Evangelicals Collide on Bias Policy," *New York Times*, June 9, 2014, www.nytimes.com/2014/06/10/us/colleges-and-evangelicals-collide-on-bias-policy.html; Robert B. Gregory, "Bowdoin: One Year Later," *First Things*, June 30, 2015, www.firstthings.com/web-exclusives/2015/06/one-year-later.

stemmed from a new antidiscrimination policy based on a 2010 Supreme Court ruling, which supported a public California law school's constitutional right to deny funding and recognition to student groups such as the Christian Legal Society that maintained exclusive criteria for leadership.[62] At Bowdoin, the Bowdoin Christian Fellowship had always required that its leaders be Christians. Unable to reach a compromise between the college's bias policy and their conviction that a Christian ministry should be led by individuals who are themselves Christians, the ministry lost student-activities funding, and longtime volunteer advisers Robert and Sim Gregory lost swipe-card access to university property.

Amid these losses, members of the onetime Bowdoin Christian Fellowship found a new direction by looking to the evangelical study center movement. For the Gregorys and Christian students at Bowdoin, this model was extremely attractive. Not only did it offer an intellectually vibrant form of evangelicalism well-suited to university life, but the model of a freestanding study center located adjacent to a university promised campus access without the restrictions of university policies. Within a year the Gregorys were able to found the Joseph and Alice McKeen Study Center and join the Consortium of Christian Study Centers. "It is a paradox," Robert Gregory noted in the wake of these events, "that barriers of exclusion often create stronger communities of inclusion."[63] Now, rather than existing as a relatively self-contained InterVarsity chapter, Christian students at the McKeen Study Center are also part of a growing network who have found a home away from home in the libraries, common rooms, Bible studies, public lectures, free meals, and a host of other activities that make Christian study centers among the more inviting spaces on modern campuses.

---

[62]The case was *Christian Legal Society v. Martinez*. For more, see Robert Barnes, "Supreme Court to Consider Case Against California Law School," *Washington Post*, April 18, 2010, www.washingtonpost.com/wp-dyn/content/article/2010/04/17/AR2010041702908.html; Charles J. Russo, "Mergens v. Westside Community Schools at Twenty-Five and Christian Legal Society v. Martinez: From Live and Let Live to My Way or the Highway?," *Brigham Young University Education & Law Journal*, June 1, 2015, 453-80.

[63]Gregory, "Bowdoin: One Year Later." In some ways the phenomenon that Gregory notes here is similar to Rod Dreher's much-discussed Benedict option, which calls Christians to neither aggressive culture war nor fearful retreat but rather solidifying their commitment to their own local faith communities. For more, see Rod Dreher, *The Benedict Option: A Strategy for Christians in a Post-Christian Nation* (New York: Sentinel, 2017), especially 166-75; Dreher, "The Idea of a Christian Village: How to Conserve and Strengthen Christians in a Culture Hostile to Our Faith; An Exclusive Excerpt from *The Benedict Option*," *Christianity Today*, March 2017, 35-41.

CONCLUSION

JUST OVER FIFTY YEARS from the time L'Abri and Regent College first began to captivate the imagination of American evangelicals with their holistic desire to create spaces where people could encounter God and learn to think Christianly about all of life, the movement they helped launch is alive and well. While some study centers, such as Ligonier Valley, have ceased to exist as residential learning communities, others continue to thrive as they balance enduring emphases with a willingness to contextualize their approach to a shifting academic and cultural landscape. After facing near-insolvency in the mid-1990s, New College Berkeley found a sustainable model for maintaining its longstanding role as the evangelical voice within Berkeley's Graduate Theological Union. The C. S. Lewis Institute, which after a period of introspection re-created itself in 1999 with a renewed emphasis on relational learning through its Fellows Program, now has regional centers in eighteen cities and counts over thirty-five thousand followers on Twitter.[1] The wing of the study center movement represented by the Consortium of Christian Study Centers has also experienced growth not just in numbers but also in influence as campus-based study centers follow the example of places such as the Charlottesville Center for Christian Study and Chesterton House at Cornell by establishing inviting and hospitable places for study, formation, rest, and relationship on the edge of some of the nation's most elite public and private universities.

In terms of influence and academic engagement, the campus-based branch of the study center movement represented by the Consortium of Christian Study Centers is uniquely poised to help Christian students cultivate an ability to think Christianly about a host of vocations and issues even as they engage with the breadth of spiritual, intellectual, and cultural perspectives available on the campuses of today's pluralistic universities. As early as 2011, Mark Noll identified the existence of study centers such as these and the formation of the Consortium

---

[1] "CSLI Locations," C. S. Lewis Institute, www.cslewisinstitute.org/CSLI_Locations (accessed June 27, 2019).

of Christian Study Centers as one of several "hopeful signs" of increased intellectual engagement among evangelicals, and in recent years study centers have been founded adjacent to the campuses of Duke University, the University of North Carolina, the University of Wisconsin-Madison, and Indiana University among others.[2] Another quantifiable indicator of the vitality of many of these study centers is their ability to generate income to maintain and expand their programming, staff, and buildings. At the time of this writing, Chesterton House, the Christian Study Center of Gainesville, the North Carolina Study Center, and the Center for Christian Study have each either begun or recently completed significant capital campaigns to expand their buildings and ministries.[3]

One of the most notable examples of the innovative ways in which study centers are beginning to mobilize an increasingly well-financed and engaged pool of students and supporters for their approach to parachurch campus ministry is Upper House at the University of Wisconsin-Madison. Formally launched by the Stephen & Laurel Brown Foundation in January 2015, Upper House is located on the second floor of a twelve-story, 1.1-million-square-foot mixed-use building located in the heart of the University of Wisconsin-Madison campus. Upper House's eye-catching design, ambitious scope, and innovative funding model have afforded it a significant voice in the study center movement—which could well see a growth in Upper House–like study centers as well-financed individuals and organizations look for ways to minister on university campuses where traditional campus ministries face uncertainty, and in some cases expulsion, due to antibias laws and questions about the stability of religious liberty.[4]

To some extent these larger cultural and legislative shifts seem to have already exerted an influence on the growth of the university-based study center movement. Of the Consortium of Christian Study Centers' twenty-eight member study centers, nearly half have been founded since 2010, when the US Supreme Court allowed universities to begin implementing far-reaching

---

[2]Mark A. Noll, *Jesus Christ and the Life of the Mind* (Grand Rapids: Eerdmans, 2011), 154-67.
[3]"Our History," Upper House, www.upperhouse.org/about/history-our-story/ (accessed June 27, 2019).
[4]Tish Harrison Warren, "The Wrong Kind of Christian," *Christianity Today*, September 2014, 54-58; Ed Stetzer, "InterVarsity 'Derecognized' at California State University's 23 Campuses: Some Analysis and Reflections," *Christianity Today*, September 6, 2014, www.christianitytoday.com/edstetzer/2014/september/intervarsity-now-derecognized-in-california-state-universit.html. Though the parachurch ministry was eventually permitted back on campuses, parachurch ministries that maintain historic Christian orthodoxy continue to remain wary of the scope of antibias legislation.

CONCLUSION 257

Figure 8.1. Upper House at the University of Wisconsin-Madison.

antibias regulations.[5] Furthermore, the model of independent study centers with freestanding space for offices and student meetings holds obvious strategic appeal to campus ministries and individuals who, like former Bowdoin College InterVarsity directors Robert and Sim Gregory, desire to minister to students but know that the university's welcome mat can be pulled at any time. It is quite possible that the future of the Christian study center movement on America's secular campuses will be deeply influenced by what happens when the wider evangelical world becomes aware of the significance of the study center model. It is an awareness that appears to be growing.[6] In early 2018 the Ravi Zacharias Institute called an invitation-only conference in Atlanta to address the future of campus ministry. Notably, Drew Trotter and four directors from the Consortium of Christian Study Centers member study centers were among the roughly seventy parachurch leaders invited to this

---

[5]For a list of the Consortium of Christian Study Center member study centers, see "Member Study Centers," Consortium of Christian Study Centers, https://studycentersonline.org/membership/member-study-centers/ (accessed June 27, 2018).

[6]Molly Worthen, "Hallelujah College," *New York Times,* January 16, 2016, www.nytimes.com/2016/01/17/opinion/sunday/hallelujah-college.html; Yonat Shimron, "Christian Study Centers Strive to Help Students Integrate Faith, Intellect," *Christian Century,* February 12, 2018, www.christiancentury.org/article/news/christian-study-centers-strive-help-students-integrate-faith-intellect-0.

meeting.[7] The reason so many invitations were extended to study center heads seems to have been at least partially due to the appeal of the study center model of independent, freestanding ministry centers located adjacent to secular campuses.

In the midst of a season of growth fueled by both the pull factors (e.g., the compelling example of thriving study centers), such as those that influenced the founding of Chesterton House, and push factors (e.g., anxiety related to religious liberty and the potential for curtailed campus access), such as those that led to the formation of the McKean Study Center, the Consortium of Christian Study Centers and the larger study center movement face important decisions related to motivations for developing new study centers and the way in which these study centers function alongside the university. As the prominence of study centers grows, and as the study center model expands its appeal to a wider subset of individuals, it is all the more important that leaders within the movement have a clear vision for both where the movement has been and where it intends to go. The preceding pages have charted this history. The few remaining pages will explore how the origins and history of a handful of influential study centers can inform the movement's ability to help future generations develop the tools to both live and think Christianly on campus and in all of life.

Looking Back, Looking Ahead

Most of the students who frequent study centers today have never heard the names Francis Schaeffer or James Houston, and few could tell you much about L'Abri or Regent College. Whether current visitors know it or not, however, the study centers they make use of for Bible studies, all-night study sessions, free lunches, concerts, and a host of other spiritual, intellectual, and social activities continue to bear significant debt to the innovation and guiding impulses of these two learning communities and the multiple study centers their example inspired. As the stories of the C. S. Lewis Institute, the Ligonier Valley Study Center, New College Berkeley, the Center for Christian Study, and the Consortium of Christian Study Centers demonstrate, the individuals who founded many of the most significant second-generation American study centers were influenced by at least one—but more often *both*—of their Swiss and Canadian predecessors.

---

[7]Andrew Trotter, email to author, June 27, 2019; "The National Campus Ministry Leaders Summit," Ravi Zacharias International Ministries, www.rzim.org/read/rzim-global/ncmls (accessed July 2, 2019).

Individually, L'Abri and Regent College each had much to offer a generation of evangelicals experiencing new levels of affluence and educational attainment in the midst of social upheaval and expanding vocational opportunities. Schaeffer and Houston recognized the shifting longings and struggles facing American youth during the 1960s earlier than most of their evangelical peers and responded with an invitation that was localized, relational, and expansive enough to make room for a wide array of vocational, intellectual, and cultural interests. To spend time at L'Abri or Regent College in the late 1960s was to enter into communities who deeply believed that loving God was the work of the heart, the mind, and the hands as one's understanding of the gospel worked itself out into any number of vocational interests and propensities.

That L'Abri (implicitly) and Regent College (explicitly) catered to laypeople rather than clergy was not inconsequential. An emphasis on helping lay Christians develop sound theological perspectives was part of the larger post–World War II emphasis on the laity, but it was not something that many other midcentury evangelical leaders had explored or developed in highly visible ways. Previously, most training of laypeople in Bible institutes and training programs such as Harold Ockenga's Boston Evening School of the Bible had focused on basic biblical literacy and training for Sunday school teachers, missionaries, and evangelists. Even later, when Harold Ockenga and Charles Fuller harnessed some of the best minds twentieth-century evangelicalism had to offer to found an educational institution, their efforts resulted in the founding of a seminary dedicated primarily to the training of clergy*men*.[8] At L'Abri and Regent College, an emphasis on theological training for the laity meant that young evangelical men *and women* could study theology together and talk through its implications for a wide range of fields—fields that many, as laypeople rather than professional clergy, had personal interest in and experience with. Even in communities such as L'Abri and the Ligonier Valley Study Center, where the formal ordination of women was held to be unbiblical, female students participated in discussions with male peers with few if any limitations. For at least a handful of young evangelical women, the opportunity to study and contribute meaningfully to theological discussions at places such as L'Abri, Regent College,

---

[8]Garth M. Rosell, *Boston's Historic Park Street Church* (Grand Rapids: Kregel, 2009), 142-43. George M. Marsden, *Reforming Fundamentalism: Fuller Seminary and the New Evangelicalism* (Grand Rapids: Eerdmans, 1987).

and the Ligonier Valley Study Center helped build confidence for advanced theological study in the future.

Through these opportunities L'Abri and Regent College helped a generation of young people, especially young evangelicals, develop a more expansive theological, cultural, relational, and vocational imagination. Indeed, part of what made L'Abri's appeal so strong during its first two decades was Schaeffer's ability to capture the imagination of a generation by talking about a personal, relational God whose lordship extended to all of life—including the arenas of literature, art, and film, which American evangelicals had largely neglected or abandoned. If all of life was affected by the gospel and within the purview of Christian vocation, the possibilities for meaningful endeavor were virtually infinite. This was likely especially true for everyday evangelicals who grew up in homes where highbrow art was unappreciated and often nonexistent. For these individuals, communities such as L'Abri and Regent College held an aspirational appeal and helped them develop not only a taste for art beyond the pop art that defined American culture but also relationships with individuals from more culturally elite and socially powerful backgrounds. Most evangelicals in the 1960s and 1970s likely knew no one who studied at Harvard, at least not until they visited L'Abri. As L'Abri connected individuals with a wide array of social, economic, cultural, and educational backgrounds and inspired them to think creatively about how the gospel might influence their various fields of interest, the Swiss community and its wider relational network helped mobilize evangelicals to pursue advanced study and thrive among the power elite.[9]

But as important—and overlooked—as L'Abri's influence in this sphere was, L'Abri alone could never have inspired the Christian study center movement as represented by the Consortium of Christian Study Centers and its member study centers. L'Abri was a powerful imaginative force within evangelicalism, but its connection to the wider scholarly community was minimal. While this may in part have been due to L'Abri's relatively isolated location, it is more attributable to Schaeffer's own eccentricity, individualism, and insecurity. Whatever its exact cause, Schaeffer and L'Abri lived in a sheltered intellectual space due to an overall failure to seek peer-to-peer interaction with the wider

---

[9] D. Michael Lindsay, *Faith in the Halls of Power: How Evangelicals Joined the American Elite* (Oxford: Oxford University Press, 2007), 106-7; Lindsay, "Evangelicals in the Power Elite: Elite Cohesion Advancing a Movement," *American Sociological Review* 73, no. 1 (February 2008): 60-82.

scholarly world. Schaeffer could help evangelicals imagine a wide array of vocational endeavor, but his example and the example of L'Abri could do little to help them imagine meaningful participation in the wider academic world at an institutional level. Schaeffer might have ministered to thousands of university students, but the university was not his home.

For a university-centric vision, the study center movement had to look not to Switzerland but to Canada. It was Houston with his deep Oxonian sensibilities and the team of scholars he led at Regent College who first fueled the study center movement's imagination for meaningful interaction—to say collaboration would be an overstatement—with modern secular universities. Regent College benefited from the same impulse for relational intentionality that fueled L'Abri and the formation of over two thousand experiments in communal living between 1965 and 1970, but unlike L'Abri and the vast majority of intentional communities, Regent College gave its students an example of what it looked like to be in community with not only each other but also the wider academic world.[10] Whereas leading evangelical scholars might stop by L'Abri from time to time, at Regent they were given a warm welcome and a large platform either as full-time faculty members or as paid summer school faculty.

Additionally, early Regent leaders such as Houston, Ward Gasque, and Carl Armerding all worked diligently to forge relationships with the larger academic world. Houston, especially in the early years of Regent, used his training in geography to build relationships at the neighboring University of British Columbia. Gasque and Armerding committed themselves to forging wider relationship with the academic world through publishing, writing regular book reviews, and active involvement in academic organizations such as the Society of Biblical Literature. The importance of academic community and its appreciation for the give-and-take among peers existed even within the microcosm of Regent College itself. Unlike L'Abri, Regent was defined and sustained not by one presiding head or family but rather by a team of credentialed scholars. Houston's title and experience at Oxford set him apart from younger scholars such as Gasque and Armerding, but it was a difference of degree, not kind.

Furthermore, as Regent brought in esteemed scholars such as F. F Bruce for its summer schools and added individuals such as Bruce Waltke and J. I. Packer

---

[10]Robert Houriet, *Getting Back Together* (New York: Coward, McCann & Geoghegen, 1971), xiii.

to its faculty, the peer-to-peer relationships both within Regent and from Regent to the larger academic world offered evangelicals a compelling model for building cross-institutional scholarly relationships. Among the study centers whose history is traced in the preceding pages, those who were influenced by a combination of L'Abri and Regent demonstrated from the start a propensity toward engagement with the wider scholarly world, whereas a study center such as the Ligonier Valley Study Center modeled more exclusively on L'Abri limited institutional power and access to the speaker's lectern to a much smaller group that usually included family, one or two favored peers, and a sizable number of internally trained protégés. At Regent and the study centers it inspired, the situation was much different. Even today Regent's model of scholarly cross-pollination continues to bear fruit among study centers that are quick to welcome a wide array of Christian scholars.

It was not only relationships to people that set the tone for the study center movement. The way in which L'Abri, Regent College, and many of the study centers that came after them related to space and place also carried deep significance. At Regent and L'Abri both the built environment and the geographic location played a role in turning the ethos of the community toward a posture of hospitality. To spend time at L'Abri was to encounter radical hospitality. For decades the Schaeffers' family home, replete with fireplaces, porches, and carefully cultivated places for shared meals and conversations, was the center of community life—a trait that communities such as the Hiskeys' initial ministry at Cornerstone and the Sprouls' ministry at Ligonier Valley largely adopted. During Regent's early years, when classes were held in the basement of the Vancouver School of Theology, home-based hospitality played an essential role in cultivating community and in granting personal access to professors and their families. This intentional emphasis on relationship—an enduring emphasis of Houston's teaching and writing—when combined with the example of L'Abri helped sow an emphasis on hospitality and relationship into early study centers such as Charlottesville's Center for Christian Study.[11] At the Center for Christian Study, the importance of maintaining a hospitable space only grew with time. When Trotter headed up an extensive renovation in the mid-nineties,

---

[11]James Houston, "Embracing the Personal in Christian Education," in *For Christ and His Kingdom: Inspiring a New Generation*, by Houston and D. Bruce Hindmarsh (Vancouver: Regent College Publishing, 2012), 45-59.

he and the architects made sure that the building would, like L'Abri, have fireplaces, a larger kitchen, and plenty of room for both large lectures and one-on-one conversations. It is no wonder that before long members of the study center were talking about the building itself as a member of the staff. Place mattered.

Place also mattered geographically. For communities such as L'Abri, Regent, and to a lesser extent Ligonier Valley, local geography was a draw itself, and visitors frequently commented on the importance of the natural beauty surrounding these study centers. Again, however, it was Regent College and its proximity not only to a thriving city and vast natural beauty but also to one of Canada's most significant public universities that captured the attention of many who went on to found the university-based study centers that now provide the growing edge of the study center movement. Throughout Regent College's first decade, no individual was more influential in this turn toward the university than Houston. From his first involvement in the Vancouver experiment, Houston understood the project as an effort to gain Christian access and influence within an increasingly influential academic system. His repeated call for a robust Christian presence on university campuses gave shape to his early efforts at Regent College as well as his involvement in other efforts to replicate Regent on other university campuses as he spent much of Regent's first decade living out his admonition that Christians should "not desert the campus for the church."[12]

Though Houston eventually shifted his focus toward workplace discipleship, his initial emphasis on engaging modern universities held lasting influence for a study center movement and its continuing emphasis on maintaining a thoughtful Christian presence on the campuses of secular universities. Geographic proximity to the intellectual vibrancy and cultural-shaping power of major universities forced those who led and frequented study centers to wrestle with a far more diverse set of intellectual challenges and experiences than many evangelicals would encounter at home, at church, within Christian college settings, or within the larger evangelical culture. This regular, unavoidable interaction with some of the nation's most culture-shaping institutions offers university-based study centers a chance to function today as God's avant-garde as they contextualize the gospel for a new generation, just as interaction with European

---

[12] James M. Houston, "The Christian Presence in the University," *Crux* 10, no. 4 (Summer 1973): 23.

culture allowed individuals such as Houston and Schaeffer to develop innovative solutions beyond those of other evangelical leaders who were enmeshed more thoroughly within American evangelicalism. If interaction with European museums, universities, and larger cultural shifts shaped L'Abri and Regent College to innovate in ways American evangelicalism alone never could, so university-based study centers, due to their proximity to the robust and diverse climate represented by modern universities, have an opportunity to play a similar role for modern Christians. In order to do so, the Consortium of Christian Study Centers and its member study centers need to have a clear sense not only of their history but also of how this history affects their ability to model faithful presence and nurture holistic flourishing within the campuses they call home.

Cultivating Faithful Presence

In the decade since its publication, James Hunter's book *To Change the World* and the model of faithful presence has proved a helpful framework for many leaders within the Consortium of Christian Study Centers and the university-based study center movement they represent. When Trotter dedicated the consortium's initial author symposium to a discussion of *To Change the World*, it was an intentional decision to establish the consortium as a faithfully Christian participant in the life of the university. For Trotter and many of those gathered at the meeting, this emphasis made sense. Unlike earlier leaders in the movement who were less at home within the modern university, Trotter and most of those present at the 2011 consortium meeting had PhDs and longstanding affinities for the university itself—an institution Trotter increasingly viewed as a friend with whom one sometimes differed rather than an adversary.[13] Trotter's sentiment is winsome, but what does it look like in practice, and how does the movement's history shape the way in which the Consortium of Christian Study Centers and its members centers work out their ministries of faithfulness and presence?

In practice, developing local study centers to be truly faithful, truly present institutions requires ongoing intentionality. As Hunter notes, to be fully faithful and fully present within the modern university community means avoiding

---

[13]David C. Mahan and C. Donald Smedley, "University Ministry and the Evangelical Mind," in *The State of the Evangelical Mind*, ed. Todd C. Ream, Jerry Pattengale, and Christopher J. Devers (Downers Grove, IL: IVP Academic, 2018), 70-71; Andrew Trotter, interview with author, 2015, Charlottesville, VA.

CONCLUSION

other frequently adopted approaches toward institutional influence: "defensiveness against," "relevance to," and "purity from."[14] For evangelically inclined study centers, it is the first and third of these models that have proved the most tempting. Since the early twentieth century theologically conservative Christians in America have had a penchant for establishing parallel organizations prone to reactionary defensiveness and cultural insularity, and the study center movement has not entirely avoided these tendencies.[15] Even L'Abri, with all its countercultural appeal and engagement with art and the prevailing philosophies of the day, carried traces of cultural withdrawal within its defining image as a shelter. As much as L'Abri served as a short-term shelter where people could find temporary physical and spiritual reprieve before stepping back into wider engagement with society, it offers a useful model for a study center movement that is still deeply committed to spiritual formation and hospitality. But to the extent that L'Abri existed as an isolated community without strong ties to the larger academic world, it offers a model not of presence but rather of institutional absence.

In terms of presence, other models, such as that of Regent College and New College Berkeley, are more helpful. Not only were leaders within these communities active within their academic guilds, but they were also able to form some degree of peer-to-peer relationships with neighboring educational institutions and faculty members. For today's university-based study centers, building relationships with university faculty remains a powerful means of connecting students and study center leadership to the thought life of the wider university. These relational connections between study center staff and university faculty are vital for helping study centers maintain an intellectual and not just geographical presence on university campuses. Christian faculty members represent an especially important point of connection between study centers and the university communities they serve.[16] As the preceding history shows, this has always been the case, as individuals such as Ken Elzinga have offered the movement academic clout and institutional support beyond the grasp of most study centers.

---

[14]James Davison Hunter, *To Change the World: The Irony, Tragedy, and Possibility of Christianity in the Late Modern World* (New York: Oxford University Press, 2010), 237.

[15]For some examples, see Joel Carpenter, *Revive Us Again: The Reawakening of American Fundamentalism* (New York: Oxford University Press, 1997).

[16]Noll highlights the growing number of Christian academics who are serving as faculty and publishing notable books. See Noll, *Jesus Christ and the Life of the Mind*, 156-57; Noll, "Evangelical Intellectual Life: Reflections on the Past," in Ream, Pattengale, and Devers, *State of the Evangelical Mind*, 26-30.

It is also important that study center leaders and those to whom they minister cultivate a wider span of relationships rooted in an abiding sense of common grace that spurs deep friendships around shared intellectual interests if not shared faith commitments. On modern, secular campuses, it is likely that no Christian ministry is better poised than study centers to be faithfully present in this way.

As the Consortium of Christian Study Centers and its member centers grow in size, staff, and programming, and as the potential of the study center movement to function as a back door to university influence amid restricted parachurch access, the Consortium of Christian Study Centers and its member centers also need to continue to work proactively to maintain faithfulness to historic Christian orthodoxy in the face of forces from the right and left that may seek to co-opt the movement for political or more narrowly organizational ends.[17] But faithfulness does not only entail avoiding structures of thinking that run contrary to historic orthodoxy; it also entails tuning the institutional life of an organization to the deep resonances of Scripture so as to constructively model the goodness of the kingdom of God and confront the countering tendencies, no matter how subtle. For many study centers, maintaining a faithfully Christian presence will mean working more proactively in the coming years to address the social, racial, and gender disparities that mark a movement whose leadership has always skewed heavily male and white. While Trotter and other members of the consortium are actively working to address these disparities, and while some gains are being made, maintaining a Christian presence that faithfully models the expansiveness of God's call to live and think Christianly across lines of race and gender requires further intentionality.

In addition to the growing awareness of these issues that movement leaders such as Trotter have demonstrated in recent years, outside forces in the culture have drawn the attention of study center leaders to issues of race in new and hopeful ways. Once again it was Charlottesville that helped to lead the way. In August 2017 the nation watched in shock as a mob of heavily armed white supremacists descended on Charlottesville and University of Virginia grounds for what was heralded as a "Unite the Right" rally.[18] In the wake of such a public hate-filled

---

[17] For opposing examples, consider L'Abri's eventual role in the rise of the religious Right and the Austin-based Christian Faith-and-Life Center's role in the rise of Students for a Democratic Society.
[18] Maggie Astor, Christiana Caron, and Daniel Victor, "A Guide to the Charlottesville Aftermath," *New York Times,* August 13, 2017, www.nytimes.com/2017/08/13/us/charlottesville-virginia-overview.html (accessed September 12, 2019).

event, organizations across the Charlottesville community sought to counter hate and racism in practical ways. For Bill Wilder and the Center for Christian Study the response was immediate and prolonged. Soon after the rally Wilder sent a letter titled "Mourning with Hope for Charlottesville" to the larger study center community.[19] In the following months the study center used its platform in town to provide a thoughtful, Christian response to the rally by hosting events in early 2018 that sought to "address both the structural and relational issues at the heart of racism." In addition, Wilder and the study center worked with Louis Nelson, the study center's board chair and professor of architectural history at the University of Virginia, to develop a video series titled "Race and Place in Charlottesville" that detailed the deep history of racism in the town.

Another powerful study center response to the events of August 2017 came from Karen Marsh and Theological Horizons. Founded in 1990 by Karen and her husband Charles, a well-known professor at the University of Virginia, since 2000 the campus ministry has been centered in the Bonhoeffer House just off University of Virginia grounds, and in early 2017 Marsh and her board of directors made the decision to join the Consortium of Christian Study Centers.[20] From its earliest years the Marshes' desire to confront racism in all its forms has inclined the ministry toward intentional and prolonged engagement with the issue. In recent years, Theological Horizons in conjunction with the Project on Lived Theology hosted African American civil rights activist John Perkins. His 2016 lecture "Has the Dream Become a Nightmare? Prospects for Reconciliation in the Wake of the New Racism" challenged listeners' perceptions and anticipated the opening of Theological Horizons' Perkins House. The intentionally interracial residential community opened its doors just days after the August 2017 rally. Now in its third year, the Perkins House continues to demonstrate Theological Horizons' commitment to bridging racial divides at the University of Virginia and in the larger Charlottesville community.[21]

---

[19]William Wilder, email, August 29, 2019. All references to the Center for Christian Study's response are taken from this email.
[20]Theological Horizons, "Who We Are," www.theologicalhorizons.org/mission-vision (accessed September 13, 2019).
[21]Karen Marsh, email, August 30, 2019. See also, Caroline Newman, "Honoring Civil Rights Hero, New House Bridges UVA, Local Neighborhood," *UVAToday*, August 28, 2017, https://news.virginia.edu/content/honoring-civil-rights-hero-new-house-bridges-uva-local-neighborhood (accessed September 12, 2019); The Perkins House Charlottesville, http://perkinshousecville.org/ (accessed September 12, 2019).

As significant and timely as these two study centers' responses to racial divides are, race is not the only equality issue that leaders within the study center movement must take into account. As the moment continues to grow it is important that its leaders remain attentive to other cultural and socioeconomic divides that affect students' access to study centers. As a quick glance at the consortium's list of member study centers reveals, the university-based study center movement is most heavily represented among the nation's most selective colleges and universities. The correlation between study centers and elite universities is understandable. Not only are students who enroll at these institutions likely to possess higher levels of intellectual ability and potential for vocational influence, but elite schools also have networks of parents and alumni who not only care about cultivating an ability to think Christianly but also possess the financial capacity to underwrite the significant costs of starting and maintaining a freestanding study center. Unless the university-based study center movement expands its scope to include a larger, more diverse pool of universities, it will continue to highlight the division between what Michael Lindsay describes as "cosmopolitan" and "populist" evangelicalism.[22] Any discussion of the evangelical mind and the ability to think Christianly has to account for significant differences between the two groups.

At one point the study center movement was one of the most prominent means of addressing this gap. Study centers were open to anyone who could physically get there, even if they got there via hitchhiking, or in the case of Sylvester Jacobs, a one-way ticket to Europe.[23] In some cases there was a minimal fee, but these fees paled in comparison to current tuition rates and the high bars elite universities set for enrollment. Furthermore, even university-based study centers such as the Center for Christian Study once had evening programs, summer courses, and internship opportunities that they offered to the wider community for free or for a minimal fee. Today, access to university study centers is much more limited, and it is primarily university admission offices who decide who will have a chance to make use of the study center.

As the study center movement firms up its place adjacent to the nation's top universities, individual study centers and their leaders need to continue to think carefully about the many implications of faithful presence. On one level this

---

[22]Lindsay, *Faith in the Halls of Power*, 218-23.
[23]Sylvester Jacobs, phone interview, July 25, 2019.

will mean that the movement's leaders continue to hone their ability, and the ability of the students who pass through a study center's doors, to think Christianly in its fullest sense while being present enough to engage with the full thought life of the university, including expressions of beauty, truth, and goodness that derive from sources that are not explicitly Christian. It also means that study centers will need to be even more intentional about how they cultivate not only their own institutional presence but also the presence of an increasingly diverse student body within their walls and leadership structures. In this regard cultivating faithful presence may entail asking hard questions about which of the faithful are actually present, not only in study center programming but also in the movement's leadership structures.

Nurturing Holistic Flourishing

If cultivated well, an emphasis on faithful presence will help the Consortium of Christian Study Centers and its member study centers take part in the larger goal of nurturing holistic flourishing at the universities they serve. At its essence faithful presence is simply a means for creating spaces in which there is "a commitment . . . to the highest ideals and practices of human flourishing in a pluralistic world."[24] In their recent manifesto to professional theologians, Miroslav Volf and Matthew Croasmun further expand on the concept of flourishing by connecting it directly to the coming of the kingdom of God or the establishment of God's home on earth. Though the church lives in the tension of the "now and not yet" or advent structure of life as it waits for the consummation of God's kingdom described in Revelation 21, it does not wait passively but continues to nurture the content of the kingdom—righteousness, peace, and joy—as described in Romans 14:17. In the process, the church inspires those around it to imagine flourishing that results from life lived well (righteousness), life that goes well (peace), and life that feels as it should (joy).[25]

This flourishing is the call and the hope of the Christian life, and it is this flourishing that theology, the church, and parachurch ministries at their best all point to and heighten humanity's appetite for. By maintaining a faithful presence attuned to the holistic needs of students' minds, bodies, and spirits,

---

[24]Hunter, *To Change the World*, 279.
[25]Miroslav Volf and Matthew Croasmun, *For the Life of the World: Theology That Makes a Difference* (Grand Rapids: Brazos, 2019), 153-54, 164-85.

study centers have a powerful opportunity to help students on secular university campuses develop a taste for the beauty, truth, and goodness of God in all aspects of creation and an anticipation of the flourishing that will accompany the coming of God's kingdom. Study centers have never and will never singlehandedly save the evangelical mind or transform Christians' ability to think Christianly on a wider scale, but by and large that has seldom been their goal. Rather than seeking to develop large ministry platforms or mass-produce their teachings, most study centers today are committed to much more localized, relational goals attuned to nurturing faithful presence among "the people and places they experience directly."[26] In so doing, study centers provide a compelling example of embodied presence, holistic care, and openhanded hospitality that contributes to the flourishing—mind, body, and spirit—of those who pass through their doors and the university community as a whole.

---

[26]Hunter, *To Change the World*, 253.

BIBLIOGRAPHY

"175 Attend Luncheon." *Praxis* 7, no. 3 (Fall 2003).

Abbott, Walter M., and Joseph Gallagher. *The Documents of Vatican II*. London: Chapman, 1966.

"About Study Centers." Centers for Christian Study International. Accessed May 2, 2016. http://studycenters.org/about/study-centers/.

"Accreditation Update." *New College Berkeley Notes* (Fall 1986).

"Accreditation Update." *New College Berkeley Notes* (Spring 1987).

"Ad Hoc Committee on Regent College—Request for Affiliation." UBC Senate Summary. November 14, 1973.

Adkins, Dinah. "The Revival of Religion." *The Daily Progress*, April 10, 1977.

"Affiliation." *Regent College Bulletin* 4, no. 1 (Winter 1974).

Albanese, Catherine L. *American Religions and Religion*. Boston: Wadsworth Cengage, 2007.

Alemany, Tara R. "Your Hosts." Forest Haven, New Hampshire. July 9, 2012. http://foresthavennh.org/about/your-hosts/.

Anderson, Doug. "C. S. Lewis: Visioner of Reality." *Radix* 13, no. 3 (December 1981): 12-15.

Armerding, Carl E. "Reflections of a Canadian Theological Educator—A Personal History." Pages 62-75 in *Studies in Canadian Evangelical Renewal: Essays in Honour of Ian S. Rennie*, edited by Kevin Quast and John Vissers. Markham, ON: FT Publications, 1996.

———. "Theological Education in the Brethren: 1934–1984." Unpublished paper.

Astin, Alexander W., Sarah A. Parrott, William S. Korn, and Linda J. Sax. *The American Freshman: Thirty Year Trends, 1966–1996*. Los Angeles: Higher Education Research Institute, Graduate School of Education & Information Studies, University of California, Los Angeles, 1997.

Astor, Maggie, Christiana Caron, and Daniel Victor. "A Guide to the Charlottesville Aftermath." *New York Times*, August 13, 2017.

"Background and Development of the Institute." *Summer Study Institute* (1976).

Baehr, Theodore. "Tangled Christian Telecommunication." *Christianity Today*, November 20, 1981, 34-35.

"Barb Bared." *Right On* 1, no. 1 (July 1969): 1.

Barnes, Robert. "Supreme Court to Consider Case Against California Law School." *Washington Post*, April 18, 2010. www.washingtonpost.com/wp-dyn/content/article/2010/04/17/AR2010041702908.html.

"Be Challenged . . . Be Fed . . . New College, Berkeley . . . Courses for the First Fall." *New College Berkeley Notes* 2, no. 4 (Summer 1979).

"A Beat with a Different Drum." *Praxis* 2, no. 1 (Spring 1998).

Bebbington, David. *Evangelicalism in Modern Britain: A History from the 1730s to the 1980s*. London: Routledge, 1993.

Bellah, Robert N. *Habits of the Heart: Individualism and Commitment in American Life*. Berkeley: University of California Press, 1985.

Biehl, Bobb. "Would You Like to Know a Bit About Me?" Bobbbiehl.com. Accessed June 13, 2016. http://bobbbiehl.com/about/.

Black, Edith. "Rediscovery of Faith." *Right On* 5, no. 8 (February 1974): 3.

Blaiklock, E. M., ed. *Why I Am Still a Christian*. Grand Rapids: Zondervan, 1971.

Blamires, Harry. *The Christian Mind: How Should a Christian Think?* Ann Arbor, MI: Servant Books, 1978.

Boersma, Hans, Craig M. Gay, and D. Bruce Hindmarsh. "Introduction: A Festschrift for James M. Houston." *Crux* 48, no. 3 (September 2012): 4-5.

Bonhoeffer, Dietrich. *Life Together*. New York: Harper & Row, 1954.

Botton, Kenneth V. "Regent College: An Experiment in Theological Education." PhD diss., Trinity Evangelical Divinity School, 2004.

Bradshaw, Wade. *By Demonstration, God: Fifty Years and a Week at L'Abri*. Carlisle, UK: Piquant Editions, 2005.

Brasher, Brenda E. *Godly Women: Fundamentalism and Female Power*. New Brunswick, NJ: Rutgers University Press, 1998.

Bratt, James D. *Abraham Kuyper: Modern Calvinist, Christian Democrat*. Grand Rapids: Eerdmans, 2013.

Braude, Anne. "Women's History Is American Religious History." in *Retelling U.S. Religious History*, edited by Thomas A. Tweed, 87-107. Berkeley: University of California Press, 1997.

"A British Scholar at Ligonier." *Tabletalk* 1, no. 2 (July 1, 1977).

Bronowski, Jacob. *The Ascent of Man*. Boston: Little, Brown, 1974.

Brown, Steven P. *Trumping Religion: The New Christian Right, the Free Speech Clause, and the Courts*. Tuscaloosa: University of Alabama Press, 2002.

Bruce, F. F. "Regent College, Vancouver." *The Witness* 100, no. 1199 (October 1970): 418-19.

Buckley, Jack. "How Should We Then Live?" *Radix* 8, no. 5 (June 1977): 12, 14.

———. "The Inklings of Oxford: An Introduction." *Right On* 3, no. 10 (April 1972): 5.

———. "Media: Life Together." *Right On* 6, no. 1 (August 1974): 4.

Budziszewski, J., ed. *Evangelicals in the Public Square: Four Formative Voices on Political Thought and Action*. Grand Rapids: Baker Academic, 2006.

Bulman, Raymond F., and Frederick J. Parrella, eds. *From Trent to Vatican II: Historical and Theological Investigations*. New York: Oxford University Press, 2006.

Burkinshaw, Robert K. *Pilgrims in Lotus Land: Conservative Protestantism in British Columbia, 1917–1981*. Montreal: McGill-Queen's University Press, 1995.

"By 1985 You Will Have a Video Recorder in Your Home." *Tabletalk* 1, no. 8 (February 1, 1978).

"A Campaign for Inerrancy." *Christianity Today*, November 4, 1977, 51-52.
Carlson, Betty. *From the Mountains of L'Abri*. Westchester, IL: Good News Publishers, 1977.
———. *A Song from L'Abri*. Westchester, IL: Good News Publishers, 1975.
———. *The Unhurried Chase*. Wheaton, IL: Tyndale House, 1970.
Carpenter, Joel A. *Revive Us Again: The Reawakening of American Fundamentalism*. New York: Oxford University Press, 1997.
"Cedarwood Housing Facility Now Ready." *Tabletalk* 2, no. 4 (June 1978): 1.
"A Celebration of Spiritual Roots: Center for Christian Study's 30th Anniversary." *Praxis* 2, no. 4 (Winter 1998).
"Center Expansion Makes Room for a Familiar Vision." *Praxis* 1, no. 1 (Fall 1997).
"The Challenge." *Tabletalk* 2, no. 8 (October 1978): 1.
"Christian Study Centers Extend Evangelical Presence at Elite Universities." *Religion Watch: An Online Publication of Baylor Institute for Studies of Religion*. Accessed March 16, 2016. www.religionwatch.com/christian-study-centers-extend-evangelical-presence-at-elite-universities/.
Clark, Robert M. "Robert M. Clark." *Regent Reflections* (1995).
Cochrane, John. "The Effect of Increased Education—And a Proposal!" *Calling* (Fall 1965): 9-11.
Coffman, Elesha J. *The Christian Century and the Rise of the Protestant Mainline*. New York: Oxford University Press, 2013.
Coho, Robert Michael. "Why I Give to Ligonier." *Tabletalk* 2, no. 8 (October 1978).
"Cold Winter, Warm Hearts." *Tabletalk* 1, no. 8 (February 1978).
"College News: New College Degrees Approved." *New College Berkeley Notes* 5, no. 2 (Fall-Winter 1982).
Colson, Charles W. *Born Again*. Old Tappan, NJ: Chosen Books, 1976.
"Community Members Explain Crusade Stance." *Cavalier Daily*, March 15, 1972.
Conference on the Inspiration and Authority of Scripture, John Warwick Montgomery, and Ligonier Valley Study Center, eds. *God's Inerrant Word: An International Symposium on the Trustworthiness of Scripture*. Minneapolis: Bethany Fellowship, 1974.
Conkin, Paul Keith. *Cane Ridge, America's Pentecost*. Madison: University of Wisconsin Press, 1990.
"Convocation." *Regent College Bulletin* 5, no. 2 (n.d.).
"Convocation IV." *Regent College Bulletin* 4, no. 2 (Spring 1974).
Cox, Harvey. *The Secular City*. New York: Macmillan, 1965.
Critchlow, Donald T. *Phyllis Schlafly and Grassroots Conservatism: A Woman's Crusade*. Princeton, NJ: Princeton University Press, 2005.
"CSLI Locations." C. S. Lewis Institute. Accessed June 27, 2019. www.cslewisinstitute.org/CSLI_Locations.
"D. Alan Williams." University of Virginia Library. Accessed March 7, 2017. http://search.lib.virginia.edu/catalog/uva-lib:2166698.

Daenuwy, Astari, and Drew Trotter. "Opening the Center Doors: Astari Daenuwy Interviews Drew Trotter, Director of the Center for Christian Studies." *Wide Awake* (Spring 1999).

"David W. Gill Appointed President of New College Berkeley." *New College Berkeley Notes* 8, no. 4 (August 1986).

Davis, J. M. "Concerning the Proposal for a Post Graduate Study Center." *Letters of Interest* (October 1965): 14.

"Decisions for Christ." *Newsweek*, October 25, 1976.

Dey, Eric L., Alexander W. Astin, and William S. Korn. *The American Freshman: Twenty-Five-Year Trends*. Los Angeles: Higher Education Research Institute, Graduate School of Education, UCLA, 1991.

DiQuattro, Esther. "Reaching." *Tabletalk* 7, no. 1 (February 1983): 5.

———. "Reaching." *Tabletalk* 7, no. 2 (April 1983): 5.

———. "Reaching." *Tabletalk* 7, no. 4 (September 1983): 5.

Dolan, Michael. "The Piano's Jazz Master of Mechanics." *Washington Times*, January 12, 1984.

Dong, Donna. "Dorothy Sayers an Artist for All Seasons." *Right On* 3, no. 10 (April 1972): 6.

Dorrien, Gary J. *The Remaking of Evangelical Theology*. Louisville, KY: Westminster John Knox, 1998.

Dovre, Paul J., ed. *The Future of Religious Colleges: The Proceedings of the Harvard Conference on the Future of Religious Colleges, October 6-7, 2000*. Grand Rapids: Eerdmans, 2002.

Dowland, Seth. *Family Values and the Rise of the Christian Right*. Philadelphia: University of Pennsylvania Press, 2015.

Downing, David. "Christian Elements in J. R. R. Tolkien." *Radix* 13, no. 3 (December 1981): 10-11.

"Dr. John Gerstner Joins Ligonier Staff." *Tabletalk*, October 1980. Ligonier Ministries holdings.

Draves, William A. *The Free University: A Model for Lifelong Learning*. Chicago: Association Press, 1980.

Dreher, Rod. *The Benedict Option: A Strategy for Christians in a Post-Christian Nation*. New York: Sentinel, 2017.

———. "The Idea of a Christian Village: How to Conserve and Strengthen Christians in a Culture Hostile to Our Faith; An Exclusive Excerpt from *The Benedict Option*." *Christianity Today*, March 2017, 34-41.

Duriez, Colin. *Francis Schaeffer: An Authentic Life*. Wheaton, IL: Crossway Books, 2008.

Durnbaugh, Donald F. *The Believers' Church: The History and Character of Radical Protestantism*. Scottdale, PA: Herald, 1985.

"Dwight House Serving as Student Residence." *New College Berkeley Notes* 5, no. 2 (Fall-Winter 1982).

Dyrness, William. "President's Column: Change." *New College Berkeley Notes* 7, no. 3 (Summer 1986).

———. "President's Column: End of Year Countdown!" *New College Berkeley Notes* 8, no. 1 (Fall 1985).

Edgar, William. *Schaeffer on the Christian Life: Countercultural Spirituality*. Wheaton, IL: Crossway, 2013.

Edwards, Mark Thomas. *The Right of the Protestant Left: God's Totalitarianism*. New York: Palgrave Macmillan, 2012.

Elliot, Elisabeth. *A Chance to Die: The Life and Legacy of Amy Carmichael*. Old Tappan, NJ: Revell, 1987.

Ellul, Jacques. *The Technological Society*. New York: Knopf, 1964.

Ellwood, Robert S. *One Way: The Jesus Movement and Its Meaning*. Englewood Cliffs, NJ: Prentice-Hall, 1973.

Enroth, Ronald M., Edward E. Ericson, and C. Breckinridge Peters. *The Jesus People: Old-Time Religion in the Age of Aquarius*. Grand Rapids: Eerdmans, 1972.

Eskridge, Larry. *God's Forever Family: The Jesus People Movement in America*. New York: Oxford University Press, 2013.

"Exam Snacks." Center for Christian Study. Accessed April 29, 2015. http://studycenter.net/examgoodies.

"Faith, Healing, and the Meaning of Jesus: The 2006 Veritas Forum at UVa." *Praxis* 10, no. 4 (Winter 2007).

Ferranti, Jennifer. "Rosenberger Case." *Christianity Today*. August 1, 1995. www.christianitytoday.com/ct/1995/august1/5t9062.html.

"The Field Mouse." *Tabletalk* 1, no. 3 (August 31, 1977).

"The Field Mouse." *Tabletalk* 2, no. 7 (September 1978).

"The Field Mouse." *Tabletalk* 3, no. 4 (May 1979).

Finke, Roger, and Rodney Stark. *The Churching of America 1776–2005: Winners and Losers in Our Religious Economy*. New Brunswick, NJ: Rutgers University Press, 2005.

"First Convocation." *Regent College Bulletin* 1, no. 2 (Summer 1971).

Fiske, Edward B. "A Look at the Man and the Shelter That Continues to Attract Evangelicals from Around the World." *Moody Bible Institute Monthly* (October 1975).

Flippen, J. Brooks. *Jimmy Carter, the Politics of Family, and the Rise of the Religious Right*. Athens: University of Georgia Press, 2011.

Fox, Richard Wightman. *Jesus in America: Personal Savior, Cultural Hero, National Obsession*. San Francisco: HarperSanFrancisco, 2004.

Fraser, Neil M. "Regarding a Post-graduate Study Center." *Letters of Interest* (November 1965): 13.

"A Friend for All Seasons." *Praxis* 2, no. 2 (Summer 1998).

Fry, Timothy, trans. *The Rule of Saint Benedict in English*. Collegeville, MN: Liturgical Press, 1982.

Gallagher, Sharon. "From Right On to Radix: Notes on Our Purpose, Vision, and Name." *Right On* 8, no. 1 (August 1976): 2.

———. "From Right On to Radix: A Short History." *Radix* 11, no. 1 (August 1979): 3-4.

———. "How Should We Then Live?" *Radix* 8, no. 4 (April 1977): 12-14.

———. "Radical Evangelicalism: A Conference Report." *Radical Religion* 1, no. 3 & 4 (Summer-Fall 1974): 61-64.

Gallagher, Sharon, and Robert L. Burt. "A Conversation with Sharon Gallagher." *New Conversations* (Winter/Spring 1976).

Garber, Steven. *The Fabric of Faithfulness: Weaving Together Belief and Behavior*. Downers Grove, IL: InterVarsity Press, 2007.

Gasque, Laurel. *Art and the Christian Mind: The Life and Work of H. R. Rookmaaker*. Wheaton, IL: Crossway Books, 2005.

Gasque, Laurel, and W. Ward Gasque. "Frederick Fyvie Bruce: An Appreciation." *Ashland Theological Journal* 23 (1991). http://biblicalstudies.org.uk/pdf/ashland_theological_journal/23-1_01.pdf.

Gasque, W. Ward. "Evangelical Theology: The British Example." *Christianity Today*, August 10, 1973.

Gay, Julie Lane, Loren Wilkinson, and Maxine Hancock. "Introduction." *Crux* 50, no. 1 (2014): 2-3.

Gelman, Eric, Janet Huck, Connie Leslie, Carolyn Friday, Pamela Abramson, and Michael Reese. "The Video Revolution: How the VCR Is Changing What You Watch." *Newsweek*, August 6, 1984.

Gerstner, John H., and R. C. Sproul. *Soli Deo Gloria: Essays in Reformed Theology: Festschrift for John H. Gerstner*. Nutley, NJ: Presbyterian and Reformed, 1976.

Gill, David W. "Autobiography." David W. Gill. Accessed September 9, 2015. http://davidwgill.org/Autobiography.html.

———. "Chapters in My Life: David Gill." *Radix* 12, no. 1 (August 1980): 4-6.

———. "Jacques Ellul and Francis Schaeffer: Two Views of Western Civilization." *Fides et Historia* 13, no. 2 (Spring-Summer 1981): 23-37.

———. "Letters from the Catacombs." *Right On* 4, no. 2 (August 1972): 2.

———. "A Marginal Life." David W. Gill. accessed October 5, 2016. www.davidwgill.org/autobio/.

———. "New College Berkeley: An Idea Whose Time Has Come." *New College Berkeley Notes* (Fall 1977).

———. *The Opening of the Christian Mind: Taking Every Thought Captive to Christ*. Downers Grove, IL: InterVarsity Press, 1989.

———. "The President: Ward Gasque." *New College Berkeley Notes* (Fall 1978).

———. "The Radical Christian: Education." *Right On* 5, no. 11 (May 1974): 7.

———. "Radical Christian: The End (Part Two)." *Radix* 10, no. 6 (June 1979): 9.

———. "The Radical Christian." *Right On* 4, no. 4 (October 1972): 3.

———. "Schaeffer!" *Right On* 3, no. 11 (May 1972): 7.

———. "Uprooting & Planting." *Radix* 9, no. 1 (August 1977): 3.

———. "The Word of God in the Ethics of Jacques Ellul." PhD diss., University of Southern California, 1979.

Gitlin, Todd. *The Sixties: Years of Hope, Days of Rage*. New York: Bantam Books, 1993.

Glancy, J. Edwards, and Joel S. Woodruff. "Celebrating Forty Years of Heart and Mind Discipleship: A Brief History of the C. S. Lewis Institute." *Knowing and Doing* (Spring 2016): 1-10.

Gottschalk, Earl C., Jr. "Hip Culture Discovers a New Trip: Fervent, Foot-Stompin' Religion." *Wall Street Journal*, March 2, 1971.

Graham, Billy. *The Jesus Generation*. Grand Rapids: Zondervan, 1971.

Graham, David. *We Remember C. S. Lewis: Essays and Memoirs*. Nashville: Broadman & Holman, 2001.

Gregory, Robert B. "Bowdoin: One Year Later." *First Things*, June 30, 2015. www.firstthings.com/web-exclusives/2015/06/one-year-later.

Guinness, Os. *The Dust of Death: A Critique of the Establishment and the Counter Culture—And a Proposal for a Third Way*. Downers Grove, IL: InterVarsity Press, 1973.

———. "Fathers and Sons." *Books and Culture*. 2008. www.booksandculture.com/articles/2008/marapr/1.32.html.

———. *Fit Bodies, Fat Minds: Why Evangelicals Don't Think and What to Do About It*. Grand Rapids: Baker Books, 1994.

Hale, Grace Elizabeth. *A Nation of Outsiders: How the White Middle Class Fell in Love with Rebellion in Postwar America*. New York: Oxford University Press, 2011.

Hall, Matthew E. K. *The Nature of Supreme Court Power*. New York: Cambridge University Press, 2010.

Hamilton, Michael S. "The Dissatisfaction of Francis Schaeffer: Thirteen Years After His Death, Schaeffer's Vision and Frustrations Continue to Haunt Evangelicalism." *Christianity Today*, March 3, 1997, 22-30.

Hankins, Barry. *Francis Schaeffer and the Shaping of Evangelical America*. Grand Rapids: Eerdmans, 2008.

———. "'I'm Just Making a Point': Francis Schaeffer and the Irony of Faithful Christian Scholarship." *Fides et Historia* 39, no. 1 (Winter-Spring 2007): 15-34.

Hart, D. G. *The University Gets Religion: Religious Studies in American Higher Education*. Baltimore: Johns Hopkins University Press, 1999.

Hatch, Nathan O. *The Democratization of American Christianity*. New Haven, CT: Yale University Press, 1989.

Hearn, Virginia. *Our Struggle to Serve: The Stories of 15 Evangelical Women*. Waco, TX: Word Books, 1979.

———. "Women's Place in the Evangelical Milieu: Is Progress Possible?" *Radix* 8, no. 4 (April 1977): 18-19.

Hearn, Walter. "A Biochemist Shares His Faith." Pages 67-82 in *Why I Am Still a Christian*, edited by E. M. Blaiklock. Grand Rapids: Zondervan, 1971.

———. "Somewhere Between: A Journey Toward Simplicity." *Radix* 8, no. 4 (April 1977): 10-11, 16-17.

Hedstrom, Matthew. *The Rise of Liberal Religion: Book Culture and American Spirituality in the Twentieth Century*. New York: Oxford University Press, 2013.
Heinz, Donald. "The Christian World Liberation Front." Pages 143-61 in *The New Religious Consciousness*, edited by Charles Y. Glock. Berkeley: University of California Press, 1976.
———. "Coming Clean: An Invitation to the Barb et. al." *Right On* 5, no. 3 (October 1973): 3, 8, 10.
Heisey, Terry M., et al. *Evangelical from the Beginning: A History of the Evangelical Congregational Church and Its Predecessors—the Evangelical Association and the United Evangelical Church*. Lexington, KY: Emeth, 2006.
Hendrix, Ronald, and Miriam Hendrix. "L'Abri Fellowship: The Ministry of Francis Schaeffer." *The Lookout* (January 3, 1971).
Henry, Carl F. H. *Confessions of a Theologian: An Autobiography*. Waco, TX: Word Books, 1986.
Herberg, Will. *Protestant, Catholic, Jew: An Essay in American Religious Sociology*. Garden City, NY: Anchor Books, 1960.
Higgins, Thomas W. "Kenn Gulliksen, John Wimber, and the Founding of the Vineyard Movement." *Pneuma* 34 (2012): 208-28.
Hindmarsh, D. Bruce. *The Spirit of Early Evangelicalism: True Religion in a Modern World*. New York: Oxford University Press, 2018.
"A Historic Moment: The Installation of Jeffrey P. Greenman as President." Regent College. November 2, 2015. www.regent-college.edu/about-us/news/2015/a-historic-moment-the-installation-of-jeffrey-p-greenman-as-regents-fifth-president.
"History." Canadian Inter-Varsity Christian Fellowship. Accessed February 23, 2016. http://canadianivcf.org/history.
"History." Evangelism Explosion International. Accessed June 13, 2016. http://evangelismexplosion.org/about-us/history/.
"History." Rivendell Institute. Accessed May 2, 2016. www.rivendellinstitute.org/about/history/.
"The History of the McKenzie Study Center." Gutenberg College. Accessed April 29, 2016. http://msc.gutenberg.edu/about/history/.
Hite, Charles. "Charlottesville's Center for Christian Study." *The Daily Progress*, September 27, 1975.
Hofstadter, Richard. *Anti-intellectualism in American Life*. New York: Vintage, 1966.
Houriet, Robert. *Getting Back Together*. New York: Coward, McCann & Geoghegen, 1971.
Houston, James M. *The Aims and Spirit of Regent College in the Early 1970s*. CD. Regent Audio, 1974.
———. "The Christian Presence in the University." *Crux* 10, no. 4 (c. Summer 1973): 21-23.
———. "C. S. Lewis as Prophet for Postmodernism." C. S. Lewis Institute. April 22, 2010. www.cslewisinstitute.org/node/1112.
———. "Embracing the Personal in Christian Education." Pages 45-59 in *For Christ and His Kingdom: Inspiring a New Generation*, by Houston and D. Bruce Hindmarsh. Vancouver: Regent College Publishing, 2012.

BIBLIOGRAPHY

———. "Having a Christian Mind." *Witness*, April 1964.
———. *I Believe in the Creator*. Grand Rapids: Eerdmans, 1980.
———. "An Idea Whose Time Has Come." *Regent College Bulletin* 2, no. 1 (Winter 1972).
———. "Letters." *The Canadian C. S. Lewis Journal* 1, no. 1 (Spring 1979).
———. *The Mentored Life: From Individualism to Personhood*. Vancouver: Regent College Publishing, 2012.
———. "Reflections on C. S. Lewis." *Right On* 3, no. 10 (April 1972): 5.
———. "Regent College Vancouver: A New Venture in Christian Scholarship." *Thrust* (January 1969): 3-8.
Houston, James M., and D. Bruce Hindmarsh. *For Christ and His Kingdom: Inspiring a New Generation*. Vancouver: Regent College Publishing, 2012.
———. "An Interview with James Houston About His Friend C. S. Lewis in Honor of the Lewis Anniversary." Titus One Nine: The Weblog of the Rev. Canon Dr. Kendall Harmond. January 14, 2014. http://kendallharmon.net/?p=42056.
Houston, Rita. "Summer School Perspective." *Regent College Bulletin* 4, no. 3 (Summer 1974).
"How to Use Christian Film and Video." *Christianity Today*, September 24, 1984, 35-53.
Howard, Thomas Albert. "Should I Send My (Christian) Child to a (Secular) State University?" Anxious Bench. February 16, 2014. www.patheos.com/blogs/anxiousbench/2014/02/should-i-send-my-christian-child-to-a-secular-state-university/.
Hunt, Keith, and Gladys M. Hunt. *For Christ and the University: The Story of InterVarsity Christian Fellowship-USA, 1940–1990*. Downers Grove, IL: InterVarsity Press, 1992.
Hunter, James Davison. *American Evangelicalism: Conservative Religion and the Quandary of Modernity*. New Brunswick, NJ: Rutgers University Press, 1983.
———. *Culture Wars: The Struggle to Define America*. New York: Basic Books, 1991.
———. *To Change the World: The Irony, Tragedy, and Possibility of Christianity in the Late Modern World*. New York: Oxford University Press, 2010.
"In the Shadow of Mr. Jefferson." *Continuing: Presbyterian Church in America* 3, no. 9 (1976): 7-8.
"An Industry on the Move." *Christianity Today*, April 1987, 50, 54-55.
International Council on Biblical Inerrancy. "Chicago Statement on Biblical Inerrancy." *Journal of the Evangelical Theological Society* 21, no. 4 (December 1978): 289-96.
Irvin, Dale T., and Scott W. Sunquist. *History of the World Christian Movement*. Vol. 2. Maryknoll, NY: Orbis, 2012.
Ivers, Gregg, and Kevin T. McGuire. *Creating Constitutional Change: Clashes over Power and Liberty in the Supreme Court*. Charlottesville: University of Virginia Press, 2004.
"J. R. R. Tolkien: Man of Another Age." *Right On* 5, no. 3 (October 1973): 9.
Jackson, Dave, and Neta Jackson. *Living Together in a World Falling Apart*. Carol Stream, IL: Creation House, 2009.
Jacobs, Sylvester. *Portrait of A Shelter*. Downers Grove, IL: InterVarsity Press, 1973.
Jacobs, Sylvester, and Linette Martin. *Born Black*. London: Hodder and Stoughton, 1977.

"January Term." *Tabletalk* 2, no. 7 (September 1978): 5.

"The Jesus People." *Newsweek*, March 22, 1971.

Johnson, Dale A., and Franky Schaeffer. "A Conversation with Franky Schaeffer." *Right On* 6, no. 1 (August 1974): 3, 8.

Johnson, Eithne. "The Emergence of Christian Video and the Cultivation of Videoevangelism." In *Media, Culture, and the Religious Right*, edited by Linda Kintz and Julia Lesage, 191-210. Minneapolis: University of Minnesota Press, 1998.

Johnson, Karl. "Our Story." Chesterton House. Accessed May 2, 2016. http://chestertonhouse.org/about/our-story.

"Join R. C. in an LVSC Club Today!" *Tabletalk* 7, no. 1 (February 1983).

Jones, Lauren, and Mitchell Powers. "After Teaching 45,000 Students, Elzinga in a Class by Himself." *UVA Today*. January 27, 2015. https://news.virginia.edu/content/after-teaching-45000-students-elzinga-class-himself.

Kullberg, Kelly Monroe. *Finding God at Harvard: Spiritual Journeys of Thinking Christians*. Grand Rapids: Zondervan, 1996.

Lakeland, Paul. "The Laity." In *From Trent to Vatican II: Historical and Theological Investigations*, edited by Raymond F. Bulman and Frederick J. Parrella, 193-208. New York: Oxford University Press, 2006.

Latourette, Kenneth Scott. *A History of Christianity: Beginnings to 1500*. Rev. ed. Peabody, MA: Prince, 1953.

Lauter, Paul, and Florence Howe. *The Conspiracy of the Young*. New York: World, 1970.

Leamer, Laurence. *The Paper Revolutionaries: The Rise of the Underground Press*. New York: Simon & Schuster, 1972.

"Leaping Ahead Program for College Credit." *Tabletalk* 4, no. 2 (February 1980): 1.

Lewis, C. S. *The Abolition of Man*. New York: Macmillan, 1947.

———. *Mere Christianity*. New York: Macmillan, 1952.

———. Preface to *On the Incarnation*. Translated by John Behr. Crestwood, NY: St. Vladimir's Seminary Press, 2011.

Lichtman, Jane. *Bring Your Own Bag: A Report on Free Universities*. Washington, DC: American Association for Higher Education, 1973.

"Ligonier—A Place for You." *Tabletalk* 2, no. 5 (n.d.): 3.

"Ligonier Celebrates Sixth Year." *Tabletalk* 1, no. 4 (September 1977): 1.

"Ligonier Is for Learning." *Tabletalk* 1, no. 3 (August 1977).

"Ligonier Packs Them In on Monday Night." *Tabletalk* 2, no. 7 (September 1978): 9.

"Ligonier Trains Campus Leaders." *Tabletalk* 1, no. 5 (October 1977): 1.

Lindsay, D. Michael. "Evangelicals in the Power Elite: Elite Cohesion Advancing a Movement." *American Sociological Review* 73, no. 1 (February 2008): 60-82.

———. *Faith in the Halls of Power: How Evangelicals Joined the American Elite*. New York: Oxford University Press, 2007.

Lindsell, Harold. *The Battle for the Bible*. Grand Rapids: Zondervan, 1976.

Lindskoog, Kathryn. "Bright Shoots of Everlastingness: C. S. Lewis's Search for Joy." *Radix* 10, no. 6 (June 1979): 6-8.

Little, Bruce A., ed. *Francis Schaeffer: A Mind and Heart for God*. Phillipsburg, NJ: P&R, 2010.

Longfield, Bradley J. *The Presbyterian Controversy: Fundamentalists, Modernists, and Moderates*. New York: Oxford University Press, 1991.

Lovegrove, Deryck W. *The Rise of the Laity in Evangelical Protestantism*. New York: Routledge, 2002.

Luhr, Eileen. "A Revolutionary Mission: Young Evangelicals and the Language of the Sixties." Pages 61-80 in *American Evangelicals and the 1960s*, edited by Axel R. Schäfer. Madison: University of Wisconsin Press, 2013.

"The Luke Club." *Tabletalk* 6, no. 2 (April 1982).

Mahan, David C., and C. Donald Smedley. "University Ministry and the Evangelical Mind." Pages 59-99 in *The State of the Evangelical Mind*, edited by Todd C. Ream, Jerry Pattengale, and Christopher J. Devers. Downers Grove, IL: IVP Academic, 2018.

Malik, Charles. *Of Two Minds*. Westchester, IL: Cornerstone Books, 1980.

Marsden, George M. *C. S. Lewis's "Mere Christianity": A Biography*. Princeton, NJ: Princeton University Press, 2016.

———. *Fundamentalism and American Culture: The Shaping of Twentieth-Century Evangelicalism, 1870–1925*, 2nd ed. New York: Oxford University Press, 2006.

———. *Reforming Fundamentalism: Fuller Seminary and the New Evangelicalism*. Grand Rapids: Eerdmans, 1987.

Marsh, Charles. *The Beloved Community: How Faith Shapes Social Justice from the Civil Rights Movement to Today*. New York: Basic Books, 2005.

———. *The Last Days: A Son's Story of Sin and Segregation at the Dawn of a New South*. New York: Basic Books, 2001.

———. *Strange Glory: A Life of Dietrich Bonhoeffer*. New York: Vintage Books, 2014.

Martin, Linette. *Hans Rookmaaker: A Biography*. Downers Grove, IL: InterVarsity Press, 1979.

Martin, William C. *With God on Our Side: The Rise of the Religious Right in America*. New York: Broadway Books, 1996.

May, Elaine Tyler. *Homeward Bound: American Families in the Cold War Era*. New York: Basic Books, 1999.

McCasland, S. Vernon. *The John B. Cary Memorial School of Religion of the University of Virginia*. Indianapolis: United Christian Missionary Society, 1944.

McDonald, Jeffrey S. *John Gerstner and the Renewal of Presbyterian and Reformed Evangelicalism in Modern America*. Eugene, OR: Pickwick, 2017.

McGrath, Alister E. *C. S. Lewis: A Life; Eccentric Genius, Reluctant Prophet*. Carol Stream, IL: Tyndale House, 2013.

———. *J. I. Packer: A Biography*. Grand Rapids: Baker Books, 1997.

"Meet the Staff: Jackie Shelton." *Tabletalk* 1, no. 4 (September 1977).

"Meet the Staff: Pat Erickson." *Tabletalk* 1, no. 2 (July 1977).

"Meet the Staff: The Sprouls." *Tabletalk* 2, no. 2 (April 1978): 5.

Meier, Paul, and Jim Hiskey. *Winning Is a Choice: How the Champions Do It, and How We Can Too*. Carol Stream, IL: Tyndale House, 2007.

"Member Study Centers." Consortium of Christian Study Centers. Accessed July 3, 2019. https://studycentersonline.org/membership/member-study-centers/.

Mercadante, Linda. *Bloomfield Avenue: A Jewish-Catholic Jersey Girl's Spiritual Journey*. Cambridge, MA: Cowley, 2006.

Miller, Steven P. *The Age of Evangelicalism: America's Born-Again Years*. New York: Oxford University Press, 2014.

Mills, C. Wright. *The Power Elite*. New York: Oxford University Press, 1956.

Mintz, Jerry, ed. *The Handbook of Alternative Education*. New York: Macmillan, 1994.

"The Mission of Ligonier." *Tabletalk* 5, no. 7 (October 1981): 1.

"The Mission of Ligonier." *Tabletalk* 5, no. 8 (November 1981): 1.

"Mission to Intellectuals." *Time*, January 11, 1960, 64.

"Monday Night Summer Lecture Series." *Tabletalk* (July 1978).

Moreland, J. P. *Love Your God with All Your Mind: The Role of Reason in the Life of the Soul*. Colorado Springs: NavPress, 2012.

Morrison, Theodore. *Chautauqua: A Center for Education, Religion, and the Arts in America*. Chicago: University of Chicago Press, 1974.

Mouw, Richard J. *Abraham Kuyper: A Short and Personal Introduction*. Grand Rapids: Eerdmans, 2011.

"Moving Beyond the Margins." *Praxis* 2, no. 3 (Fall 1998).

Myers, Ken. *All God's Children and Blue Suede Shoes: Christians & Popular Culture*. Westchester, IL: Crossway Books, 1989.

"The National Campus Ministry Leaders Summit." Ravi Zacharias International Ministries. Accessed July 2, 2019. www.rzim.org/read/rzim-global/ncmls.

Nelsen, Frank C. "Evangelical Living and Learning Centers: A Proposal." *Christianity Today*, May 26, 1972, 7-8.

"New Berkeley Liberation Program." *Right On* 1, no. 1 (July 1969): 4.

"New Directors Join Board." *Tabletalk* 3, no. 6 (July 1979): 1.

"The New Rebel Cry: Jesus Is Coming!" *Time*, June 21, 1971.

"New Year Starts Big." *Tabletalk* 3, no. 1 (February 1979): 1.

Newman, Caroline. "Honoring Civil Rights Hero, New House Bridges UVA, Local Neighborhood." *UVAToday*, August 28, 2017.

Newman, Michael Z. *Video Revolutions: On the History of a Medium*. New York: Columbia University Press, 2014.

Noll, Mark A. "Evangelical Intellectual Life: Reflections on the Past." Pages 26-30 in *The State of the Evangelical Mind*, edited by Todd C. Ream, Jerry Pattengale, and Christopher J. Devers. Downers Grove, IL: IVP Academic, 2018.

———. *Jesus Christ and the Life of the Mind*. Grand Rapids: Eerdmans, 2011.

———. *The Scandal of the Evangelical Mind*. Grand Rapids: Eerdmans, 1994.

Ockenga, Harold John. "Resurgent Evangelical Leadership." *Christianity Today*, October 10, 1965, 11-15.

"Of the Stacking of Many Books." *Praxis* 2, no. 3 (Fall 1998).

O'Keefe, Mark. "Maclellan Foundation." Philanthropy Roundtable. August 2005. www.philanthropyroundtable.org/topic/excellence_in_philanthropy/maclellan_foundation.

Olthuis, John A. *Out of Concern for the Church*. Toronto: Wedge, 1970.

"Our History." Consortium of Christian Study Centers. Accessed May 2, 2016. https://studycentersonline.org/about/history/.

"Our History." Upper House. Accessed June 27, 2019. www.upperhouse.org/about/history-our-story/.

"Our History." Washington Institute. August 26, 2011. www.washingtoninst.org/about-us/our-history/.

"Our Story." Westminster Schools. Accessed April 25, 2016. www.westminster.net/history.

Palmer, Earl. "Theological Themes in C. S. Lewis' Fiction." *Radix* 9, no. 1 (August 1977): 12-16.

Parkhurst, Louis Gifford. *Francis Schaeffer: The Man and His Message*. Wheaton, IL: Tyndale House, 1985.

Parsons, Burk. "R. C. Sproul: A Man Called by God." Ligonier Ministries. Accessed May 27, 2016. www.ligonier.org/learn/articles/r-c-sproul-man-called-god/.

Paulson, Michael. "Colleges and Evangelicals Collide on Bias Policy." *New York Times*, June 9, 2014. www.nytimes.com/2014/06/10/us/colleges-and-evangelicals-collide-on-bias-policy.html.

Peck, Abe. *Uncovering the Sixties: The Life and Times of the Underground Press*. New York: Pantheon Books, 1985.

Pellish, Shelly. "Center Welcomes Class of 2011 Families." *Praxis* 11, no. 3 (Fall 2007).

———. "Fundraising Update." *Praxis* 13, no. 2 (Summer 2009).

Perrin, K. Eric. "Back to Basics." *Christianity Today*, November 23, 1973, 56-57.

Perry, Charles. *The Haight-Ashbury: A History*. New York: Random House, 1984.

"Personalia." *Christianity Today*, August 11, 1972, 41.

Phillips, Susan S. *Candlelight: Illuminating the Art of Spiritual Direction*. Harrisburg, PA: Moorehouse, 2008.

———. *The Cultivated Life: From Ceaseless Striving to Receiving Joy*. Downers Grove, IL: InterVarsity Press, 2015.

Phillips, Susan S., and Soo-Inn Tan. *Serving God's Community: Studies in Honor of W. Ward Gasque*. Vancouver: Regent College Publishing, 2015.

Pohl, Christine D. *Making Room: Recovering Hospitality as a Christian Tradition*. Grand Rapids: Eerdmans, 1999.

"Police Dept. of Chicago v. Mosely." Oyez. Accessed June 10, 2014. www.oyez.org/cases/1970-1979/1971/1971_70_87.

"The Possibility of a Student Residence." *New College Berkeley Notes* 5, no. 1 (Summer 1982).

"Pressure in Pittsburgh." *Christianity Today*, January 4, 1974, 53-55.

"Prison Fellowship Attends Seminar." *Tabletalk* 3, no. 3 (April 1979): 1.

"Prison Ministry Seminar." *Tabletalk* 4, no. 3 (March 1980): 1.

"Professor Hoo: Ken Elzinga." *The Cavalier Daily*, February 10, 2013. www.youtube.com/watch?v=hXMTk4MBTqI.

Quebedeaux, Richard. *I Found It!: The Story of Bill Bright and Campus Crusade*. San Francisco: Harper & Row, 1979.

———. *The Young Evangelicals: Revolution in Orthodoxy*. New York: Harper & Row, 1974.

Ream, Todd C., Jerry Pattengale, and Christopher J. Devers, eds. *The State of the Evangelical Mind*. Downers Grove, IL: IVP Academic, 2018.

"Receiving and Walking: The Faith and Life Residential Year." *Praxis* 12, no. 1 (Spring 2008).

"Regent College Visit." *New College Berkeley Notes* (Spring 1978).

"Remember Those Who Are in Prison." *Tabletalk* 4, no. 4 (n.d.): 9.

Rennie, Ian S. "Emphases of the Program: Lay vs. Professional." Paper presented at "Openness to the Future: A Prelude to Planning," 1974.

———. "Regent College: A Reflective View." *Regent Collage* 2, no. 1 (June 1981).

"The Return of David Gill Dean and Associate Professor of Christian Ethics." *New College Berkeley Notes* 8, no. 1 (Fall 1985).

Reynolds, Barbara. "Dorothy Sayers: Lively Minded Believer." *Radix* 12, no. 4 (February 1981): 10-11.

Ritter, Marion, and Rosemary Cooney. "Visiting L'Abri Fellows Present 'The New Inferno' Lecture Series." *The Cavalier Daily*, March 2, 1973.

Rizzo, Gene. *The Fifty Greatest Jazz Piano Players of All Time: Ranking, Analysis and Photos*. Milwaukee: Hal Leonard, 2005.

"The Romans Club." *Tabletalk* 6, no. 4 (October 1982): 13.

Rookmaaker, H. R. *Modern Art and the Death of a Culture*. Wheaton, IL: Crossway, 1994.

Rosell, Garth. *Boston's Historic Park Street Church: The Story of an Evangelical Landmark*. Grand Rapids: Kregel, 2009.

———. *The Surprising Work of God: Harold John Ockenga, Billy Graham, and the Rebirth of Evangelicalism*. Grand Rapids: Baker Academic, 2008.

"Rosenberger v. Rector & Visitors of the University of Virginia." Cornell University Law School: Legal Information Institute. Accessed April 28, 2016. www.law.cornell.edu/supremecourt/text/515/819.

"Rosenberger v. University of Virginia." Center for Individual Rights. Accessed April 28, 2016. www.cir-usa.org/cases/rosenberger-v-university-of-virginia/.

Rossinow, Douglas C. *The Politics of Authenticity: Liberalism, Christianity, and the New Left in America*. New York: Columbia University Press, 1998.

Roszak, Theodore. *The Making of a Counter Culture; Reflections on the Technocratic Society and Its Youthful Opposition*. Garden City, NY: Doubleday, 1969.

Rowley, Jack. "Audio/Video: Video Equipment." *Tabletalk* 4, no. 1 (January 1980).

———. "How Many Can You Reach with a Video Ministry?" *Tabletalk* 3, no. 6 (n.d.): 12.
———. "Is Your Church Using Video? You Need a Video Manager." *Tabletalk* 3, no. 10 (November 1979).
———. "The Ligonier Valley Study Center Early Years." Ligonier Ministries. June 20, 2010. www.ligonier.org/blog/ligonier-valley-study-center-early-years/.
———. "LVSC Video: Small Beginnings . . . New Horizons." *Tabletalk* 6, no. 4 (October 1982).
———. "Video Education: A Reality for You." *Tabletalk* 3, no. 4 (May 1979): 12.
———. "Video Revolution Begins." *Tabletalk* 3, no. 3 (April 1979): 12.
———. "What to Consider Before Starting a Video Ministry." *Tabletalk* 3, no. 5 (June 1979): 12.
Rowley, Linda. "Tapetalk: Knowing Scripture." *Tabletalk* 7, no. 4 (September 1983): 10, 14.
Ruegsegger, Ronald W. *Reflections on Francis Schaeffer*. Grand Rapids: Academie Books, Zondervan, 1986.
Russo, Charles J. "Mergens v. Westside Community Schools at Twenty-Five and Christian Legal Society v. Martinez: From Live and Let Live to My Way or the Highway?" *Brigham Young University Education & Law Journal*, June 1, 2015, 453-80.
Ryken, Leland. *J. I. Packer: An Evangelical Life*. Wheaton, IL: Crossway Books, 2015.
Sandeen, Ernest Robert. *The Roots of Fundamentalism: British and American Millenarianism, 1800–1930*. Chicago: University of Chicago Press, 1970.
Scaer, David P. "International Council on Biblical Inerrancy: Summit II." *Concordia Theological Quarterly* 47, no. 2 (April 1983): 153-58.
Schaeffer, Edith. *Dear Family: The L'Abri Family Letters, 1961–1986*. San Francisco: Harper & Row, 1989.
———. *The Hidden Art of Homemaking*. Wheaton, IL: Tyndale House, 1985.
———. *L'Abri*. Worthing, UK: Norfolk, 1969.
———. *The Tapestry: The Life and Times of Francis and Edith Schaeffer*. Waco, TX: Word Books, 1981.
———. *What Is a Family?* Old Tappan, NJ: Revell, 1975.
———. *With Love, Edith: The L'Abri Family Letters*. San Francisco: Harper & Row, 1988.
Schaeffer, Francis A. *A Christian Manifesto*. Westchester, IL: Crossway Books, 1981.
———. *A Christian View of the Bible as Truth*. Westchester, IL: Crossway Books, 1982.
———. *The Church at the End of the Twentieth Century*. Pages 3-114 in *Complete Works of Francis A. Schaeffer: A Christian Worldview*, vol. 4, *A Christian View of the Church*. Westchester, IL: Crossway Books, 1982.
———. *Death in the City*. Pages 209-300 in *Complete Works of Francis A. Schaeffer: A Christian Worldview*, vol. 4, *A Christian View of the Church*. Westchester, IL: Crossway Books, 1982.
———. *Escape from Reason*. Pages 207-74 in *Complete Works of Francis A. Schaeffer: A Christian Worldview*, vol. 1, *A Christian View of Philosophy and Culture*. Westchester, IL: Crossway Books, 1982.
———. *The God Who Is There*. Downers Grove, IL: InterVarsity Press, 1968.

———. *He Is There and He Is Not Silent*. Carol Stream, IL: Tyndale House, 1973.

———. *How Should We Then Live?* Pages 83-280 in *Complete Works of Francis A. Schaeffer: A Christian Worldview*, vol. 5, *A Christian View of the West*. Westchester, IL: Crossway Books, 1982.

———. *How Should We Then Live? The Rise and Decline of Western Thought and Culture*. Old Tappan, NJ: Revell, 1976.

———. *The Letters of Francis A. Schaeffer: Spiritual Reality in the Personal Christian Life*. Edited by Lane T. Dennis. Wheaton, IL: Crossway, 1986.

———. *The Mark of a Christian*. Pages 181-208 in *Complete Works of Francis A. Schaeffer: A Christian Worldview*, vol. 4, *A Christian View of the Church*. Westchester, IL: Crossway Books, 1982.

———. *The New Super Spirituality*. Pages 383-401 in *Complete Works of Francis A. Schaeffer: A Christian Worldview*, vol. 3, *A Christian View of Spirituality*. Westchester, IL: Crossway Books, 1982.

———. *No Little People*. Pages 3-194 in *Complete Works of Francis A. Schaeffer: A Christian Worldview*, vol. 3, *A Christian View of Spirituality*. Westchester, IL: Crossway Books, 1982.

———. *Pollution and the Death of Man*. Pages 3-82 in *Complete Works of Francis A. Schaeffer: A Christian Worldview*, vol. 5, *A Christian View of the West*. Westchester, IL: Crossway Books, 1982.

———. *True Spirituality*. Pages 195-380 in *Complete Works of Francis A. Schaeffer: A Christian Worldview*, vol. 3, *A Christian View of Spirituality*. Westchester, IL: Crossway Books, 1982.

———. *Two Contents, Two Realities*. Pages 403-27 in *Complete Works of Francis A. Schaeffer: A Christian Worldview*, vol. 3, *A Christian View of Spirituality*. Westchester, IL: Crossway Books, 1982.

Schaeffer, Francis A., and C. Everett Koop. *Whatever Happened to the Human Race?* Pages 281-416 in *Complete Works of Francis A. Schaeffer: A Christian Worldview*, vol. 5, *A Christian View of the West*. Westchester, IL: Crossway Books, 1982.

Schaeffer, Frank. *Crazy for God: How I Grew Up as One of the Elect, Helped Found the Religious Right, and Lived to Take All (or Almost All) of It Back*. New York: Carroll & Graf, 2007.

———. *Sex, Mom, and God: How the Bible's Strange Take on Sex Led to Crazy Politics, and How I Learned to Love Women (and Jesus) Anyway*. Cambridge, MA: Da Capo, 2011.

Schindell, Kit. "Have You Met Dal Schindell?" *Crux* 50, no. 1 (2014): 46-47.

———. "Kit Schindell." *Regent Reflections* (1995): 3-4.

Schneider, Kathy. "Chancellor Street House Gives Faith New Meaning." *The Cavalier Daily*, circa 1998, 5.

"School District of Abington Township, Pennsylvania v. Schempp." Legal Information Institute. Accessed April 22, 2016. www.law.cornell.edu/supremecourt/text/374/203.

Schumacher, E. F. *Small Is Beautiful: Economics as If People Mattered*. New York: Harper Perennial, 2010.

Seigel, Jerrold. *Bohemian Paris: Culture, Politics, and the Boundaries of Bourgeois Life, 1830–1930*. New York: Viking, 1986.
Sharlet, Jeff. *The Family: The Secret Fundamentalism at the Heart of American Power*. New York: HarperCollins, 2008.
Shelton, Jackie. "Ligonier Opens New Library." *Tabletalk* 1, no. 2 (July 1978).
Shimron, Yonat. "Christian Study Centers Strive to Help Students Integrate Faith, Intellect." *Christian Century*, February 12, 2018. www.christiancentury.org/article/news/christian-study-centers-strive-help-students-integrate-faith-intellect-0.
———. "On College Campuses, Some Evangelicals Find Room to Reflect." *Religion News Service*. February 5, 2018. https://religionnews.com/2018/02/05/on-college-campuses-some-evangelicals-find-room-to-reflect/.
Simpson, Jeffrey. *Chautauqua: An American Utopia*. New York: Harry N. Abrams, 1999.
"Skinner Gets Them Together." *Christianity Today*, June 9, 1972, 45.
Smiley, Jane. "Frank Schaeffer Goes Crazy for God." *The Nation*, September 27, 2007. www.thenation.com/article/frank-schaeffer-goes-crazy-god/.
Smith, Danny, and Francis A. Schaeffer. "A Conversation with Francis Schaeffer." *Right On* 5, no. 10 (April 1974): 1, 2, 10.
Smith, Gary Scott. *A History of Christianity in Pittsburgh*. Charleston, SC: The History Press, 2019.
Sparks, Jack. *God's Forever Family*. Grand Rapids: Zondervan, 1974.
———. "Small Is Beautiful." *Right On* 6, no. 1 (July-August 1974): 4.
Sproul, R. C. *The Holiness of God*. Wheaton, IL: Tyndale House, 1998.
———. "In Memoriam: Francis Schaeffer, 1912–1984." *Tabletalk* 8, no. 4 (September 1984): 12.
———. "A Modern Reformation: Ligonier's Vision." *Tabletalk* 1, no. 6 (November 1977).
———. "On the Move." *Tabletalk* 8, no. 4 (September 1984): special supplement.
———. "The Parable of Peter the Profit-Making Pork Producer, or the Ballot Is a Bullet." *Tabletalk* 5, no. 3 (March 1981).
———. "Reaching." *Tabletalk* 7, no. 5 (December 1983): 5.
———. "Right Now Counts Forever: Frustrations of a Christian Educator." *Tabletalk* 5, no. 4 (April 1981): 2.
———. "Right Now Counts Forever: God, Violence, Pro Football." *Tabletalk* 1, no. 4 (September 1977).
———. "Right Now Counts Forever: My People Perish." *Tabletalk* 3, no. 7 (August 1979): 1.
———. "Right Now Counts Forever: Robbing Hood." *Tabletalk* 5, no. 2 (February 1981).
———. "Right Now Counts Forever: Roots in the Pepsi Generation." *Tabletalk* 1, no. 1 (May 6, 1977).
———. "Right Now Counts Forever: Terrorism." *Tabletalk* 2, no. 5 (July 1978).
———. "Right Now Counts Forever: Theology and 'Reaganomics.'" *Tabletalk* 6, no. 1 (February 1982).
———. "The Year in Review." *Tabletalk* 3, no. 8 (September 1979): 1-3.

Sproul, R. C., and R. C. Sproul Jr. *After Darkness, Light: Distinctives of Reformed Theology; Essays in Honor of R. C. Sproul*. Phillipsburg, NJ: P&R, 2003.

Stackhouse, John G. *Canadian Evangelicalism in the Twentieth Century: An Introduction to Its Character*. Toronto: University of Toronto Press, 1993.

Staub, Dick. "R. C. Sproul's Testimony: The Theologian and Author of Five Things Every Christian Needs to Grow Talks About How He Met Jesus and Why Playing the Violin Is like Reading the Bible." ChristianityToday.com. December 1, 2002. www.christianity today.com/ct/2002/decemberweb-only/12-30-21.0.html.

Steiner, Beat U. "The Replication of Regent College." Paper presented at "Openness to the Future: A Prelude to Planning," 1974.

Stetzer, Ed. "InterVarsity 'Derecognized' at California State University's 23 Campuses: Some Analysis and Reflections." *Christianity Today*, September 6, 2014. www.christianitytoday.com/edstetzer/2014/september/intervarsity-now-derecognized-in-california-state-universit.html.

Stone, Rachel Marie. "Remembering Edith Schaeffer." *Christianity Today*, April 1, 2013. www.christianitytoday.com/women/2013/april/remembering-edith-schaeffer-evangelical-woman-in-pearls-and.html.

Strachan, Owen. *Awakening the Evangelical Mind: An Intellectual History of the Neo-Evangelical Movement*. Grand Rapids: Zondervan, 2015.

———. "Carl Henry's University Crusade: The Spectacular Promise and Ultimate Failure of Crusade University." *Trinity Journal* 35, no. 2 (2014): 75-92.

The Street People: Selections from "Right On," Berkeley's Christian Underground Student Newspaper. Valley Forge, PA: Judson, 1971.

"Student Life." *Tabletalk* 1, no. 3 (August 1977).

Sullivan, Winnifred Fallers. "The Difference Religion Makes: Reflections on Rosenberger." *The Christian Century*, March 13, 1996, 292-95.

"Summer School 1973." *Regent College Bulletin* 3, no. 3 (Summer 1973).

"Summer School Revisited." *New College Berkeley Notes* (Fall 1978).

Sunquist, Scott W. *Understanding Christian Mission: Participation in Suffering and Glory*. Grand Rapids: Baker Academic, 2013.

Sutherland, Brian P. "Are You Keeping Up?" *Calling* (1970).

———. "Regent College Opens July 2." *Letters of Interest*, February 19, 1969, 20-22.

Sutton, Matthew Avery. *American Apocalypse: A History of Modern Evangelicalism*. Cambridge, MA: Harvard University Press, 2014.

Swartz, David R. *Moral Minority: The Evangelical Left in an Age of Conservatism*. Philadelphia: University of Pennsylvania Press, 2012.

"Table Talk." *Tabletalk* 1, no. 5 (October 1977).

Taylor, Charles. *A Secular Age*. Cambridge, MA: Belknap, 2007.

Tegtmeier, Dennis H. "Congregational Video: A Viable Ministry." *Christianity Today*, November 20, 1981, 36.

Thelin, John R. *A History of American Higher Education*. Baltimore: Johns Hopkins University Press, 2004.

Thiessen, Carol R. "Now a Guide to Religious Video/Tape/Disc Programs." *Christianity Today*, November 20, 1981, 35-36.

Thomas, Arthur Dicken. "James M. Houston, Pioneering Spiritual Director to Evangelicals." *Crux* 29, no. 3 (September 1993): 2-10.

———. "James M. Houston, Pioneering Spiritual Director to Evangelicals." *Crux* 29, no. 4 (December 1993): 17-27.

Thornbury, Gregory Alan. *Why Should the Devil Have All the Good Music? Larry Norman and the Perils of Christian Rock*. New York: Convergent, 2018.

"A Thundering Paradox of a Woman." *Tabletalk* 6, no. 4 (October 1982): 2-3.

Tinder, Donald. "Pro-inerrancy Forces Draft Their Platform." *Christianity Today*, November 17, 1978, 36-37.

"Travelers." *Regent College Bulletin* 4, no. 3 (Summer 1974).

Trotter, Andrew. "Ed Clowney: A Personal Remembrance." *Praxis* 9, no. 2 (Summer 2005).

———. "Engaging Issues of Truth, Meaning and Purpose." *Praxis* 6, no. 4 (Winter 2002).

———. "From the Executive Director." *Praxis* 1, no. 2 (Winter 1997).

———. "From the President: Culture Dissolved." *Praxis* 6, no. 1 (Spring 2002).

———. "From the President: Signs . . . and Sometimes Wonders." *Praxis* 6, no. 3 (Fall 2002).

———. "Lions and Witches and Myths, Oh My!" *Praxis* 10, no. 1 (Spring 2006).

———. "Movies Tell Us About Ourselves." *Praxis* 7, no. 2 (Summer 2003).

———. "An Open Letter to Our Friends." *Praxis* 12, no. 3 (Fall 2008).

———. "Responsibility." *Praxis* 12, no. 4 (Winter 2009).

Turner, John G. *Bill Bright and Campus Crusade for Christ: The Renewal of Evangelicalism in Postwar America*. Chapel Hill: University of North Carolina Press, 2008.

VanderVennen, Robert E. *A University for the People: A History of the Institute for Christian Studies*. Sioux Center, IA: Dordt College Press, 2008.

Veerman, Ralph D. "Ligonier News: Ethics." *Tabletalk* 9, no. 4 (August 1985): 2.

Vettel, Eric. "A Place for Study, a Place for Living." *Praxis* 7, no. 3 (Fall 2003).

"The View from Lausanne." *Christianity Today*, August 16, 1974, 35-37.

Volf, Miroslav, and Matthew Croasmun. *For the Life of the World: Theology That Makes a Difference*. Grand Rapids: Brazos, 2019.

Wacker, Grant. *America's Pastor: Billy Graham and the Shaping of a Nation*. Cambridge, MA: Belknap, 2014.

"Wade Bradshaw." Trinity Church. Accessed May 2, 2016. www.trinitycville.org/Wade-Bradshaw.

"Wanted: Jesus Christ," *Right On* 1, no. 2 (1969): 4.

Warren, Tish Harrison. "The Wrong Kind of Christian." *Christianity Today*, September 2014, 54-58.

Wasser, Frederick. *Veni, Vidi, Video: The Hollywood Empire and the VCR*. Austin: University of Texas Press, 2001.

"Wednesday Study Rolls On—Rain or Shine." *Tabletalk* 2, no. 5 (July 1978): 1.

Wells, Ronald A. "Francis Schaeffer's Jeremiad: A Review Article." *Reformed Journal* 32, no. 5 (May 1982): 16-20.

———. "Whatever Happened to Francis Schaeffer?" *Reformed Journal* 33, no. 5 (May 1983): 10-13.

"What Is a Study Center?" Consortium of Christian Study Centers. Accessed May 2, 2016. https://studycentersonline.org/about/what-is-a-study-center/.

White, Terry D., and Stephen Grill. *Winona at 100: Third Wave Rising; The Remarkable History of Winona Lake, Indiana*. Winona Lake, IN: BMH Books, 2013.

Wigger, John H. *Taking Heaven by Storm: Methodism and the Rise of Popular Christianity in America*. New York: Oxford University Press, 1998.

Williams, Daniel K. *God's Own Party: The Making of the Christian Right*. New York: Oxford University Press, 2010.

Winner, Lauren F. "From Mass Evangelist to Soul Friend." ChristianityToday.com. October 2, 2000. www.christianitytoday.com/ct/2000/october2/7.56.html.

Woodbridge, John D. "Harold O. J. Brown." *First Things*, July 10, 2007. www.firstthings.com/web-exclusives/2007/07/harold-oj-brown.

Woods, C. Stacey. *The Growth of a Work of God: The Story of the Early Days of the Inter-Varsity Christian Fellowship of the United States of America as Told by Its First General Secretary*. Downers Grove, IL: InterVarsity Press, 1978.

Woodward, Kenneth L., John Barnes, and Laurie Lisle. "Born Again!" *Newsweek*, October 25, 1976, 68-78.

Woolverton, John F. "Evangelical Protestantism and Alcoholism 1933–1962: Episcopalian Samuel Shoemaker, the Oxford Group and Alcoholics Anonymous." *Historical Magazine of the Protestant Episcopal Church* 52, no. 1 (March 1983): 53-65.

Worthen, Molly. *Apostles of Reason: The Crisis of Authority in American Evangelicalism*. New York: Oxford University Press, 2013.

———. "Hallelujah College." *New York Times*, January 16, 2016. www.nytimes.com/2016/01/17/opinion/sunday/hallelujah-college.html.

Wuthnow, Robert. *The Restructuring of American Religion: Society and Faith Since World War II*. Princeton, NJ: Princeton University Press, 1988.

Yoder, John Howard. *The Politics of Jesus*. Grand Rapids: Eerdmans, 1972.

"Young Congregation Outgrows Its Quarters." *The Daily Progress*, January 20, 1979.

Zablocki, Benjamin David. *The Joyful Community: An Account of the Bruderhof, a Communal Movement Now in Its Third Generation*. Baltimore: Penguin Books, 1971.

Zaleski, Philip, and Carol Zaleski. *The Fellowship: The Literary Lives of the Inklings: J. R. R. Tolkien, C. S. Lewis, Owen Barfield, Charles Williams*. New York: Farrar, Straus and Giroux, 2015.

Zeldman, Jeff. "Monty Alexander: New Looks at Old Standards." *Washington Post*, January 12, 1984.

Zell, Wes. "Hospitality and the Move-In Day Crowd." *Praxis* 8, no. 2 (Summer 2004).

———. "Living Sanely When Life Is Fired Point-Blank: Os Guinness Addresses Students at Veritas Forum 2009." *Praxis* 13, no. 2 (Summer 2009).

———. "Move-In Day Lunch Draws 400." *Praxis* 10, no. 3 (Fall 2006).

———. "Study Center Spaces: A Site That Supports Kingdom Work of All Kinds." *Praxis* 11, no. 2 (Summer 2007).

ARCHIVES LIST

Alderman Library Clippings Files, University of Virginia, Charlottesville, VA

Center for Christian Study Archives, Center for Christian Study, Charlottesville, VA

Christian World Liberation Front Collection, Graduate Theological Union Library, Berkeley

Francis A. Schaeffer Collection, Southeastern Baptist Theological Seminary, Wake Forest, NC

James Houston Fonds, Regent College, Vancouver

Keith Sheppard Grant Collection, Regent College, Vancouver

Ligonier Ministries Archives, Ligonier Ministries, Sanford, FL

Michael Collison Fonds, Regent College, Vancouver

New College Berkeley Archives, New College Berkeley, Berkeley

In addition to formal archives, this project also made use of the personal archives of Carl E. Armerding, Jane Spencer Bopp, David W. Gill, Dale Myers, Beat Steiner, and Drew Trotter.

INTERVIEW LIST

Bernard Adeney-Risakotta, Skype, August 16, 2016
Carl Armerding, Vancouver, October 23, 2015
Théna Ayers, Vancouver, October 26, 2015
Stuart Boehmig, FaceTime, May 23, 2016
Jane Spencer Bopp, Charlottesville, VA, April 11, 2014
Wade Bradshaw, Charlottesville, VA, September 16, 2015
Margaret Cullen, email, July 27, 2018
Kenneth Elzinga, Charlottesville, VA, February 28, 2014
Sharon Gallagher, Berkeley, December 3, 2015
Ward and Laurel Gasque, Vancouver, October 23, 2015
David Gill, Skype, December 15, 2015
Jackie Shelton Griffith, Skype, May 31, 2016
Os Guinness, Mclean, VA, October 19, 2015
Walter and Virginia Hearn, Berkeley, December 1, 2015
James Hiskey, phone, February 23, 2015
James M. Houston, Vancouver, October 24, 2015
Sylvester Jacobs, phone, July 25, 2019
Claire Brittain Kimmel, Skype, April 7, 2016
Linda Mercadante, phone, December 12, 2015
David Mahan, phone, May 23, 2016
Earl Palmer, phone, August 17, 2016
Susan and Steve Phillips, Berkeley, December 2, 2015
Daryl Richman, phone, May 27, 2014
Jack Rowley, phone, April 4, 2016
R. C. Sproul, phone, February 12, 2016
R. C. Sproul Jr., phone, May, 24, 2016
Beat Steiner, Charlottesville, VA, April 9, 2016
Beat and Barb Steiner, phone, March 25, 2014; March 8, 2016
John Terrill, phone, August 4, 2016
Andrew J. Trotter Jr., Charlottesville, VA, March 6, 2014; March 27, 2014; April 6, 2016
David Turner, Charlottesville, VA, April 22, 2014
William Wilder, Charlottesville, VA, February 7, 2014; April 9, 2016

FIGURE CREDITS

Figure 1.1. Courtesy of Swiss L'Abri

Figures 1.2, 1.3, 1.4, 1.5. Courtesy of Linda Mercadante

Figures 1.6, 5.2. Courtesy of Stephen Sparks

Figure 1.7. © Sylvester Jacobs. Used by permission.

Figures 2.1, 2.2, 2.3, 2.5, 2.6, 2.7, 2.9, 3.1, 3.4. Courtesy of the John Richard Allison Library Archive, Regent College

Figures 2.4, 2.8, 2.10. Courtesy of Regent College

Figure 3.2, 3.3. Courtesy of Jim and Lorraine Hiskey

Figure 3.5. Courtesy of the C. S. Lewis Institute

Figures 4.1, 4.2, 4.3, 4.4, 4.5, 4.6, 4.7, 4.8. Courtesy of Ligonier Ministries

Figures 5.1, 5.3, 5.4. Courtesy of David Gill

Figure 5.5. Courtesy of New College Berkeley

Figures 6.1, 6.3, 7.1, 7.2, 7.3. Courtesy of the Center for Christian Study

Figure 6.2. Courtesy of *The Daily Progress*

Figures 7.4, 7.6. Courtesy of Brittany Fan

Figure 7.5. Courtesy of Elisa Bricker

Figures 7.7, 7.8. Courtesy of Chesterton House

Figure 8.1. Courtesy of Upper House

INDEX

accreditation, 110, 114, 174, 179-81, 184
Action Ministries, 14, 189-93, 199-200, 203, 210-11, 222
Adeney-Risakotta, Bernard, 171-72, 179-81
affluence, 2, 40-41, 198, 207, 259
Alexander, John, 54
Anselm House, 246
  name change from MacLaurin Institute, 246
antibias policies, 253, 256-57
anti-intellectualism, 1, 152, 205
apologetics, 126, 132, 137, 159, 212, 252
Armerding, Carl E., 49, 56, 59, 74-75, 83-86, 112-14, 118, 175, 261
art, 2, 8, 15, 22-23, 29, 33-35, 39, 41-45, 57, 59, 82-83, 94, 158-59, 161, 163, 213, 229, 260
Augsburger, Myron, 197
Ayers, Thena, 35-36, 77-80, 133
baby boomers, 2, 37, 86, 152, 182, 228
  and increasing enrollment in college, 2, 50
Barrs, Jerram, 23, 30, 78
Beat poets, 40
Bellah, Robert, 184, 186
Berkeley Barb, 157
Berkeley Christian Coalition, 165, 171, 179
Biehl, Bobb, 138-40, 144, 146-47
Black Panther Party, 158
Boehmig, Stu, 127, 139-40
bohemian sensibilities, 5, 153, 155
Bonhoeffer, Dietrich, 3, 100, 162
Bonhoeffer House, 267
Books and Culture, 247
bourgeois, 24, 40
Bowdoin College, 253-54
Bradshaw, Wade, 245
Bright, Bill, 155
Brown, Harold O. J., 24, 208

Bruce, F. F., 52, 54, 57-58, 77, 102, 105-6, 124, 261
C. S. Lewis College, 102, 108-15
  accreditation, 110
  affiliation, 111
  enrollment, 113
  finances, 110-11, 113-14
  leadership of, 108
  summer study institute, 102, 106-8
C. S. Lewis Institute, 91, 111, 115-19, 213, 245, 250, 255, 258
  naming of, 115
  programming, 115-16, 255
Calling, 49-50, 62
Calvary Chapel, 154
Calvin College, 10, 24, 32-33
Calvin, John, 6, 136
Cambridge Evangelicals, 121
Cambridge University, 222, 225
Campus Crusade, 155-56, 159, 192-93, 198, 207, 233
campus ministries, 98, 131, 159, 198, 204, 231-32, 239, 256-57
Canadian Inter-Varsity Fellowship, 35, 55
Center for Christian Study, 7, 189-90, 193, 199-218, 221-49, 252-53, 255-56, 258, 262, 267-68
  building, 234-38, 241, 262
  Christian Law Fellowship, 204, 207
  finances, 203-4, 216-18, 223, 234-35, 237
  founding, 200-201, 237
  Fraternity-Sorority Fellowship, 218
  growth, 234-35
  and hospitality, 233, 235-36, 240-42
  influence of, 223, 234, 237-38, 243-44, 247-49
  and L'Abri, 224-25, 240-43, 263
  lay theological education, 211, 213, 218, 223
  leadership, 209

  location, 203
  Medical Fellowship, 204
  and parental involvement, 239-43
  programing, 201, 207-9, 212-16, 223-33, 237-42, 267-68
  and Regent College, 213-14, 224, 243
  summer program, 213-15, 218
  and undergraduates, 241-42
  and unity among campus ministries, 204, 231, 239
Chalet les Melezes, 18-19, 22-23, 26-27, 29, 36, 38, 41, 43-44, 252
Chesterton House, 246-49, 253, 255-56, 258
Chicago Statement on Biblical Inerrancy, 138
Children for Christ, 16, 38
Christian Legal Society v. Martinez, 254
Christian Liberation University of Berkeley, 166-67
Christian spirituality, 17, 118, 186
Christian Study Center of Gainesville, 256
Christian Study Centers International, 246, 248-49
Christian World Liberation Front, 1, 152-61, 165-71, 173-74, 179
  and art, 158-59
  methods of, 155-56
Christianity Today, 17, 55, 91-92, 138, 154, 208, 226, 242, 247
church and state, 103, 194, 196
Clowney, Edmund, 114, 206, 214
Coalition of Christian Outreach, 124
Coe, Douglas, 100, 102-4, 108, 111, 114-17

INDEX

Colson, Chuck, 45, 106, 130, 142
common grace, 252, 266
commune, 15, 154, 162
community, 3, 6, 8, 10, 13, 15, 17, 19-21, 23, 25-26, 29, 31, 34, 38, 41-42, 45-46, 48-49, 55-56, 59, 70, 72-78, 92, 94, 97, 99-100, 106, 109-11, 118, 126-28, 134-35, 144, 147, 149, 152, 155, 161, 165, 167-72, 178-79, 182-84, 187, 189, 190-95, 197, 199, 200-202, 204-5, 207, 209-10, 212-13, 215-17, 221, 228, 232, 239, 241-42, 247, 250-53, 260, 261-62, 264, 267-68, 270
   and C. S. Lewis College, 97, 106, 109-11, 115
   and the Center for Christian Study, 199, 201-2, 204, 207, 209, 212, 215-17, 221, 232, 239, 241-42
   and the Christian World Liberation Front, 152, 155
   and Cornerstone, 99-100
   and the Crucible, 167, 170
   and L'Abri, 6, 13, 15, 17, 19-21, 25-26, 29, 31, 34, 38, 41-42, 45-46, 126, 161, 167, 189, 209-10, 213, 215, 260, 262, 265
   learning, 152, 172, 189, 202, 213
   and the Ligonier Valley Study Center, 126-28, 134-35, 147, 149
   and New College Berkeley, 172, 178-79, 183-84
   and Regent College, 6, 48, 55-56, 59, 70, 72-78, 189, 209, 215, 261-62
   work-study, 170-71
Consortium of Christian Study Centers, 7-8, 10, 187, 245-46, 248-58, 260, 264, 266-69
   birth of, 245-46, 248-50
   and gender, 187, 266-67
   influence of, 252, 255, 257-58

members, 187, 255-56, 266, 268
   and race, 266-67
   relationship to the academy, 251-53, 257-58
contextualization, 5, 39
Cornerstone, 99-104, 106, 108-10, 200, 202, 213, 262
cosmopolitan evangelicalism, 41, 44, 57, 81, 177, 268
counterculture, 4, 70, 84, 86, 153, 155, 157-58, 165, 171-72, 181, 187, 189, 198, 228
Covenant College, 24, 125
Covenant House, 167
Covenant Theological Seminary, 41, 79, 245
   and the Francis Schaeffer Institute, 245
   and the Francis Schaeffer Lectures, 245
creationism, 81
The Crucible, 13, 152, 165, 167-72, 174, 178, 202
   enrollment, 169
   courses, 170-72
   membership fees, 169
culture war, 252, 254
Day Spring Institute, 246
discipleship schools, 169
Dobson, James, 138, 143-44
Dobson Effect, 143-44
Duke University, 4, 256
Dwight House, 166, 169, 171, 179, 184
Dyrness, William, 41, 178-80
ecology, 33, 82, 172
Edgar, William, 30-31, 41
Ellul, Jacques, 70, 164, 174
Elmbrook Study Center, 222-23, 250
Elzinga, Ken, 103, 189-94, 200-201, 203, 205-6, 210, 212-13, 222, 237-39, 265
Escape from Reason, 25, 27, 122
Escobar, Samuel, 57, 95-96
Evangelical Fellowship of Canada, 63
evangelical mind, 1, 10, 47, 247, 251, 268, 270
Evangelical Women's Caucus, 80, 167-68

evangelicalism, 1-2, 5-6, 16-17, 23-24, 26, 29, 33, 35, 41, 44, 46-48, 57, 81, 85, 96, 107, 119-20, 123, 138, 145, 152, 154, 157, 162, 164, 168, 190-91, 195, 199, 202, 214, 226, 254, 259-60, 264, 268
   definition of, 1
   thinking, 152
Evangelicals for Social Action, 168
evangelism, 16, 92, 123, 131, 139, 155, 158, 165, 189, 198, 209, 212, 217, 234
   video, 143
existentialism, 5
Faith-and-Life Community, 3-6, 266
Faith in the Halls of Power, 46
faithful presence, 10, 251-53, 264, 268-70
Farel House, 13, 20, 26, 41, 159
the Fellowship, 99, 102, 117
Fellowship House, 102, 114
Fellowship of Christian Athletes, 193, 204
feminism, 77, 80-81, 172
   biblical, 172
film, 15, 27-28, 34-35, 40, 42, 134-35, 143, 160-61, 163, 209, 229-30, 245, 260
   and Francis Schaeffer, 15, 27-28, 34-35, 40, 42, 163, 209, 229-30, 260
First Presbyterian Church, Berkeley, 173
flourishing, 7-8, 10, 15, 216, 264, 269-70
free speech, 153, 158, 166, 234
free universities, 13, 152, 166, 168-69, 171, 174
Free University, Amsterdam, 14, 121, 135, 198
Free University of Berkeley, 166
Fuller Theological Seminary, 17, 49, 51, 55, 65, 72, 79, 160, 178, 181, 183, 190, 259
Gallagher, Sharon, 13, 34, 157, 160-62, 163, 165, 167-68, 172-73, 175, 177, 184-85, 229
   editorship of *Right On*, 160, 162, 165

INDEX

and New College Berkeley, 177, 184-85
Garber, Steven, 36-37, 245
Gasque, Laurel, 74-75, 83, 178, 185
Gasque, Ward W., 49, 52, 56, 59, 74-75, 79, 81, 83-85, 112, 160, 175-79, 261
gender, 77, 81, 131-32, 141, 168, 188, 266
geography, 51-52, 54, 60, 82, 93, 117, 261, 263
Gerstner, John H., 121, 135, 138,
Gill, David, 7, 13, 157-78, 180-81, 183-84, 188, 214
 and Francis Schaeffer, 13, 159, 163
 and New College Berkeley, 172-77, 180-81, 183-84, 188
 and *Right On*, 160-64, 173
The God Who Is There, 13, 25, 27, 122, 159
Gordon College, 32, 122, 242
Gordon-Conwell Theological Seminary, 193, 222
Graduate Theological Union, 167, 170, 173, 179, 180, 183-86, 255
Graham, Billy, 45, 55, 154-55, 162, 190, 193, 195
Gregory, Robert B, 253-54, 257
Griffith, Jackie Shelton, 128, 133-35
Guinness, Os, 24, 32, 34-35, 41-42, 44, 57, 159-60, 207, 211, 214, 232
Hatfield, Mark, 106, 113-14
Harvard University, 24, 41, 121-22, 206, 230-31, 260
Hearn, Virginia, 164, 167-68, 170, 173, 178
Hearn, Walter, 164, 167
Henry, Carl F. H., 55, 178
Hillman, Dora, 124-26, 145, 148-49
Hiskey, Jim, 7, 13, 99-102, 104-5, 107-10, 113-16, 175, 200, 262
holistic flourishing, 7, 10, 264, 269-70
Hollywood Free Paper, 157
 subscribers of, 157

hospitality, 3, 8, 16-18, 29, 31, 38-39, 40, 44, 73-76, 80, 100, 121, 126-27, 199, 215, 224, 231, 238-42, 252-53, 262-63, 265, 270
 at the Center for Christian Study, 215, 224, 238-42
 at Cornerstone, 100, 262
 home-based, 16-17, 74-76, 96, 122, 127, 262
 at L'Abri, 16-18, 29, 31, 38-39, 40, 44, 80, 100, 215, 224, 262-63, 265
 at the Ligonier Valley Study Center, 126-27, 262
 at Regent College, 73-76, 215, 262
Houston, James M., 2, 6, 9, 14, 33-34, 48, 51-56, 58-76, 81-87, 91-119, 152, 158, 163, 174-76, 178, 182, 188-89, 199-200, 209-11, 214, 217, 224, 243, 258-59, 261-64
 and the academy, 6, 63-64, 87, 117-18
 aura of, 84-85, 112
 contemplating leaving Regent College, 108, 112-15
 emphasis on personal relations, 86, 95, 112-13, 117-19
 experience at Oxford, 85-86, 261
 lay theological education, 6, 96, 119, 200
 and professionalism, 61-62, 117
 and the replication of Regent College, 101, 103-7, 110-11, 113-14, 116, 119, 189
 spiritual direction, 85-86, 118
 spiritual theology, 118-19
 thinking Christianly, 64, 115
 and the trajectory of the personal, 60-61, 73, 262
How Should We Then Live?, 27-28

Howe, Richard, 246, 249
Hunter, James Davidson, 206, 239, 251-52, 264
Hurtado, Larry, 111
Independent Board for Presbyterian Foreign Missions, 16, 18
inerrancy, 81-82, 138, 205
Inklings, 162-63
Institute for Advanced Christian Studies, 55
Institute for Christian Studies, 9-10, 167
International Council on Biblical Inerrancy, 138
International Council of Christian Churches, 22
International Jacques Ellul Society, 164
InterVarsity Christian Fellowship, 23, 26, 49, 54-55, 79-80, 98, 155, 192, 253
 Urbana mission conference, 49
InterVarsity Press, 25
Jacobs, Sylvester, 108, 268
Jesus Christ, 13, 156, 159, 193, 230
 as a revolutionary, 156
Jesus movement, 47, 72-73, 152, 154, 157, 159, 169, 189, 193, 196, 198-99, 205
Jesus people, 72, 152, 154, 160
 in the media, 154
Johnson, Karl, 246-48, 251
Kennedy, D. James, 136
Koop, C. Everett, 208
Kullberg, Kelly Monroe, 230
Kuyper, Abraham, 34, 59, 121
L'Abri, 2-7, 10, 13-48, 57, 70-71, 74, 78-80, 100, 105, 107, 110, 120, 123, 125-27, 129-32, 134, 159-63, 167-70, 174-75, 182, 189, 197-98, 200-202, 206, 208-10, 212, 214-15, 224-25, 227, 230, 240, 242-43, 245, 247, 250, 255, 258-65
 and art, 15, 29, 43-45, 161
 as an aspirational community, 41-46, 260
 beauty at, 15, 29, 43-44, 263

as credential, 29, 46
Dutch L'Abri, 22, 57, 157
English L'Abri, 23
film at, 27-28, 161
financial stability of L'Abri, 26
growth of, 25-26
as a hospitable community, 38-40, 262, 265
as an intellectual community, 31-37
and isolation from the academy, 32-33
lasting influence of, 46
prayer at, 17, 22, 29-31, 41, 44-45, 78
as a spiritual community, 29-31
tapes, 201-2
laity, 6, 48, 62, 64, 72-73, 77, 86, 130, 136, 174-76, 178, 180-81, 187, 211, 223, 224, 242, 259
Lausanne Congress on Evangelism, 96
lay theological education, 6, 14, 62-63, 68, 77, 93, 119-20, 122-23, 126, 130, 137, 147, 150-51, 177-78, 182, 188, 211-12, 224, 226-28, 259-60
shifts in, 227-28
and women, 177, 259-60
leisure and Christian education, 129-30, 214-15
Lewis, C. S., 36, 60, 70-71, 86-87, 93, 98, 108-9, 162-63
and American evangelicalism, 36, 163
and James Houston, 60, 70-71, 93, 98, 108-9, 163
library, 2, 9, 51-52, 54, 75, 80, 94, 97, 100, 110, 114, 117, 134, 169, 176, 178, 180, 183-85, 190, 201-2, 209, 235-36, 238
tape, 100, 134, 159, 169, 201-2
Life Together, 3, 114, 173
Ligonier Ministries, 120, 147, 149-51
founding of, 147
Ligonier Valley Study Center, 120-21, 123, 125-51, 200, 202,

217, 225, 227, 224, 244, 258-60, 262
and college students, 132
expansion of the board, 142, 147, 149
finances, 137-39, 145-47
gender at, 132-33, 134-35, 259-60
growth of, 126-27, 130-31, 137-39, 145
and L'Abri, 131, 225, 258, 262
and lay theological education, 120, 126, 130-13, 227
mass communication, 144-45
mission of, 137
move to Orlando, 149
natural beauty, 129-30
programing, 131-32, 135, 217
staff, 128, 130, 134-35, 140, 144, 147, 149
and video, 142
line of despair, 17
literature, 4, 35, 59, 260-61
Logos, 170
Lookout Gallery, 83
MacArthur, John F., 136, 144
Macaulay, Ranald, 23, 198
Maclellan Foundation, 233
Mahan, David, 246, 251
marketplace, 109, 118, 183
Marsden, George, 32-33, 232, 247
Marsh, Karen, 267
Martin, William J., 54, 56, 93
McKean Study Center, 253, 258
McKenzie Study Center, 244
Menlo Park Presbyterian Church, 173
Mercadante, Linda, 21, 38-40, 43, 77-78, 80-81, 133
Mere Christianity, 87
mere Christianity, 71, 87
middle class, 40, 50, 155-56, 198
mind, 1-2, 7, 10, 17, 25, 31, 35, 37, 41, 47, 64, 80, 82, 94, 96, 120, 123, 132, 136-37, 197,

202-3, 209, 214, 221, 224, 230-31, 238, 247, 251, 259, 268-70
Christian, 64, 94, 224, 231. *See also* evangelical mind
heart and, 197, 221, 230
Montgomery, John Warwick, 138, 159, 170
Mouw, Richard, 33, 114
Myers, Ken, 229
National Prayer Breakfast, 13, 98-99, 118
Navigators, 192
New College Berkeley, 153, 173-87, 227, 255, 258, 265
accreditation, 178-81
affiliation, 184-85
courses, 178
enrollment, 180-81
faculty, 178
finances, 178-81, 183-85
founding, 173
and lay theological education, 153, 174-78, 180-83, 187-88
Noll, Mark, 1, 7-8, 247, 251, 255, 265
North Carolina Study Center, 256
Ockenga, Harold John, 16, 55, 259
oil fields, 201
ordination, 7, 77, 134, 259
of women, 77, 134, 259
Outrageous Ideas of Christian Scholarship, The, 247
Oxford University, 6, 34, 51, 53, 58-59, 61, 70, 73, 85, 91, 93, 98, 162, 261
Packer, J. I., 54, 57-58, 77-78, 81, 106, 111, 113, 138, 214, 261
Palmer, Earl, 107, 114, 163, 172-73, 175, 177
Park Street Church, 24
Pederson, Duane, 138, 157
Philadelphia Conference on Reformed Theology, 134-35
Phillips, Susan, 184-87
and spiritual formation, 186
Pinnock, Clark, 66, 80-81, 138
Pittsburgh Experiment, 124

INDEX

Pittsburgh Offensive, 123-24, 131
Pittsburgh Theological
  Seminary, 121
place, 4, 8, 15, 20, 33, 39, 70-76,
  116, 120, 127-28, 132-33, 142-43,
  151, 159, 186, 199-200, 210,
  233-39, 251, 262-63, 267, 270
pluralism, 158
Plymouth Brethren, 6, 8, 48,
  50-52, 71, 73-74, 77, 81, 111,
  160, 175, 177
  Exclusive, 158
  Open, 50-51, 58
politics, 6, 26-28, 45, 118, 155,
  160, 196
postmodernism, 71, 84
Praxis, 237, 244
praying family, 15, 22, 30
Presbyterian Church (USA), 81
Presbyterian Church in
  America, 134
Princeton Theological
  Seminary, 78-79, 81, 173
Princeton University, 27
Prison Fellowship, 130
psychology, 85, 161
race, 266-68
Radix, 156, 165, 199, 229
Ravi Zacharias Institute, 257-58
Reformed Theological
  Seminary, 223
Reformed Theology, 6, 22, 59,
  120-21, 123, 134-36, 150, 166,
  174, 205, 208, 225
Regent College, 2-3, 6-7, 9-10,
  14, 33, 36, 41, 48, 53-120, 134,
  153, 158, 163, 168-69, 173-79,
  181-83, 185, 187, 200, 202,
  208-9, 211-15, 224-28, 230,
  236, 243, 245, 255, 258-65
  and affiliation with UBC,
    66, 68, 94, 97
  and art, 57, 59, 82-83
  economic stability, 66, 70,
    94
  enrollment, 66, 68-70, 76,
    94-95, 97, 104, 111-12
  faculty, 53, 55-57, 62-63,
    65-70, 73-77, 80-85, 94,
    97, 103-4, 108, 110-12, 116,
    174, 176, 261-62, 265
  female faculty, 80

and lay theological
  education, 64, 68, 77, 93,
  101-2
and the lay vs. professional
  debate, 64-70
natural beauty, 59, 67, 71
replication of, 94-98, 101,
  103-7, 110-11, 113-14, 116,
  119, 173-75
summer school, 53, 56-58,
  119, 168
relational network, 1, 5, 7-8, 10,
  22, 45-46, 79, 102, 110, 138,
  143, 158, 164, 176, 193, 204,
  215, 231, 244, 250, 254, 260,
  268
Rennie, Ian, 56, 64-66, 71, 108
Richman, Daryl, 189, 190-93,
  195, 200-205, 209-12, 215, 217,
  222, 243
Right On, 13, 152, 156-57,
  160-65, 168, 171, 173, 199
  founding, 156-57
  influence, 157
  name change of, 165
  pioneering new voices, 164
Rivendell, 246
*Ronald Rosenberger et all. v.
  Rector and Visitors of the
  University of Virginia et al.*,
  234-35, 244
Rookmaaker, Hans, 22-23, 30,
  32, 41, 57, 59, 75, 178, 198
Rowley, Jack, 123, 126, 128, 130,
  143-47, 149-50
Ryan, Joseph "Skip," 206-7, 211,
  221-22
Sayers, Dorothy, 162, 170
*The Scandal of the Evangelical
  Mind*, 1, 247
Schaeffer, Edith, 5-6, 14-16, 18,
  20, 22-26, 28-30, 38-39,
  41-45, 74, 78, 210
  appearance of, 38-39,
    41-42, 44
  and art, 18, 39, 41-45
  and Christian
    womanhood, 44
  and the cultivation of
    beauty, 6
  influence on L'Abri, 14,
    42-44

and L'Abri, 18, 20, 22, 25-26,
  29
and prayer, 15, 22, 26, 30
Schaeffer, Francis A., 2, 5-6,
  13-48, 70-71, 74, 78-79, 82,
  84, 94-96, 100, 105, 115,
  122-23, 125, 127, 131-32, 152,
  159-61, 164, 170, 174, 178, 188,
  197-202, 205-10, 213, 217,
  224-25, 229-30, 243, 245, 247,
  252, 258-62, 264
  appearance, 5, 37, 40-41
  and art, 15-16, 33-35, 41-45,
    178
  as author, 12, 15, 21, 25-27,
    46, 122-23, 127, 159, 161,
    163, 170, 208, 210
  and the Center for
    Christian Study, 188,
    197-202, 205-10, 213, 217,
    224-25, 229-30, 240, 243
  and Cornerstone, 100, 105
  and Europe, 16, 38, 264
  as evangelical celebrity,
    26-27, 31, 38, 98, 125, 164,
    202
  and film projects, 27-28,
    163, 208
  and fundamentalism, 15-18
  and hospitality, 17, 38, 80,
    127, 240, 262
  influence of, 2, 5-6, 13-14,
    17, 23, 25-26, 29-30, 32,
    34-35, 41-42, 45-46,
    78-79, 100, 152, 159-60,
    178, 188, 202, 206, 208-10,
    213, 224, 229, 243, 245,
    258, 260-61, 264
  intellectual isolation of,
    32-34, 70, 81, 105, 252,
    260-61
  and L'Abri, 6, 13-48, 74,
    78-80, 100, 105, 123, 125,
    131-32, 159-61, 163, 200,
    202, 206, 210, 224, 230,
    243, 247, 258, 260-62, 264
  and the Ligonier Valley
    Study Center, 125, 131
  as missionary, 13, 16, 19, 24
  and New College Berkeley,
    174, 178
  as pastor, 5, 13, 16, 38

and prayer, 19, 22-23, 30
and Regent College, 33-34,
    71, 74, 79, 82, 94-96
spirituality of, 29-31
Schaeffer, Frank, 24, 27-28,
    163
Schindell, Dal, 83
Schloss Mittersill, 250
science, 59, 61, 82, 86, 93, 167
separation of church and state,
    196, 234
sexism, 79, 81, 168
Sheppard, Marshall, 48-53, 62,
    72, 74, 81, 83-84, 110
Skinner, Tom, 57, 193-95, 214
Small Is Beautiful, 28, 162
Smiley, Jane, 40
Smith, Jane Stuart, 210
Society of Biblical Literature,
    261
space, 26, 38, 66, 73, 76-77, 100,
    126-27, 130, 149, 169, 179, 185,
    192, 197, 200-201, 206, 223,
    233, 235-38, 241, 252, 254-55,
    257, 260, 262, 269
    theology of, 236
    See also place
Sparks, Jack, 45, 154-56,
    159-60, 162, 165, 167, 171-72
Spiritual Counterfeits Project,
    169
spiritual formation, 4, 186, 210,
    265
sports, 128-29
Sproul, R. C., 7, 14, 81, 106,
    120-51, 202, 205, 214, 224,
    243, 250, 262
    hospitality of, 122, 262
    influence of Francis
        Schaeffer on, 122-23,
        125-26
    and lay theological
        education, 122-23, 126,
        136-37
    ministry to students at
        Westminster College,
        121-22
    national profile, 144-45, 151
    on the new reformation,
        136-37
Sproul, R. C., Jr., 121, 135
Steiner, Beat, 7, 14, 37, 96-98,
    104, 189-90, 193-98, 200-203,
    208-10, 242
Stephen & Laurel Brown
    Foundation, 256
Stott, John, 98, 102, 106, 113,
    178, 202, 214
study center, 1-10, 13-15, 37, 80,
    92, 99-101, 110, 119-21, 123-51,
    174, 182, 185, 187-88, 190, 198,
    200-218, 221, 228-70
    church-based, 243, 250
    city-focused, 250
    definition of, 8, 250
    destination, 250
    female leadership, 187, 267
    funding models, 256-57
    independence of, 253,
        257-58
    movement, 2-4, 6-10, 13-15,
        37, 119, 150-51, 187, 223,
        225, 232, 243, 249-58,
        260-66, 268
    and religious liberty, 256
    and secular universities,
        174, 251-53, 257
    university-based, 247, 250,
        255-56, 268
Supreme Court, 194, 196, 234,
    244, 254, 256
Tabletalk, 133, 136, 140-42,
    144-48
    launch of, 140
    as a marketing tool, 140-42,
        146
technological society, 70, 151,
    164
theological education, 6, 14, 36,
    48, 68, 77, 79, 93, 119-20,
    122-23, 126, 130-32, 137,
    144-45, 147, 150-51, 153, 156,
    162, 175, 177-78, 182, 187-88,
    200, 211-12, 223-24, 226
    of the laity, 48, 77, 93,
        119-20, 122-23, 126,
        130-32, 137, 147, 150-51,
        153, 156, 162, 175, 177-78,
        182, 187-88, 200, 212,
        223-24, 226
Theological Horizons, 187, 267
think Christianly, 1, 6, 8, 64,
    97, 104, 115, 132, 188, 229-30,
    251, 255, 258, 266, 268-70

To Change the World, 251, 264
Tolkien, J. R. R., 162-63
Trinity Evangelical Divinity
    School, 79, 211, 222-23, 225
Trinity Presbyterian Church,
    Charlottesville, 204-8, 211,
    216-17
    and the Center for
        Christian Study, 207, 211,
        216-17
Trotter, Andrew, 7-8, 37,
    221-53, 257, 262, 264, 266
    and the Center for
        Christian Study, 222-45,
        247-50
    and the Consortium of
        Christian Study Centers,
        7-8, 245-47, 250-53, 257,
        264, 266
    education, 225
truth, 5, 15-17, 24, 29, 35, 37, 39,
    86, 137, 169, 196, 232, 239,
    269-70
Turner, David, 37, 206, 210-18,
    222-25, 228, 242-43
Tyndale Fellowship, 54
Tyndale House, 54-56, 107
Unite the Right, 266-67
University of British Columbia,
    35, 51-52, 66, 68, 72, 78-79,
    93-94, 110-11, 261
University of California,
    Berkeley, 13, 36, 107, 153,
    158-60, 174
University Christian
    Ministries, 199, 203, 205,
    207-9, 211, 217-18
University of Maryland, 13,
    98-100, 103, 106-7, 109, 111, 200
University of North Carolina,
    256
University of Pittsburgh, 124,
    135
University of Southern
    California, 161, 165, 172
University of Texas, 3-4, 52, 93,
    107
University of Virginia, 14, 96,
    98, 103, 189-99, 204, 207,
    209-10, 221-22, 227, 229,
    231-32, 234, 238-39, 243, 252,
    266-67

INDEX

evangelical access to, 192, 194-97
and parachurch ministries, 192-95, 198, 204, 206-7
University of Wisconsin, 4, 91, 98, 256-57
Upper House, 256-57
Vancouver School of Theology, 66-68, 73, 76, 80, 262
Veritas Forum, 230-34
video, 120, 123, 142-51, 202, 208, 267
  video revolution, 143-44, 146
Vietnam War, 158
Vineyard School of Discipleship, 169
vocation, 2, 6, 29, 35-37, 41, 176, 187, 209, 213, 245, 255, 259-61, 268

  thinking Christianly about, 6, 29, 176, 187, 213, 255, 260
  vocational options, 2, 37, 41, 259-60, 261
  vocational reorientation, 35
  vocational revolution, 37
Volf, Miroslav, 269
Waltke, Bruce, 77, 202, 214, 261
Washington Institute for Faith, Vocation, and Culture, 36, 245
Wells, David, 41, 214
Westminster College, 120-21
Westminster House, 246
Westminster Schools, 222
Westminster Theological Seminary, 32, 41, 121-22, 206, 223, 243
Westmont College, 24, 34, 160
Whatever Happened to the Human Race?, 208-9

Wheaton College, 24, 57, 162
Wide Awake, 234, 44
Wilder, William, 238, 267
women, 6-7, 44, 51, 77-81, 85-86, 109, 115, 131-35, 164, 168, 177, 191, 213, 259
  theological education of, 6-7, 51, 109, 115, 132-35, 168, 177, 213, 259
Woods, Stacey, 55
Woodson, Dorothy, 20, 31
Woodson, Hurvey, 198
World Evangelical Fellowship, 81
worldview, 5, 34, 37, 109, 159
Young Life, 65-68, 107, 124, 134, 204, 206, 238
Young Men's Bible Study Conference, 58-59
Zeoli, Bill, 28